Ancient Greek Housing

T0372696

The temples and theatres of the ancient Greek world are widely known, but there is less familiarity with the houses in which people lived. In this book, Lisa Nevett provides an accessible introduction to the varied forms of housing found across the Greek world between c. 1000 and 200 BCE. Many houses adopted a courtyard structure which she sets within a broader chronological, geographical and socio-economic context. The book explores how housing shaped – and was shaped by – patterns of domestic life, at Athens and in other urban communities. It also points to a rapid change in the scale, elaboration and layout of the largest houses. This is associated with a shift away from expressing solidarity with peers in the local urban community towards advertising personal status and participation in a network of elite households which stretched across the Mediterranean. Instructors, students and general readers will welcome this stimulating volume.

LISA C. NEVETT is Professor of Classical Archaeology at the University of Michigan, Ann Arbor. Her books include *House and Society in the Ancient Greek World* (1999), *Domestic Space in Classical Antiquity* (2010), *Theoretical Approaches to the Archaeology of Ancient Greece* (edited, 2017) and *An Age of Experiment: Classical Archaeology Transformed* (co-edited, 2018). Between 2014 and 2019 she co-directed a field project at Olynthos (northern Greece) which included the excavation of a Classical house. Starting in 2022 she has co-directed a further field project at Pella (also in northern Greece) which aims, among other goals, to reveal additional domestic buildings and their associated material.

Ancient Greek Housing

LISA C. NEVETT

University of Michigan, Ann Arbor

CAMBRIDGE
UNIVERSITY PRESS

Shaftesbury Road, Cambridge CB2 8EA, United Kingdom

One Liberty Plaza, 20th Floor, New York, NY 10006, USA

477 Williamstown Road, Port Melbourne, VIC 3207, Australia

314–321, 3rd Floor, Plot 3, Splendor Forum, Jasola District Centre, New Delhi – 110025, India

103 Penang Road, #05–06/07, Visioncrest Commercial, Singapore 238467

Cambridge University Press is part of Cambridge University Press & Assessment, a department of the University of Cambridge.

We share the University's mission to contribute to society through the pursuit of education, learning and research at the highest international levels of excellence.

www.cambridge.org
Information on this title: www.cambridge.org/9780521198721

DOI: 10.1017/9780511979262

First published 2023

Printed in the United Kingdom by TJ Books Limited, Padstow Cornwall

A catalogue record for this publication is available from the British Library.

Library of Congress Cataloging-in-Publication Data
Names: Nevett, Lisa C., author.
Title: Ancient Greek housing / Lisa C. Nevett, University of Michigan, Ann Arbor.
Description: Cambridge ; New York, NY : Cambridge University Press, 2023. | Includes bibliographical references and index.
Identifiers: LCCN 2022051470 (print) | LCCN 2022051471 (ebook) | ISBN 9780521198721 (hardback) | ISBN 9780521124638 (paperback) | ISBN 9780511979262 (epub)
Subjects: LCSH: Dwellings–Greece–History–To 146 B.C. | Housing–Greece–History–To 146 B.C. | Dwellings–Social aspects–Greece. | Social archaeology–Greece. | Greece–Social conditions–To 146 B.C.
Classification: LCC DF99 .N467 2023 (print) | LCC DF99 (ebook) | DDC 307/.0938–dc23/eng/20221025
LC record available at https://lccn.loc.gov/2022051470
LC ebook record available at https://lccn.loc.gov/2022051471

ISBN 978-0-521-19872-1 Hardback
ISBN 978-0-521-12463-8 Paperback

Contents

Figures

Maps

Preface

This volume builds on and moves beyond ideas from my previous work, while at the same time aiming to present evidence and interpretations in a way that is accessible to a non-specialist audience. In my first book, *House and Society in the Ancient Greek World* (Nevett 1999), I sought to break away from what had, until then, been the traditional approach to the archaeological evidence for ancient Greek houses, which focused on placing excavated structures into architectural typologies. Instead, I evaluated the information offered by the architecture alongside that from other sources: the objects found in and around houses; contemporary written evidence; and the iconography of painted pottery. As well as investigating the cultural context of the houses I was examining, I drew on theoretical frameworks employed in the wider sub-discipline of household archaeology. My goal was to understand how the different spaces of a house were once used by their inhabitants, and hence, to reveal something of the social lives of Classical households. I argued that the traditional architectural typology divided into separate categories forms of house which were functionally similar, and I identified a broader group of structures which I termed 'single-entrance, courtyard houses', highlighting their main architectural features. This type, I suggested, was shaped by a particular view of how the residents of a respectable household – particularly the male householder and his female relatives – should relate both to the outside world, and to each other. I suggested that the type was characteristic of houses of the fifth and fourth centuries BCE from across the Greek world.

Since *House and Society* appeared there has been an increasing interest in the ancient Greek domestic sphere and a change in the scope of study. Other attempts have been made to synthesise groups of material and to explore how domestic buildings functioned as inhabited structures. At the same time, new evidence has come to light, adding to our picture of the way in which house-forms varied across time and space. In this context, the present volume takes up the investigation of ancient Greek housing where *House and Society* left off. The scope is wide, both in chronological and geographical terms. The book covers a period of about nine hundred years, from the tenth to the second century BCE. Significant attention is thus paid to: the process of differentiation between residential and other kinds of building (Chapter 2); the development and social significance of the single-entrance, courtyard house itself (Chapter 3); evaluation of just how widespread the single-entrance, courtyard house might have been across culturally Greek areas more generally (Chapters 4 and 5); and finally, to charting the transformation and disappearance of the single-entrance, courtyard house during the late Classical and Hellenistic periods (Chapters 6 and 7). In organising this evidence, I have employed the chronological framework used by modern scholars of ancient material, although I have not applied this rigidly, attempting instead to explore various groups of material according to similarities between them and to the underlying social trends they seem to suggest. Thus, for example, I have focused in Chapter 2 on housing on the Greek mainland and Aegean islands; in order to give a fuller picture I have supplemented this with information from the Asia Minor coast (modern Turkey) but have reserved full discussion of early Greek sites in the wider Mediterranean for consideration alongside the later settlements in these areas in Chapter 5. At the same time, I have broadly confined discussion of the larger houses, especially those with two courtyards, to Chapters 6 and 7, even though chronologically they overlap with some of the houses discussed in Chapters 3–5. When selecting material for inclusion, I have tried to highlight the phase or phases of a site for which the best evidence survives.

This volume moves beyond the static, normative model for domestic organisation constructed in *House and Society*, broadening the scope to investigate the social and cultural significance of continuities and discontinuities in domestic organisation across time and space. I highlight generational shifts in the meaning encapsulated by the domestic sphere, from the earliest differentiation of houses from buildings with other roles in the Early Iron Age, through the use of urban Classical houses to materialise membership of the wider community, to the large Hellenistic double-courtyard- and peristyle-structures which signalled a re-orientation of their occupants' allegiances away from their neighbours towards a Mediterranean-wide social and economic elite. At the same time, I point out the existence of local, non-elite housing cultures, which can be detected throughout the period discussed, but which are particularly characteristic of the Early Iron Age and Archaic settlements as well as being prominent in Hellenistic times.

The amount of archaeological material available is such that this volume cannot provide a comprehensive listing of all the relevant information

about Greek housing of the first millennium BCE; nor does it offer a
detailed discussion of all of the sites mentioned: there are simply too many
sites and houses, so that the result would have been unwieldy (and unread-
able). I have, therefore, placed the main emphasis on examples from
mainland Greece. In order to give a flavour of the extent of the distribution
of the single-entrance, courtyard house, I have also drawn very selectively
on sites from other regions, not only on the west coast of Asia Minor, but
also in modern Sicily and southern Italy, on the northern Black Sea coast
(in and around modern Crimea), and on the north African coast (modern
Libya). Because there was no politically unified 'Greece' as we know it
today, the 'culturally Greek' world explored here refers to a group of
communities sharing some linguistic, mythical-religious, and material-
cultural traits, although there were significant differences between them
as well. The lives of their inhabitants drew not only on some elements that
modern scholars might classify as characteristically 'Greek' but also on
others we might associate with other cultures, and this was done to varying
degrees depending on the location and time period. As suggested in
Chapter 5, in the context of ongoing discussion about the extent to which
specific cultural groups can be identified in the material record and potential methods for doing so, the architecture of houses, together with the
organisation of domestic activities, provides one among a number of
potential barometers of cultural variability across time and space.
Nevertheless, these are sources which should be handled with care: the
construction of a house and the use of its internal space can be (and as
I suggest below, was) consciously manipulated to symbolise individual
identity and status, or to articulate the acceptance or rejection of social
norms (for example).

Over the past twenty years or so, the subject of ancient Greek housing
and domestic social life has entered the student curriculum at school- and
university-levels. I have received a number of comments to the effect that
House and Society has been used for teaching in both of these contexts,
despite the fact that the book has a somewhat narrow focus and was written
in a technical manner which was not aimed at a student audience. In this
context, as well as investigating the chronological and geographical boundaries of the single-entrance, courtyard house, the current volume is
intended to provide an approachable overview of a selection of the vast
array of primary evidence for ancient Greek housing now available. In the
hope of making this material accessible to those without extensive background knowledge I have minimised the use of technical terminology, as
well as avoiding the use of footnotes and references in the text. A glossary is

provided for those terms that were unavoidable, and for anyone wishing to follow up individual points further I have provided a Bibliographic Essay containing detailed references to the sources on which my discussion is based. Also with a non-specialist audience in mind, I have incorporated numerous figures as an aid to visualising the individual structures under consideration: many of these hint at the three-dimensional forms of the original buildings, with the caveat that the locations of doorways are sometimes unknown. I have also included translated extracts of many of the ancient texts to which I refer. In bringing together bibliography and sources in this way, I hope to encourage readers not only to evaluate the evidence for themselves, but also to follow up their own interests by carrying out new research which moves beyond the selection of issues and evidence discussed here.

Acknowledgements

As the origins of this project imply, the ideas presented here are the result of years spent exploring, assembling and re-assembling a kaleidoscope of evidence for Greek housing in different ways to consider a range of social questions. I am deeply grateful to Anthony Snodgrass for supporting my first forays into this research area, as well as to the late Jim Coulton for suggesting the expression 'single-entrance, courtyard house', which continues to prove so useful. The present volume has taken far longer to write than it should have: writing was ultimately finished in the spring of 2020 under 'pandemic conditions', with severe limitations on library access and no possibility of travel. Fortunately, it was already mostly complete in 2013 when I took on a significant administrative responsibility at the University of Michigan (directing the Interdepartmental Program in Classical Art and Archaeology), a post I held for seven years while continuing to teach a full course load and with only a single term of leave. In summer 2014, along with colleagues from the Greek Archaeological Service and British School at Athens, I also embarked on a field project at the site of the city of Olynthos, involving scholars and students from Michigan and from numerous institutions across Europe and North America. It has been a joy to work with all of these participants in different ways throughout this time. It has also been a privilege to have the opportunity to collect new kinds of data which will help to address many outstanding questions about domestic organisation, even if at the same time it raises as many new ones. Discussions in the field and in the process of studying our material have helped me to structure my thoughts and sharpen my analysis. In particular, Bradley Ault has been a constructive interlocutor and helpful sounding board on numerous interpretative issues, as well as facilitating the use of information from Halieis. Bettina Tsigarida has generously shared her extensive knowledge and ideas about excavated houses and information about the palace at Pella and, most of all, her infectious enthusiasm for the archaeology of northern Greece. The kindness of other colleagues has also contributed to the final text: Alexander Mazarakis Ainian kindly gave me offprints detailing some of his work at Skala Oropou. Vaso Missailidou also helpfully provided offprints relating to her excavations at Aphytis. Elpi

Naoum led a memorable tour at Petres, shared information about the site and facilitated the use of images of the houses. Mme Sylvie Bouchoule of the University of Nancy II permitted me to study Émile Burnouf's scholarly archive and facilitated my visit to Nancy. Parrish Wright and Laurel Fricker efficiently helped with sourcing and organising some of the source material for the illustrations and commented on versions of the text. Special thanks are due to Lorene Sterner for beginning the daunting task of preparing the many drawings that are an integral part of the book and are fundamental for understanding my discussion of the individual houses. Max Huemer and Laurel Fricker deserve my eternal gratitude for stepping in and methodically carrying that task to completion. The work could not have been undertaken without the generous support of the Frier Fund of the Classical Studies Department and the research funds provided by the College of Literature, Science and the Arts at the University of Michigan, for which I am very grateful. Sabbatical leave and a Michigan Humanities Award gave me an opportunity to write some of the material included here. I gladly acknowledge the many students at Michigan who have taken my courses on ancient housing, especially those in my graduate seminars on ancient domestic space: they have helped me continually to refresh and re-think many of the ideas presented here, and I know they will continue to do so into the future. I also thank a number of scholars and institutions who generously granted permission to reproduce various images, as noted individually in the captions of the Figures. (I regret that the cost of obtaining permission obliged me to omit many others in the final stages of preparing the book for publication.) I am grateful to Sally Bjork who re-photographed some of the images for reproduction. David Potter kindly read and commented on a chapter of the text, while Cambridge University Press's two readers made numerous constructive suggestions across the entire volume which have significantly improved it. I am indebted to Michael Sharp for his patience in awaiting the long-overdue typescript and to him and to Katie Idle for all of their advice along the way. I am grateful to the copy editor, Linda Duarte and indexer, Pam Scholefield, for their work on the volume. Most of all, I thank my husband David Stone, who has continued to believe in and support all of my academic endeavours, even when they seemed to be without end, and who has consistently shouldered more than his share of our own domestic activities to give me time to work. This book is for him, and for our daughter Charlotte, who once dreamed that we were excavating a perfectly preserved house from its roof on downwards; may that dream one day come true!

Chronology

Early Iron Age	ca. 1050 BCE–ca. 700 BCE
Geometric Period	ca. 900 BCE–ca. 700 BCE
Archaic Period	ca. 700 BCE–480 BCE
Classical Period	480–323 BCE
Hellenistic Period	323–31 BCE

1 | Introducing Ancient Greek Housing

This chapter sketches out the nature and scope of the evidence available for Greek housing during the first millennium BCE. Drawing on textual sources, the significance of the house in ancient Greek (mainly Classical Athenian) culture is investigated. Some of the processes (both human and natural) which have shaped the material remains of the houses themselves are outlined.

The Idea of a House

A house is more than simply a building. In modern western culture it is a deeply symbolic structure: ownership of a house or home is a dream to be striven for even (if the economic crisis of the early twenty-first century is any guide) where attaining that goal requires unsustainable sacrifices in other aspects of life. At the same time, a house is also a vehicle for self-expression. Its location, style and decoration often proclaim its occupants' membership of specific social, economic, ethnic or other groups (either consciously or subconsciously); somewhat paradoxically, its decoration also often simultaneously demonstrates their individuality. These two conflicting messages can often be in tension with each other within the context of a single building.

In the ancient Greek world, too, housing carried strong symbolic associations. Archaeology and texts both show that we should be careful not to assume that these associations were the same as our own. The words for 'house' (*oikia*) and 'household' (*oikos*) are closely related and in some ways the house seems to have embodied the survival and continuity of the household, transcending individual generations of human lives. Relevant written sources offering an insight into the symbolic aspects of Greek houses derive mainly from the context of fifth- and fourth-century BCE Athens. These texts must be read with a critical awareness of their context: they present the personal perspectives of their writers (with all the geographical, social, gender and other biases those may entail) and they are constrained by the conventions of the various genres in which they are composed. It is important to remember that attitudes are likely to have changed through time and space. Indeed, some of those changes are explored through the material record in the later chapters of this book. But the written sources do, nevertheless, offer a sense of some of the range of associations houses may have evoked, at least in Classical Athenian culture. They, therefore, represent a helpful starting point for thinking about some of the parallels and contrasts between ancient Greek and modern western attitudes towards housing.

A superficial reading of the Classical Attic texts suggests that, as in many cultures, elite, male Athenians (the authors of these accounts) construed the house as a female domain, in contrast with the public sphere, which is often portrayed as male. But as we shall see, a closer look reveals that this is a rhetorical trope which does not, in fact, convey the full range of associations carried by a house. The physical building itself was also articulated as being central to the (male) householder's identity and to the well-being of the household. A particular form of punishment, known as 'kataskaphe', was carried out in Athens and elsewhere. This involved (among other things) the complete destruction of a convict's entire house and presumably also the dispersal of its contents. The material significance of this act of punishment will become increasingly clear as we explore the symbolism of the house through Athenian texts and look at the character of the Greek domestic environment using archaeological evidence. Broadly speaking, however, kataskaphe dismantled the household by removing its living space. This meant eliminating both stored foodstuffs and the durable goods which might have been used to produce, or been exchanged for, further supplies. Kataskaphe was also a deeply symbolic act. It must have erased a man's social identity by depriving him of the location in which he could be found by, and entertain, his friends and associates. It would also have destroyed the paraphernalia of domestic cult, which may have included both apotropaic Herms (stone markers with sculpted heads sacred to the god Hermes) at the house entrance and altars located in and around the central courtyard. It may also have dispersed his household.

Housing was not only important spiritually and materially, but it also carried symbolic weight, and in a variety of textual sources it is taken as emblematic of an owner's character and personal conduct. At Classical Athens, a degree of moderation and self-restraint is articulated as the expected norm in this, as in other aspects of life. For example, the orator Demosthenes, speaking during the mid fourth century BCE, comments repeatedly that the prominent statesmen of earlier generations – Aristeides, Miltiades, Themistokles and Kimon – lived modestly in houses which were no different from those of their less illustrious fellow citizens (Text Extract 1). We do not, of course, have any way of knowing whether Demosthenes was right, and his comments are made for comparative purposes, contrasting the modest houses with the magnificent religious buildings of the Periklean Akropolis and with the opulent buildings of the Macedonian king, Philip II. Nonetheless, the fact that Demosthenes is able to use such claims to rhetorical effect suggests that there was probably at least some degree of contemporary public support for restraint of ostentation and expenditure on houses but that, at the same time, there may have been citizens beginning to indulge themselves in precisely this manner. (As we shall see in Chapter 7, this interpretation is supported by the archaeological evidence for the housing of this period more broadly.)

Demosthenes' perspective is shared by other authors: a similar point is made by Xenophon, also writing in the fourth century BCE, who suggests that it is much better to spend money on beautifying the city as a whole than on decorating one's own private house (Text Extract 2). Restraint over the lavishness of housing is also mentioned by Plutarch, writing four centuries later, when discussing the fourth century BCE Athenian tyrant Lykourgos, one of whose actions was said to have been to introduce a law preventing individual houses from becoming too extravagant (Text Extract 3). But the level of decoration in housing at Athens was perhaps viewed as unrepresentative of that in the Greek world more generally, even at a later date, if the comments of Herakleides Kritikos are to be believed: writing in the mid third century BCE, he claimed that there were still few lavish houses in Athens (Text Extract 4). (His description of this city contrasts with his picture of Tanagra, in Boiotia, which he says is most beautifully built, the houses having fine porches.)

At the same time as being a public symbol, an individual's house also seems to have been regarded as very much his own domain. The act of crossing the threshold placed an obligation on a visitor to act according to specific social codes. Writing in the first century CE, Plutarch comments that a visitor should give a warning of his approach so as not to catch a glimpse of some domestic activity which should not be witnessed by an outsider (Text Extract 5). In the context of Classical Athens, major transgressions by would-be callers come to the fore. Plato and Xenophon offer several descriptions of situations in which visitors did not follow the normal protocols, instead arriving drunk and demanding to see the owner of the house even if he was busy (for example, Alkibiades arriving at Agathon's house in Plato's *Symposium*, 212 C-D: Text Extract 6). In Athenian legal speeches, episodes in which a man enters another man's house without permission are portrayed by the prosecution as outrageous. The transgression is often compounded by the fact that such uninvited guests are said to have burst in on female members of the household. (See Text Extract 7; the gender dynamics represent part of a wider sensitivity about social contact between women and unrelated men, a theme taken up again in Chapters 4 and 7.)

A number of sources imply that as well as these kinds of social rules covering the behaviour of visitors, there were also expectations about appropriate domestic behaviour which applied to the residents of a house. In Athenian drama some disapproval is displayed towards wives who leave their houses too frequently or without proper reason. (For instance, in a very fragmentary text, the comic playwright, Menander, writing in the late fourth to early third century BCE, portrays a man chastising his wife for going into the street outside: Fragment 546 K). Passing over the threshold thus seems to have been a symbolic act for both visitors and residents, and its significance is perhaps confirmed by numerous references to door-keepers. In theory, their job seems to have been to control who came into the house, although they are sometimes depicted as failing to keep out unwanted guests, as was the case with Alkibiades in Plato's *Symposium*, mentioned above (Text Extract 6). At the other extreme, the doorkeepers themselves are portrayed as capable of ignoring normal social rules, as in Plato's description of Kallias' doorman, who tries to exclude even callers who observe the social etiquette and have genuine reason to enter (Text Extract 8). A house also played a more pragmatic role – as an economic asset. Inscriptions from a range of locations including Athens and also the city of Olynthos in northern Greece (discussed in detail in Chapter 4), attest to the mortgaging and sale of urban houses (Text Extract 9).

Even taken together this textual information offers only partial coverage of a narrow range of topics and is limited in its geographical scope. It also draws on sources ranging over several centuries in time. The authors, nevertheless, reveal glimpses of what appears to be a durable and deeply entrenched system of beliefs surrounding domestic life. The fact that a number of texts of different genres describe incidents (real or fictitious) in which there was a failure to observe apparent norms, suggests that such norms were widespread and that there may have been some degree of ambivalence about them, such that they may not always have been followed in the course of day-to-day life. The house, therefore, seems to have constituted something of a contested space – a context in which social rules and boundaries were negotiated through the behaviour of, and interaction between, different social groups (male: female; resident:

non-resident; younger: older; higher status: lower status, etc.). Study of ancient Greek housing thus potentially enables us to explore some of these tensions and boundaries.

The model sketched above offers a few strands of information about some aspects of the symbolism attached to housing by specific individuals, during particular periods and in certain locations, pointing up some major differences between ancient Greek and modern western conceptions of the house as a social and symbolic space. But the cultural significance of housing is likely to have changed through time and space within the Greek world. Our textual sources are too few, and too limited in their chronological, geographical and social coverage, to provide a full and nuanced picture. Instead, it is necessary to turn to the archaeological evidence, which is the main subject of this book. The remainder of this chapter explores the nature of the evidence itself, laying out some of the general characteristics of Greek houses during the first millennium BCE. The history of research on this material is sketched, including some of the main issues which have been discussed. These sections serve as a background for the more detailed chapters that follow, which ask what the evidence of housing can tell us about Greek domestic life and about Greek society more generally, highlighting patterns of continuity and change across time and space.

The Nature of the Archaeological Evidence for Ancient Greek Housing

Houses have survived at large numbers of sites of different dates from across the ancient Greek world. There are many characteristics they have in common: on the Greek mainland the most widely used building technique was to form a low stone wall or socle on which was erected a superstructure composed of sun-dried mud bricks. Mudbrick is easy to obtain, relatively straightforward to work with, and has good insulating properties. In fact, this building method was used in Greece into the twentieth century, and still continues in use in some other parts of the world. Its disadvantage, though, is that the mud is very vulnerable to damage by water, which dissolves the bricks, turning them back into mud. The stone socle raised the bricks above ground level, preventing rainwater from pooling against exterior walls and dissolving them. There is some evidence to show that, as with much more recent buildings constructed in this way, the exterior walls were sometimes provided with a coating of lime plaster which would

Figure 1.1 Exterior wall showing the remains of a plaster coating. Delos, Lake House. (Author's photograph, courtesy of the Ephorate of Antiquities of the Cyclades. The rights to the monument shown belong to the Hellenic Ministry of Culture and Sports (Law 3028/ 2002). Delos is under the supervision of the Ephorate of Antiquities of the Cyclades, Ministry of Culture and Sports.)

have guarded against rain splashes. On Delos, where the exterior walls are constructed entirely of stone and therefore survive better than mudbrick, evidence survives of several coats of plaster including an outer layer coloured white (Figure 1.1). These structures and evidence from other stone-built houses at Ammotopos suggest that such houses would have presented the passerby with a relatively blank façade, pierced only by a single street door with perhaps a few openings for ventilation high in the wall. A small number of other features may have provided hints about the identity and status of the occupants within, however: in a few cases the use of large blocks of well-cut ashlar masonry in the socle of the façade may have served to differentiate a particular house from those around it. The financial inscriptions mentioned above seem likely to have been set into the façades of the houses to which they applied, where they would have warned any prospective purchasers that a particular property was encumbered, or attested to the house changing hands. Presumably, they might also have conveyed information about the identities of the owners, their wealth and who their associates were, since guarantors and witnesses to the transactions are listed (Text Extract 9).

Pitched roofs with deeply overhanging eaves are also likely to have been used to keep rain away from the exterior walls (as has been suggested for the heröon building at Lefkandi: see Chapter 2). Evidence for the exact design rarely survives archaeologically although in large interior spaces it was sometimes supported by internal posts, as indicated by post-holes or stone bases. During the Early Iron Age, such roofs were normally thatched, but by the fifth and fourth centuries BCE terracotta roof tiles were widespread on domestic buildings. They would have been supported on wooden beams and sometimes seem to have been removed when the houses were abandoned, since they are not always found in large numbers during excavation. It is frequently assumed that at least part of the roof would have been pitched inwards towards the courtyard (as shown in Figure 3.4), enabling the household to collect rainwater from the roof in a cistern for household use. Among the various types of pan- and cover-tile, other designs are occasionally found. For instance, a few examples resemble the *opaion* mentioned in textual sources – a tile with an opening to vent the smoke from a hearth. More substantial 'chimney pots' were also used, and an example has been found on a Classical house near the Agora at Athens. Elaborate, decorative, exterior fixtures include painted and moulded terracotta tiles and antefixes designed to decorate the roof, painted terracotta simas (panels which ran along the tops of walls beneath the eaves) and carved stone column capitals: examples of all these elements have been found in the large and ostentatious House of Dionysos at Pella (discussed in Chapter 7). Flat, clay roofs may also sometimes have been used for certain parts of the house or in particular building styles, especially for some of the smaller rooms or more modest structures. The main alternative to this kind of mudbrick construction was to build walls entirely of stone, a method particularly common in Crete and the Aegean islands. Stone is obviously a more durable material than mudbrick, although more, and more specialised, labour was required for quarrying, transportation and construction. In stone buildings, the roof was probably often flat, composed of wooden cross-beams and stone slabs with weatherproofing of compressed clay, as in the Geometric-period houses of Zagora on Andros.

Both mudbrick and stone houses frequently had open courtyards which were sometimes paved or cobbled. Floors were commonly composed of compacted earth which was sometimes topped with rolled clay. From the Classical period onwards more durable surfaces began to be provided, at first in only one or two rooms, and then more widely throughout the house. These consisted of cement, sometimes with inlaid pottery sherds or small pebbles. The earliest mosaic floors, introduced around 400 BCE, consisted of black and white pebbles placed in geometric or figural patterns; later they were composed of specially cut stone tesserae (small cubes) in a range of different colours. The decorative effect of mosaic floors was increasingly enhanced by plaster walls with designs in both true fresco and fresco secco techniques (that is to say, painted either before or after the plaster had dried). At first, simple panels were created in different colours, but by the Hellenistic period figural designs were being used as well as painted architectural features which were enhanced by moulded plaster (the so-called masonry style, a forerunner of Roman wall painting).

The transitions between the interior and exterior of the house, and between different rooms, were sometimes marked by thresholds. In earlier houses these were normally composed of small stones, but by the Classical period they were sometimes made from a single large, stone block, normally with cuttings where wooden doors would have been set. In stone-built houses door lintels and jambs were sometimes monoliths – single large blocks of stone, which retain the cuttings for bars and bolts. Doorways seem to have been one of the main routes through which light entered the interiors of these buildings. To some extent they were supplemented by windows, but window glass was not used until the Roman period and then only rarely. This meant that openings to the outside let in not only light, but also potentially rain, heat, cold or drafts. If there had been large openings to the exterior, passersby in the street would have been able to look in. In the later houses at Delos, which were built of stone and preserved to a considerable height, there are only a handful of window openings to the exterior: these have cuttings in their stone sills suggesting the placement of bars for security, and shutters which could presumably have been closed, making up for the lack of window glass. As we shall see in Chapter 3, by the Classical period, most houses had an internal courtyard which acted, among other things, as a lightwell, enabling daylight and fresh air to ventilate the interior through doorways and probably also through adjacent inward-facing windows. The remains of stone window mullions, carved in the decorative Doric or Ionic architectural orders (styles) occasionally survive. These are no longer in situ because the mudbrick walls into which they were set have long since collapsed, but they seem to have belonged to windows oriented inwards into the courtyard (as in the House of the Mosaics and House II at Eretria: see Chapter 6). Artificial light was provided by torches, oil lamps, hearths and braziers, but the amount and quality of such light must have been relatively poor, making daylight a valuable asset and one worth taking account of in house design.

In comparison with the houses of modern, western society, those of the ancient Greek world had relatively few amenities. In addition to acting as a lightwell, the courtyard provided a bright and well-ventilated space for a range of economic activities such as processing crops or practising crafts including metallurgy, manufacture of ceramics or sculpting. Built-in features were limited in number and range. Raised stone ledges or benches against the walls provided seating or, in some houses of the early first millennium, supported storage vessels. Storage for smaller items was sometimes also provided by shelves or niches in walls. Another major fixed feature of some houses was a hearth consisting of an ash-filled area, sometimes demarcated by stone slabs (Figure 4.6). This was used for cooking, heating and lighting. Water was supplied by a well or cistern, normally located in the courtyard, although not every house had its own water source. From the Classical period onwards, some urban dwellings were provided with terracotta drains to carry waste water out to the street, and there were fixed toilets in some. Archaeological evidence dating to the late fifth and early fourth centuries BCE reveals ceramic vessels used for this purpose, as at Olynthos, where a urinal was found in situ in an exterior wall. A number of houses at Delos, which date to the second to first centuries BCE, are provided with small rooms enclosing multiple-seat toilets. This type of installation consisted of a wooden or stone seat with holes cut into it, above a channel along which water could be directed to carry away the waste. Archaeologically, it is this channel which typically survives (Figure 1.2). More often, though, terracotta chamber pots would have been used, and at least one terracotta object identified as a child's 'potty' survives from the ancient Agora in Athens. From the sixth century BCE onwards, bathing sometimes took place in a terracotta bathtub (Figure 1.3). Such vessels had fixed locations but were not plumbed in; instead, they relied on water being poured in from smaller containers. The bather had only sufficient space to sit (with knees bent) on a raised bench at one end, rather than stretching out flat as in a modern, western tub. Water would have collected around the foot end and could have been scooped up again in order to wash the upper body. By the end of our period, bathing facilities in some locations were becoming more elaborate: in Sicily, for instance, a larger, cement bathing installation was sometimes fed with water heated by a furnace in a neighbouring room. Finally, from the fifth century BCE, if not earlier, some houses possessed upper storey rooms over at least part of the lower storey. These were supported on wooden beams set into the walls and were accessed via a stairway. In some cases flights of stairs may also have led from the ground floor up to exterior workspaces on flat roofs.

The processes involved in planning and constructing these houses are difficult to investigate. Local resources and the environment must have

Figure 1.2 Toilet showing the paved floor with the water channel behind. Delos, Hermes House.
(Author's photograph, courtesy of the Ephorate of Antiquities of the Cyclades. The rights to the monument shown belong to the Hellenic Ministry of Culture and Sports (Law 3028/ 2002). Delos is under the supervision of the Ephorate of Antiquities of the Cyclades, Ministry of Culture and Sports.)

played a role alongside social factors (as shown in Chapter 5). In many of the regions discussed in this volume the climate is warm and dry for much of the year, making it possible, and even desirable, to carry out domestic activities outdoors or in a roofed but well-ventilated space. In a few places where the climate is cooler or damper, such as the mountains of Epiros, courtyards were sometimes diminished in size. Further afield in culturally

Figure 1.3 Replica of a terracotta bathtub in situ at Olynthos (house A v 6; a mend with lead clamps is visible).
(Author's photograph, courtesy of the Ephorate of Antiquities of Halkidiki and Aghios Oros. The rights to the monument shown belong to the Hellenic Ministry of Culture and Sports (Law 3028/2002). Olynthos is under the supervision of the Ephorate of Antiquities of the Halkidiki and Aghios Oros, Ministry of Culture and Sports.)

Greek communities on the northern Black Sea coast, the earlier houses were typically semi-subterranean, possibly mitigating against harsh winter conditions. Settlement location also to some extent determined the materials available: for example houses on the Aegean islands, where timber was relatively scarce but flat stones relatively plentiful, were typically built of stone, in contrast with those on the mainland, where mudbrick normally prevailed. At the same time, the topography of the settlement site must have influenced the size and form of houses to some extent, perhaps explaining the narrow, linear houses of Azoria and Kavousi Kastro (Chapter 5). Nevertheless, some communities adopted regular plans despite unfavourable terrain, as at Vroulia on the island of Rhodes (Figure 2.13). In some cases, significant investment was required to minimise such difficulties, as at Priene, where extensive terracing was used to facilitate the construction of a linear street grid and courtyard houses (Chapter 5). A further influence on the forms taken by settlements and houses was the history of the individual community: the city of Athens, for example, grew up over time, with irregular plans and oddly shaped house plots between (Chapter 3). But many cities which were newly planned and -built during the fifth and fourth centuries BCE were organised on a regular grid, with straight streets intersecting at intervals which produced rectangular 'insulae', or blocks of buildings, between, offering spaces for orthogonally planned houses. Inscriptions from Black Corcyra on the Dalmatian coast and from Pergamon, show how cities delegated responsibility for laying out areas of land and maintaining the urban environment, to individuals and groups within the community. This would have led to a co-ordinated approach to the planning and construction of housing. Such planning and oversight can be seen in the way that houses share party walls, not only in the new foundations like Olynthos, but also in established cities like Athens. It is unclear whether individuals were responsible for the construction of their own homes or whether the task was a specialist one. In the context of Olynthos, Nicholas Cahill has suggested convincingly that the creation of a row of houses was a collaborative project. The outer walls of each block were built at one time, necessitating co-operation. On the other hand, the styles of construction used for the socles were different in different houses, implying that several teams of builders had been at work. Cahill speculates that those teams consisted of members of the households planning to live in the houses, helped by their extended families together with friends. In such a situation, the final layout of the house would have been governed not only by the dimensions of the plot and the need to use drainage patterns which would fit with those of the neighbours, but also perhaps by the requirements of the first set of occupants. Jamie Sewell has argued, in addition, that economic and technological factors also played a role in shaping the houses at the site, and that structures which were of comparable size and similar layout were built because the materials for each house were provided in standardised dimensions and quantities. This is an intriguing idea and fits with the generally agreed upon hypothesis that the houses in question may have been built over a relatively short period to accommodate households moving into the city from elsewhere. Nevertheless, in relation to Olynthos, at least, it may overestimate the degree of formal similarity between properties. The layout and room dimensions are, in fact, quite variable, while it is actually the total area and common range of facilities that are the most striking similarities between the houses as a group. (Sewell's theory may also overestimate the desire and capacity of the city to provide materials.)

The 'family, friends and neighbours' model is not the only way one could envisage the process of construction involving teams of workers: if an individual row of houses was to be built in a short time for incoming residents, teamwork might simply have been the most efficient method – involving either groups of future residents, or existing citizens anticipating the arrival of new settlers. The use of such construction methods in the Classical Greek world has been documented in monumental buildings through observation of masonry styles, while small numbers of inscriptions preserve contracts for constructing temples, showing that specific elements were allocated to different craftsmen. The identities of those who were involved in laying out and building houses like those at Olynthos and elsewhere will probably remain unknown and may well have varied from place to place and time to time. What this discussion shows is that a given house will potentially have been shaped by a variety of factors, including the personal preferences of individual households, the materials and time available, and the local historical or political circumstances, as well as more general cultural expectations. For archaeologists, the challenge is to distinguish these and other influences from each other by looking at the houses themselves and also by viewing them within their broader architectural, geographical and chronological contexts.

In addition to the architectural features of a house, excavation also uncovers evidence for the furnishings and possessions of its former inhabitants in varying numbers. In comparison with those one would expect in a modern western household, these 'finds' are normally relatively sparse, although they increase in quantity, variety and sophistication through the period covered here. Organic materials, such as wood and textiles, do not survive archaeologically except in rare circumstances, so the presence of such items as furniture and cushions usually has to be deduced indirectly. They are sometimes represented on painted pottery, and they are also listed on the Attic Stelai (inscriptions detailing objects confiscated by the Athenian state and put on sale as punishment following the conviction of the general Alkibiades and his associates in 415/14 BCE). Neither source is straightforward to interpret for various reasons: the text on the stelai is incomplete; the precise meaning of the vocabulary used is not always certain; and the documents may not have consisted of complete inventories of the houses involved. The images on pottery needed to be similar enough to the experience of viewers to be readily interpretable, but this does not mean that the furnishings they depict can be taken as in any way 'typical'. These sources do, nevertheless, provide insights into some of the sorts of items that may once have been kept in some houses.

The stelai list a range of perishable goods including grain, wine, olives, olive oil and firewood, alongside containers such as baskets and boxes. Pieces of furniture include stools, chairs and tables. Other kinds of items may have a better chance of surviving archaeologically, including agricultural tools such as hoes and pruning hooks, which may have been made of metal. A few pieces of personal clothing are listed such as cloaks and sandals. In general, though, the lists highlight the contrast between attitudes towards property in the ancient Greek world and those of the modern west. The overwhelming majority of the items seem to be utilitarian and for the use of the household as a whole. It is tempting to wonder whether the owners of the household took away prized personal items before the property was confiscated, though this is a question we cannot, of course, answer. The images on painted pottery show rooms fitted out with similar furniture to that listed, with couches, tables and stools. Patterned textiles, particularly cushions, are a prominent element.

Archaeologically, the vast majority of artefacts found in excavated houses are ceramic. From the beginning of our period, these include vessels for serving, storage, and cooking, but also other items such as equipment for domestic cloth production (loom weights and spindle whorls). By the fifth century BCE, this range has broadened to include decorative elements such as wall plaques and architectural mouldings. The comfort and appearance of individual rooms would have been enhanced by the presence of the textiles mentioned above, which, in many cases, were probably produced by members of the household, and would have been used for cushions and throws. Small amounts of metal (mainly bronze, but also iron) served a variety of purposes, including fixtures or fittings such as nails, handles and door knockers and portable braziers. Bronze, silver and exceptionally even gold, were also used for items such as drinking cups and containers for mixing wine with water. Wood, ivory and bone were formed into boxes, pins, combs and other personal items. By the late fourth and third centuries BCE glass was occasionally used as inlay for wooden containers or furniture, and even for small perfume bottles.

As noted above, the number and variety of objects found in domestic contexts changes through time, with later houses generally yielding more, and more costly, possessions. But there are many exceptions to this generalisation since there are several other factors at work. These include the location of the settlement, the socio-economic status of the original occupants of the house, the circumstances of its abandonment, its state of preservation, and the aims and methods of the excavators. In practice, these factors will all have interacted to shape the assemblage surviving from any one house, but it is helpful to consider the potential effects of each one in isolation. Taking first the question of location: it seems that access to trade routes and raw materials may have affected the quantities of basic items present since there are certain regions in which, even as late as the third century BCE, households seem to have had relatively few possessions in comparison with contemporary households elsewhere. For example, in Olbia, a Greek city north-west of modern Crimea, there seems to have been a shortage of even one of the most basic domestic commodities of all – pottery: not only were the quantities found by excavators relatively small, but there were unusually large numbers of vessels which had broken and then been mended with lead, suggesting that they were valuable, or even irreplaceable.

In relation to the social status of the original occupants of the houses, throughout the period discussed in this volume the status and resources of a household will have been important factors in determining house size as well as the number and range of artefacts found within. At the start of our period, the majority of dwellings were small, single-room structures, with an average area of about 80 m² and without surviving evidence of architectural elaboration. There is some variation in size, but while larger buildings may have been associated with wealthier individuals and/or households, the house rarely seems to have been used to symbolise status in a straightforward way. Elites asserted their social position through a variety of other means, including burials and, later, sanctuary dedications, as well as practices such as feasting. By the mid fourth century BCE, better-off members of society were investing increasing resources in their houses, creating larger structures with more rooms and more architectural decoration. As noted in Chapter 3, for many urban dwellers in the fifth and fourth centuries BCE, owning a house which conformed to a particular set of architectural conventions may have expressed citizen status, or at least, an aspiration to behave like a man of citizen status in a citizen state. It therefore seems to have been important to have a structure that 'fitted in' with those around it.

By the third century BCE, members of the elite routinely spent large amounts on building and furnishing their houses. At the same time, however, there must have been a considerable proportion of the population who continued to live in much smaller, less elaborate structures and with fewer possessions. Excavators have focused the majority of their attention on higher-status buildings. Poorer households are, therefore, likely to be under-represented archaeologically, but they can certainly be detected at a few sites: in the context of fifth-century BCE Athens, for example, the smallest houses discovered in the area around the Agora consist of only two or three rooms and an open courtyard. At Olynthos, a few house plots on the North Hill were subdivided to provide accommodation for several households at around the same date. In second- and first-century BCE Delos, recent work has emphasised the presence, alongside elaborate,

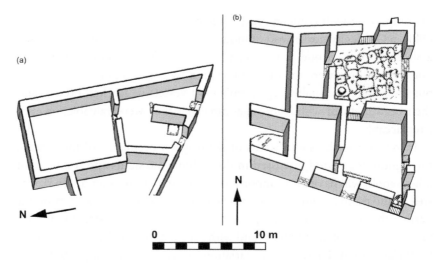

Figure 1.4 a and b: Examples of small residential/commercial premises from Delos.
(Drawn by Lorene Sterner based on Trümper 2005b, Fig. 8.1.)

wealthier residences, of a number of small establishments combining commercial facilities with modest residential accommodation (Figure 1.4). Textual evidence also points to the existence of 'synoikiai' – multiple-family dwellings or apartments, from at least the fifth century BCE. Such structures have yet to be positively identified archaeologically, but some forms of permanent or temporary residential accommodation are beginning to be isolated. A possible example is 'building Z' at the Kerameikos, which in its best-preserved phase (phase 3) some scholars have identified as a brothel (Figure 1.5). Even if this identification is correct, to judge from the array of domestic pottery, weaving equipment and personal items, individuals may have resided in the building at least for part of the time, while its scale also suggests the possibility that it may have served as a communal dwelling.

The circumstances leading to the abandonment of individual houses are highly variable and obviously help to determine what was left behind to be found during an archaeological investigation. In some cases, houses were vacated hurriedly with only limited time for residents to prepare, and perhaps little opportunity to take their possessions with them when they departed. For example, at Olynthos, historical sources tell us of the siege, capture and ultimate destruction of the city in 348 BCE by king Philip II of Macedon, who is said to have killed or enslaved all the inhabitants. In such

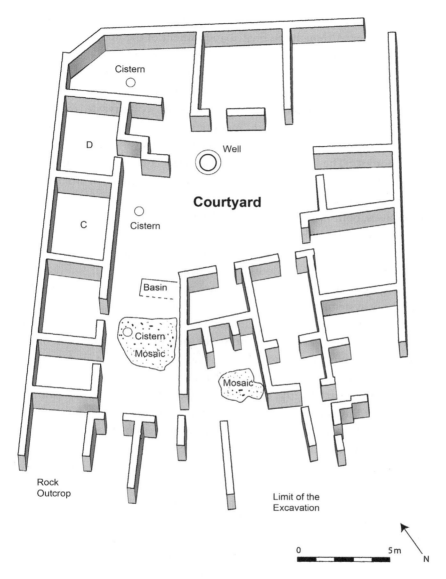

Figure 1.5 'Building Z' in the Kerameikos, Athens (phase 3).
(Drawn by Lorene Sterner based on Ault 2016, Fig. 4.4.)

circumstances the occupants are unlikely to have been able to carry away many of their things, but the houses may have been looted by Philip's army and a few seem to have been burned. Excavators found evidence of the hurried abandonment of the city in the form of caches of valuables which had been buried under the earth floors of some of the houses. These included several hoards of coins and also larger items such as a portable bronze brazier. Although the final abandonment of the houses at Olynthos is likely to have been rapid, the circumstances meant that their contents may not have been organised in their normal fashion. Even the fixtures and fittings could have been affected: the historian Thucydides, describing the flight of the rural population from the Attic countryside during the Peloponnesian War in 431 BCE, mentions that the inhabitants took with them not only their household equipment but also the woodwork from their homes. The portability of structural components implied by Thucydides is borne out in the evidence from a number of inscriptions. Leases dating between the fourth and second centuries BCE for farmhouses, both in Attica and on the island of Delos, specify that wooden fixtures and fittings belonged to the tenant and they were, therefore, presumably removed at the end of the tenancy. Similarly, the Attic Stelai also include items such as doors and ladders.

Salvaging of fixtures, fittings, furniture and possessions is likely to have been more systematic where the occupants of a structure moved out in a leisurely, pre-planned fashion. The scale of such activities normally has to be inferred during excavation from the amount and condition of the material remaining: for example, at the Classical farmhouses in Attica near the Dema wall and near the Cave of Pan at Vari, the last inhabitants seem to have been particularly thorough in cleaning their houses prior to departure. Only small fragments of pottery remained in crevices in the bedrock, and at the Dema house even most of the roof-tiles were missing. At Athens there is some evidence that, as well as salvaging possessions, the process of leaving a house may have involved ritual activity. This may have introduced new configurations of material not characteristic of the house's use as a dwelling: a number of properties excavated in and around the Agora yielded pyres in the floor deposits of some of the rooms. There is also, occasionally, evidence that while certain rooms in a structure may have been abandoned, others continued to be occupied (for example, in house C in the Athenian Agora, discussed in Chapter 3, a shop or work-shop with direct access from the exterior seems to have remained in use after the remainder of the complex had fallen into disuse). It is possible that derelict buildings served as dumps used by the occupants of neighbouring properties. The process of abandonment would, therefore, have led not only to the removal of some items, but also to the introduction of others which were not part of the original domestic assemblage.

The abandonment process is thus likely to have transformed a house to a greater or lesser degree, depending on the circumstance of its final occupants' departure, their level of resources, and the behaviour of neighbours (including whether the building was re-occupied at a later date). Other transformations will have taken place as the structure became part of an archaeological, rather than an inhabited, landscape. The extent to which structural elements, fixtures and possessions are preserved differs from site to site. A key influence is the micro-environment in and around a building. In most of the locations discussed in this book, there is a moderate amount of moisture in the air and soil. Under these circumstances organic materials such as wooden roof beams begin to rot even if they have not been removed. At the same time, mudbrick walls degrade very quickly once roofs and protective surface coatings are no longer in good condition. The individual sections of brick collapse and, in most cases, dissolve back into mud, leaving the stone socle which outlines the plan of the building but reveals little about its superstructure.

Where houses are built principally of stone, they are normally better preserved. The town of Delos (discussed in Chapter 7) offers a striking example: here, roof- and floor-beams have long since disappeared and the uppermost courses of stone have collapsed, but the house walls often still stand to a height of several metres, preserved beneath the stone tumbled from the upper parts of the superstructure. These buildings thus retain the openings for doors, windows and stairways, and reveal where structural alterations have been made, such as blocking doors or inserting additional walls which do not bond (are not integrated physically) with those of the original structure. During excavation, painted wall plaster is sometimes found on both interior and exterior walls, although exposure to air, rain and sunshine following excavation means that much of this has now disappeared. While at such sites organic materials like wood, food and textiles do not generally survive, it is occasionally possible to retrieve traces of foodstuffs parched by fire. These include grain, fruit seeds and olive pits; as, for example, at the large, fourth-century BCE farm site of Tria Platania, on the eastern slopes of Mount Olympos (discussed in Chapter 7). Here, large storage jars found in situ contained pips from grapes, while archaeobotanical evidence for a wide variety of other foodstuffs was also found in the soil, including wheat, olives, beans, lentils, peas, blackberries and cherries. In a few instances, fragments of textiles may also be preserved in charred form, although this is most common at burial sites where a body has undergone cremation (as in the male burial under the heröon building at Lefkandi, discussed in Chapter 2), rather than in domestic contexts. If the soil is not too acidic, animal bones and shells can sometimes also offer some information about food production and diet. For example, in the tower compound at Thorikos in Attica (discussed in Chapter 3), the excavators were able to determine that the inhabitants of one house ate pork and shellfish, discarding bones and shells under a staircase in the courtyard.

In exceptionally dry climates or in small areas of a site or building which have been serendipitously free of moisture, mudbrick can survive. At the Graeco-Roman village of Karanis (Fayum, Egypt) the desert environment has preserved the mudbrick walls of numerous houses to a height of several storeys. As with the stone walls at Delos, here archaeologists have been able to study details of the superstructure such as the locations of windows and wall niches, and also occasional painted plaster decoration. Wooden structural elements such as door leaves and window shutters are often preserved here as well, although the wood has lost its structural qualities, resulting in the collapse of beams supporting floors and roofs. Textiles and other organic materials are also present here, too, directly attesting to a variety of aspects of life which elsewhere have to be inferred indirectly. At the other end of the spectrum, wood, seeds and other organic substances can also be preserved where levels of groundwater are high. Saturation soon after the abandonment of a house excludes oxygen and prevents the action of bacteria which cause decomposition. Such situations are rare among Greek sites, but they do sometimes apply to small deposits like those found in wells, where groundwater has been consistently high since Antiquity. An example, excavated in the Athenian Agora (the main square of the ancient city) in 1937, contained two wooden buckets and a wooden comb, all dating to the Late Roman period.

A final consideration affects the interpretation of those artefacts which have survived and been recovered by archaeologists. It is tempting to regard objects found in different locations around the house as representing items left behind by the inhabitants as they went about their daily routines. This would mean that activities carried out in various locations could be 'read' from the items found there. In practice, however, there are a range of explanations for an item arriving at the spot in which archaeologists find it. It may, of course have been used there, but it may also have been stored there until required elsewhere. Furthermore, at the time a house was abandoned, an individual object may no longer have been being used for the purpose for which it was originally made: it could have been set aside as rubbish but disposed of within the boundaries of the house (for instance, in a pit under the floor or in a courtyard – as in the koprones or rubbish pits in the houses in Athens and at Halieis in the Argolid, discussed in Chapters 3 and 4) or it could have been intended to be stored temporarily pending disposal elsewhere. Given the relative scarcity of possessions, they must also have been intensively recycled – either intact or in fragments – for other purposes: at Olynthos, for example, a small, fine ware jug was used for mixing mortar to prepare a floor. Even broken pottery sherds had secondary functions – for instance as building materials – as in House I at Eretria (discussed in Chapter 6), where they were used in the mortar matrix of the walls, layered between the stone core and plaster surface. The observations of excavators in attempting to distinguish between artefacts deposited in connection with these different types of scenario are clearly crucial if artefacts are to be used to assist in reconstructing patterns of activity within the domestic context.

Past Research on Ancient Greek Housing

Regardless of the processes leading to the deposition of objects within a house or the effects of decay, the information recovered from any excavated house is heavily dependant on the aims and methods of the archaeologists carrying out the investigation. Until the late-nineteenth century little archaeological research had been done to uncover and understand the remains of the houses of Classical Greece. Early ideas about their architecture and organisation were, therefore, based on the ancient textual sources and on analogies with the extensively excavated remains of houses from Roman Herculaneum and Pompeii, in Italy. At the turn of the century, ancient Greek houses began to be excavated in increasing numbers. Substantial blocks of multiple-room houses with central courtyards were unearthed during large-scale campaigns at Priene, Delos and Olynthos (Map 1).

For most of the twentieth century the interpretation of these and other excavated sites continued to be dominated by a reliance on texts. Priene and Olynthos, in particular, were used as 'type-sites' to exemplify two different house designs whose patterns of organisation were said to correlate with descriptions given by the Roman architect Vitruvius. In the 'prostas'-type, which is sometimes also found on mainland Greece as at Abdera, the courtyard and main room are articulated through a deep but relatively narrow porch, identified as Vitruvius' 'prostas' (Figure 1.6 and see Text Extract 10). At Olynthos, by contrast, a number of the rooms are accessed via a broad portico, identified as a 'pastas' (Figure 1.7), which occasionally ran around all four sides of the courtyard to form a 'peristyle'. As we shall see in Chapter 7, however, the peristyle-house is exemplified by a number of the larger residences on Delos (Figure 1.8).

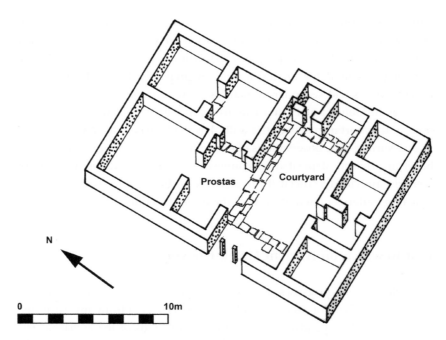

Figure 1.6 Example of a 'prostas' type house: Abdera house C.
(After Nevett 1999, Fig. 1.)

The textual sources thus formed the basis both for distinguishing the types, and also for creating the labels that were associated with the various configurations of the physical remains. The word peristyle itself is derived from the Greek term 'peristylion', meaning 'having columns all around', a fair description of the courtyards for which excavators generally use this word. Terminology from the texts was also borrowed for other elements of the excavated buildings; for example, a variety of ancient authors mention a space called the 'andronitis' or 'andron', which is used for male drinking parties or 'symposia'. Some black- and red-figure vases appear to show such parties (Figure 1.9), with the participants reclining on couches. A number of excavated houses incorporate one room (or, more rarely, several rooms) in which the floor has a raised border, and the door is placed off-centre, as if to accommodate couches along the walls. It seems a fairly good guess that such features can be associated with the surviving descriptions and images, and that these rooms can reasonably be termed androns (the plural of andron). In the case of other terms, however, things are less clear-cut. For example, texts also make reference to a 'gunaikon' or 'gunaikonitis' – usually translated as women's quarters – in opposition to the andron or andronitis. Yet it is unclear where such a space

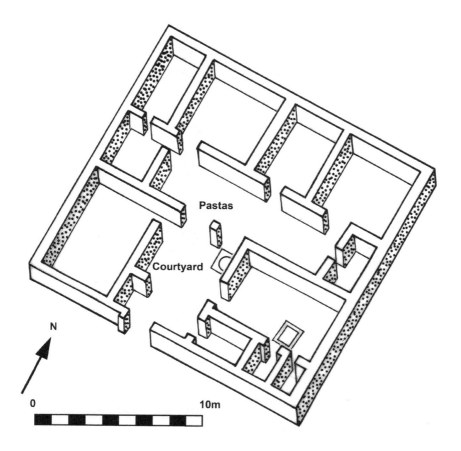

Figure 1.7 Example of a 'pastas' type house: house A vii 6 from Olynthos. (After Nevett 1999, Fig. 2.)

would have been located and what its features would have been. Indeed, it seems probable that the term does not refer to a specific room but rather indicates the domestic part of the house, away from the andron.

Being aware of the fact that the basis for applying some of these Greek words to the archaeological material is not always very strong is not merely a question of pedantry: the use (or misuse) of these terms can result in circular arguments and can be actively misleading since they can form the basis for assumptions about the role of a room in daily life. At the same time, the inhabitants may not necessarily always have used space in the way the builders envisaged, particularly where a house was occupied for several generations. The ancient vocabulary is, therefore, employed only sparingly here and texts are not relied upon to draw direct inferences about the possible uses of the rooms concerned. Rather, discussion of their roles is

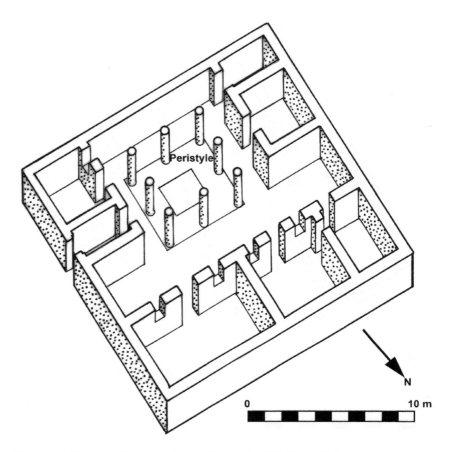

Figure 1.8 Example of a 'peristyle' type house: the Hill House, Delos. (After Nevett 1999, Fig. 3.)

based directly on the architectural and (where available) artefactual evidence for the activities which may have taken place there.

The major campaigns of exploration at Olynthos and Karanis, both carried out during the 1920s and 1930s, were unusual in paying attention to housing at a time when most classical archaeologists were drawn to monumental religious and civic buildings like temples and theatres. As noted above, however, the late nineteenth and early twentieth centuries also saw the excavation of significant numbers of houses at a few other ancient Greek sites, including Priene and Delos. The primary goal of the excavators was normally to explore the layout of individual structures and the way in which they fitted into the urban plan. Limited interest was also taken in the domestic artefacts – particularly as a means of dating a structure, or where they were perceived to be of intrinsic artistic interest.

Figure 1.9 Attic red-figure stamnos with a 'symposium' scene.
(British Museum 1843.1103.99, attributed to the Peleus Painter, ca. 450–440 BCE. © Trustees of the British Museum, reproduced by permission.)

The work carried out at Olynthos and Karanis was well ahead of its time in that inventories were made listing some of the pottery, metalwork and other domestic artefacts uncovered, along with information about where in individual houses some of them were found. The stated aim of this approach was similar in each case and was relatively straightforward, namely, to provide a context for ancient literature. (The excavators of these sites were re-orienting the priorities of accepted archaeological practice quite radically. It is perhaps no coincidence, therefore, that the field director at Karanis, Enoch Peterson, had previously worked for the excavator of Olynthos, David Robinson, at his earlier excavation of Pisidian Antioch, in southern Turkey.)

Through most of the twentieth century, the goals of many excavators of ancient Greek houses remained relatively static, with priority given to understanding their architecture and layout. Increasing numbers of directors were, however, inspired to fuller recording of the associated artefacts, and particularly, the locations in which they were found, even if those data were not always fully published. This was particularly the case in the settlements of the early first millennium BCE. For example, at Nichoria (discussed in Chapter 2), which was excavated in the 1970s, sufficient information was recorded to enable a distribution map to be drawn up of the objects found in one structure, Unit IV.1. Towards the end of the twentieth century, the aims of studies of ancient housing began to shift. The influence of ideas from other academic disciplines (particularly household archaeology, first developed for analysing other cultures in different parts of the world) offered the possibility of using excavated houses in order to address questions about ancient society. In the early first-millennium contexts these questions included the nature of the social structure and the origins of later cult practices. For the fifth and fourth centuries BCE the character of relationships between the two sexes was a major issue. At the same time, the introduction of computers made the storage and analysis of data much faster and more straightforward, enabling (for example) statistical analyses of Robinson's original data from Olynthos.

Scholarship on the topic of ancient Greek housing has been transformed since the late 1980s, when two landmark publications suggested in different ways, and on very different scales, that the forms taken by Greek houses were intimately connected with fundamental aspects of political and social life. This assumption has formed the basis of a variety of further work which has sought to re-evaluate excavated evidence as a means of addressing social questions. These studies have incorporated ideas and analytical techniques developed by archaeologists working in other cultural contexts. Today, it is clear that Greek housing can be used actively as a tool for understanding Greek society, rather than simply to illustrate social-historical accounts based on texts. This body of material offers unique insights into aspects of culture not addressed by written sources, a means of redressing some of the biases inherent in those sources by allowing access to the activities of a wider variety of social groups in a greater range of locations, and it enables a more dynamic view of change through time.

Large numbers of Classical and Hellenistic houses have now been excavated and studied, from locations across the Greek world. As knowledge has improved, it has become clear that there was considerable variety

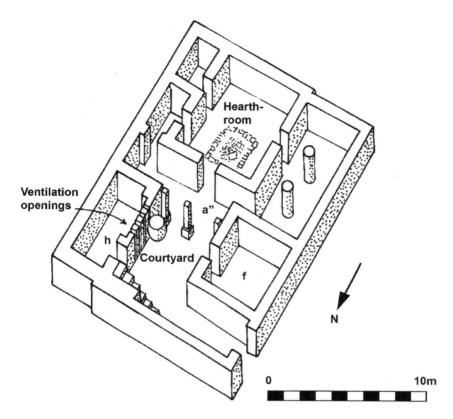

Figure 1.10 Example of a 'hearth-room' house: House 1 at Ammotopos.
(After Nevett 1999, Fig. 4.)

in scale and plan. Like the houses at Priene and Olynthos, many are organised around an open courtyard with the rooms entered individually via some kind of portico. One exception to this general pattern is a type of house known as the 'hearth-room house', which was identified and described more recently than the other types (Figure 1.10). Here, the layout is dominated by a large interior space featuring a central hearth and giving access to many of the other rooms. The courtyard is relatively small and typically only a few rooms open off it. So far, this type seems to have been relatively rare, being found on the central western Greek mainland (at Ammotopos and Kassope in Epiros – see Chapter 4) although houses from elsewhere sometimes include some of its organising principles. There has recently been a dramatic increase in the information available from the island of Crete, where there also seem to have been distinctively different patterns of spatial organisation from those found in other areas, with internal courtyards developing relatively late and being comparatively rare (discussed in Chapter 5).

The future promises an increase in the breadth and sophistication of the questions asked of the archaeological remains of houses, with associated demands on excavators to recover more information, for example comprehensive lists of artefacts and the locations in which they were found. At the same time, an important expansion is taking place in the variety of types of data, requiring more widespread adoption of a number of scientific techniques. These include analysis of fragments of bone and botanical remains, which reveal patterns of activity across the house and offer an insight into diet and foodways (among other things). At the same time, the introduction of soil micromorphology and geochemical studies is adding a new dimension, leading, for example, to improved understanding of the nature of early metallurgy and how it was integrated with other domestic activities. More widespread use of these and other scientific techniques in the field promises greatly to expand our knowledge of the range and organisation of domestic activities, and of the role ancient Greek houses and households played in relation to wider society.

Today's excavation projects uncover relatively small numbers of houses in comparison with their predecessors. At Olynthos, for example, Robinson's excavations fully or partially uncovered a total of approximately one hundred houses during only four seasons of work. Part of the reason this was possible was that, in common with many other directors of this era, Robinson had long field seasons and was able to pay for the participation of large numbers of local workers (for instance, his notebooks show that, during the 1928 season, there were two hundred people working simultaneously at the site). But it is also the case that projects carried out at that time neglected much information which is now regarded as significant and the collection of which makes excavation much slower and more laborious. For instance, today it is standard practice to explore the stratigraphy (the vertical sequence of deposits) making diagrams of the different levels as viewed from the side (section drawings), as well as horizontal plans. Such information is vital in enabling archaeologists to identify and distinguish between different phases of occupation and can even be used to isolate material coming from collapsed upper storeys. For example, both Ioulia Vokotopoulou's work at Olynthos during the 1990s and the work of the more recent Olynthos Project have demonstrated that at least two different levels are potentially distinguishable in houses from the site. Nevertheless, no section drawing from David Robinson's original excavation is included, either in his publication or in the original field notes.

Even in terms of the recovery and recording of artefacts, in which he was so ahead of his time, Robinson would today be criticised: the small numbers noted from each room suggest that he focused on those which were largely complete, discarding others which, although fragmentary, may have held important information about the organisation of activity in a house. (For example, the number of ceramic items recorded from house A viii 10, including the unpublished items listed in the notebooks, totals 16, although in addition, two deposits were recorded as containing 'much coarse pottery'; by comparison, the number of ceramic items recovered from house 7 at Halieis, excavated in the 1960s and 1970s, totalled around 6,230 and is estimated to represent the remains of at least 824 different vessels. The preliminary findings of the Olynthos Project in house B ix 6 suggest that it was particularly the coarse and plain pottery that Robinson's team neglected to preserve or record, although Robinson left no indication of his criteria for retaining or discarding material.)

Despite the availability to today's archaeologists of mechanised and computerised equipment, therefore, modern excavations are able to proceed at only a fraction of the speed of those of Robinson and Peterson. For example, exploration of a single Archaic house at Euesperides (modern Benghazi in Libya) by the Libyan Society during the 1990s took three field seasons. This slow rate of progress means that, at most sites, our knowledge is restricted to a much smaller number of structures. To some extent the effect of this can be mitigated by the use of new, non-destructive geophysical techniques such as electrical resistance and magnetometry, which, if soil conditions are right, can reveal the plans of unexcavated structures, as at the site of Plataia in Boiotia, where such work revealed the pattern of streets, building blocks and even the internal walls of individual structures. Similar results were obtained more recently at Olynthos by the Olynthos Project.

In the context of this book, one challenge in attempting to piece together the 'big picture' is to integrate the information derived from excavations which have focused on architecture, with that from the small number of projects which have had more ambitious goals and have published a wider range of information. It is unclear how representative our current excavated sample might be of the full spectrum of houses occupied by ancient Greek households. As noted above, there is likely to be a bias towards the recovery of houses belonging to higher status households, which must have been larger, more substantially constructed, and consequently, better preserved and more visible. These are also the structures which tend to be more attractive to excavators because they offer more information from which to understand the organisation of the original building. At the same time, they often contain features considered to be aesthetically pleasing, such as mosaics, whose discovery was, at least in the context of some of the earlier excavations, a major motivation for excavation. It is, therefore, likely that smaller, flimsier, low status structures are under-represented in our sample of excavated houses. At the same time, regional variation may have been obscured to some extent by the fact that the amount of excavation that has taken place in different parts of the Greek world varies. It therefore seems likely that as research intensifies and more data are gathered, an increasingly detailed picture will emerge of similarities and contrasts between houses in different regions or dating to different time-periods.

Greek Domestic Architecture ca. 950–500 BCE

Reinventing the House

This chapter explores archaeological evidence for housing in mainland Greece and the eastern Aegean islands along with Greek settlements on the west coast of Asia Minor. The period covered runs from around 950 BCE to about 500 BCE. During the second millennium BCE, much of this region had been occupied by sophisticated, urban societies featuring a range of different types and sizes of domestic (and other) buildings which made use of a variety of technologies. By our period, however, a wave of widespread dislocation and destruction had been followed by a new era of settlement in small, village communities. It is the nature of the households in these communities that is our central theme. As we shall see, a growth in the scale and complexity of the settlements themselves was accompanied by a broadening of the variety of buildings being created and by an increase in the size and segmentation of the individual houses. Our first task, however, is to ask some basic questions about how to interpret the archaeological remains themselves.

Definitions and Origins: What Is a House?

In a modern, western city, distinguishing between residential buildings and those with other functions is generally relatively easy, even for a casual observer standing in the street. Houses and apartment blocks have their own characteristic features including: their scale; the number, size and arrangement of their doors and windows; and the nature of their relationship with neighbouring buildings, roads and walkways. But identifying an excavated ancient building as a 'house' is often less straightforward. Uncertainties and ambiguities are introduced by evidence which is missing because of the way the building was abandoned, preserved or excavated (see Chapter 1). But perhaps even more important, there are also cultural issues to be addressed. In many contemporary urban contexts, a residential building stereotypically plays a clearly defined and relatively limited range of roles: above all, it is a place to eat, sleep and relax with other residents and with invited visitors. There is a distinction between these 'private' functions and more 'public' ones. In other cultures, and during other periods, however, activities modern Euro-Americans consider 'private' or 'domestic' in character may be combined with a number of others, including (but not limited to) production of a variety of goods for consumption within or outside the household, bulk storage of agricultural produce, housing livestock, transacting business and receiving uninvited guests.

Unlike the later periods covered in this book, there is no direct written evidence from the beginning of the Early Iron Age to provide a cultural context within which to explore the way in which housing may have been conceptualised. How, then, was a house defined in this period? What roles did it fill and how may those roles have varied through time and space? A starting point for addressing these questions is provided by some of the most detailed published information about an Early Iron Age house, that from Unit IV.1 at Nichoria on the southern Greek mainland. More extensive evidence from other sites, including Eretria, Skala Oropou and Zagora, provides a context for assessing how representative the Nichoria example might be and for studying how individual houses were integrated into larger communities. A final example, the enigmatic Toumba building at Lefkandi, crystallises many of the issues discussed in the chapter.

Nichoria Unit IV.1

Evidence for several Early Iron Age structures was found at Nichoria in the south-west Peloponnese. The best-preserved of these is Unit IV.1 (as it was named by the excavators) (Figure 2.1). This building was occupied from the early tenth century BCE until about 800 BCE, when it was abandoned after being burned. It is apsidal in plan (that is, it has a curved wall at one end) and is oriented approximately east-west. The walls consisted of low socles formed by at least four courses of irregular stones and there was a superstructure of mud bricks. These were reinforced against both exterior and interior faces with wooden posts, while further wooden posts, seated on stone bases, supported the roof. An open area in front of the porch may have provided space for domestic activities. The building underwent at least one major episode of remodelling. There has been debate about its original layout and about the number and location of the doors. In its larger, later form the maximum dimensions were approximately 8 × 20 m, providing nearly 130 m^2 of interior space. This was divided into an open porch at the east end, a large main room in the centre, and a small area in the apse. Because most of the materials used were not very sturdy or

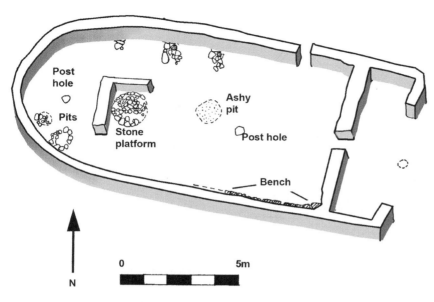

Figure 2.1 Nichoria building IV.1.
(Drawn by Lorene Sterner based on Mazarakis Ainian 1992, Fig. 4b.)

durable, some details of the construction and modification are unclear, and little is known for certain about the superstructure.

Terracotta building models of a slightly later date, which were dedications to the gods at several cult sites, seem to show buildings of the same or similar form. These suggest that there would have been a pitched (sloping) roof. The Perachora model (Figure 2.2) appears to represent small, triangular openings at the tops of the side walls for ventilation. These are paralleled in a stone house at tenth- to eighth-century BCE Zagora on Andros (discussed below), where an intact wall toppled over from vertical to horizontal, preserving the form of the wall face. Such openings are likely to have been small, however, and the main route by which smoke was vented or light and air entered Unit IV.1 was probably through doorway(s) to the exterior. The principal entrance was via the porch located at the east end, although in one phase there may also have been a secondary doorway in the north wall (as shown in Figure 2.1).

Nichoria Unit IV.1 is to some extent typical of a number of houses built in Greece during the tenth, ninth, eighth and even seventh centuries BCE: comparable examples have been excavated in a range of different regions including Attica, Euboia, Greek Macedonia and the Aegean islands. Comparable structures have also been found in settlements on the west coast of Asia Minor yielding Greek pottery. The buildings vary

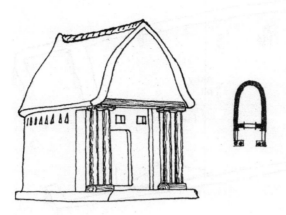

Figure 2.2 Reconstructed form and plan of a terracotta building model
from Perachora.
(After Payne et al. 1940, Plate 9b; scale not indicated.) Reproduced with permission of the
British School at Athens.

considerably in size, with single-room houses predominating. Two of the
larger examples, from phase 1 at Assiros in northern Greece, cover 120 m^2
and 125 m^2. Among the smallest is an oval house at the location of Old
Smyrna, Izmir (in Turkey) which covers only about 10 m^2. The arrangement of interior space in the various structures is also variable: particularly
in the larger examples, there could be internal partitions which created as
many as four or five separate rooms which were often entered in sequence.

Detailed information about the artefacts found in these buildings is
usually lacking, making it difficult to know how they were used and
whether there were functional distinctions between them. Nevertheless,
the evidence from Unit IV.1 is particularly revealing because the excavators
did record and publish the scattered objects found incorporated into its
mud floor. These accumulated from the activities of the building's occupants over a long period, and in some cases individual items are difficult to
attribute to a specific architectural phase. They do, however, offer an
indication of some of the activities the occupants may have engaged in
inside and around the building. The porch was furnished with large storage
jars for agricultural produce; their visibility may have had a symbolic
significance, suggesting that the household had substantial reserves of
agricultural wealth. Once inside, there was a stone bench against the south
wall of the main room, close to the entrance. In the centre of the room an
ash-filled pit may have been used for cooking. At the opposite end, a

circular stone platform may also have served as a fireplace. Animal bones mixed with ash littered the floor in this area and may have been swept from the platform itself. A large number of knucklebones also found here may have been used as gaming pieces. In fact, animal bones, some with cut- and tooth-marks were spread throughout both the main room and also the room in the apse. Cups, jugs and kraters (large, deep bowls) were found almost throughout the building, especially on the porch and around the fireplace. Ten spindle whorls (used in textile production) were also found against the walls of the main room, most of them on the north side. In the apse room, two deposits of legumes (peas or beans) lay on the floor, along with fragments of further storage jars. Two stone-lined pits, possibly also used for storage, had been dug into the floor itself. These show that agricultural goods were kept here as well as on the porch. A number of other miscellaneous items were recovered in this room, including an iron axe, an iron knife and the bronze central boss from a shield.

The long period of occupation and the architectural changes made to Unit IV.1 both suggest that the way in which interior space was used may have changed through time. The items found on the floor are, therefore, likely to represent a palimpsest resulting from different activities under-taken at different points in the building's history. For this reason, it is potentially misleading to try to assess in any detail where different activities were located within the interior. There may also have been variation over the short-term in the way in which space was used. For example, one scholar, Kare Fagerstrom, has suggested that the porch may have func-tioned for eating and drinking during summer months, while the interior hearth and fireplace provided more comfortable locations in winter. (This kind of routine might explain why pottery associated with drinking accu-mulated over such a wide area.) The range of items found in and around the house clearly attests to a variety of the activities making up the lives of the building's inhabitants. Tasks included: the storage of food and prepar-ation of meals of peas, beans, and meat; drinking; textile production; and even, perhaps, games of knucklebones. The shield boss and axe are evi-dence of other activities which were probably performed outside the confines of the house itself.

The dominant role played by vessels for food and drink in the overall assemblage, and a scarcity of artefacts in general, both create a rather different impression from the much more numerous and eclectic range of goods and possessions one might expect to see in a modern, western house. This can partly be explained by the fact that some of the items originally present in Unit IV.1 may have been removed when the building was abandoned by its final inhabitants. At the same time, because organic materials such as wood and textiles have not survived there are elements of the furnishings, utensils and personal items which have not left signs of their presence. In contrast, the pottery fragments and animal bones associated with eating and drinking have been preserved relatively well. It is also the case that in contrast with modern, western households, which are typically integrated into a market economy, purchasing food in small quantities for relatively immediate consumption, the household at Nichoria seems to have been part of a very different system. This was a subsistence economy in which the household itself produced much or most of its own food and would, therefore, have had to store in bulk basics like the legumes found in the apse. At the same time, the objects found at Nichoria had to be manufactured individually by hand and raw materials such as metals had to be imported over long distances via potentially unreliable trade networks. This meant that artefacts such as the shield boss were relatively costly in terms of labour and materials. Therefore, even if we were to be able to step back in time into the house at Nichoria with all of its original furnishings and possessions intact, it would probably still look relatively bare compared with what might be expected in the contemporary industrialised world.

The layout of the Nichoria house also shows other ways in which the experience of living here would have been rather different from that of living in a western house or apartment today. The available space, around 130 m^2, is relatively generous – equivalent to a three-bedroom apartment in modern Athens. In the absence of detailed evidence about the nature and size of households in Early Iron Age Greece, comparisons with other cultures can help to suggest parameters for the numbers of occupants. Anthropologists have found that, especially in larger households, there tends to be about 10 m^2 of space per person. This would give an estimated figure of about 13 individuals for the Nichoria building. Such a method of calculation is obviously very approximate for a variety of reasons: the quantity of space allocated per person varies greatly between societies. In the modern west we might expect a small nuclear family (parents and one or two children) to occupy this kind of home. By contrast, a recently built apartment complex in Guangzhou, China's third largest city, includes units comprising a living room, two bedrooms and a bathroom which are designed to accommodate up to six adults in an area of only 33 m^2. The relationship between house and household also changes through time: Unit IV.1 was in use over a long period and the numbers of residents must have fluctuated with the 'life cycles' of the occupying family or families as spouses moved in and babies were born, increasing the size of the resident group, while as time passed individuals will have died and mature children may have moved out.

Ethnoarchaeologists have observed that in some cultures there is a connection between the social and economic status of the occupants and the amount of living space at their disposal, with wealthy and/or high status households occupying larger dwellings. Unit IV.1 is relatively large in comparison with some of the other houses known from tenth- and ninth-century BCE Greece. Indeed, the excavators suggest that it may have belonged to the 'chief' of the village in which it stood. It is impossible to be certain how many people would have lived here at any one time or what the relationships between them might have been. Its size may suggest either that it was constructed for an extended family which perhaps included several generations and/or siblings with their spouses and families, or that it may, on occasion, have been used to accommodate significant numbers of visitors. Interior space here was also divided very differently from that in many contemporary societies: as far as we can see, the main functional distinction was between storage (in the apse) and living space (in the main room), with no separate areas for sleeping, eating, cooking or bathing. Most domestic activities must have been performed in the single large, central room, in full view of everyone else in the house, and perhaps also outside in the adjacent courtyard during fine weather. Visual and aural privacy (in the sense of not being seen or overheard), which can often be taken for granted in a large, multiroom house, cannot, therefore, have existed in Unit IV.1 or in other similar structures.

Early Iron Age Housing in Context: Eighth-Century BCE Settlement at Eretria

Unit IV.1 offers a detailed impression of an Early Iron Age dwelling and of the distribution of objects in its interior, but the layout of the Early Iron Age settlement at Nichoria as a whole is not easily reconstructed. Individual Early Iron Age houses can, however, be contextualised elsewhere in a few other locations. A particularly extensive picture is offered by the eighth–century BCE community at Eretria, on the island of Euboia. Today, this settlement lies buried beneath the modern town, which means that its original size and the density of occupation are difficult to reconstruct, but the stone socles of a number of mud brick buildings have been uncovered in several different areas. Comparison between them shows that there was some variation within the community in terms of house size and layout, and this has been interpreted as evidence that there may have been differences in the social statuses of the occupants.

In a southern neighbourhood near the ancient seashore lies the Roussos plot (Figure 2.3), where a series of buildings were constructed, destroyed and replaced in as many as six different phases dating between the middle of the eighth century and about 700 BCE. The result is that the surviving stone socles now represent a network of overlapping structures (Figure 2.4). One apsidal building, which may have been the earliest and was certainly the largest, had an area of about 40 m^2. Later, the south part of the plot was occupied by a series of oval and apsidal structures which were smaller in size, offering about 25–30 m^2 of interior space. Their furthest extent may have been defined on the south side by a straight boundary wall. These apsidal and oval buildings seem to have co-existed with a cluster of small, rectilinear ones which were roughly square in shape, each offering about 16 m^2 of interior space. At least one had a stone-built bench inside, similar to that found in Nichoria Unit IV.1. As we shall see later, such features have also been found in other buildings of this form and date.

The structures of the Roussos plot can be compared with those found elsewhere in Eretria. To the north, away from the shore, further curvilinear buildings have been excavated by Petros Themelis in an area referred to by some archaeologists as the 'Quarter of the Panathenaic Amphorae'. In the last quarter of the eighth century BCE an oval structure, house A, was built, with an area of approximately 55 m^2. To its east stood a perimeter wall which seems to have functioned to stabilise the foundations, preventing erosion by the nearby stream and retaining the soil on which the house stood. Artefacts found in and around the building include fragments of a table amphora (a large, closed container for liquids), a krater, a jug, and two drinking cups. A fire during the late eighth century BCE seems to have destroyed the house. At around 700 BCE a second apsidal building, house B, was constructed a short distance to the north-west. At around the same time, house A was also repaired and reinhabited. The occupation of this whole area lasted for about three generations: it seems to have been abandoned by about 625–600 BCE. The pottery found in both phases of house A parallels some of the kinds of shapes found at Nichoria, attesting to the consumption of drink. Under the earthen floor of house B, however, excavators found evidence for a rather different activity: a deposit of small gold ingots and scrap gold had been placed in a cup and buried, presumably with the intention of being recovered at a later date and perhaps reworked into new gold items.

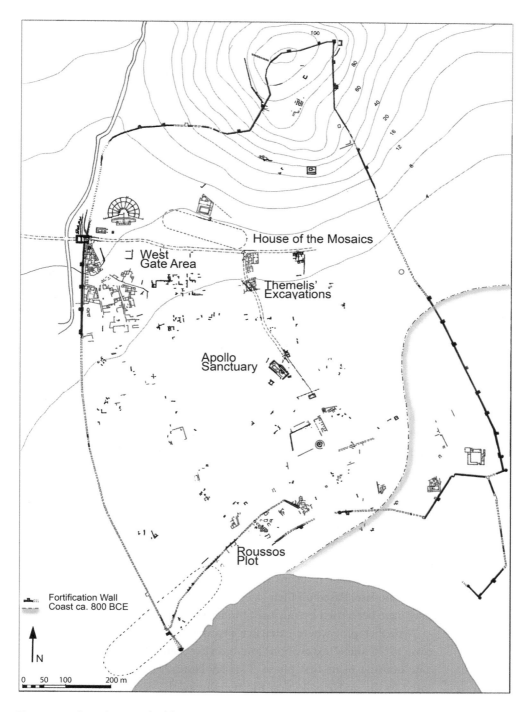

Figure 2.3 Plan of ancient buildings excavated at Eretria showing the locations of the areas mentioned in the text.

(Drawn by Lorene Sterner based on Sapouna Sakellaraki 1995, Fig. 9 and Lang 1997, 284–89.)

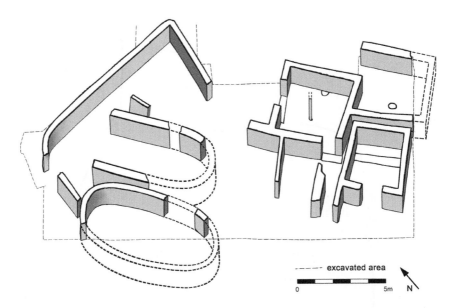

Figure 2.4 Early Iron Age structures on the Roussos plot, Eretria in their final phase of occupation.
(Drawn by Lorene Sterner based on Mazarakis Ainian 2007, Fig. 17.6.)

Rapid though the pace of rebuilding seems to have been in this northern area of Eretria, each phase of occupation was still longer than those of the buildings on the Roussos plot. The individual structures were also placed further apart and were somewhat larger, providing a more spacious living environment for the inhabitants. These differences have led one scholar, Alexander Mazarakis Ainian, to propose that the residents of the two neighbourhoods were of contrasting social statuses, the inland area being occupied by an elite group with more resources at its disposal, while the southern area may have housed less well-off traders and fishermen. Despite the differences in the scale of the houses in these two neighbourhoods, they are all an order of magnitude smaller than Unit IV.1 at Nichoria. This fact may be significant in terms of the numbers of people they were built to accommodate. Based on their size, it seems likely that the Eretria structures may have been used by nuclear families of perhaps four to six individuals.

A further plot where extensive investigation has been carried out lies close to Themelis' excavations and has also been interpreted as comprising elite housing in its first phase. This lay beneath the later sanctuary dedicated to the god Apollo and the remains of the early structures are very fragmentary but have been tentatively reconstructed (Figure 2.5). A cluster of apsidal and oval buildings dates to around the mid eighth century BCE

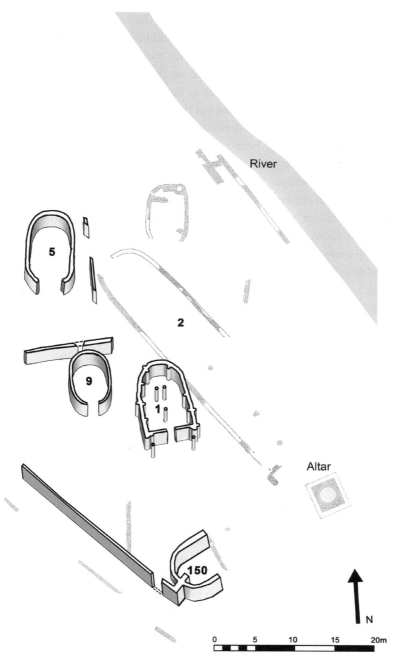

Figure 2.5 Early Iron Age buildings in the later Sanctuary of Apollo, Eretria. (Earlier buildings are reconstructed, later ones are shown in plan).
(Drawn by Lorene Sterner based on Mazarakis Ainian 1997, Fig. 104 and Verdan 2012a, Fig. 4.)

and traces of metalworking were found right across the area from this phase. One of the structures, labelled building 5 by archaeologists during recent re-investigation of the plot, was oval in form and had an area of about 65 m^2. Close to the entrance on the south side was found a hearth which the excavators interpreted as having been used for domestic activities, although they did not rule out the possibility that these may have been carried out alongside metalworking. A smaller apsidal building to the south (9) also seems to have been residential in character.

A third building on the same plot, building 1 (also known as the 'Daphnephoreion' or 'bay hut') is the best known Eretrian structure of this period and its interpretation has proved controversial. This is apsidal and has an area of about 60 m^2, comprising a shallow porch and a larger interior room with a hearth. Wooden posts originally supported the roof of the main room and the projecting corners of the porch. The walls of the building had pairs of wooden posts against their inner and outer faces. For this reason the excavators initially thought that the superstructure was made of woven twigs and branches, rather than mud brick. Further exploration has shown that this was not the case: like other eighth century BCE buildings, building 1 was, in fact, constructed of mud brick on a stone socle. The twin sets of posts probably served to stabilise the walls.

When building 1 was initially published, its excavators suggested that it was a temple. They were led to this conclusion partly because they took the construction materials and technique to be symbolic, an imitation of a cult building described by the Roman writer Pausanias in the second century CE. The interpretation also fitted with the later history of this area: immediately next to building 1, a further structure, building 2, was subsequently erected. Its foundations were apparently recessed to avoid one of the supporting posts of building 1, suggesting that the two may have co-existed for a time. Building 2 is a monumental 'hekatompedon' (literally, a structure measuring one hundred Greek feet in length). It uses the same basic construction techniques as its neighbours, consisting of a stone socle, mud brick superstructure and internal posts supporting the roof. The scale is totally different, however: the building is almost 35 m long and covers around 270 m^2. Several aspects of its construction and location suggest that it functioned as a temple, including its large size. In addition, a sacrificial altar and a pit containing offerings were located directly outside the doorway, which faced very approximately eastwards – a spatial relationship typical in later Greek temples. The artefacts found in the area, some of which were imported from as far away as the region of modern Lebanon, include pottery vessels, glass beads, bronze figurines and gold bands.

Subsequent excavations to the south brought to light a further building, 150. Its orientation towards the altar in front of the later monumental temple (2), suggested that it may also have played some kind of religious role. In the early seventh century BCE the entire area seems to have been cleared for the construction of a monumental, rectangular, stone temple to Apollo.

Given this later history it is perhaps tempting to assume that at least some of the earliest buildings on the plot, especially building 1, might also have played a religious role. Building 2 would then represent the continuation of a sacred function already present. As we have seen, the earliest material associated with these structures seems to point towards a domestic and manufacturing role, rather than a recognisable cult function. Nevertheless, in comparison with the other structures of this date at Eretria, building 1 is relatively large, and this has led to the suggestion that it may have represented the house of a high-status individual, a leader within the community. This fits in with general ideas about the nature of Early Iron Age society: based on a variety of archaeological evidence which has been interpreted with reference both to later texts and also ethnographic parallels, most communities are assumed to have had leaders or chiefs. These were men who were able to achieve and reinforce high social status by attracting followers through various means, including through control over access to resources such as surpluses of agricultural produce and/or imported and exotic goods. The leader's house may have served as a location for feasts and other social occasions to which his followers were invited.

Against this background, Alexander Mazarakis Ainian has proposed an attractive explanation, both for the history of buildings of the later Apollo sanctuary at Eretria, and also for the emergence of specialised cult buildings during the eighth century BCE more generally. He suggests that in Early Iron Age society religious ritual was initially associated with the house of a leader and that gradually, through time, such ritual came to occupy its own separate spaces – the earliest sanctuaries. This would explain the apparent change in the role played by this part of Eretria, from an elite residence to a dedicated cult place. The presence of metalworking, which today we would think of as an industrial activity to be carried out in a location separate from living accommodation, might seem surprising. Yet as we shall see, throughout antiquity workshops were often interspersed with, or even contained within, Greek domestic buildings. Furthermore, metals were not plentiful commodities during this period; control of their supply and working by leaders may have been a means of exercising power over their communities in a similar way to the control of agricultural surpluses and imported goods. It should therefore be no surprise to see this 'industrial' function represented in what may have been a high-status, residential context.

Another aspect of the eighth-century BCE structures at Eretria – the presence of boundary walls close to some of the houses – has been explained by Mazarakis Ainian in the light of his own excavation at a settlement lying across the straits from Eretria, on the mainland at Skala Oropou. This work has brought to light curvilinear buildings similar to those from Eretria, some of which can be shown to have been grouped within perimeter walls. One such enclosure in the central area of the site is relatively well-preserved and has been excavated in its entirety, along with several structures lying outside it (Figure 2.6). The perimeter walls mark out a space that is trapezoidal in shape with a jog on its eastern side and cover a total area of a little less than 250 m². The interior may have been accessible via three separate entrances. (If all were in use simultaneously then it seems likely that the wall provided a boundary marker or screen, rather than offering security, since the latter would be simpler with only a single entrance to protect or monitor.) Occupation of the enclosure lasted from the later eighth century into the seventh century BCE and inside

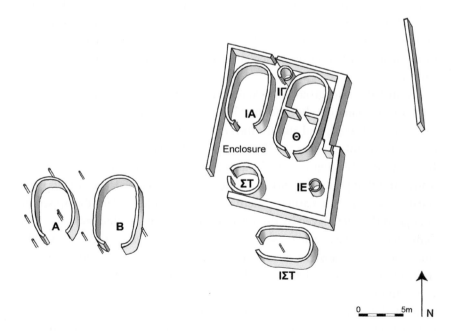

Figure 2.6 Early Iron Age buildings from the central area at Skala Oropou. (Drawn by Lorene Sterner based on Mazarakis Ainian 1997, Fig. 104.)

were arranged, at various times, a number of structures of varying shapes and sizes.

The largest, eastern, building, building Θ ('theta'), was occupied for a considerable period and underwent two major phases of reconstruction, being enlarged from about 45 m² to 56 m² before being reduced again. Inside, a well-preserved mud brick wall divided the space into two separate rooms, the inner one having a wide stone bench around the apse. Objects found here include fine ware kraters, jugs and cups, as well as lamps and a range of fragments of coarse pottery and storage vessels. Metal artefacts including lead fishing weights were also found. The smaller, western, oval building (building IA) had an area of about 34 m². A hearth or kiln lay at its centre and there was some evidence of metalworking, including two stone anvils and some slag. Domestic items were also uncovered here, including loom weights, spindle whorls, and a selection of fine ware cups and kraters. Mazarakis Ainian suggests that building Θ may have been used for communal feasting or drinking, while building IA served for a wider range of household activities. Aside from the evidence for metalworking, the range of activities represented in the two buildings is comparable to that suggested by the finds from Nichoria. Interestingly, two small circular buildings in the southern area of the enclosure (ΣΤ and IE) may have served a more specialised function or functions: a range of exotic goods found here have been identified as religious offerings. The buildings seemed to lack domestic finds and features. Mazarakis Ainian argues that the enclosure as a whole should be thought of as a single domestic unit comprising several separate buildings all functioning together as parts of a single larger whole. As he points out, there are parallels for the kind of house-compound arrangement he is suggesting, in present-day, non-western societies, where different activities such as sleeping and cooking are performed in separate structures within a single enclosure. In the Early Iron Age Greek context he suggests that a similar pattern of organisation can be identified tentatively also at Eretria. The material from the central area at Skala Oropou currently provides the most detailed published evidence of the artefacts associated with such a compound, which offer some insight into how the different structures in this type of enclosure were used.

The nature of the association between the buildings in this kind of compound is very significant because it potentially has a profound effect on the way in which we define a 'house' archaeologically in the Early Iron Age Greek context. Mazarakis Ainian's interpretation raises the possibility that even if an entire structure of this date is excavated, it may not always constitute the whole 'house' if that 'house' were distributed across multiple structures. Future work, particularly on the range of finds from buildings within enclosures of this kind, should shed further light on these different interpretative possibilities. It may be that no single model will describe all the archaeological examples found, but rather, some structures may have been independent while others formed part of larger groupings. Furthermore, those within a compound might have served variable combinations of roles at different points in the life cycle of a household, or at different stages during the existence of the compound itself. In addition to providing evidence about social organisation, the association between domestic activities and metalworking at Skala Oropou parallels the situation at Eretria and reinforces the assumption that manufacturing took place in close proximity to residential space during this period. The circular structures in the compound of building Θ provide a further indication of the potential of residences to play a spiritual role, supplementing the evidence from the Apollo sanctuary plot in Eretria.

Evidence for Social Change?: Housing at Zagora

As we have already seen, by around 700 BCE a new type of building which was square or rectangular in plan, had begun to appear at Eretria. One hundred metres east of the plot excavated by Themelis, a square building measuring 7.7 m by 7.7 m with a preserved area of around 60 m², was located beside an apsidal one. A section of wall found to the north could be part of a perimeter wall which may have surrounded both structures. No other walls of this period are reported, so it seems that the square building was probably free-standing. This new rectilinear design offered approximately the same amount of living-space as the neighbouring apsidal structure, but its shape has important practical implications. Not much is known about the superstructure of such buildings, but it is possible that they had flat, rather than pitched roofs. If this was the case, they may have been economical in using less timber for the roof structure than the pitched roofs of curvilinear buildings, and they might also have provided additional space for outdoor activities on the roof itself. There are also more obvious advantages: in comparison with curvilinear structures, rectilinear ones are more adaptable, they can potentially be built close together or even abut their neighbours, sharing party walls. This means that larger numbers of houses could be packed into a smaller area of land and could require fewer materials to construct. They could also be enlarged relatively easily by creating additional rooms adjoining existing ones. The inhabitants of

Eretria capitalised on these advantages to some extent. For example, among the cluster of orthogonal structures on the northern part of the Roussos plot, two units on the south-east side share a party wall, while to the north a third is contained within its own separate walls but fits closely into the angle formed by the junction of the other two (Figure 2.4).

Communities of similar rectilinear houses with one or two rooms have been found elsewhere, for example in the seventh century BCE at Emborio on Chios, where the individual dwellings, some with external courtyards, are scattered over the slopes of a steep akropolis (Figure 2.7). The implications of the rectilinear design can be seen most clearly, however, at another island site, Zagora on Andros, which was established during the late tenth century and abandoned by the close of the eighth century BCE never to be re-occupied. An absence of modern construction activity, means that several large areas could be excavated, giving a sense of the organisation of the community as a whole as well as offering a picture of the development and functioning of the individual houses.

Zagora is located on a high headland which juts out into the sea and is separated from the water by sheer cliffs. A fortification wall was built to protect the neck of land that gave access from the interior of the island of Andros. Space for the settlement itself was thus confined and this may have been an incentive to pack the houses close together. All of them were rectilinear in plan and each one abutted a neighbouring property on at least one side, sharing a party wall. Interestingly, the individual units were generally similar, not only in their basic layout, but also in their construction history. During the earlier phases of occupation, rows of one- or two-room houses were built in stone. Most had a porch, or more rarely, an antechamber, and some were approached through an exterior courtyard (Figure 2.8). Inside, the main room was usually rectangular and slightly deeper than it was wide. The dimensions and proportions of both porch and interior room varied somewhat, but a single house covered an area of approximately 50–80 m^2. The main internal features were wooden posts which supported a flat roof. There was typically also a stone bench along the rear wall which sometimes extended along the side walls as well. This bench was used as a base on which to stand storage vessels, as indicated by depressions in its upper surface. The excavators suggested that differences in the size and location of individual houses may have corresponded to social distinctions between occupying families.

Information about the complete inventories of individual residential units and the locations in which items were found has not been published, but, like the earlier Unit IV.1 at Nichoria, the artefacts found at the site

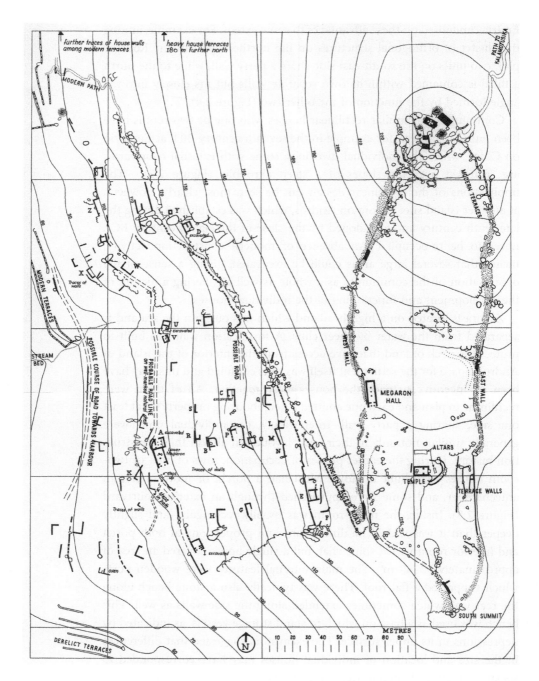

Figure 2.7 Plan of the Archaic settlement at Emborio, Chios.
(After Boardman 1967, Fig. 4.) Reproduced with permission of the British School at Athens.

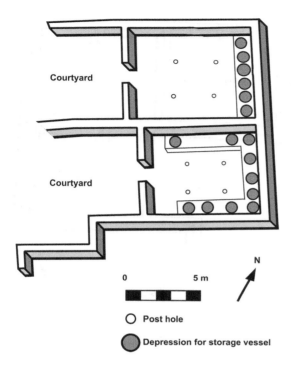

Figure 2.8 Zagora on Andros, two single room houses (Units H26/27/
42/43/47 phase 1).
(Drawn by Laurel Fricker based on Cambitoglou et al. 1988, Plate 11.)

consisted predominantly of pottery used for food and drink. Among the
rarer objects were two stone scarabs (beetle-shaped amulets or seals),
originally manufactured in the eastern Mediterranean, along with pottery
imported from Corinth and from Athens. Such finds show that the inhabitants were integrated into trading networks through which they were able to
obtain a variety of different goods from a range of sources.

Through time extensive modifications were made to houses across the
settlement at Zagora. Many of the rooms featured several successive floor
levels and individual units were expanded by constructing new additions or
by amalgamating adjacent properties (Figure 2.9). A pre-existing main
room was frequently subdivided into a larger front area and two smaller
rear chambers which lay side-by-side. The amount of space available was
often increased by adding a new living-area consisting of one or two rooms
which faced the original complex across an open area, rather than abutting
the front walls. One explanation for this arrangement is that although the
rectilinear plans of the houses offered the potential for adding further
rooms, their tightly packed arrangement meant that the only available

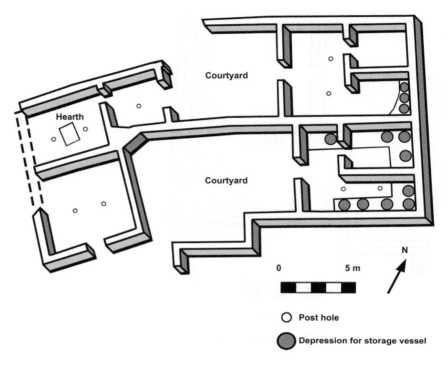

Figure 2.9 Zagora on Andros, two single room houses after expansion (Units H26/27/42/43/47 phase 2).
(Drawn by Laurel Fricker Cambitoglou et al. 1988, Plate 11.)

space was immediately in front of the existing building. Adding rooms here would have meant that little air or daylight could have filtered to the original space at the very back, which would then have been three or four rooms deep. Such a plan may have been considered impractical in the context of a society where artificial lighting was restricted to hearths and torches, while the only ventilation came via doors and window openings to the exterior. In this context the decision to expand the Zagora houses by adding further rooms at some distance from their original nuclei makes practical sense and may also have preserved outdoor areas used for domestic activities. The reason for this expansion is not entirely clear: Lin Foxhall has suggested that the strategy may have accommodated additional nuclear family units which were created as members of an original household married and split off to form their own households, although the limited evidence for the use of space suggests that rooms with similar functions were not usually duplicated in the older and newer parts of a single structure. It is important to note that a desire to increase the amount of living space available and also to partition space into more separate, often smaller, rooms is seen widely in Greek communities over a longer timeframe. Cultural change may therefore have played a role, perhaps demanding more visual and aural separation for different groups of occupants from each other, along with the separation of living and storage areas.

The basic range of activities attested in the houses at Zagora, as suggested by the range of artefacts recovered, is in many ways similar to those of Nichoria and Eretria, with storage, preparation and consumption of food and drink featuring prominently, alongside textile production. The character of the settlement as a whole was very different, however. The fact that the individual houses were much more densely concentrated with only narrow passageways between would have given the inhabitants a rather different experience of living within their community. Both the existence of a fortification wall and the layout, with party walls, indicate that households worked together in a co-ordinated way to plan and construct their settlement. This collaboration in some ways parallels the construction of building 2 at Eretria, the monumental temple, which must also have required pooling of labour and resources. The aims of each enterprise were different, however, with the inhabitants of Zagora focusing on their living environment and their physical safety, while those at Eretria channelled their efforts into creating a symbol of their religious observance and collective identity. Eretria continued to flourish during the centuries which followed (examples of houses from the fourth century BCE are discussed in Chapter 6), but Zagora was abandoned by the end of the eighth century BCE for reasons which are unknown to us today. Its abandonment raises an important question about whether the settlement and its inhabitants can be taken as in any sense representative of others of the same date, or whether it constituted some kind of architectural, and perhaps also social, experiment, which failed. This question needs to be addressed by understanding Zagora in the broader context of developments in settlement- and house-construction during the Early Iron Age.

Nichoria, Eretria and Zagora in Context: Early Iron Age Housing Across the Central Aegean

Residential buildings of tenth-, ninth- and eighth-century BCE date have been explored at a number of other sites in a range of different parts of the Greek world including mainland Greece, the Aegean islands and also in settlements on the west coast of Asia Minor (modern Turkey) where Greek-style pottery was in use. For the tenth and ninth centuries BCE, these range in scale from about 10 m^2 to about 100 m^2, with the largest having multiple rooms while the smallest are undivided. There are also a number of forms: while some are apsidal or oval, the majority are orthogonal (meaning that they have straight walls meeting at right angles). The small number and eccentric distribution of the examples currently known is perhaps unlikely to offer a sample which is representative of the original range of dwellings of the period, and as further evidence comes to light a more reliable picture will surely emerge.

For the eighth century BCE, a larger sample of securely datable houses have been preserved and completely excavated, although it is important to be aware that a few sites such as Zagora provide relatively numerous examples. For this period there is a similar range of sizes to that found during the tenth and ninth centuries. The mean (average) is still only two rooms and an area of just over 90 m^2. The number of curvilinear, as opposed to orthogonal, plans may decline somewhat but it is difficult to place too much weight on this comparison since the sample size is small in the earlier period. In addition, orthogonal houses may be over-represented because their arrangement – with walls abutting – makes them relatively easier for excavators to find and more economical to excavate in large numbers than is the case with more widely spaced, curvilinear buildings.

The artefacts recovered from these houses show little variation: they are generally functional and indicate the relatively narrow range of basic activities we have already seen, principally the storage, preparation and consumption of food and drink. Like others from the same period, the buildings themselves were utilitarian with few internal walls, but where space was subdivided to some degree the main distinction suggested by the artefacts is between storage- and living-accommodation. As at Nichoria, there would have been little scope for more functionally specialised areas or personal space for individual members of the household. In most cases a variety of domestic tasks must have been undertaken in a single space and a number of individuals may have worked simultaneously.

There are one or two exceptions to the generalisations given above, and these may correspond with differences in the size, make-up and/or (as has been frequently assumed) the status of the social groups they accommodated. The most extreme example is the tenth-century BCE building at Lefkandi Toumba. This is worth looking at in detail because it crystallises many of the questions and issues raised by trying to interpret the material from this period as a whole.

Challenging the Stereotypes: The Mystery of the Monumental Building at Lefkandi Toumba

The structure at Toumba, Lefkandi on the west coast of Euboia, close to Eretria, is the most impressive, and yet one of the most enigmatic, buildings of the Greek Early Iron Age (Figure 2.10). Built in the tenth century BCE, it is apsidal and oriented east-west, with the entrance at its east end. As at Nichoria, the upper parts of the walls were composed of mud bricks, although here they rested on an unusually high socle of rough stone slabs. A series of wooden posts was set against the inner faces of the walls and a second row ran down the centre of the building, supporting the thatched roof. A third set of posts surrounded the exterior, perhaps supporting the overhang of the eaves to form a veranda or perhaps some sort of fence. At the east end of the building a porch sheltered the door. At least part of the interior was divided into small chambers. (Our knowledge of the layout is incomplete because the central section of the building was destroyed before archaeologists were able to excavate and study it.)

Although the construction technique has been compared with that of the smaller 'megaron' at the nearby settlement site of Xeropolis, the scale of the Toumba building is unparalleled by any other Greek structure so far known from the period. At close to 50 m in length and 14 m wide, it is only slightly shorter than George Washington's original White House (51 m: Figure 2.11). But what might account for the monumental scale of the Toumba building? In order to address this question, it is necessary to explore what role it may have played by looking at it in more detail.

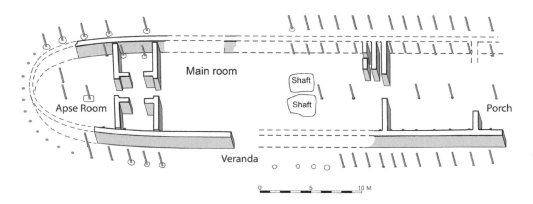

Figure 2.10 The building at Toumba, Lefkandi, Euboia.
(Drawn by Lorene Sterner, based on Popham and Sackett 1993, Plate 5.)

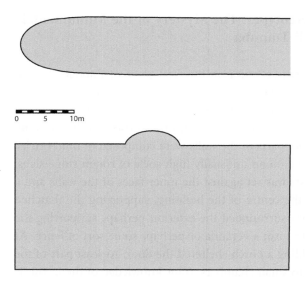

Figure 2.11 Comparison in scale between the building at
Lefkandi Toumba and George Washington's original
White House.
(Drawn by Lorene Sterner.)

The Toumba site is an attractive one with commanding views down the
hillside to the sea. No evidence of any other buildings of this date has been
found in the immediate vicinity – in fact, archaeological investigation of
the adjacent slopes has instead revealed extensive cemeteries lying only
100–300 m to the east and south-east. Xeropolis, mentioned above, is the
closest known settlement of Early Iron Age date and is about 800 m away.
The building's context is therefore at first sight unhelpful as a guide to its
role. Nevertheless, a crucial element to take into account in interpreting the
building is a pair of deep, rock-cut, shafts below the floor of the central
room, each of which contained burials. The southernmost shaft held the
cremated remains of a man, wrapped in cloth and placed in an elaborate
bronze amphora of a type produced in the eastern Mediterranean more
than a century earlier. Further items had been placed in the grave along
with the amphora, including a bronze bowl which had been used as a lid, as
well as a spear head, sword and whetstone. Beside this cremation the body
of a woman had been laid out: she was adorned with a variety of jewellery.
The most striking was a gold necklace which was produced in Babylonia
(in present-day Iraq) and may well have been one thousand years old at the
time she was interred with it. The sequence of events leading up to the
burials is unclear: a knife placed close to the woman's body might suggest

that she was sacrificed and buried alongside the man at the time of his own death. Nevertheless, the archaeological evidence does not definitively show that the two interments took place simultaneously, nor that the woman died of anything other than natural causes. Indeed, one archaeologist has suggested that the female burial is the more important of the two and that the male cremation was intended as a companion for her. The second, northern shaft contained the bodies of four horses, two with iron bits still between their teeth. The presence of these horses, together with the items of precious metal and heirlooms, suggest that the occupants of the southern shaft grave were high status individuals who had expensive possessions. But what was the nature of their connection with the building in which they were found? And what was the purpose of the building itself?

Unfortunately, the destruction of the central part of the structure means that it is impossible to determine whether it was already standing when those shafts were cut, or whether the burials preceded its construction. It did not stand for very long, however: relatively few artefacts are associated with the floors, and those clay floors themselves are not very heavily compacted as one might expect after a period of prolonged use. At some point the building began to collapse or was deliberately dismantled; the apse was then taken down and parts of the roof and upper walls deliberately destroyed. The interior was filled with earth brought from elsewhere and a massive tumulus or 'toumba' was painstakingly raised over the top. Further burials were placed in and around the mound until around the end of the ninth century BCE, while settlement continued to the end of the eighth century BCE at nearby Xeropolis.

The intended role of the Lefkandi Toumba building has been much debated: was it originally a large house, turned to funerary use on the death of its occupants? Was it conceived as a mausoleum or a 'heröon', to house only the dead, perhaps honouring individuals who were viewed as heroes or were thought to be in some sense superhuman? Much of the evidence can be read either way: the location, for example, can be seen as fitting the hypothesis of a residential building for a member of the elite because of its commanding position; but the surroundings, amidst extensive cemeteries, would also support a mortuary interpretation. Because we lack the crucial stratigraphic information which would reveal the construction sequence we can never distinguish definitively between these two alternatives. Instead, it is perhaps relevant to think more about the cultural context of the building.

In writing up the architecture, J. J. Coulton, one of the excavators of the Toumba building, stressed the similarities in construction between this and other Early Iron Age Greek structures such as Nichoria Unit IV.1. He did also highlight a few features which may have made the Lefkandi structure stand out, however: the walls incorporate unusually high, well-made stone socles and mud bricks of different colours, which might have been arranged to make patterns on the exterior. (Indeed, painted patterns found on terracotta models of the late ninth and eighth centuries BCE such as the one from Perachora shown in Figure 2.2 may be attempts to reproduce this kind of effect.) More striking is the external colonnade or fence, which would have differentiated the building from other contemporary structures both in terms of its design, and also by enhancing the most dramatic visual effect of all, namely, its sheer, monumental scale. The resulting impression of these elements on the original viewers can only be guessed at today, when we are accustomed to seeing a multiplicity of enormous structures in a wide variety of forms and materials. It is clear, however, that the Toumba building would have embodied the importance of those associated with it. The ability to mobilise the labour and resources necessary for its construction indicates an individual or group with high status in the community as a whole.

A second consideration is also important: as we have seen, the use of architectural space seems to have been fluid in Early Iron Age Greece. Assigning a clearly defined role to the individual structures we have been looking at is not always easy: there are ambiguities over whether building 1 at Eretria played a residential or a religious role; over whether its neighbours were houses or workshops; and over whether or not the compound at Skala Oropou functioned as a single residential complex. These interpretative difficulties are not always simply a consequence of missing data. They also result from the way space was conceptualised in Early Iron Age Greece itself: the range of materials and building designs in use was relatively narrow. Only gradually do we see increasing evidence of attempts to distinguish spaces for various types of activity or categories of individual, either within a single structure or in distinctively different ones. By contrast, most of the buildings we have seen were inherently multi-functional and flexible in the roles they played. This means that trying to fit individual examples into our own set of analytical categories (residential, industrial, religious, mortuary) may be anachronistic and therefore a somewhat fruitless exercise. The Lefkandi Toumba building may not have been constructed with a single, narrowly defined purpose in mind; instead its importance lay (and lies) in its power to enhance the status of the individuals associated with it, through its monumentality.

Early Iron Age Structures and the Study of Greek Housing

While the Lefkandi Toumba building is so far unique, our other examples of Early Iron Age buildings show that the interpretative problems it poses are not. Archaeologists need to be flexible in defining a 'house' and willing to set aside assumptions derived from their own cultural experiences. These include ideas about what kinds of activities are, or are not, suited to a residential setting, as well as about what size and arrangement of space might be appropriate. It is also necessary to be open to a variety of possible occupants: in the modern, western world an individual residential unit (a house, flat or apartment) is often stereotyped as home to a small number of individuals – a single person living alone, a couple, or one or two parents with a child or children. In reality, however, households are much more variable and can incorporate extended family members and also unrelated individuals. Differing expectations about the definitions and roles of house and household have important consequences for architectural form and interior arrangement, which vary through time and space depending on the requirements of an individual community and on its accepted cultural norms. Interpretations of ancient Greek buildings therefore need to keep in mind the possibility that a variety of living arrangements may have existed. Indeed, one suggestion made about the Toumba building at Lefkandi is that it was the residence of an extended social group or clan, with a number of households each occupying part of the interior in a manner similar to the ethnographically documented long-house structures in present-day Amazonia.

The context of a house also plays an important role in its interpretation. Comparisons between buildings within a single settlement or landscape, and assessments of the relationships between structures from different locations, are both important. For example, if other buildings on the scale of the one at Lefkandi Toumba are brought to light in future, the presence or absence of domestic pottery or the presence and location of any associated burials may shed further light on the role or roles played by the Toumba building.

To what extent can we link these details in to a larger picture of the character of Early Iron Age society? The diversity of architectural forms in the Greek world during this period suggests that social structure may have varied regionally: for example, while the colossal Lefkandi heröon could potentially have accommodated a cluster of families, a smaller building such as one of the original houses at Zagora was surely inhabited by a more restricted group. As we have already seen, differences in the sizes and locations of buildings within a single settlement have sometimes been interpreted as indicators of social hierarchy – as with the two settlement areas at Eretria. Many scholars have also argued that these communities were led, or ruled, by a 'wanax' ('king'), 'chief' or 'big man'. While the details of these models differ somewhat, depending on which evidence is emphasised and what parallels are used, there is a common basic understanding: there was only a limited degree of social and economic inequality, with communities led by individuals who were able to mobilise followers by controlling access to resources such as foodstuffs, imported goods or metals. A leader's power may have been displayed conspicuously by holding feasts to which those followers were invited. Such power may have been more or less transient, perhaps in some places relying on an element of heredity, in others based simply on an ability to retain the support of other community members. As we have seen, Alexander Mazarakis Ainian has also suggested that there may have been a religious component, with some leaders' dwellings serving as religious centres as well as homes.

While the precise details have been debated, broadly understood, such models help to make sense of some of the evidence. Prominent storage of significant quantities of food, along with large numbers of serving vessels, as at Nichoria, reinforced a culture of feasting and the patron status of a leader. The presence of rare, imported goods such as the heirlooms at Lefkandi, were emblematic of an ability to use long distance contacts to obtain prestige goods. Above all, the scale of a building like the Lefkandi heröon required mass community participation in its construction, showing that some individuals – presumably including the couple buried beneath its floor – were able to garner significant material support from large numbers of followers. These features open up a tiny window into the conceptual world of Early Iron Age Greece: although to contemporary, western eyes the buildings seem relatively unsophisticated (not to say uncomfortable as places to live), the scale of the Lefkandi heröon suggests that there was a concept of monumentality, and that this was combined with a sense that status and power could be expressed through a building, as well as through other elements of material culture, including heirlooms.

In summary, the overall impression these Early Iron Age structures give is of structures that were diverse in their form and size. Some of this diversity can be explained by regional variation, with the agglutinative, multi-roomed structures being commonly found in northern Greece, the single-room apsidal buildings on the mainland further south, and the rectangular, stone houses in the islands. Superficially, the agglutinative and single-room 'megaron' (rectangular or apsidal with the entrance at one end) types imply radically different patterns of social relations. Whereas the presence of multiple rooms would have enabled individuals and activities to be spatially separated, the single-room megaron would have forced everyone and everything into the same single space. In practice, however, some of the larger megaron structures, such as the Nichoria house, were subdivided by interior walls. At the same time, at least some of the smaller ones, like those at Skala Oropou, may have represented elements of larger compounds in which the individual megara constituted specialised 'rooms'. Regional differences in patterns of social relations may not, therefore, have been as great as might first appear. Further information on artefact assemblages and their distributions, particularly from potential house compounds, should help to clarify this question in future.

These buildings also seem to have been similar in terms of the range of activities they hosted: few fixed architectural features are found – hearths and benches being the main ones. But the artefacts suggest a range of basic subsistence functions: bulk storage of foodstuffs in large storage jars or smaller vessels set on benches; preparation and serving of food and drink in jugs and cups; production of textiles using terracotta loom weights and spindle-whorls. Rarer activities include craft production such as iron working. There is also some indication that these buildings could play a symbolic role: in addition to the monumentality of the Lefkandi heröon, which surely expresses the power of the couple entombed there through their ability to mobilise the labour to construct such a large building, everyday items such as storage vessels may also have assumed a symbolic role. In some cases they are elaborately decorated, and they could be kept for generations, carefully mended with lead if they were broken. Their location may have contributed to their symbolic value: at Nichoria, for example, some were placed in the porch of the house where they would have been seen by passers-by or visitors.

The eighth century seems to have witnessed a change. It is during this period that specialised buildings appeared with a clearly non-residential role – such as the hekatompedon at Eretria. It seems that by this time communities may have been thinking about architectural space in a different way, as something more specialised and more functionally defined than had previously been the case. Perhaps it is no coincidence that during this same period in a few places residential space began to be partitioned to a new degree – as in the second phase at Zagora and possibly in compound houses at Skala Oropou and Eretria. In such buildings distinctions seem to be made between living accommodation, storage, workshop and even religious space.

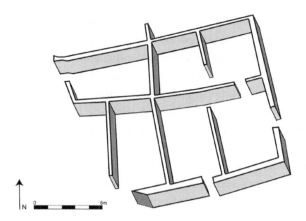

Figure 2.12 Residential complex at Kastanas Level 8 (ca. 800 BCE).
(Drawn by Lorene Sterner based on Hänsel 1989, Fig. 130.)

Despite this trend, it is important to note that even as late as the sixth century BCE, single room houses dominate our evidence. The move from a lesser to a greater partitioning of space is also not universal: for example, there are communities in northern Greece, such as Assiros or Kastanas (Figure 2.12), where agglomerative blocks of multiple rooms were succeeded by less spatially divided megaron-type buildings. The amount of social co-operation was also variable: a settlement like Zagora, with its fortification and party walls between houses demanded a high degree of group planning while the independent placing of megaron-type structures or compounds, like those at Eretria, need not have done so. While the more co-operative communities appear in some respects to be fore-runners of the later polis or citizen state, the abandonment of Zagora suggests that such co-operation did not, in itself, guarantee the success of a community. Differences like these underline the heterogeneity in types of settlement and social structure during the period, which has often been stressed by scholars of Greek Early Iron Age archaeology.

Coda: The Transformation of Early Iron Age Communities in Greece and the Eastern Aegean: Evidence for Housing during the Archaic Period (Seventh and Sixth Centuries BCE)

Curvilinear building forms, such as those seen at Lefkandi and Nichoria, seem gradually to have disappeared from culturally Greek areas and only a handful have been found in use later than the end of the seventh century

BCE. (an example is an apsidal house at Larisa on the Hermos, in Asia Minor, which has been dated to around 600 BCE). Nevertheless, the distinctive 'megaron'-style layout of the apsidal structures we have looked at, with the porch and entrance on one of the short sides, and a small number of spaces reached sequentially behind, does continue into the Archaic period in the context of rectilinear houses. At Vroulia on Rhodes, for instance, despite the steep terrain, a double row of adjoining residential buildings dating to around 600 BCE consisted, for the most part, of two or three rooms each, possibly with a courtyard to the south (Figure 2.13). At the same time, the single-room house still accounts for roughly fifty percent of known examples throughout the seventh and sixth centuries, BCE. At Limenas on Thasos, for example, poorly preserved remains of sixth- and fifth-century BCE date close to the Hermes Gate apparently include a single-room building in an area occupied by a later housing block. At Hypsele on Andros, a settlement of small, stone-built

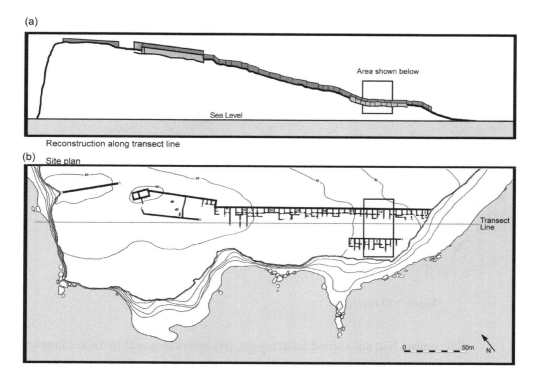

Figure 2.13 Plan, section and reconstruction of the settlement at Vroulia, Rhodes.
(a. drawn by Lorene Sterner; b. drawn by Lorene Sterner based on Lang 1996, Fig. 64; ca. after Hoepfner 1999, p. 198, courtesy of Wolfram Hoepfner.)

(c)

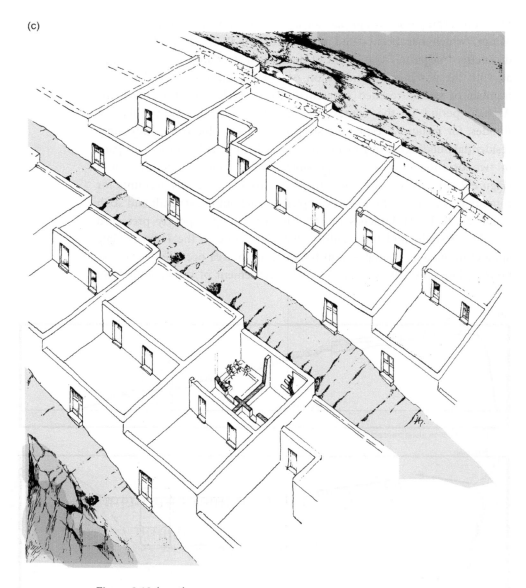

Figure 2.13 (*cont.*)

houses laid out around an akropolis, has been compared to the community at Zagora. However, although it was occupied from the ninth century it seems to have continued in use through to the fourth century BCE. Only limited information about the houses is so far available, but the individual structures were orthogonal and consisted of one or a few rooms, sometimes with rectangular stone hearths.

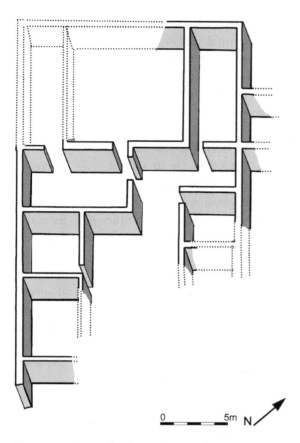

Figure 2.14 Example of an orthogonal building with a new mode of organisation: Kopanaki house A.
(Drawn by Lorene Sterner based on Kaltsas 1983, Plan B and Fig. 2.)

Throughout the Greek mainland and beyond there are some indications that the potential of orthogonal structures to form paratactic complexes (in which individual rooms were placed adjacent to each other sharing party walls) began to be pursued in new ways, as in Dystos house k (seventh or sixth century BCE); and a house at Kopanaki (Peloponnese, mid-sixth century BCE) (Figure 2.14). These make use of elements associated with earlier buildings, including open courtyard spaces, orthogonal construction and multiple rooms, but those features are combined with a new spatial syntax: the rooms are arranged alongside an unroofed courtyard space and are typically accessed individually from there so that each one is relatively 'private', rather than being subject to through traffic by individuals passing from one to the next. In some instances a portico or transverse anteroom intervenes between the courtyard and the interior rooms – as in one, or possibly two, houses beneath the central part of Insula II near the Hermes Gate at Limenas on Thasos, consisting of a courtyard, pastas and two rear rooms. Karl Reber has commented that in southern Greece this arrangement, referred to in some of the literature as a 'three-room group', originally constituted the core roofed area of a dwelling, before later being supplemented by additional roofed spaces. Something like this arrangement was also used at sites on the northern mainland, as for example in House A in the south-east sector at Argilos. In its second phase, dating to around 500 BCE, the Argilos building consisted of a courtyard, anteroom and two small rooms behind. The partial remains of a house interpreted as being of similar design and belonging to the sixth century BCE have also been identified in the West Quarter at Skala Oropou: one room contained a terracotta bath-tub and a hearth. (The house also made use of terracotta roof tiles, which became ubiquitous into the fifth century BCE and were better suited to roofing orthogonal buildings than curvilinear ones.) Archaic houses on Crete, and further afield in culturally Greek communities in Magna Graecia, tend to follow somewhat different patterns of organisation from those on the mainland and eastern Aegean islands, and consideration of them is therefore reserved for Chapter 5, where the long-term development of housing in these regions is considered.

While the evidence is useful, in comparison with earlier and later periods, excavated houses of seventh- and sixth-century BCE date are scarce and fragmentary. This may partly be the result of a tendency for small settlements to be abandoned – as we have seen at Zagora. Their inhabitants presumably moved to larger population centres which continued to thrive during the centuries (or even millennia) that followed. Because of the extended length of occupation at these larger sites, the remains of sixth-century BCE houses have been obliterated, or lie covered by the foundations of later buildings. The availability of information about housing of this period has also been affected by other local circumstances. For example, the Persian army's destructions of cities such as Athens and Olynthos (in 480/479 BCE) seem to have razed to the ground private houses as well as public buildings, giving rise to widespread re-building and sometimes making earlier levels difficult to reconstruct and interpret.

In sum, while Archaic housing in Greece and the eastern Aegean islands is frustratingly difficult to explore because of the scarcity of evidence, what we can say is that the Archaic period in general saw the emergence of residential buildings which were characterised by several features: a southern courtyard; a pastas; and one or more rooms to the north. These point towards a new type of structure which becomes characteristic of the Greek world during the Classical period, and which suggests a fundamental change in patterns of social life: namely, the single-entrance, courtyard house. The layout of this house-form and the social implications of its organisation are explored in detail in Chapter 3, taking housing in Athens and its hinterland, Attica, as an example.

3 | Classical Athens and Attica

The Anatomy of Housing in a City and Its Territory

This chapter explores the physical characteristics and social significance of houses from the city of Athens, its dependent settlements and the surrounding Attic countryside, dating to the Classical period (between 480 and 323 BCE). Taken together, Athens and Attica offer an unparalleled opportunity to compare structures from a variety of different environments, including not only the city but also outlying villages or deme centres and rural farms. This evidence shows that houses with four to five rooms or more share some characteristic elements in their basic layout: a single entrance designed to screen the interior from the street; an open courtyard; an anteroom or portico adjacent to that courtyard; and rooms which radiate from the central court-portico area and were reached individually from there, rather than being entered in series. These shared features together point to a distinctive form of dwelling, the 'single-entrance, courtyard house'. Underlying this form was a collective pattern of social expectations which included: restricting and/or monitoring movement in and out of the house; separation of male visitors from the remainder of the household; and potential for the surveillance of individuals moving around the interior of the house. Together, these elements suggest a desire to regulate social contact between members of the household and outsiders. Such ideas are a strong element of various textual passages by Classical Athenian authors, which imply that, ideally, limitations were placed on the movement and social contacts of citizens' wives. At the same time, the single entrance and interior courtyard provided physical security for the material goods belonging to the household, including those stored and used in the open courtyard as well as those kept inside the building.

Housing in the City of Athens

Context and Evidence

During the later fifth century BCE, the city of Athens was a bustling community with an estimated 35,000 people living within the urban centre, defined by its fortification walls. In the city itself, extensive evidence for houses has been found on the south and south-west sides, where large numbers were explored during the nineteenth century before the growth of the modern city. One particular scholar, Émile Burnouf, was especially interested in the residential districts, estimating that he had excavated about 800 rooms, which he assumed belonged to domestic buildings. Burnouf worked in the area between the Areopagos, Pnyx and Hill of Nymphs and also in the Koile Valley between the Long Walls (which connected Athens to its port, Peiraios) (Figure 3.1). He commented that there was no trace of settlement outside those walls and concluded that the structures he found must, therefore, have been contemporary with their period of use (the fifth century BCE). (The historian Thucydides

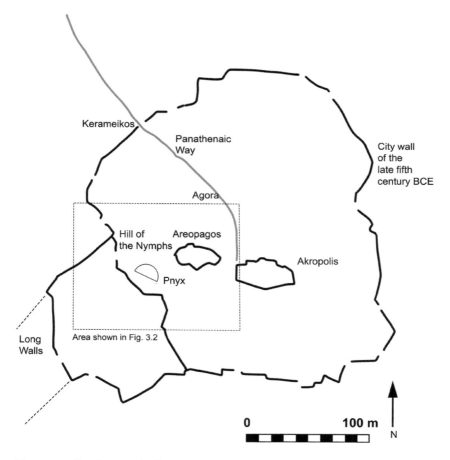

Figure 3.1 Sketch map of Athens.
(Drawn by the author, adapted from Nevett 2011b, Fig. 1.)

specifically refers to the allotment of space within the Long Walls to refugees from the Attic countryside fleeing Spartan invasion in 431 BCE.) Due to the time in which he was working, Burnouf's accounts offer an unparalleled, but tantalisingly brief and often imprecise, overview of these neighbourhoods. He gives details of only a handful of the individual structures he investigated, which he says are not representative of the evidence overall, and he does not report any of the ceramics or other material associated with the architecture. This means that in most cases it is impossible to date the remains he describes. Some, at least, may have been Classical, but they need not necessarily all have been contemporaneous with each other, and others may have been Hellenistic or Roman. (In at least one instance he identifies an impluvium (sunken pool), a feature not usually found in Greece until the second or first century BCE.)

During the late nineteenth and early twentieth centuries, more systematic excavations uncovered housing on the north slopes of the Areopagos and in the valley between the Areopagos and the Pnyx, where the houses were particularly well-preserved under layers of silt which had washed down hill. In ancient times this was a central part of the city, close to the Agora, the main square which was a focus for important civic buildings as well as being a commercial centre. According to the ancient writers, the city plan of Athens was notoriously disorganised, with narrow, winding streets (Text Extract 4). The archaeological evidence reveals roads of packed earth which were sometimes surfaced with gravel, potsherds, broken tiles or cobbles, and which varied considerably in width. The widest avenues can be up to 6 metres across, with wheel ruts testifying to the passage of carts along them. Smaller, secondary streets measuring around 3 metres wide led off these avenues, while narrow, winding lanes gave access on foot to many of the individual houses. Much of the terrain in the city is hilly and in some cases the roads sloped steeply, or even, in the lanes, incorporated flights of steps. Open gutters often ran alongside, channelling excess rainwater (Figure 3.2).

Different residential neighbourhoods seem to have had their own distinctive characters: Burnouf comments that on the Areopagos the houses appeared to be scattered in a random fashion whereas those behind the Pnyx were organised in rows with streets between. He also notes that the further the distance from the Akropolis, the more regular the street layout became, and his comments accord well with more recent mapping of the street network of Classical Athens. These contrasts might perhaps reflect a gradual expansion of the city, with residential areas being laid out at different times. The Persian sack of Athens in 480 BCE, together with the

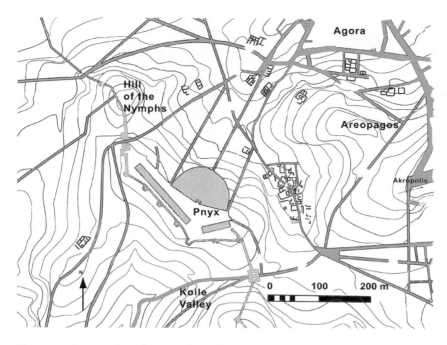

Figure 3.2 Layout of south-west Athens showing the topography together with the Classical roads (dark grey), monuments (light grey) and some of the excavated houses. (Drawn by the author, adapted from Nevett 2011b, Fig. 2.)

subsequent reconstruction work, destroyed the remains of earlier buildings with the result that information about Athenian housing in the seventh and sixth centuries BCE is scarce. In some areas, however, continuous use for housing can be shown over a long period: for example, between the Areopagos and Hill of the Nymphs, evidence for domestic buildings dates back to at least the sixth century BCE and continues into the second and first centuries BCE. In some individual buildings, it is also possible to trace the origins of the post-480 BCE layout to an earlier phase, as with those on the south-east side of the Akropolis and on the north slope of the Areopagos. Burnouf also suggests that houses in different locations had contrasting characters: those closest to the Akropolis were the smallest, while those further away were larger, especially when higher up the hill-sides. It is possible that this indicates socio-economic distinctions between the inhabitants, with the wealthier households occupying hilltops which offered cool breezes in summer, as Burnouf inferred; but the fact that he was comparing structures which may not have been built at the same time means that we cannot rule out the possibility that such contrasts were due to changes through time in housing styles.

Figure 3.3 Athens, House of the Parakeet Mosaic (also known as the House of the Roman Mosaic) showing large ashlar blocks of Akropolis limestone. The house was originally constructed in the fourth or third century BCE and continued to be occupied into the Roman period, when the mosaic was added.
(Author's photograph reproduced courtesy of the Ephorate of Antiquities of Athens – Ancient Agora/Areopagos. © Hellenic Ministry of Culture and Sports/Organization of Cultural Resources Development (H.O.C.RE.D.).)

What was it like to visit one of these neighbourhoods during the fifth century BCE? On a stroll down a street the visitor might have encountered houses constructed in irregularly shaped blocks of adjoining properties, often sharing party walls. Each one had a stone socle composed of several courses of polygonal (irregular) or ashlar (squared) masonry, often in akropolis limestone and normally measuring about 45 cm in thickness (for an example, see Figure 3.3). Above, the superstructure would have been mud brick and risen one or two storeys in height (Figure 3.4). Space in an upper storey may sometimes have been increased by a projecting balcony or upper room, as revealed by occasional traces of column supports. In most cases, the house façade was pierced only by a single door, which was often placed at one corner of the building, or at least, was off-centre in the façade, its location marked today by a stone threshold block. It is possible that, as suggested by textual evidence, in some cases the entrance may have been highlighted by a hermaic stele (a stone marker

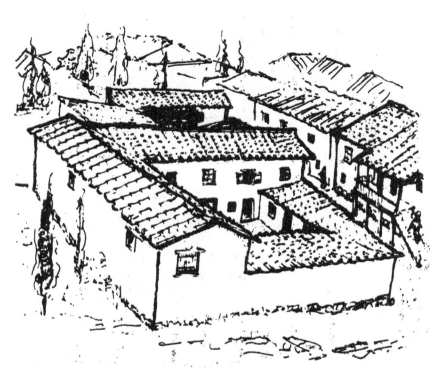

Figure 3.4 Reconstruction of houses C and D from near the Great Drain.
(Drawing reproduced from Ellis Jones 1975, Fig. 22, courtesy of the Belgian School at Athens.)

featuring a head depicting Hermes, together with a phallos: Figure 3.5).
Such figures have been found in large numbers in the vicinity of the Agora
but mostly in secondary contexts where they were re-used as building
materials in the walls of later structures or thrown into pits.

Various other features were probably visible on the house façades:
although the mud brick superstructures of the walls have not survived,
better-preserved, stone-built houses from Ammotopos (fourth century
BCE) suggest that window openings on the exterior walls may have been
few and located high up, probably serving as much for ventilation as they
did for lighting (Chapter 4). A comparable situation is implied for the later
fourth century BCE by the Aristotelian *Constitution of Athens*, in which
city officials are said to prevent the construction of windows opening
outwards onto the street (Text Extract 11). Windows are, nevertheless,
represented on a few Attic vessels of fifth and fourth century BCE date
(Figure 3.5); many of them may have faced inwards into an open
courtyard, rather than outwards onto the street. Other features were

Figure 3.5 Attic red-figure krater showing Herakles with his infant son. The setting is generally interpreted as an outdoor sanctuary but has several elements in common with a domestic courtyard, namely: a hermaic stele (far left), columns (upper left) and a shuttered window (top centre).
(Munich Antikensammlungen 6026, courtesy of the State Collections of Antiquities and Glyptothek, Munich.)

probably more prominent from the exterior: the façades of some of the houses lining the ancient road between the Agora and the Akropolis carried inscribed blocks giving information about sales or mortgage agreements in which they were used for security, as on the so-called House of Aristodemos, named by the excavators after the owner specified in the inscription. (Other such inscriptions have been found in the vicinity of the Agora, although as with the Herms, almost none are in their original locations.)

In the smallest houses like those on the west side of the block excavated at the North Foot of the Areopagos, the street entrances gave directly into enclosed courtyards (Figure 3.6). Elsewhere the court was entered via a lobby or passageway, as in the central house in a group of three located on the Areopagos (Figure 3.7). In the larger houses, the view from the entrance area into the courtyard beyond was often obstructed. In the north-east corner house from the North Foot of the Areopagos, this is done with a screen wall, but other arrangements such as right-angled passages are also found, as in house C near the Great Drain (Figure 3.8).

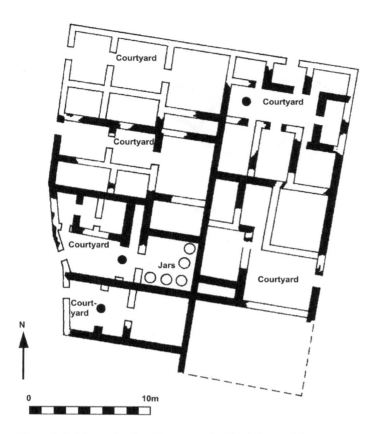

Figure 3.6 Athens, insula of houses at the North Foot of the Areopagos.
(Adapted from Nevett 1999, Fig. 17.)

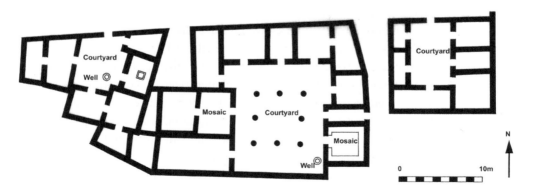

Figure 3.7 Group of three houses on the North Shoulder of the Areopagos.
(Adapted from Nevett 1999, Fig. 20.)

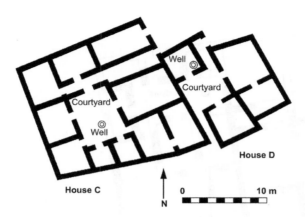

Figure 3.8 Houses C and D near the Great Drain (fifth century BCE phase).
(Adapted from Nevett 1999, Fig. 19.)

In houses of all sizes a central courtyard was key to the organisation of space. It offered a well-lit place for domestic activities and also a means of providing light and air to the interior rooms. Most of those rooms – including any in an upper storey – would have been reached via a staircase located here. During the fifth century BCE most courtyards were surfaced with packed clay. If there was a well or cistern from which water could be drawn, it would normally have been located here. This water could have been supplemented by supplies carried home from a public fountain house. In several cases, stone-lined pits are also located in the court or just outside the house in the street, as in the north-east house of the insula at the North Foot of the Areopagos. One interpretation of these is that they were planting pits for trees. Nevertheless, it seems possible that large trees grown in such proximity to houses would have disturbed the earth floors and undermined walls. Furthermore, in the city of Halieis, where the contents of similar pits were investigated intensively, they proved to contain large quantities of broken pottery and were interpreted as 'koprones' or cess pits. The Athenian pits may have served a comparable function, receiving household waste such as broken pottery, along with sewage. (They were not connected to a main public sewer and hence would have required periodic emptying – a task attested in some textual sources.)

There was often a roofed portico or pastas running along one or more sides of the court, as reconstructed for the central house on the North Shoulder of the Areopagos (Figure 3.7) and some of the smaller houses on the North Foot of the Areopagos (Figure 3.6). The pastas gave access to some of the main rooms which were typically located on the north side of the court. It provided shelter for the entrances from summer sun or from rain, and enabled residents to move around somewhat more comfortably. At the same time, as we shall see below, the larger spaces of this type may have offered well-ventilated but shady locations where a variety of domestic tasks could be carried out in hot weather. In two-storey houses there must have been an equivalent shaded gallery above the pastas, giving access to the upper storey rooms.

On a few occasions, as in the northernmost part of House C near the Great Drain, a room was entered only from outside the house and was unconnected with the rest of the interior (Figure 3.8). There are typically no fixtures in such spaces and few or no finds are reported, so there is little evidence to go on in interpreting their roles. It seems possible that they represent retail or workshop spaces, perhaps arranged to give easy access to individuals unconnected with the household, without compromising the security or morality of those within the house proper.

A final distinctive feature is found only in a minority of Classical Athenian houses, but has often been thought of as a characteristic element of Classical Greek domestic structures, and that is the space archaeologists habitually refer to as the 'andron', its architectural features apparently designed to support the symposium or male drinking party, as noted in Chapter 1. If textual sources can be taken as a guide, symposia seem to have taken place after the evening meal. Participants reclined one or two to a couch. Wine mixed with water was served and (in the literary descriptions, at least) the main focus of the occasion was on conversation and entertainment. Some of the surviving texts suggest that high levels of intoxication could be reached, depending not only on the number of servings of wine poured but also on their strength, which was controlled by a master of ceremonies – the symposiarch – who diluted the wine with water as was the custom. Paintings on ceramic vessel shapes which may have been used at symposia and which appear to show such occasions (Figure 1.9), have been interpreted as suggestive of the kinds of activities that may have taken place, including musical performances, the game of kottabos (which involved flicking the lees of the wine at a target), and sexual activity. The images cannot be interpreted as photographic representations, but they are supported by functional aspects of some of the vessels used. For example, a common form of kylix (a high-stemmed cup with a wide, flat body) which was in use in the later sixth century BCE carried large painted eyes and would have formed a mask when held up to drink, the foot of the cup representing a large, mis-shapen nose (Figure 3.9). Trick cups have also

Figure 3.9 Attic red-figure 'eye-cup', ca. 520–500 BCE.
(British Museum 1842.0407.23, made by Hischylos, painted by Epiktetos. © Trustees of the British Museum, reproduced by permission.)

been found with hidden openings which challenged the user to drink without spilling their contents down his front. Other vessels assumed shapes inspired by human anatomy, including kylikes with feet in the shape of male genitals, which presumably had to be grasped by their users (the painted images suggest that it was customary to hold a kylix from underneath, by its foot, unless playing kottabos). Together, this evidence points to an occasion which could engender anything from serious discussion and debate, through ribald humour, to intoxicated behaviour, depending perhaps on the symposiarch, or on the stage of the evening. Given the potentially disruptive, even transgressive, nature of the symposium, it will come as no surprise that some households seem to have constructed an andron as an enclosed room within which participants in symposia could safely be isolated from members of the household during such occasions.

Among the houses found near the Agora, some were furnished with an andron. One example, excavated in its entirety, is the so-called House of the Greek Mosaic, constructed around 300 BCE on the slope of the Areopagos (Figure 3.10). Here a shallow anteroom, which had the andron behind, lay on the visitors' right as they passed down the narrow entrance corridor and into the courtyard. The floors of both anteroom and andron were decorated with mosaics formed of coloured pebbles set into a mortar

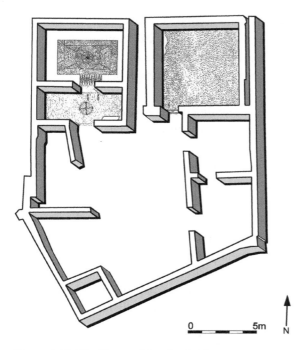

Figure 3.10 The House of the Greek Mosaic.
(Drawn by Max Huemer based on Agora Drawing: PD 1245 (DA 6809).)

bedding and aligned in contrasting geometric patterns. The doorway of the room itself was placed off-centre, suggesting the placement of couches around the walls. These would have stood on the plain, raised border of yellow plaster which had space for perhaps nine couches, accommodating a maximum of eighteen drinkers in all. This was a relatively large house and the andron was one of the two biggest rooms, occupying the most comfortable location to the north of the courtyard where the sun would penetrate only in the cool of the winter when it was low in the sky. Both the decoration and the location of the andron are indications of the room's importance. In some other houses the stone socles of the andron walls are also constructed differently from those of the other rooms, as in the House of the Parakeet Mosaic illustrated above (Figure 3.3). Here the monumental limestone blocks presumably advertised the room's presence even from the outside to passers-by who did not enter the house, as well as guiding those who may have been invited for their first symposium, to the correct location within. While many, or perhaps even most, Classical Athenian houses lacked an andron, a small number of others have been recognised from their distinctive architectural features during rescue excavations elsewhere in the city. For example one decorated with a panelled, black and white pebble mosaic floor was found in a late-fifth century BCE house (House 'Theta') during the excavations at the site of the New Akropolis Museum, and the rooms are still visible, preserved beneath the raised museum building.

Classical Athenian houses had few functionally specialised rooms with built-in features like the kitchens of today with their ovens, cupboards and worktops. In a handful of instances waterproof cement flooring suggests that one particular space may have been used for bathing. Running water was lacking; washing arrangements made use of various terracotta and stone vessels which had to be filled and emptied manually. Numerous fragments of large, shallow, pedestalled basins (louteria) have been found in fills and well-deposits around the Agora and at least some of these may originally have been used for washing, as shown on contemporary red-figure vase-paintings (for example, Figure 3.11). A sixth century BCE terracotta hip-bath of the type mentioned in Chapter 1 has been found during the Agora excavations: such a bath may originally have been set into a waterproof floor.

An important role of the house was storage of foodstuffs. Because there was no refrigeration, this required a cool, dark space. A small house on the west side of the block at the North Foot of the Areopagos (Figure 3.6) included a room where five large storage jars were set into the ground. The excavators do not comment on whether anything was found inside these particular vessels, but they may originally have contained grain, lentils, beans, olives, olive oil, or wine, traces of which have been found in other vessels of this date and were staple foods. Currently, the most abundant evidence for the ceramic vessels in which food and drink were stored, prepared, cooked and eaten comes from debris such as the fills of wells which are assumed to contain refuse from domestic contexts. This does not tell us about where storage, cooking or dining took place or how such activities may have been separated or combined, but it does show the range of cooking equipment available and emphasise its portability. To compensate for the fact that fixed hearths were relatively rare, small terracotta ovens and cooking bells would frequently have been used. These could have been moved about as required, perhaps burning indoors during the winter but in the courtyard or pastas during the summer, to avoid over-heating the interior rooms. Terracotta grills – like one of two found in the house block on the North Foot of the Areopagos – would have enabled meat or vegetables to be cooked directly over the flames. A range of ceramic coarse ware pots and pans could have been placed over the heat

Figure 3.11 Attic red-figure hydria showing women using a louterion to wash. (British Museum 1844.0614.1, ca. 480 BCE, attributed to the Kleophrades painter. © Trustees of the British Museum, reproduced by permission.)

from a stand or brazier. Such vessels represent less than 50 per cent of the recorded ceramic assemblage, however: the remainder is accounted for by plain and black-slipped wares for household use and for serving food and drink. A substantial proportion (about a third) are kraters (large, deep vessels: see Figure 3.5), jugs or cups. All of these were probably used for mixing, pouring and consuming liquids, suggesting the importance of drinking in Classical Athens. Given that textual and iconographic evidence both point to the cultural significance of wine, it seems safe to assume that some, at least, of these vessels were used for its consumption. By comparison there are only about half as many plates and dishes for serving food, raising the possibility that individuals might have eaten from shared platters rather than each having their own.

Artefacts also reveal household production and storage of a variety of other commodities, for domestic use, for sale, or both. Especially frequent are terracotta spindle whorls and weights from warp-weighted looms. In the insula on the North Foot of the Areopagos, for example, a group of nine such weights came from a single room, while in house C by the Great Drain twenty loom weights with a spindle whorl were found in one room. In some cases, the organisation of space, together with the artefacts located there, suggests that commercial shops or workshops were incorporated into houses. Examples found by the excavators of the Agora houses include: part of a cobbler's shop, identified by numerous hob nails and bone eyelets; several marble workers' workshops with fragments of partially worked stone along with sculptors' tools and pits used for polishing the finished products; a coroplast's workshop (for the manufacturer of terracotta figurines), revealed by figurine fragments along with vats and channels for refining the clay; and, in house D, a metalworking establishment attested by fragments of iron and bronze.

To what extent can we talk of a 'typical' house in Classical Athens? Burnouf comments that single-room structures were the most frequent type he found, but he does not document any of them in detail and he may have been viewing as separate properties, spaces which were really part of a single house. He also reports finding dwellings consisting of a central courtyard with just three rooms arranged in a Π-shape around it. Buildings of this type, located on the hillsides to the west and south-west of the Agora, were also recorded by the German scholars Ernst Curtius and Johannes Kaupert in the later nineteenth century. Cuttings where the rock was levelled to make floors, staircases and lanes were re-examined here in the 1970s. These structures are in some ways quite different from the dwellings found in the vicinity of the Agora. In particular, the rooms tend to be arranged sequentially, rather than being entered individually from a central courtyard, and there are sometimes two different entrances. The more recent identification of some of these cuttings (from the area of Aghia Marina on the eastern spur of the Hill of the Nymphs: Figure 3.2) as belonging to sacred, rather than to domestic, buildings, is a salutary reminder of some of the difficulties involved with using this evidence. There are, unfortunately, too many uncertainties about dating and interpretation to sustain detailed analysis.

A further structure to consider is building Z from the Kerameikos (already mentioned in Chapter 1). This had a long life, originating in the early fifth century BCE and undergoing a series of reconstructions through to the early first century BCE. The role it played is difficult to understand owing to its complex history and the fact that the location of its southern boundary remains unexplored. The excavators interpret the first two phases, which date from the early and late fifth century BCE, as belonging to a house. They suggest that during subsequent phases the building was reconstructed to serve as a tavern, textile workshop and possibly a brothel. The most extensive artefact inventory comes from phase 3, dating to the third quarter of the fourth century BCE (Figure 1.5). A minimum of sixteen different rooms were reached via at least three different circulation spaces, the largest of which was probably an open courtyard with a well. Superficially, the general arrangement of building Z recalls a courtyard house with a prostas or pastas to its north-west, in front of rooms C and D. But the building is much larger (covering about 500 m^2) and the rooms are arranged in a much denser pattern than we have seen elsewhere in Athens. The artefact assemblage is eclectic and comprises a range of ceramics, tools, loom weights and personal items. They suggest the presence of large numbers of individuals – perhaps using the building as a tavern or brothel but alternatively, perhaps as some kind of apartment complex or establishment renting out rooms. Such shared dwellings are attested in textual sources but are difficult to identify archaeologically.

Taken together, the Athenian evidence suggests there was significant diversity in the size and organisation of dwellings in the Classical city. At the same time there are some underlying principles which governed their organisation. As noted above, these include: a single street entrance; the interruption of the view into the house from the street outside; the use of the courtyard as a transitional space through which the residents had to walk in order to move between rooms; and the presence of a portico. This, then, is the basic configuration of the larger Classical Athenian houses.

Already established by the later fifth century BCE, the same organisational pattern seems to have been retained through a number of generations until at least the later fourth century BCE. Many Athenian houses of the fifth century survived into the fourth century BCE but were modified. For example, in the block at the North Foot of the Areopagos the sanitary systems were upgraded during the fourth century: stone or terracotta drains were constructed leading from the individual houses and into public drains in the street while the koprones went out of use. Other modifications were made to houses C and D near the Great Drain: the courtyards were surfaced with paving or cobbles to give a more durable finish which could withstand rain better. Houses C and D were later amalgamated to provide combined workshop and residential quarters, and then subsequently re-divided before the complex was finally abandoned in the mid-fourth century BCE. Some other buildings were occupied for longer periods: the House of the Parakeet Mosaic was still in use during the second century CE, when the eponymous mosaic was laid in the andron. But towards the end of the fourth century BCE, the effects of the contraction in population which followed Athens' defeat in the Peloponnesian War are apparent in the archaeological record, as many of the other houses in the vicinity of the Agora were abandoned and the land on which they stood was not re-occupied until the third century BCE or later.

Understanding Urban Athenian Households

Who would have inhabited the houses we have been exploring? Textual sources suggest that the basis of a household was normally the nuclear family group of a man, his wife and any children. But a variety of other individuals could also live with them, such as elderly parents, orphaned nieces and nephews, or unrelated friends and lodgers. Ownership of enslaved people may also have been widespread: they perhaps represented up to one sixth of the Athenian population during the late-fifth century BCE and a significant proportion of them would have played domestic roles. The make-up of a household must also have changed through time over both the short and long term. Each household had its own life cycle, growing and shrinking as its members were born, then aged, moved away or died. The mortgage and lease documents show that houses, like other property, were economic assets which could be bought, sold, used as security to obtain loans or rented out to provide an income. Changing hands in this way meant that over time a single house may have been occupied by a series of different households, despite the fact that the literary texts often seem to represent an ideal in which the property was of central importance to a family, to be looked after and passed on to future generations. In short, then, the households occupying a single excavated house must have represented a dynamic kaleidoscope of different social configurations, and this must account, at least in part, for alterations made to the architecture through time.

Some of the smaller houses may have been occupied by individuals of lower social status – perhaps non-citizens or metics (foreign workers), who were not permitted to own their own property and would, therefore, have had to rent places to live. But the larger houses, which are better-represented archaeologically, are likely to have belonged to wealthier households and it is in these structures that we see a range of features suggesting some of the social conventions operating in Classical Athens. At this end of the spectrum, textual evidence suggests that a single kin group may have possessed more than one house, and members of that group may not, therefore, always have lived in the same place at the same time. In any one case it is impossible to use archaeological material to identify either the precise status and composition of the occupying household at a particular moment in time, or the relationships between its members. Nor is it possible to pinpoint the activities of specific individuals. Nevertheless, in aggregate the excavated evidence does yield some common characteristics which seem to be designed to promote or restrict movement and social interaction in particular ways. These can be used in conjunction with the Attic texts and ceramic iconography to make suggestions about Athenian domestic social life.

The pattern of architectural features and internal organisation of Athenian houses, outlined above, was not coincidental: enclosing the exterior courtyard space within the rooms had both practical advantages and socio-cultural significance. From a functional point of view the arrangement ensured the presence of light and air in the interior, even when houses shared party walls with neighbours (which would have prevented most of the property's boundary walls from being used for windows and ventilation). The single street entrance, the measures taken to interrupt sight lines between interior and exterior, and the arrangement of space around the courtyard, all served to isolate the occupants from the street outside. At the same time, the larger houses offered a selection of different rooms in which individuals could work, socialise or rest. The interiors of these would have been quite dark, particularly those receiving only secondary light from the pastas. It would, therefore, have been relatively difficult to see into them from outside in the court, but much easier for those inside to observe activity in the court. The overall layout would have meant that anyone wanting to enter or leave the house, or to move from room to room, would have had to pass through the court-pastas area, and so could potentially have been observed by other members of the household present in either of these spaces or in one of the interior rooms.

These characteristics of the layout correspond with information gathered from disparate textual sources which suggest that, among wealthier households at least, privacy for the household as a whole was considered very important. At the same time, there was also concern for control over the residents, and a key aspect of enforcement was surveillance. A variety of texts suggest that this was a strong influence on the behaviour of respectable adult women – the wives and daughters of Athenian citizens, whose freedom to leave the house at will and to form relationships may have been restricted by social expectations. These expectations may have been linked with a concern to demonstrate that any children inheriting property and citizen status were legitimate heirs. As noted in Chapter 1, traditional interpretations of the texts have often gone further, suggesting that even within the house itself these women would have occupied separate quarters, living apart from male household members (see Text Extract 7). Nevertheless, although the terms 'andron' (or 'andronitis') and 'gunaikon' (or 'gunaikonitis') in the Classical Athenian context are usually translated as 'men's room' and 'women's room', closer examination of the texts reveals inconsistencies in the way in which the terms are applied. In Xenophon's *Oikonomikos* (Text Extract 12) they appear to indicate quarters for enslaved people of each sex, but in Lysias' *Against Eratosthenes* (Text Extract 13) and indeed in Roman writer Vitruvius' *On Architecture* (Text Extract 10) they designate the spaces in which the house owner and his wife, respectively, may have spent time.

From an archaeological perspective, the evidence from Classical Greece in general does not suggest a strict division of space into separate male and female areas, since space is typically organised around a single open courtyard with rooms entered individually. Until detailed information is published on the distribution of artefacts in the houses excavated around the Agora, it is difficult to identify which spaces may have been most important in Athenian women's daily activities. Nevertheless, it seems likely that the courtyard and pastas played a key role: these were light and well-ventilated areas with access to water for domestic chores. The distribution of artefacts from comparable houses in other ancient Greek communities shows that items such as loom weights and cooking vessels are often found here (see, especially, the evidence from Olynthos, discussed in Chapter 4). It is possible that where there was an upper storey this may have been used by female members of the household, as Lysias suggests. Even if that were the case, however, the problem he highlights with access to facilities such as water, would have been constant, and it seems unlikely that any theoretical restriction of female activity to the upper storey could actually have been observed rigorously in practice. Furthermore, in many instances there is no evidence of an upper floor, and none of the houses we have seen is obviously divided into two different ground floor areas. Overall, therefore, the evidence we have looked at here does not support binary interpretations of the use of domestic space, and in fact the pattern of organisation centred on the court works in an opposite way, integrating the rooms into a single complex.

Social conventions operating in the larger households of Classical Athens were therefore probably more subtle than literal readings of the texts have suggested: while male and female household members may have been engaged in different activities within the domestic sphere and may thus often have occupied different spaces, it is unlikely that such an integrated house plan would have been used if custom had dictated their strict separation. It seems more probable that, as with some other, better-documented, societies, where contact between men and women was restricted (such as Islamic North Africa during the nineteenth century), it was contact between respectable women and unrelated men which was problematic. The creation of the andron, noted above, seems to respond to such a situation, providing a location where male visitors could be entertained in isolation behind a closed door. While guests were present in the courtyard, women could have withdrawn to the interior rooms, but once the guests were safely inside the andron, normal domestic activities could have resumed, with female members of the household using the courtyard as necessary. The andron often had a small anteroom, and this would have meant that the courtyard was invisible to guests even if the door of the room itself were opened, for example, to bring in further supplies of wine. As noted above, the majority of excavated houses did not have an andron. In its absence, a more multi-purpose room could have been used, or even the portico or courtyard. In such a situation, scheduling of activities is likely to have been as important as rigid spatial boundaries in observing social conventions, with different users present at different times of day. Those conventions are also likely to have been aimed at restricting contact between narrowly defined groups of individuals – the wives and daughters of citizens and unrelated men – rather than between men and women, per se.

The interior arrangements of Athenian houses thus seem to express specific social expectations – privacy and isolation for the household as a whole from the wider community, surveillance of individuals by each other as they moved through the house carrying out their day-to-day business, and separation between visitors and those not directly involved in entertaining them. For citizen men it may have been important to demonstrate support for these social customs to the wider population of the city through the architecture of their houses. Ownership of a house with this particular layout may have affirmed indirectly the legitimacy of offspring and their right to inherit not only the wealth of the oikos but also the status of citizen, which had to be confirmed by fellow members of the deme from which the male householder's family originated. The physical house can, therefore, be seen to have had a symbolic, as well as a strictly functional dimension. This symbolism also may have gone further: for example, possession of an andron may have been a claim to status, proof of the householder's wealth and, indirectly, a statement that he was the sort of man who hosted symposia and, therefore, needed a room like this.

In sum, although the houses known archaeologically from Classical Athens vary considerably in shape and size, the larger ones do share a variety of underlying organisational characteristics which can be linked with specific social conventions. Whether those conventions were always observed in practice is difficult or impossible to know. But the overall picture demonstrates the symbolic importance of the house as a structure, something which is also clear from the contemporary Athenian textual evidence reviewed in Chapter 1. That importance perhaps stems from the fact that the house was located at the interface between the spheres of polis (citizen-state) and household – the exterior represented the household to the wider community, a role which the interior also performed for any visitors who were permitted to enter. Architecture, layout and decoration must, therefore, all have been instrumental to varying degrees in creating an impression which materialised the status of the male householder. The location of the andron off the courtyard, rather than separated from the other rooms, suggests that the display of the interior to visitors was intentional: perhaps offering visitors a brief view of a well-ordered household also served to enhance the householder's status. The organisation of space in these houses is at odds with the rather superficial binary opposition which has sometimes been drawn in the ancient Greek context between the sphere of the polis, which has been viewed as male, and that of the house, which has been viewed as female. Instead, the emerging picture is more complex and demonstrates the way in which the correct ordering of the domestic sphere may have been closely linked with the male citizen's status and reputation, as well as with that of his wife.

Planned Housing Development in an Attic Context: Peiraios

The city plan of Athens, with its winding streets and irregularly shaped housing plots, presents a strong contrast with its port, Peiraios. Historical sources suggest that prior to the fifth century BCE Peiraios was relatively insignificant, with few buildings. During the fifth century, however, the Athenians made a deliberate decision to expand the settlement as well as construct a fortification linking it with Athens itself (the Long Walls, referred to above). Aristotle attributes the plan to a single individual, Hippodamos of Miletos, who he says was the first Greek to focus attention on urban organisation. Whether or not this was the case, the surviving archaeological evidence shows that the settlement was planned on an orthogonal grid. The insulae between incorporate both the major civic buildings and also blocks of housing. There are a variety of opinions about the extent of this grid, but the community's regular layout clearly represents a striking contrast with the less formal plan of Athens itself: Peiraios must, therefore, have had a very different atmosphere (Figure 3.12). As we shall see in later Chapters, grid plans were regularly used in other Greek cities and the existence of regularly sized insulae has implications for the houses located in between. Such urban plans have been interpreted in a well-known study by Wolfram Hoepfner and Ernst-Ludwig Schwandner as evidence that concepts of equal distribution of wealth and equal shares in property underlay the ideas of political equality current in Athens during the fifth century BCE. They argue that these ideas were instrumental in determining the layout of cities and housing quarters across the Greek world at this time. (Although in some cases, such as at Halieis in the Argolid, discussed in Chapter 4, the regular grid plan is apparently not

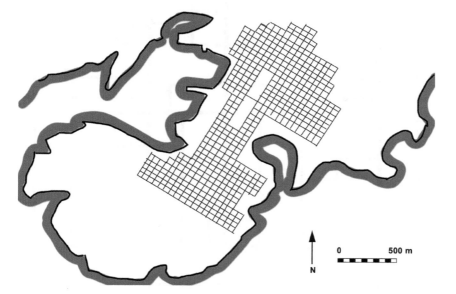

Figure 3.12 Peiraios, sketch map of the peninsula with the reconstructed urban grid of the Classical settlement.
(Drawn by the author based on information from Hoepfner and Schwandner 1994, Fig. 14.)

accompanied by an equal distribution of space for each house, the central point that the physical organisation of space was closely linked to the conceptual sphere revolutionised many classical archaeologists' ways of thinking about the interpretation of the built environment.)

The remains of the Classical houses in Peiraios are very fragmentary, having been much disturbed by more recent building activity. Insulae known from excavation consist of eight houses arranged back-to-back in two rows. In collaboration with Giorgos Steinhauer, Hoepfner and Schwandner have reconstructed the organisation of a 'typical' block of houses by combining fragments of a number of structures dating between the fifth and third centuries BCE (Figure 3.13). In the resulting 'model', a single house measures approximately 20 by 12 m – a relatively long and narrow shape. It is entered through a passageway at the south which leads

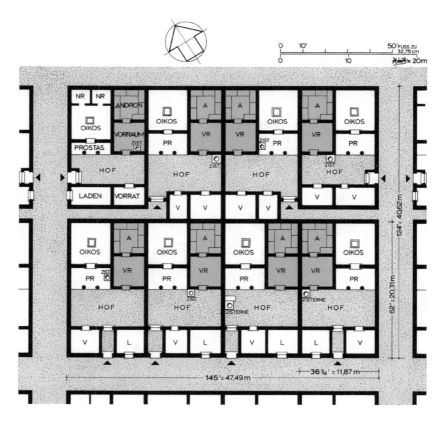

Figure 3.13 Peiraios, house block reconstructed by Hoepfner and Schwandner. (After Hoepfner and Schwandner 1994, Fig. 31, courtesy of Wolfram Hoepfner.)

into a courtyard at the centre. To the north, the rooms comprise, first, a large living room or 'oikos' with two ancillary rooms at the rear; second, an anteroom and seven-couch andron (several houses preserve evidence of raised borders and pebble mosaics). There is no pastas-type portico: instead, a narrower prostas is shown in front of the oikos. To the south of the courtyard, Hoepfner and Schwandner reconstruct anciliary rooms (storerooms and shops).

Peiraios thus presents both a radically different type of street plan from Athens, and also a form of domestic architecture which, if reconstructed correctly, looks unlike any house currently known from Athens itself. On closer inspection, though, the layout in fact preserves many of the functional characteristics of the larger houses in the vicinity of the Agora. There is a single entrance, which may have been protected by two sets of doors, one at either end of the entrance passage. Once inside, space is arranged around the courtyard, which gives access to the majority of interior rooms. The main difference lies in the portico, which is reduced in size, offering access only to what may have been the main living room, rather than to a whole range of rooms to the north of the courtyard. In practical terms this may have meant that there was less shaded, exterior space in which to carry out domestic activities during the hot summer months, although the small size of the courtyard may have meant that at some times during the day, parts of it were shaded by the surrounding rooms. So, although these houses look superficially different from their counterparts in the city of Athens itself, in practical and social terms they are likely to have worked in a similar way. The use of a prostas rather than a pastas may be due to the narrow shape of the plot, which did not offer space for a long portico (although presumably the choice to divide up an insula in this way was a deliberate one which took into account the desired organisation of the individual houses).

Classical Housing in Smaller Attic Communities

Discussion in this chapter has so far concentrated on urban housing, but there is also evidence of residential accommodation located outside the urban centres of Athens and Peiraios, in the surrounding deme centres, villages and rural farmsteads. While some houses in these locations are organised in similar ways to their urban counterparts, there is also systematic variation which is probably linked with the different social and practical requirements of dwelling in these non-urban locations.

The Attic chora, or rural territory of Athens, covered an area of some 2,500 km² (Figure 3.14). During the late fifth century BCE, it may have been inhabited by around 280,000 people. Some of this population may have been seasonally, if not permanently, resident in rural farmsteads, examples of which have been investigated in a number of locations. Nevertheless, many or most probably lived in the small towns and villages dotting the landscape both on the coast and in inland areas. These settlements were integrated into a network of demes, which were political

Figure 3.14 Sketch map of Attica showing the locations of sites mentioned in the text. (Drawn by the author.)

and administrative subdivisions of the Athenian state. The deme centres provided the foci for local economic, social and also political life, particularly for those who did not travel to Athens on a regular basis. In common with Peiraios, a few of these deme settlements were evidently organised on regular grid plans, as with the habitation area at Sounion, which was probably laid out during the fifth century BCE (Figure 3.15). In contrast, the more extensively investigated remains at Thorikos and Ano Voula (ancient Halai Aixonides) had layouts similar to what we have already seen in the city of Athens itself: excavations in both locations have revealed densely built-up areas with streets on irregular plans which seem to have grown up through time.

Thorikos is located on the lower slopes of a conical hill, Velatouri, a short distance from the sea (Figure 3.16). Settlement in the area has a long history, going back at least to the third millennium BCE and including Early Iron Age housing. The landscape is rich in mineral resources and by the fifth century BCE Thorikos served as a centre for mining and processing silver ore. The community boasted a variety of shared facilities including religious buildings, an early theatre, a fortification wall and several cemeteries. In the Industrial Quarter, the main, stone-paved, street is 3.1–3.5 m wide and makes a gradual ascent up the hillside, so that it would have been usable by carts (Figure 3.17). Some of the other roads are narrower and steeper, catering only to pedestrian traffic. Like those we have seen at Athens, the houses are very variable in size, layout and the range of facilities they encompass. Space is generally organised around an open courtyard, but even in the largest the organisational principles seem to have been somewhat different from those seen in Athens and Peiraios: instead of the courtyard serving as the main route for moving about the house, at Thorikos the rooms are often organised in separate suites in which one leads off another sequentially. For example, house 1 in the Industrial Quarter, was constructed around 430 BCE and terraced into the hillside around two separate courtyards (Figure 3.18a). A series of living rooms were entered from the western courtyard, two of them with red plastered walls. A support for a gallery overlooking the western court indicates that there was an upper storey above at least some of the rooms. The eastern court seems to have been the focus for storage facilities, yielding large numbers of sherds from amphorae, and it seems to have had its own entrance at the eastern tip of the house, separate from the doorway on the southern side which led into the residential quarters. Shortly after the initial construction of the property the two sections were

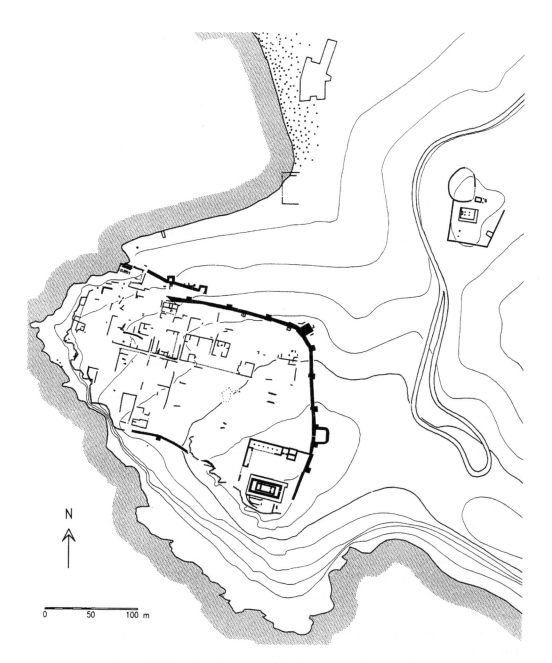

Figure 3.15 Cape Sounion, plan of the deme centre showing the topography and the regular street grid.
(After Goette 2001, Fig. 58, courtesy of Hans R. Goette.)

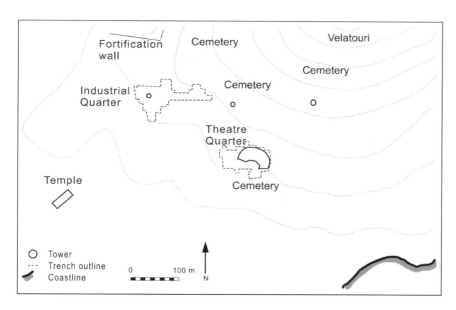

Figure 3.16 Thorikos, sketch plan of the deme centre.
(Drawn by the author based on Nevett 2005, Fig. 6.2a.)

Figure 3.17 Thorikos, view along a street in the Industrial Quarter with house 1 to the left.
(Author's photograph, courtesy of the Ephorate of Antiquities of Eastern Attika. The rights to the
monument shown belong to the Hellenic Ministry of Culture and Sports (Law 3028/2002).
Thorikos is under the supervision of the Ephorate of Antiquities of Eastern Attika, Ministry of
Culture and Sports.)

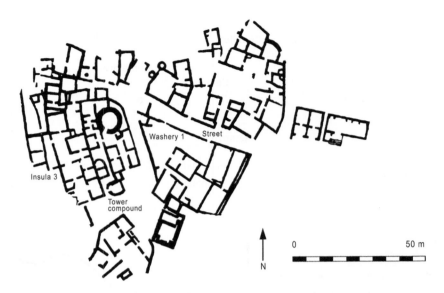

Figure 3.18a Thorikos, sketch plan of House 1 in the Industrial Quarter, with surrounding buildings.
(Drawn by the author based on Nevett 2005 Fig. 6.2b.)

separated to form independent units. Other, smaller, houses from the site have only a single courtyard although some of them also seem to have featured more than one entrance from the street.

A prominent aspect of the built environment, both within the deme centre at Thorikos and in the surrounding area, was the presence of numerous washeries – facilities for ore processing: in total over 200 such complexes have been found. Their characteristic features were cisterns connected to large cement floors with channels and settling basins for washing and drying the ore. The interior rooms of these complexes often include mills for grinding the rock before it was washed, but there are also further rooms which may have been used as residential accommodation. An example is washery 1, also located in the Industrial Quarter. Here a large, triangular courtyard accommodated processing facilities (Figure 3.18b). A group of six rooms to the south is interpreted as residential. As in the houses from the site, some are arranged sequentially, rather than radiating directly from the courtyard. This combination of workshop and residential space parallels buildings seen in the city of Athens. It is unclear what the social status of the residents would have been: although

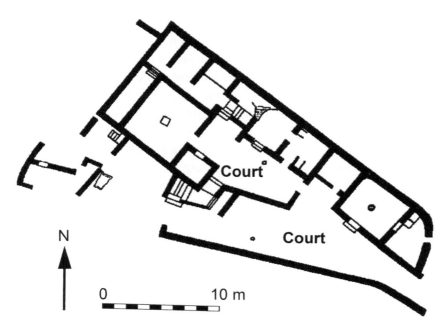

Figure 3.18b Thorikos, sketch plan of the excavated structures of the
Industrial Quarter.
(Drawn by the author based on Nevett 2005 Fig. 6.2b.)

it seems likely that many of the workers in the silver industry – and
hence presumably many of the residents of Thorikos itself – may have
been enslaved, it has as yet been impossible to find clear evidence of this
in the archaeology. In addition, the provision of civic amenities such as a
theatre within the community suggests that there was also a significant
citizen population.

Across the street to the west of washery 1, insula 3 demonstrates
another, distinctively different, characteristic of some of the Thorikos
residences, which is the incorporation of circular-planned towers into
domestic complexes. The tower here, which was built in the mid-fifth
century BCE, measures 7.25 metres in diameter on the exterior. Stone
walling up to 1.5 metres thick survives to head height, suggesting that the
superstructure was probably entirely of stone (although towers with stone
socles and mud brick superstructures are known from other settlements).
There were multiple entrances and access routes into and around the
tower, with a door on the ground floor, a second entrance on the first floor

reached via an external staircase, and a further staircase on the interior. The tower was built into a series of terraces and its original height is now unknown, but it stands on the north side of a small, split-level courtyard which was entered from the south via a corridor and served as a focus for the other rooms of the complex. On the east, south and west sides these were reached individually from the court, but the remainder were clustered around the tower and entered sequentially in two groups. Those in the north-west corner may have been used for crop processing as the stone bed for an olive press was found here, suggesting the production of olive oil on a significant scale. Most of the material associated with the complex seems to have been domestic in character, however, consisting of various kinds of pottery associated with food storage, preparation and consumption; lamps; and refuse from meals (ash and animal bones).

Three other circular towers have been found at Thorikos and similar features also occur at other deme sites, including Ano Voula, on the west coast of Attica. The deme centre at Ano Voula is likely to have been largely reliant on agriculture and would, therefore, perhaps have been more typical of the character of Attic villages generally than Thorikos (where the mining industry must have had a major impact on the economy). Excavation amongst the present-day buildings in several locations there has revealed an akropolis, habitation areas and a cemetery. In addition, a variety of inscriptions dating to the fifth and fourth centuries BCE show a lively local political and religious life, attesting to some of the activities of the community's officials. In the largest excavated area, the Kalampoka plot, a network of winding streets separated several irregularly shaped insulae comprising residential buildings and small shrines (Figure 3.19). The remains of three circular towers survive here and are paralleled by at least one more, excavated elsewhere in the settlement. While some of them may have been free-standing, the most intensively investigated example forms part of a larger complex dating to the late fifth or early fourth century BCE. The tower is similar in scale to that at Thorikos (approximately 6 m in diameter; again, the original height is unknown). Although not all of the doorways in this insula can be identified, a tentative interpretation of the layout can be suggested, based on the plan. There are apparently three residential units side-by-side. The two western ones appear to comprise some elements familiar from the housing of Athens, Peiraios and Thorikos. Each has what appears to be a courtyard at the centre. The largest rooms are on the north side, approached via a pastas or anteroom. (The division between this space and the court takes the form of a low stone socle rather

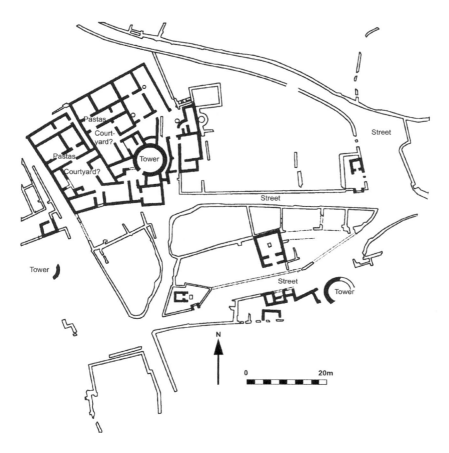

Figure 3.19 Ano Voula, buildings and streets of the Kalampoka plot, showing the tower compound (top left).
(Drawn by the author based on Nevett 2005, Fig. 6.4.)

than a row of bases. It may either have supported a solid wall, or a low parapet on which columns or supports rested.) The southern and eastern parts of the insula are more irregular, perhaps because of the inclusion of the circular tower, which must have made arranging the surrounding spaces awkward. This irregularity may also reflect modifications made to the layout during the life-time of the insula, which apparently included blocking a passageway from the north of the western unit. A connecting doorway between the eastern and central units may similarly be a modification of an earlier plan, perhaps linked with the construction of the tower and surrounding spaces, which may have blocked an original southern entrance. In its final phase, then, the insula perhaps consisted of two properties, with the western unit owning the irregular southern section including the tower (since the tower appears to have been entered from this western structure), while the eastern and central units were combined. (These are only suggestions and would need to be tested through detailed stratigraphic and architectural study.) Other houses from the site are preserved in a more fragmentary form and are, therefore, even more difficult to interpret.

Domestic Life in the Deme Centres

The housing of the deme centres thus made use of a number of elements familiar from the urban houses in Athens and Peiraios: construction was of mud brick with stone socles. An open courtyard formed the central circulation space and was often supplemented by a portico sheltering the entrances to some of the main rooms. The number of excavated houses in any of these locations is small. There is therefore no way of knowing how representative either group is, but there are several characteristics which are worth highlighting as they may have social and cultural significance.

The structures excavated in the demes are for the most part larger than those in the city itself. While their plans follow the pattern of organisation of some of the larger Athenian houses, the central court was sometimes less important for accessing individual rooms, with suites entered sequentially instead, which would have reduced the possibility of monitoring movement into and around the house. At the same time, access to the house itself was often freer, with two, or even three, different entrances regularly provided, facilitating movement of people and goods into and out of the house, but reducing the level of security and seclusion. Inside, there is only limited evidence for any kind of decoration – while painted plaster was found in house 1 at Thorikos, no andrones have been found either here or at Ano Voula. In addition, building styles were often rougher, making use of irregularly shaped blocks for the wall socles. Together, these features suggest that life in the deme houses may have been somewhat different from in the larger urban centres. Within the confines of a smaller community it may have been the case that ostentatious architectural statements of adherence to the norms of behaviour required of urban dwellers were not a prominent feature of housing. Households perhaps did not need to signal their status or conformity to social ideals for outsiders, since members of the smaller community were more likely to have first-hand knowledge of each other. At the same time, as is the case in many of the houses in Athens itself, the lack of identifiable andrones does not necessarily mean that symposia did not take place in these deme houses – they could have been held in more informal circumstances – in multifunctional spaces, or in the courtyard (although as in their urban counterparts, this would have given them a rather different atmosphere from that of the enclosed space of an andron).

A final, obvious, contrast between the urban and deme houses is the presence of the towers which were incorporated into some of the deme structures. Their role has long been debated: the doors of some of them could be barred from both inside and out, and they potentially offered a secure location for storage or retreat in a time of danger. Sarah Morris and John Papadopoulos have suggested that both these and towers lying outside settlements were used to lock up teams of enslaved people who provided labour for agriculture and mining. This use fits with an episode mentioned by Demosthenes, in which enslaved women who lived in a tower were able to fend off attackers attempting to steal goods from the house (Text Extract 14). Nevertheless, this is just one source, and given the multi-functional use of space in Greek domestic contexts generally, a wider range of roles perhaps seems more plausible – securing valuables of any kind, such as agricultural produce, raw materials, or household goods, may also have been important, given that these communities were small and some were perhaps vulnerable to raiding from the sea. At a symbolic level, possession of a tower may also have amounted to a statement of wealth, both because it may have been relatively difficult to build, and also because owning (or residing in) a property with one suggested that the household had significant assets which needed securing.

Country Living: Evidence for Housing in Rural Attica

Exploration of the landscape in several parts of Attica has shown that the later fifth century BCE saw the most intensive occupation of the rural landscape of pre-modern times. In particular, detailed investigation of the area covered by the ancient deme of Atene has revealed a countryside dotted with evidence of activity, including scatters of pottery sherds, burials, terrace walls, cisterns, walled enclosures, threshing floors, courtyards and roofed buildings. Such elements are often found clustered in a single location. The size of the buildings involved is quite variable, ranging from a single room up to an open courtyard associated with seven or eight separate interior spaces. Some of the most durable architecture takes the form of isolated towers, as for example at the southern tip of Attica in the countryside around Sounion. Just like their counterparts in deme settlements, rural towers may have played a variety of roles, including as lookouts or defensive structures. In some cases, however, they are associated with other remains such as courtyards, cisterns, walls, threshing floors and/or inscriptions cut into the surface of rocky out-crops, suggesting that they formed part of larger farming and residential complexes (for example the Cliff Tower, shown in Figure 3.20). Such buildings are often known only from evidence gathered during surface survey and not through excavation. This makes it difficult to get a full and detailed picture of the variety of activities carried out or to judge the degree to which there may have been an architecturally standardised layout.

One of the most detailed pictures of a rural farmstead comes from the excavations at the so-called Dema House, in the interior of the Attic peninsula. In many respects, the structure is similar to the urban houses of Athens itself, not only in terms of its construction, which was mud brick on a stone socle with a pitched, tiled roof, but also its layout (Figure 3.21). The Dema house was built around 420 BCE and destroyed within a generation, with limited re-occupation during the fourth century BCE. It is relatively large, covering an area of about 350 m^2. Space is organised around an open courtyard which accounts for a third of this space and was supplemented by a broad pastas on its north side, sheltering the entrances to the main rooms. As in the city houses, those rooms were reached individually from the court, rather than in series.

The last occupants of the Dema house cleared out most of their belongings before they left, but a few objects remaining in and around the building give an impression of some of the activities carried out there: for example, sherds of large storage jars in the southern and eastern parts of the house may attest to storage of agricultural produce, while pieces of mill stone survive from crop processing. Associated pottery includes a range of household and table wares as well as trans-port amphoras and cooking ware – all consistent with domestic activi-ties. No evidence of a tower was reported, although a similar house at Vari (Figure 3.22) and another close to Ano Voula at Cape Zoster, which date to the fifth and fourth centuries BCE respectively, did have square rooms with thickened walls which may have risen higher than the remainder of the building and served as some kind of tower (their original heights are unknown).

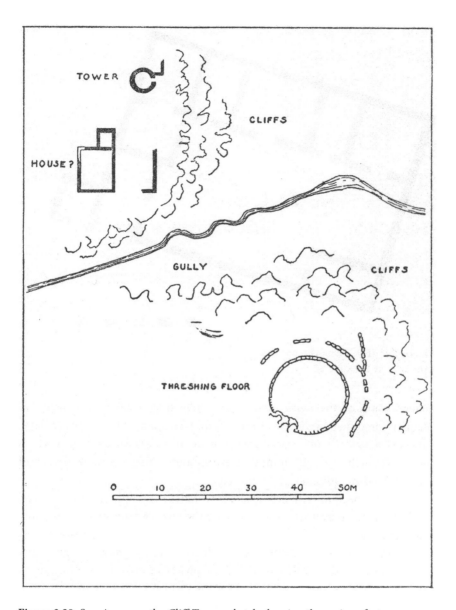

Figure 3.20 Sounion area: the Cliff Tower: sketch showing the various features associated with the structure.
(After Young 1956, Fig. 2, c, courtesy of the Trustees of the American School of Classical Studies at Athens.)

These various structures had a variety of features in common with their urban counterparts, including a single entrance and an open central courtyard-portico area which acted as the main circulation space, giving access to the surrounding rooms. The addition of towers in some instances

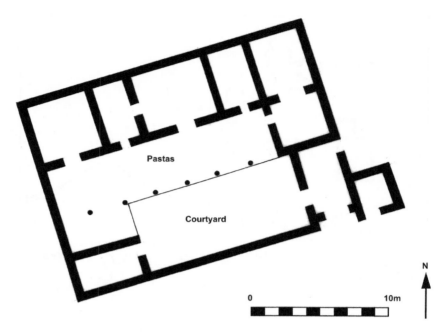

Pastas

Courtyard

N

0   10m

Figure 3.21 The Dema House, Attica.
(After Nevett 1999, Fig. 15.)

echoes some of the deme houses and may have offered a measure of security for valuables. Many of these farm structures were relatively large. That extra space is often accounted for by an extensive courtyard which may have facilitated agricultural activities and perhaps offered a place of safety for farm equipment and animals.

There has been intense debate about whether rural buildings would have been occupied all year round, or whether they would have been in use only during the parts of the year when intensive agricultural labour was necessary – for example during the harvest. It has been pointed out that if the owners (or indeed lessees – as we have a variety of documents attesting to the leasing of such properties) lived for the rest of the year in the city or in one of the deme centres, they would have been able to participate more fully in communal political and cultural life. In practice there may have been examples of both patterns of occupation, but however they were used, farmsteads still constitute a distinctive form of domestic structure. Comparison with the complexes from Cape Sounion and Atene suggests that the Dema house and others like it may not have been typical. Their substantial construction and regular layouts may indicate that the occupants were unusually wealthy. Such houses may have constituted country

Figure 3.22 The Vari House, Attica. View from the interior of the tower, across the courtyard to the pastas and northern rooms.
(Author's photograph, reproduced by permission of the Ephorate of Antiquities of Peiraios and the Islands. The rights to the monument shown belong to the Hellenic Ministry of Culture and Sports (Law 3028/2002). The Vari House is under the supervision of the Ephorate of Antiquities of Peiraios and the Islands, Ministry of Culture and Sports.)

retreats, incorporating features of urban housing to an unusual degree. Following the Peloponnesian War, the population of rural Attica seems to have contracted: many isolated farms were abandoned during the fourth century BCE and not re-occupied.

Farm buildings constitute the main form of isolated residential building in the Classical Attic landscape, but other types of specialised structure are occasionally found. In particular, ore washeries are present, not only within the settlement at Thorikos, but also widely scattered through the surrounding countryside both singly and in clusters. Curiously, in some cases such washeries include androns. An example belongs to a complex at Soureza, south-west of Thorikos, dating to the fourth century BCE, which incorporated a mosaic floor and plaster walls. While we cannot be sure exactly why such a room was constructed here, it might perhaps indicate a need to entertain business associates in connection with ore processing and/or the periodic use of the complex by urban dwellers, as suggested for the largest farmhouses. An andron occurring in a single farm complex at Atene might perhaps be explained in the same way.

Conclusion: Houses in Classical Athens and Attica, and the Single-entrance, Courtyard House

As we have seen, housing in Athens and Attica varied considerably in scale and form. The smallest urban dwellings were very simple, composed of one to three rooms and a courtyard, but with few, if any, identifiable architectural features. These are likely to represent the accommodation of households of relatively low socio-economic status who had little freedom of choice in how to construct and maintain their houses because of resource constraints. This form of building is perhaps the most consistent over time, its layout changing little, although more research is needed on the distribution of finds and activities to understand whether there was a comparable degree of continuity in the use of space. Because of their size and simple construction, houses of this type are probably significantly under-represented in the archaeological record. Such small dwellings can be distinguished from a number of larger structures comprising four or five rooms or more, which constitute a functional type, namely, the single-entrance, courtyard house. As noted above, this is characterised by certain basic organisational features, including a single entrance separated from the interior, a central courtyard with adjacent pastas, prostas or anteroom, and a radial (as opposed to sequential) pattern of spatial organisation. On current evidence this house-form seems to have been fundamentally an urban one, although some of its basic features are echoed in the larger rural farmsteads.

It is impossible to pinpoint the emergence of the single-entrance, courtyard house precisely in time. Its creation was surely supported by a gradual increase in the resources available to some households, requiring them to occupy larger amounts of space in which to store their material goods (possessions, foodstuffs and any materials for craft production). This increase in the scale of the larger properties often went hand-in-hand with more substantial construction techniques, including the use of cut stone blocks in the wall socles and the provision of terracotta-tiled roofs, which must have required strong timber supports. Nevertheless, social factors were surely also involved in determining the exact form taken by such houses. It is impossible to know whether in such cases household size also changed, although this may have happened, through the creation of extended family households or the inclusion of unrelated individuals such as enslaved people. The fact that such houses seem to materialise a sensitivity about social contact between the women of the household and outsiders suggests that in Athens it may have been linked with the idea that lineage and inheritance were important determinants of the right to citizenship. Athenian concern for citizenship rights is apparent from at least 451 BCE, when the statesman Perikles introduced a law restricting eligibility to those whose fathers and also mothers, could be shown to be descended from citizen families. Inhabiting a house with this design may, therefore, have been a symbolic statement that the household supported the ideals of the citizen state. Restricting women's movements may have been viewed as ensuring paternity and thereby protecting the integrity of the citizen body. The single-entrance, courtyard house can thus be identified tentatively as embodying ideals of citizenship, although it is likely to have been emulated by other groups, and of course the extent to which daily patterns of behaviour conformed to the ideals suggested by the architecture is difficult to assess. Interestingly, those ideals do not seem to have been communicated to the same extent through deme houses. As suggested above, the individual residents of these smaller communities may have known each other better, so that symbolic demonstrations were less significant. The fact that some of the large rural farmsteads do seem to have been organised in a manner closer to the urban houses may also be important. This, together with the presence of andrones in some of the mining complexes, may possibly reflect the activities of city-based households in the rural landscape.

As this chapter shows, then, the single-entrance, courtyard house is not a rigidly defined architectural type. Rather, it describes a collection of organisational characteristics. While some of them, such as the central courtyard, go back several centuries in some areas (as seen in Chapter 2), in Athens and Attica it is hard to find houses which bring the elements together consistently before the fifth century BCE. Furthermore, even within this relatively small geographical area there is significant variation in the exact forms taken by houses, with some households occupying structures of modest size and few rooms which lack the characteristic features of their larger peers. Major questions to be addressed in the following chapters are how widespread these different types of building were, how long they persisted and what some of their social or cultural implications may have been. We also explore evidence for alternative patterns of domestic organisation and consider their possible significance.

4 | Housing in Mainland Greece during the Classical Period

Towards a Shared Ideal?

Introduction

This chapter builds on the discussion in Chapter 3 in order to consider how far housing on the Greek mainland was organised in a similar way to that in Athens and Attica, during the fifth and earlier fourth centuries BCE. The discussion is complemented by the following chapter which expands the horizons further to investigate housing across the wider culturally Greek world. By exploring the spatial extent of the single-entrance, courtyard house, and considering the potential social significance of some of the continuities or variations in form and organisation, these chapters together address the question of how representative this house-form, with its associated social norms, may have been, of the Greek world as a whole.

The present chapter shows that the single-entrance, courtyard house was widespread through the Greek mainland. As suggested for Athens (Chapter 3), it can be interpreted as materialising a set of ideal patterns of activity which may have been considered appropriate for households of a particular status, but which may have been aspirational as much as real for many. At the same time, there are clear instances where the single-entrance, courtyard house seems not to have been present. In some cases, this seems likely to be a consequence of the occupants' lack of economic resources – some houses were simply too small to incorporate its key features, as we have already seen in the vicinity of the Athenian Agora. Other examples, however, parallel some of the housing of the Attic demes in following alternative configurations of space which are likely to result from prioritising different social, cultural and/or environmental considerations. What some of those factors may have been is explored below in relation to the individual cases.

As we have seen in Chapter 2 with housing from earlier periods, the geographical distribution of the evidence is uneven, and much of the surviving material is fragmentary. In southern Greece, especially the Peloponnese, excavated houses are very scarce in comparison with the northern Greek mainland. For the future, as more sites are investigated in detail, the picture will no doubt become more subtle and complex.

At present, brief overviews can be offered of selected regions, although the number of houses and sites represented in each is quite variable. The regions are defined in part based on geographical criteria and in part with regard to characteristics of the houses themselves.

Northeastern Greece

Olynthos

We begin our journey in northern Greece, with the city of Olynthos, a site first excavated between 1928 and 1938. It has dominated the literature on Classical Greek housing ever since, owing to the large scale of the excavations and the amount of information collected and published. Unusually detailed records about the distribution of artefacts found during those early excavations help to supplement the kind of architectural evidence we looked at in Chapter 3. Patterning in the distribution of the artefacts offers an opportunity to consider more fully how the activities of different household members may once have mapped onto some of the physical spaces of the houses. The relatively well-preserved houses and detailed publication offer an opportunity for close inspection of a range of their physical characteristics. At the same time, the large number of excavated houses reveals a range of features that recur frequently, offering a baseline against which to assess the significance of variations in architecture found elsewhere.

The city of Olynthos is located on the Halkidiki peninsula in northern Greece. It lies about 250 kilometres from Athens, as the crow flies. In Classical times, this region was thought of as the edge of the Greek world, abutting as it did the kingdom of Macedon to the west and the culturally diverse interior of the Balkans to the north. The city itself spreads across two low hills and spills onto the eastern plain below (Figure 4.1). Its oldest district, the South Hill, was probably laid out during the sixth century BCE. Textual sources suggest that in 432 BCE, when it was a relatively small community, Olynthos became the centre of an 'anoikismos', a movement of the inhabitants of settlements from the surrounding area to live in the city. In 423 BCE, it also became the centre of a political alliance – the Halkidian League – aimed at resisting domination by its neighbours in Macedonia and Thrace, and by Athens to south. At much the same time, and presumably as a result of these political and demographic changes, archaeological evidence shows that the settlement itself was expanded: a new housing district was laid out on the North Hill, a larger hill-top north of the original centre.

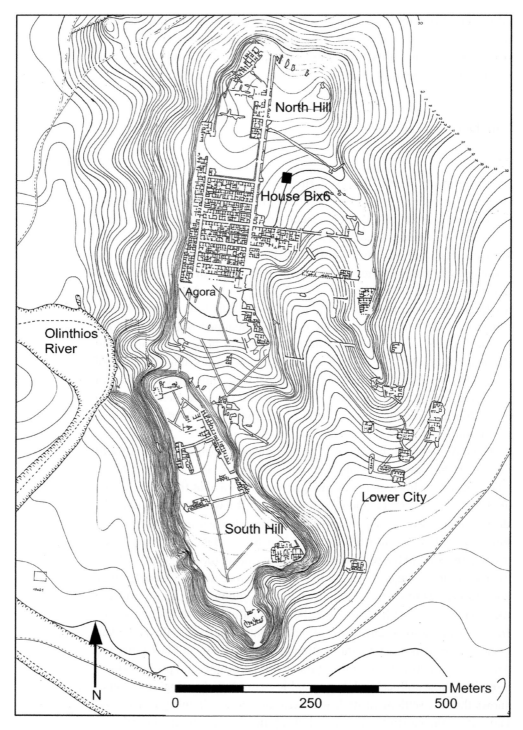

Figure 4.1 Olynthos, topographic plan showing the excavated areas.
(Drawn by David Stone.)

The first excavator of Olynthos, American scholar David Robinson, dug many trenches on the South Hill, locating what he referred to as the 'Religious and Municipal Center' (including a building with ashlar masonry socles and painted stucco), as well as many structures he identified as houses. Nevertheless, the topography was difficult to understand because the streets and buildings appeared to follow irregular plans which meant that in many cases it was impossible to tell where one property ended and the next began. Robinson, therefore, chose to focus on the North Hill. This was laid out on a rectilinear street grid. The houses were occupied for three or four generations and were probably abandoned in 348 BCE, when textual sources record the capture and destruction of the entire city following a siege by king Philip II of Macedon. Archaeological evidence of fighting has been found across the site, including hoards of coins and other items buried under house floors, scattered evidence of burned destruction and looting in some neighbourhoods, and even bronze arrowheads or lead sling bullets, the latter sometimes with the name 'Philip' moulded onto the surface. Olynthos seems to have been obliterated so completely that Robinson found only very limited evidence of possible re-occupation in the form of late coins which were concentrated at the northern end of the North Hill. While this destruction must have been a catastrophe for the ancient residents, it means that the site is an excellent source of information for archaeologists – the city was not significantly disturbed by subsequent construction, and it was possible to excavate large, contiguous areas to understand the typical organisation of the houses. Most recently, the legacy data provided by Robinson's project have been supplemented by the results of new field work at the site by the Olynthos Project. This includes geophysical investigation clarifying the extent of the inhabited area and the layout of the thoroughfares and houses in unexcavated areas; field survey exploring the extent of the urban area along with the date and nature of the occupation in different neighbourhoods; and the painstaking excavation of a single house, B ix 6, using a wide range of modern scientific techniques to explore the use of space throughout the interior. Among other things, this work has shown that the South Hill was laid out on a regular plan although the streets did not run on a continuous orthogonal grid. Excavation in and around some of the houses in this neighbourhood demonstrated the complex chronological sequence of the buildings but did not investigate the layout of individual houses. The vast majority of evidence regarding the housing of Olynthos' inhabitants, therefore, comes from the North Hill.

Figure 4.2 Olynthos, view of the area excavated by David Robinson on the North Hill looking north along Avenue A and showing the restored socles of the excavated houses to either side.
(Author's photograph, courtesy of the Ephorate of Antiquities of Halkidiki and Aghios Oros. The rights to the monument shown belong to the Hellenic Ministry of Culture and Sports (Law 3028/2002). Olynthos is under the supervision of the Ephorate of Antiquities of the Halkidiki and Aghios Oros, Ministry of Culture and Sports.)

Robinson's original project found that, on the North Hill, the streets and broad avenues were set at regular intervals and intersected at right-angles (Figure 4.2). The individual housing blocks between were rectangular in plan and most were composed of ten, roughly square-shaped, houses arranged in two rows of five, sharing party walls with their neighbours on either side. Each double row was divided by a narrow alley surfaced with cobbles and provided with a water channel for drainage. An open area close to the centre of the North Hill probably served as the city's agora or civic square. Analysis of a number of scattered inscriptions from across the North Hill, which relate to financial transactions using some of the houses as security, suggests that those located closer to the agora were more valuable and highly sought-after, despite the city's small scale (its total length is only just over a kilometre).

The houses themselves follow the general type of construction discussed in Chapter 1, with mudbrick walls, stone socles (in this case normally unworked cobbles) and terracotta-tiled roofs. The layouts of most are relatively clear (Figure 4.3). The exact nature of the superstructures can

Figure 4.3 Olynthos, house A viii 2 looking northeast from Avenue A. Unusually, the house was proabably entered from here, on its west side. The limestone block (left foreground) was probably one of two flanking the entrance corridor (the corresponding one did not survive, and a modern replacement now occupies that position). Beyond lies the cobbled courtyard with the cut limestone bases for the columns or pillars of the pastas to its left. To the far left is an andron with an anteroom in front.
(Author's photograph, courtesy of the Ephorate of Antiquities of Halkidiki and Aghios Oros. The rights to the monument shown belong to the Hellenic Ministry of Culture and Sports (Law 3028/2002). Olynthos is under the supervision of the Ephorate of Antiquities of the Halkidiki and Aghios Oros, Ministry of Culture and Sports.)

only be tentatively reconstructed (Figure 4.4). Individual properties on the North Hill are mostly of a standard size, around 290 m^2 in ground area, although some which had been built up against the inside of the city wall are a little smaller, while others in the Lower City were often somewhat larger. In their basic design, the houses in these different locations are strikingly similar to each other and clearly incorporate the features of the single-entrance, courtyard organisational scheme. As in the Athenian examples, there are relatively few permanent architectural fixtures which might hint at the way in which internal space was used. Nevertheless, interpretation is assisted by the exceptional detail of the information routinely collected about some of the objects recovered during excavation (such as ceramic vessels, metal fixtures and fittings, and mill stones). This included notes about the approximate locations in which many of them were found. Some caution is necessary in interpreting these artefacts, however: in addition to the general considerations outlined in Chapter 1, at Olynthos there are some particularly acute problems with evaluating their contexts. The excavators sometimes noted changes in soil colour and

Figure 4.4 Olynthos, reconstruction of a domestic courtyard looking north towards the pastas. (After Hoepfner and Schwandner 1994, Fig.76, courtesy of Wolfram Hoepfner.)

texture, or measured how deeply buried an object was, but they did not draw any of the stratigraphic sections showing the relationships between deposits, which would be normal today. It is, therefore, difficult to distinguish (for example) between items which may have been in situ on house floors at the time the city was destroyed, and others which may have fallen from collapsed upper storeys. Despite these issues, the large number of excavated houses means that it is possible to analyse statistically the distribution of different types of objects. This yields some patterns which are likely to result from the way in which different parts of the house were used, and these help to contextualise the information from the architecture, improving our understanding of general patterns of domestic activity in the city.

An example which shows many of the typical features of the Olynthian houses, including a good number and variety of artefacts, is house A vii 4 (Figure 4.5). The property is entered from the street through a door on the south side which leads via a lobby (sometimes referred to as the prothyron) into a cobbled central courtyard (i). The lobby would have restricted the view into the house from the street, even when the door was open. Once inside, the visitor would have a full view of a pastas to the north (f), which

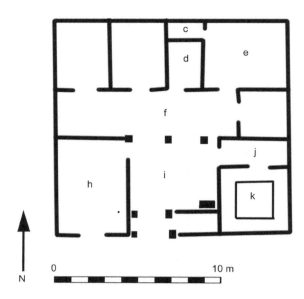

Figure 4.5 Olynthos, plan of house A vii 4.
(Drawn by the author based on Robinson 1938, Fig. 5 and Plate 99.)

gave onto a range of rooms behind. A Doric capital, found in the court, must have belonged to one of the columns or pillars supporting the pastas roof. The intention was perhaps to create a formal ambience, recalling the architectural style of the larger, more elaborate colonnades of public buildings. The effect was enhanced by the use of decorative terracotta plaques and bronze bosses. In a few other houses the portico extends onto two, three or even (occasionally) all four sides of the courtyard, forming a full peristyle (as in the so-called House of the Comedian). Some also have other evidence of decoration in the courtyard and porticoes, including painted plaster walls and even a mosaic floor (as in house A vi 3).

In common with the larger Athenian houses, the courtyard and pastas together form a key node in the circulation pattern: most of the individual rooms open off here rather than communicating directly with each other. A rectangular stone base found in the southeast corner of the court of A vii 4 was probably the base for a flight of wooden stairs. This probably led to an upper storey extending above at least the northern part of the house (a more likely reconstruction than workspace on a flat roof since the tile debris found during excavation suggests the use of a pitched roof). The upper storey rooms would probably have been reached from a gallery overlooking the courtyard (like that shown in Figure 4.4).

The court and pastas seem to have been used for a number of domestic purposes: a few houses had their own cisterns underneath the court – as in the neighbouring house to the east, A vii 6. A range of different types of pottery were also regularly found here. In house A vii 4 the courtyard contained cups and jugs, but there was also a fish hook and an arrow head. In the adjacent pastas there were weights, a needle, an earring, a lekythos (a small bottle for oil or perfume), a brooch and an additional arrowhead. The range of artefacts from this house is very comparable to that found in these spaces in other houses in the city. Statistical analysis of the distribution of artefacts through space indicates common patterns. Activities accompanying the abandonment of the buildings are perhaps more likely to be random and therefore statistical outliers. Thus, focusing on repeated patterns perhaps offers the most reliable way to detect some of the practices involved in using and storing objects, which were common to many households in their daily lives. Such information indicates that users of these spaces habitually treated the court and pastas as an extension of the interior, making use of the good light and ventilation of these areas, rather than simply using them as corridors linking the different rooms.

In house A vii 4, rooms c, d and e, to the north of the court, form an architecturally distinctive complex which is common at Olynthos and is also found elsewhere. This complex was named the 'oikos unit' by J. Walter Graham (a member of Robinson's team who worked especially closely with the architecture of the houses) and he identified it as the focus for domestic life. The main room was e. Aside from a substantial stone mortar (grinder) there were no fixed architectural features here, but a couple of forms of installation are characteristic of such spaces in other houses. Occasionally there are traces of a rubble construction which may have provided a cupboard or shelf and in a few instances a central hearth was provided which may have served to heat the room in winter (as in house A vii 2: Figure 4.6). In the Olynthos houses more generally, this type of room has yielded no particularly characteristic configuration of artefacts; instead, the wide variety suggests that the spaces may have been multi-functional.

In house A vii 4 the floor of room c was made of waterproof mortar, contrasting with most of the rest of the house, where the floors were mostly of beaten earth. A mortar basin was located in one corner of the room and may have been used for washing. At the time of excavation, the floor surface had a gap in it which was probably once occupied by a terracotta bathtub, of a type still surviving in a few other houses (Figure 1.3). In addition to baths, some houses were furnished with louteria (pedestalled basins) which may also have been used for personal cleanliness

Figure 4.6 Olynthos, house A vii 2, detail showing a reconstructed hearth in situ at the centre of room a; in the foreground is the pastas.
(Author's photograph, courtesy of the Ephorate of Antiquities of Halkidiki and Aghios Oros. The rights to the monument shown belong to the Hellenic Ministry of Culture and Sports (Law 3028/2002). Olynthos is under the supervision of the Ephorate of Antiquities of the Halkidiki and Aghios Oros, Ministry of Culture and Sports.)

(Figure 3.11). Elsewhere at Olynthos, examples of terracotta vessels have been found which may have served as urinals: a fragment of one was still in situ, set into a wall so that it drained out of house A vii 9. A further terracotta item found in the drainage alley behind house A iv 9 was interpreted as a toilet seat. Although there was a common drainage system at Olynthos for rainwater, and fresh water was piped to several fountain houses in the city, there was no piped water supply to the individual houses, and cisterns for collecting rainwater are present in only a small minority. For most households, water would, therefore, have had to be collected and carried to the house.

Adjacent to the bathing area in house A vii 4 and separated from it by a wall, lay a further small space, d, which was identified by Graham as a 'flue' based on ashy deposits noted during excavation. Although no artefacts are recorded as coming from this space, similar spaces in other houses, including B ix 6 which was excavated recently, have yielded not only ash but also broken pottery, terracotta figurines and animal bone. Robinson and Graham interpreted this type of deposit as household refuse accumulating in the base of a shaft which was intended to vent smoke through the roof, and they suggested that the rubble wall which sometimes separated this space from the adjacent living area may have been pierced higher up to allow smoke to evacuate via the flue. The combination of fireplace and bathing area seen in this house recurs across the city and is also found in

Greek houses elsewhere; it seems likely that the fire was used for warming, cooking and to heat water for baths.

Two further, also typologically distinctive, rooms identifiable in house A vii 4 are j and k. These have the same features as the andron and anteroom seen occasionally at Athens (Chapter 3) and must have shared the same purpose. Such spaces are comparatively frequent at Olynthos (they are present in about 28 per cent of the excavated houses). As is usual, the doorway of the andron in A vii 4 is off-centre to allow for the placement of couches inside. The fill removed from rooms j and k yielded traces of painted wall plaster suggesting that each space was decorated in three colours: in the andron there were red walls with a white base and a yellow band above it. The anteroom was different: the main colour was yellow with a black base and a white band. Although today the room is back-filled so that no plaster is visible, there are a few instances in other Olynthian houses where traces of coloured plaster can still be seen adhering to the exposed socles of androns (Figure 4.7).

In house A vii 4 the floors of both j and k were made of cement. In k a raised border, painted yellow, would have served as a base for the couches

Figure 4.7 Olynthos, house A vi 6: andron, with a black and white pebble mosaic floor laid in a geometric design and traces of red plaster walls (upper right).
(Author's photograph, courtesy of the Ephorate of Antiquities of Halkidiki and Aghios Oros. The rights to the monument shown belong to the Hellenic Ministry of Culture and Sports (Law 3028/2002). Olynthos is under the supervision of the Ephorate of Antiquities of the Halkidiki and Aghios Oros, Ministry of Culture and Sports.)

or cushions arranged around the walls. (As is the case with most Olynthian androns, the room could accommodate seven couches and a total of up to fourteen occupants.) In other houses the floor of both the andron and anteroom sometimes feature a more elaborate surface of pebble mosaic. A range of black-and-white and polychrome designs have been found, including geometric patterns (Figure 4.7) and even, occasionally, figured scenes (for example, the 'Villa of Good Fortune' boasted a central motif depicting Dionysos and a panther). It is unknown whether the simpler cement floors might originally have featured comparable painted designs, or whether they may have been covered by rugs or mats. Nevertheless, the general elaboration of these rooms, in addition to the court and pastas, suggests an element of display which may have been aimed at making a good impression on visitors from outside the household as well as at creating pleasant surroundings for the residents themselves.

A final distinctive space is the large room h, which has its own entrance from the street and also connects with the courtyard. Apart from the entrance arrangements and its large size, there are no architectural features which might offer an indication of what this space was used for, nor did it yield many artefacts. Similar spaces are present in many other houses in the city and are often unconnected with the remainder of the house. As a rule, they have no discernible architectural features and there are no characteristic types of finds. Robinson and his colleagues suggested that they may have served as shops, workshops or stable facilities. (Their identification was perhaps made on analogy with the houses of Roman Italy where shops and workshops are sometimes well-preserved and therefore easily identifiable. There, they are set into house facades and are often similarly independent of those houses.) Finds in some of the other houses suggest that households were engaged in a variety of commercial, agricultural or industrial production. For example, in house A 6 a pressing floor, part of an olive crusher and a group of mill stones were found. Elsewhere, crafts practised include coroplasty (the manufacture of terracottas) in house B i 5 and sculpting in A 5. The integration of residential and productive space in this way parallels what we have already seen at Athens in the houses close to the Agora.

The role played by the upper storey in house A vii 4 is unclear because the lack of information about stratigraphy prevents positive identification of finds from here. Nevertheless, in more recent work it has been possible to distinguish two separate levels of deposits in some areas. In house B ix 6, the higher one contained a range of fine ware and miniature vessels, including cups, jugs, and large lekanides (lidded bowls) that may have come from the upper storey. This might imply that those rooms included living space and were perhaps also used for ritual activities. It seems likely, however, that as with many of the ground floor rooms, those in the upstairs were used relatively flexibly since there is no clear difference in the organisation of space between those houses which seem to have had an upper storey and those which apparently did not.

The upper storey has sometimes been thought of as the location in which female members of the household may habitually have spent their time, based on the fact that several Athenian textual sources refer to the use of upper rooms by women. Nevertheless, artefacts which can specifically be associated with women such as loom weights, perfume bottles and cosmetic boxes, are found widely scattered through the domestic context, implying that women may have used a range of different domestic spaces. This seems to hold true both for houses which seem to have had an upper storey and for those which lack any evidence of one.

Although the North Hill was probably occupied for three or four generations, the excavators regarded this part of the site as having a single phase of occupation – that is, they assumed that the residents did not change the buildings significantly during the time they lived there. Upon close inspection, though, in various locations there is evidence of a number of alterations. In some cases, it seems that pre-existing structures may have been incorporated into the house blocks since there are some double walls included in buildings which are otherwise regular in plan. In other instances, the excavators revealed the foundations of walls which had been dismantled. Elsewhere, parts of properties, or even single rooms, seem to have been sold off to neighbours. For example, an andron with a doorway leading into house A vi 10 sits on land lying within what was surely the original footprint of its western neighbour, A vi 8. There are also houses which seem to have been subdivided, as in the case of C -x 7 (Figure 4.8). It is possible that changes may have resulted from political and economic uncertainty during the years immediately prior to Philip's besieging of the city, although it is perhaps more likely that they attest to the changing requirements and fortunes of different households over time.

In general it seems that activities such as cooking and food preparation, which in a modern western home tend to have fixed locations, may have taken place in varying spaces at Olynthos, depending perhaps on the season or even on the time of day. A built hearth is not present in every case, while some houses yielded portable braziers along with storage and cooking wares from a variety of locations, including the courtyard and pastas. Other items linked with domestic activity, such as loom weights,

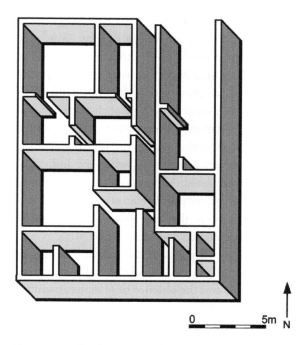

0 ____ 5m N

Figure 4.8 Olynthos, house C–x 7, showing the subdivision of space into
separate units.
(Entrances to some of the rooms are unlocated; drawn by Max Huemer based
on Robinson 1946, Plate 230.)

were similarly widely distributed. The basic pattern emerging is, therefore,
of only a limited amount of specialisation in the roles played by individual
spaces. By maintaining some flexibility in where they carried out their
various tasks, residents would have been able to take advantage of natural
daylight and of the thermal properties of different parts of their houses
throughout the day and during different seasons, as well as fulfilling the
requirements of a variety of social conventions. The relatively limited
quantity, and the portability, of domestic equipment would have enhanced
this flexibility. Taken as a whole, the single entrance and the dominance of
the court-pastas area over circulation suggest a desire to monitor, and
perhaps also to control, movement. Therefore, despite the fact that their
appearance was superficially different from that of the larger Athenian
examples (discussed in Chapter 3), their internal space seems to have been
used in a similar way, following the single entrance, courtyard model.

Finally, the Olynthian material furnishes some evidence to reinforce
the suggestion, made in Chapter 3, that the ideal of separating household
members from visitors is mostly a characteristic of larger properties. As at

Athens, some examples of small houses have come to light here which possess only three or four rooms and cover an area as little as 75 m². An example of this kind of arrangement is house C–x 7, mentioned above, in which a single plot seems to have been subdivided, forming several separate units (Figure 4.8). Although the level of preservation does not allow all of them to be reconstructed precisely, they show some typical characteristics of houses of this size. Each unit is apparently undecorated and without a specialised andron. There is also no evidence of any attempt to shield the interior of the house from the common passageway, while the individual rooms of a unit are sometimes interconnected. Although on present evidence C–x 7 seems unrepresentative of the majority of dwellings at Olynthos, it is possible that structures of a similar size were also to be found among those on the South Hill, which is less well-documented and -understood.

The socio-economic status of the occupants of the individual units of C–x 7 and other similar ones is, of course, impossible to reconstruct precisely. Nevertheless, the small size and the absence of obvious amenities or decoration suggest that they may have been of relatively modest means. Since these households did not create private environments in the interiors of their dwellings, they were perhaps unable to sustain the lifestyles enjoyed by their neighbours in the larger structures. If guests were entertained at all in such houses, there is no evidence that separate space was provided for this purpose. Such apparent disregard for the conventions followed in the larger houses may point to households which did not pursue the same ideals of social behaviour as their neighbours: entertaining guests within the household may not have been customary or if it did take place, it may have been lacking in formality and the pressure to separate guests from household members may have been absent. It is possible that houses like these belonged to a group of urban poor and/or to disenfranchised social groups. Despite the presence of a small number of such units, a surprising aspect of the North Hill houses more generally in comparison with the Attic properties discussed in Chapter 3 is their relative uniformity in size and amenities. It is, therefore, no surprise that Olynthos features promin-ently in the work of Wolfram Hoepfner and Ernst-Ludwig Schwandner, as evidence that the ideals of political equality between male citizens were also translated into the economic sphere in the form of houses of equal size.

Some of the most prominent recurring features of these houses are bathing rooms and androines. What might the relatively frequent incorpor-ation of these facilities into the domestic architecture at Olynthos signify? Several explanations are possible and are not necessarily mutually exclu-sive: in following a fairly set notion of the single-entrance, courtyard house the inhabitants of Olynthos could have been trying to be seen to espouse similar ideals to those expressed at Athens and (as we shall see below) other Greek cities. This could have been one consequence of Athenian dominance, which Ian Morris has argued spurred cultural changes in other cities, causing them to become like Athens itself. It may be that the social and practical considerations affecting housing at Olynthos were similar to those shaping housing at Athens, with some households gaining access to greater resources and feeling the need for a larger amount of space. It is also possible that the northern location of Olynthos is important and that the city's inhabitants, who lay at the fringes of the Greek world, were trying to demonstrate their 'Greekness' by ostentatiously conforming to some of the conventions of the domestic organisation perceived as characteristic of Greek communities further south. Additional readings could be suggested, especially because motivations and perceptions are likely to have varied even among the individuals and households concerned. With respect to andrones, in particular, it is also important to emphasise that although they are often seen as typical of Olynthian houses, the fact that the features modern archaeologists associate with such spaces were recognised in only one in four of the excavated examples raises questions: did the other houses have andrones which lacked such features? Or were other spaces also used for the same purpose? Did only some households participate in the kinds of social activities for which an andron was used (whether or not that equated with the roles such rooms played further south)? On present evidence, these are hard to answer, although it is perhaps relevant to point out that house B ix 6 had a room possessing some, but not all, of the typical features of such spaces – a reminder that any generalisations we make about ancient housing and the use of space are, of necessity, somewhat simplified and do not encompass the full range of variation found in a large sample of houses. The users of such spaces were individuals who made their own decisions and had their own ideas, while at the same time each house had its own unique history.

Having sketched the organisation of domestic space at Olynthos as a foil for the evidence from Athens and Attica presented in Chapter 3, it is now possible to explore some of the continuities and discontinuities in the configuration and use of domestic space across geographical space and through time. The remainder of this chapter explores housing from elsewhere in the area of present-day Greece during the Classical period, looking at evidence for similarities and differences between regions and communities, and attempting to understand some of the social and cultural factors which may have contributed to those continuities and contrasts.

Northern Greece beyond Olynthos

The detailed evidence for this region offered by Olynthos is complemented by less extensive information from a variety of other sites in northern Greece (the regions of Pieria, Greek Macedonia, Halkidiki and Thrace), where housing from several communities shows many similarities with what we have already seen. By the Classical period, the fertile landscapes in these areas were occupied by a relatively dense network of cities. On-going investigation at a number of them means that knowledge and understanding of the appearance and organisation of Classical housing here is increasing rapidly. In addition to Olynthos, the single-entrance, courtyard house type seems to have been in use in several other communities. One of the most extensively documented is on the northern Aegean island of Thasos, where details of the interior spatial organisation of at least 20 houses have been investigated, most of them located at Limenas, the ancient city lying beneath the modern town. The district close to the Silenos Gate (Figure 4.9) offers two examples of a form of relatively large house with patterns of organisation which are representative of other, similarly sized structures on the island. In insula I, starting in the mid fourth century BCE there is a change from small houses with one to three rooms and a courtyard, to the construction of two, more complex, buildings with five or more rooms each, following the single entrance, courtyard model (houses Ia and Ib). Both houses cover around 200 m^2 and in some phases they are similar in plan. In house Ia the entrance is from the south and leads, via a corridor, into a central courtyard (Figure 4.10). A staircase in the court led to an upper storey. In both cases the rooms to the north are entered via a long anteroom. (In house Ia the wall dividing this space from the court was preserved to around a meter in height, so that the anteroom seems to have been enclosed to at least that height.) Although the anteroom may have filled some of the roles we have seen for the pastas elsewhere (such as storage) its design must have had implications for the range of activities which could have been carried out there: despite the existence of doorways connecting it with the court, light and ventilation would have been limited. The rooms behind would also have been correspondingly darker and more airless, although this problem could have been mitigated if there had been openings to the exterior at the rear. This combination of courtyard, pastas-like anteroom and rear rooms is found in a number of other, less well-preserved houses at Limenas and has been viewed as typical of the spatial organisation of the island's larger houses during the Classical period. Neither house Ia nor Ib (Figure 4.11) has any space resembling the

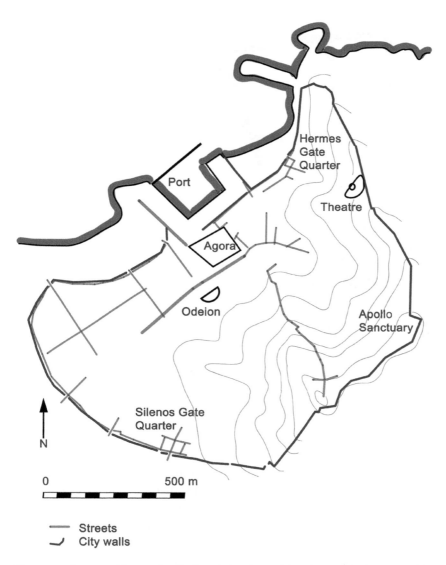

Figure 4.9 Limenas, Thasos, sketch plan of the Classical city showing the location of the housing quarters of the Silenos Gate (Porte du Silène) and Hermes Gate (Porte d'Hermès).
(Drawn by the author based on Grandjean and Marc 1996, figure on p. 74.)

andron we have seen elsewhere: the excavators did note that in house Ia room (1) contained much fine tableware, suggesting that it may have been used for dining; its relatively large size might support this interpretation, although it is also possible that crockery was being stored here for use elsewhere in the house. Since there appears to have been access to the room

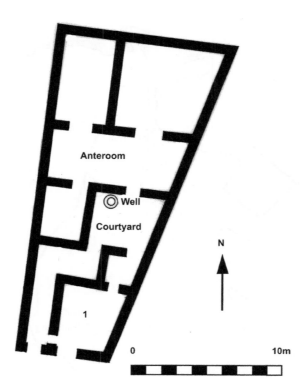

Figure 4.10 Limenas, Thasos, house Ia near the Silenos
Gate (period 4, phase 1).
(After Nevett 1999, Fig. 21.)

directly from the street during some periods of use (which would be highly
unusual for an andron) it also seems possible that the room served as some
kind of commercial premises. As these two properties illustrate, then, the
inhabitants of Limenas used a version of the single entrance, courtyard
house but with a pastas which was at least partially, if not completely,
enclosed. A similar arrangement is also found in the countryside, in farms
excavated at Marmaromandra and at Glykadi, both dating to the late
fourth century BCE.

Evidence for smaller houses is also found in and around Limenas: the
western house in insula I near the Silenos Gate originated as a single-room
house. The fragmentary remains of two-room houses, with the rooms
entered in series from one of the short ends, have been found in excavations near the city's agora. Later disturbance means that their construction
date is unclear but they seem to have been destroyed towards the end of the
fourth century BCE. Although not always well preserved, buildings such as

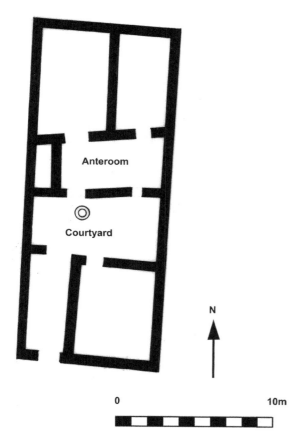

Figure 4.11 Limenas, Thasos, house Ib near the Silenos Gate (period 4, phase 1).
(After Nevett 1999, Fig. 22.)

these perhaps offer evidence of households whose socio-economic status might have been similar to that of the occupants of Olynthos house C–x 7. Overall it seems that while the layout of the Classical settlement at Limenas is somewhat less regular than Olynthos, there are parallels between the two cities in terms of their housing stock, which comprises some properties following the single-entrance, courtyard model, alongside other, smaller structures which do not.

Examples of settlements which echo this range of forms are also found elsewhere in the region: a partially excavated, fourth-century BCE house, house 3 at Torone in the Halkidiki peninsula, may perhaps also belong to the single-entrance, courtyard type. The excavators reconstruct an entrance into the central space from the east although they stress that this is a guess

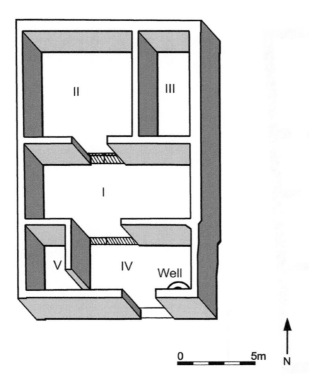

Figure 4.12 Torone, structure 3, author's interpretation.
(Drawn by Max Huemer based on Cambitoglou and
Papadopoulos 2001, Fig. 29.)

and that evidence for the actual doorway was not preserved. Comparison
with the Limenas houses suggests an alternative possibility, that the building may in fact have been entered at its southern end, through room IV, as
indicated in Figure 4.12. The most southerly space was furnished with a
well, a feature commonly found in courtyards, and although the excavators
reject the possibility that this area served as a courtyard, they do so based
on the fact that the floor is surfaced with packed clay rather than something
more durable. In fact, clay surfaces have been found in domestic courtyard
spaces elsewhere, including on the North Hill at Olynthos. A dense deposit
of tile in the northwest corner of this area may have resulted from the
collapse of a pitched roof, with tiles sliding down and into an open court, as
found (for example) during the recent excavations of B ix 6 at Olynthos,
where tiles were most numerous in the cobbled courtyard. This reconstruction would leave room I as the anteroom of a three-room group similar to
those at Limenas, with the two main rooms II and III behind. (The
entrance to III was not located during excavation, but if the layouts of

other houses can be used as a guide, it is most likely to have opened directly from I.) A particularly interesting item found in the Torone house was a portable terracotta oven which was located in room V. This parallels vessels from the Athenian Agora and reinforces the suggestion made above that, in contrast with most modern western cooking practices, in ancient Greek houses fixed facilities were not always used. Food preparation could be done with portable equipment which could be relocated according to short-term environmental constraints and social requirements.

While the northern Greek houses discussed so far resemble, by-and-large, the architectural form traditionally labelled as the pastas house, this arrangement is not the only one adopted in the region. Further east at Abdera, in Thrace, the houses generally follow a different plan. Near the northern boundary of the city, fragmentary remains on the Avramoglou plot reveal settlement remains dating from the mid seventh century to the third century BCE. Here, a partially preserved house dating to the late fifth century has a paved courtyard with stone bases for a portico running around at least two sides. Some of the interior rooms were originally decorated: the excavators noted traces of painted wall plaster and the remains of a monochrome pebble mosaic. Further evidence comes from a residential quarter near the West Gate, which has yielded structures dating from perhaps the fourth century BCE onwards and with areas ranging from about 60 m^2 up to about 200 m^2. Individual house plots here are long and narrow and the space in each seems to have been subdivided into living and service zones. A courtyard to the south of each plot features a relatively short, prostas-type porch to the north, which gives onto two rooms located at right-angles to each other. Houses B and C both possess large living rooms with elaborately decorated façades and large stone threshold blocks facing into their courtyards (Figure 1.6). Fragments of painted wall plaster found in the fill were assumed to have come from here as well. Inside are stone-built hearths like those sometimes found at Olynthos as well as at other sites in northern Greece, as for example in partially preserved houses at Aphytis in the western Halkidiki, a settlement destroyed in an earth-quake at the end of the fourth century BCE. The Aphytis structures were, in addition, equipped with stone-paved bathing areas and painted wall plaster. Similar hearths are also reported from the Classical settlement at Megali Rachi in Aiani, where small courtyard-houses were terraced into steeply sloping terrain, making use of staircases to move between levels.

Alongside the larger properties we have just looked at there is also evidence at Abdera of more modest structures with only a few rooms. On the Avramoglou plot, after the destruction of the house dating to the fifth-century BCE, two smaller residential buildings were laid out on either side of a road during the fourth century BCE. One of these consisted of a large, square, paved area leading to two further spaces, one with a water-proof plaster floor. The entire complex had an area of only 34 m^2 – smaller than some of the smallest units at Olynthos.

In sum, there is secure evidence for the existence of houses of single-entrance, courtyard type in north-eastern Greek settlements by the late fifth century BCE. Certain architectural features recur in some of the larger houses, including stone-built hearths. These, together with decorative elements such as painted wall plaster and carved column capitals found in some of the courtyards, attest to a symbolic role for the house among wealthier inhabitants of these communities comparable to that we have identified at Athens. Smaller units suggest the simultaneous presence of socio-economically less privileged households in these communities, as well.

Viewed against this backdrop, the houses of the North Hill district at Olynthos seem in many ways unusual. They are generally larger than the larger properties known from other settlements in the region, and a more consistently recurring set of room-types is identifiable based on architectural criteria, including amenities such as andrones and baths, which are found much more rarely elsewhere. As noted above, it is interesting to speculate that such characteristics might have been due to the circumstances under which this district was first settled, and/or to the prominent political role played by Olynthos during the later fifth and earlier fourth centuries BCE. It should also be remembered, however, that Robinson's project at Olynthos was exceptional in the number of houses investigated, and it is difficult to judge whether the examples of houses known from other sites are representative of the housing stock of those settlements more generally. Placing the region itself in a wider context by examining evidence from a larger geographical area will provide additional comparative evidence.

North-western Greece

Research further to the west offers insight into a region with a rather different settlement history and a contrasting political situation. Unlike the northeast, there is no single site in this region which dominates our understanding, but there are several well-preserved settlements which provide a basis for reconstructing some of the characteristics of the houses here. A notable source is the work of a joint Greek and German team in the area close to the present-day city of Arta, in Epiros. They have identified settlements in which the layout of domestic space follows a pattern of organisation which is distinctively different from anything we have seen so far: the so-called hearth-room house type, discussed in Chapter 1. The best-preserved examples are at Ammotopos (ancient Orraon), a small, walled settlement probably built in the mid fourth century BCE and destroyed by the Romans in the second century BCE. Defensive walls here enclose sufficient area for about one hundred houses which were laid out along grid-planned streets. Several structures, built entirely of limestone and preserved above 6 metres high in places, offer the most complete surviving examples of Classical houses anywhere in Greece, and suggest what the lost mud brick superstructures of some of those at other settlements might perhaps have looked like. House 1 is the only one to have been extensively investigated (Figure 1.10). It seems to have been constructed around 350 BCE. and is built of large, roughly shaped blocks, including impressive monoliths which supported a portico on the south side of the courtyard in front of the main range of rooms. The walls are preserved close to roof level (Figure 4.13). There is clear evidence for an upper storey across much of

Figure 4.13 Ammotopos, house 1, exterior view showing stone walls: the ventilation openings are at a height of approximately 2 metres above ground level.
(Author's photograph, reproduced by permission of the Ephorate of Antiquities of Preveza. The rights to the monument shown belong to the Hellenic Ministry of Culture and Sports (Law 3028/2002). Ammotopos is under the supervision of the Ephorate of Antiquities of Preveza, Ministry of Culture and Sports.)

the building in the form of a staircase and beam holes for the upper floor. The roof must have been pitched and tiled, to judge from tile fragments found during excavation and restoration work.

The paved courtyard of House 1 was reduced to a very small size in the second phase of occupation by the installation of a cooking space on its east side (h), identified on the basis of the remains of foodstuffs and domestic pottery, as well as the ventilation openings facing the courtyard (which parallel the partition between oikos and flue in some of the Olynthian houses). In contrast with the properties we have seen in other communities, the courtyard lay to the north of the main rooms, rather than to the south. It seems to have played a relatively unimportant role as a route for moving around the building: in the earliest phase of occupation it gave access only to one room with an off-centre door (f) which Sotiris Dakaris, one of the excavators, interprets as an andron, perhaps due both to the position of the doorway and to the stone benches around the walls, although the irregular shape is unusual. The main circulation spaces were the portico (a") to the south of the court, and a large interior room with a central hearth. It is noticeable that in contrast with the patterns we have typically seen elsewhere, two of the rooms have two entrances, including the large sunken space in the south west corner, which the excavators identify as a store-room. This would have been accessible easily both from the courtyard and from the hearth-room, which presumably provided the main interior living- and work-area, particularly in the first phase of occupation. The implications of these access patterns would have been that anyone present in the hearth-room could have monitored movement around the house through the open door into the portico (a"). By contrast, however, occupants of the courtyard and outer rooms would not have been aware of others moving between the hearth-room and its surrounding spaces.

A similar pattern of organisation has been suggested for the houses in the city of Kassope, close to Ammotopos (Figure 4.14). These were occupied from the fourth century down to the first century BCE, by which time the area had fallen under Roman control and Kassope was seemingly abandoned in favour of the new city of Nikopolis, to the south. The socles of these houses are very substantial, consisting of polygonal masonry surviving to a height of more than a metre in places. A series of modifications were made through time which has meant that the organisation of space in the earliest phase has had to be reconstructed, based in part on the forms of the houses in later years. Some of the most detailed information about the fourth-century BCE phase comes from house 6 (Figure 4.15). Like the others at the site, this one makes up part of a long insula in which

Figure 4.14 Kassope, view westwards down the main street. The polygonal masonry of the socles of the house façades are visible to the right (in the middle distance on the right is the market building).
(Author's photograph, reproduced by permission of the Ephorate of Antiquities of Preveza. The rights to the monument shown belong to the Hellenic Ministry of Culture and Sports (Law 3028/2002). Kassope is under the supervision of the Ephorate of Antiquities of Preveza, Ministry of Culture and Sports.)

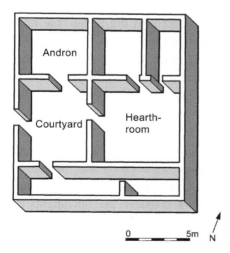

Figure 4.15 Kassope, house 6, layout during the Classical period.
(Drawn by Max Huemer based on Hoepfner and Schwandner 1994, Fig. 136.)

party walls were shared with neighbours. It sits on a roughly square plot with an area of about 225 m^2. A single entrance leads directly from the street into the courtyard. From here it was possible to enter a large, square room to the north, interpreted as a nine-couch andron, based on the off-centre doorway, although nearly all the rooms in these houses have such doorways. In addition, the court also gave access to a storage room to the south and to a large living room (the hearth-room) to the east. This in turn led into a further area to the north, which was probably divided into two separate spaces, each with its own entrance from the living room. In some of the other houses the living room was furnished with a stone hearth and a stair base, leading Wolfram Hoepfner and Ernst Ludwig Schwandner to reconstruct a ceiling rising to the height of two storeys and a gallery along one side which would have led to upper rooms above the lower storey side rooms. As at Ammotopos, the organisation of space would effectively have divided the house into an outer area arranged round the court, and an inner one, centring on the living room, although here there are no rooms with multiple entrances, possibly because of the reduced area (ca. 225 m^2 as opposed to 290 m^2) and consequently smaller number of spaces.

The layout of this house-type conforms to some of the characteristics of the single-entrance, courtyard house, with a possibility of surveillance from the hearth-room over movement around most of the house. At the same time, however, the Kassope houses do not exhibit a desire to separate the interior of the house from the street (possibly because less activity was carried out in the courtyard). Furthermore, the arrangement of space around two circulation areas, rather than one, would potentially have offered more of a binary division than we have seen elsewhere. One possible explanation is the physical environment of the region: the relatively high rainfall as well as the high elevation (and hence cooler temperatures), may have made exterior, courtyard space hospitable for a shorter part of the year than in other parts of Greece. It also seems possible that cultural factors were at play: the mountainous terrain, with the Pindos range separating the region from other areas of northern and central Greece, may have restricted the flow of people and ideas, so that these buildings may be strongly influenced by local traditions, both architectural and social. Indeed, it seems that the political organisation and the culture here were somewhat different from those of communities further south and east, where the population did not always consider the inhabitants of Epiros to be members of the same cultural group as themselves. It would therefore be unsurprising to see evidence here of strong local traditions in house design. Interestingly, as we shall see in Chapter 7, the use of an interior circulation space seems to have become more popular in later centuries, across a broader area, supporting the idea that in at least some regions, cultural factors may have been important in its adoption.

Could the division of space in hearth-room houses point to some degree of separation between the two sexes? This question is difficult to answer: extrapolating to north-western Greece attitudes towards gender articulated in Athenian textual sources would be dangerous, given the physical and cultural distance between the two. Furthermore, if food preparation was undertaken by women (rather than, say, by servants) then the answer would be 'no', since the food preparation area at Ammotopos is not part of the inner, hearth-room, complex, at least in its final phase of use. Neither of these lines of reasoning is conclusive, but on balance it seems unsafe to assume that the hearth-room pattern of organisation offers an insight into gendered patterns of activity.

Overall, even this small sample of settlements suggests that house forms in northwestern Greece may have been more variable than those seen in the northeast. Fragmentary evidence from other sites in the region, such as Leukas and Arta (ancient Ambrakia) support this impression by adding further variation to the picture. At Leukas, for example, the fourth century BCE phase underlies a slightly later one, but the fourth century houses seem to have had single entrances and small courtyards which were generally completely surrounded by rooms, although they had no form of portico. Where circulation patterns could be reconstructed, these usually seem to have required residents to pass through the courtyard, hence conforming to the single-entrance, courtyard model more closely than the hearth-room houses. In this region as a whole, houses typically seem to have had fewer distinctive amenities than can be identified in northeastern Greece: for instance, decorated andrones or waterproofed rooms and ceramic tubs for bathing are less common. Overall, then, some of the influences which appear to have shaped the single-entrance, courtyard houses of Attica and northern Greece also seem to have been relevant in this region. But there is also some degree of difference as well: in the hearth-room houses, ease of surveillance from any part of the house seems to have been less of a concern, suggesting that social control may have been of more limited importance.

Central and Southern Greece

Aside from Athens and Attica, the material from central and southern Greece is uneven in its distribution, with good evidence from Euboia and the Argolid but almost nothing (at time of writing) from the Peloponnese. Work at the site of the city of Halieis, in the Argolid, provides a baseline for understanding the housing of this region since both architecture and artefacts, together with their distribution, have been documented and published. Occupation extends back into the Archaic period. During Classical times the fortification walls enclosed not only an akropolis but also a lower town which spread over a flat coastal area and was organised following two different urban grids on slightly different alignments. The city was apparently abandoned during the early third century BCE for unknown reasons. Today, part of the lower town, including some of its houses and a sanctuary of Apollo, lie submerged owing to changes in sea-level since antiquity. Systematic excavation in the lower town during the late 1960s and early 1970s revealed two houses in their entirety, along with parts of up to eighteen others. Publication focused on the five most completely recovered examples. Careful attention was paid to the stratig-raphy, and the excavators aimed to record large numbers of artefacts, distinguishing items which may have been in use immediately prior to the abandonment of the individual houses, from others which may have been the residue of earlier phases of occupation, may have been in storage, or may have been incorporated into refuse deposits. As a consequence, the numbers of recorded finds per house are far greater than those from Robinson's work at Olynthos, giving a more detailed picture of the range of activities carried out.

House 7, which was excavated in its entirety, serves as an example of the general layout and provides an opportunity to explore the extent to which the artefacts and architectural features both point to similar conclusions about the use of internal space (Figure 4.16). Despite the regular urban grid plan there seems to have been more variability in house size here than was usual at Olynthos. House 7 is one of the larger ones excavated, covering an area of around 230 m^2. Two occupation levels were distinguished within the structure. Earlier walls underlying it were not extensively investigated, but it seems that both of the phases belong to the fourth century BCE. The house has a variety of characteristics familiar from structures we have already seen elsewhere: a single entrance takes the form of a recessed prothyron. Interior space is organised around an open courtyard. The most prominent feature is an andron with a large anteroom, in the northwest corner. The socles of the exterior walls and the façade of the andron with its anteroom consist of large blocks of conglomerate standing knee-high. Their exceptional size means that, even if they were originally plastered over, they would have attracted attention, identifying the presence and

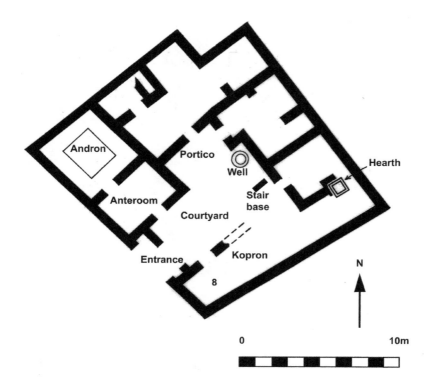

Figure 4.16 Halieis, house 7, plan.
(After Nevett 1999, Fig. 26).

location of the room to visitors entering the house and to passers-by in the street. The andron itself had a raised border which could have accommodated seven couches (Figure 4.17). Set into the yellow plaster floor the excavators found a small, plain ware jar which contained a fine ware bowl and cup. A channel cut from the centre of the floor would have directed any liquid into these vessels. Bradley Ault, who published the houses, cautiously suggests that libations – ritual offerings of poured wine for the gods which are referred to in Athenian textual sources – may have drained into here. This seems a more likely explanation than simply the functional drainage of the floor, since the vessels would presumably have been difficult to clean out and the residues could have been disposed of more easily if they had simply been allowed to disperse into the soil beneath the floor.

As at Olynthos, the courtyards of the houses at Halieis seem to have been used for a variety of different activities. In house 7 a deep well in the northern corner provided water. Ault identifies a stone-lined pit on the south side as a kopron or cess pit. It contained the fragments of at least

Figure 4.17 Halieis, house 7, balloon photograph; the andron is visible at the top left. (Photograph courtesy of the Halieis Publications Committee. The rights to the monument shown belong to the Hellenic Ministry of Culture and Sports (Law 3028/2002). Halieis is under the supervision of the Ephorate of Antiquities of the Argolid, Ministry of Culture and Sports.)

230 different ceramic vessels of all types, some 300 pieces of broken roof-tile, as well as fragments of lamps, metal items and pieces of animal bone. The pit had a capacity of ca. 4.3 m^3 and presumably had to be emptied periodically (as Ault points out). An underfloor drain carried liquid run-off from the pit eastwards and out of the house. A variety of pot sherds incorporated into the earth floor matrix in the courtyard and also in room 8 seem to represent fragments of vessels used and accidentally broken here over a long period of time, which failed to make it as far as the kopron during cleaning. They attest to the presence in the courtyard of pottery associated with a variety of additional activities, especially storage of food and drink. A stone block on the north-eastern side of this space may have served as the base for a flight of stairs leading to an upper storey located above the rooms on the north-western side of the courtyard, although no evidence for the use of these upstairs rooms was recorded.

One feature not represented in house 7 but identified in at least five other houses at Halieis is a press bed for extracting juice from grapes and/ or oil from olives. This seems to have been a particularly characteristic form of installation. House D, for example, had a cement platform occupied by a press bed and an inset catch-basin. In the same complex of rooms a crushing trough and a weight block (equipment for crushing the olives prior to pressing) were also present. It is unclear what type of production was taking place in establishments like this one: study of the landscape and long-term regional patterns of land-use in the landscape surrounding the city led to a suggestion that olive oil was exported from here during the Classical period, and the presence of domestic pressing facilities may reflect the importance of this crop to the economy of the town as a whole. Lin Foxhall has argued for an association between large-scale olive oil production and elite households, commenting that households from lower down the social hierarchy did not generally maintain specialised processing equipment although they could have produced small amounts of oil for domestic use by other means. If the Halieis facilities were dedicated to pressing olives, this would imply that the houses belonged to wealthy families. However, Foxhall sheds doubt on this interpretation, suggesting that the small amount of crushing equipment together with oddities in the forms of the press beds themselves, indicate that they were most probably used for a range of other agricultural, and possibly also industrial, purposes, rather than for olive oil production.

The amount of pottery recovered from house 7 is overwhelming at 6230 catalogued fragments, but some of the categories of material present at Olynthos are noticeably less well-represented at Halieis, suggesting that the settlements were abandoned under differing circumstances. For example, at Olynthos loom weights were found in abundance across the city, occasionally even in rows which suggest the presence of looms still in position when the houses were destroyed. In house 7, by contrast, only seven loom weights were found. These were widely scattered and four of them were in the kopron where they had presumably been deliberately discarded. For this reason it seems likely that loom weights were normally among the possessions which were taken with the departing household when a house was abandoned. Other items falling into this category include mill stones (also a frequent find at Olynthos) which may have been portable and made out of relatively high-value, imported stone. Therefore, in most houses the items that were left behind and recovered by the archaeologists seem to consist of a residue of lost and discarded possessions (some already broken) together with others considered not to be worth taking – either because they were too large, heavy or numerous, or because they were not thought to have much sentimental or financial value. House 7 nevertheless presents an interesting contrast with the Vari and Dema houses, discussed in Chapter 3, which were also excavated paying careful attention to the finds, and which also seem to have been cleared out by their departing residents. In those locations the floors seem to have been much more thoroughly cleaned, with only the smallest, most fragmentary pottery sherds remaining. Since nothing is known about the circumstances of the abandonment of any of these locations, the reason for these differences is unclear, but they are an important reminder of how influential site formation processes are in filtering the evidence archaeologists find.

The layout of house 7, and of the other houses at Halieis, is given an appearance of regularity by the orthogonal plan of the neighbourhood in which they are located. In addition, many common features recur in different properties, including the single entrance, court, portico, pressing facility and andron-anteroom complex. There is, nevertheless, considerable variation between even the few houses which have been excavated, with a wider range of house sizes and more diverse internal configurations than would be found in such a small sample of houses from Olynthos. Differences include: the precise arrangement of the entrance; the scale and location of the portico; the organisation of the domestic quarters; and the presence or absence of an andron. As at Olynthos, however, the basic idea of the single-entrance, courtyard house prevails: there is a suite of shared features and patterns of layout, including the single entrance, the multi-functional courtyard and the role that that courtyard plays as the principal circulation space.

Elsewhere in the southern Greek mainland, the best-preserved structure is one of the so-called large houses located inside the walled settlement at Dystos, on the island of Euboia (the structure is referred to variously in the literature as House 1 or House J). This covers an area of about 288 m² and dates to the mid fourth century BCE with some later modifications. Its walls are built entirely out of thick, white marble blocks, and are therefore preserved to a height of several metres. At first sight the plan appears quite unlike that of any house discussed so far, with individual rooms arranged sequentially and a square chamber seemingly super-imposed in the centre (Figure 4.18). This chamber, which has been variously interpreted as a doorman's room or an andron, apparently represents a late modification of the original layout. In the past, the building has been interpreted as a house with two open courtyard areas (spaces 3 and 5). Based on more recent

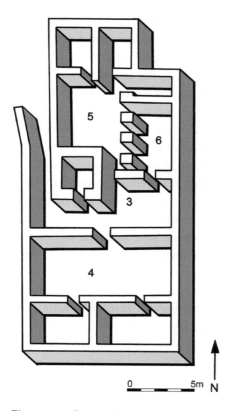

Figure 4.18 Dystos, House 1.
(Drawn by Max Huemer based on Hoepfner and
Schwandner 1994, Fig. 307.)

investigation this has been disputed, with the suggestion that only 5 was a courtyard while 3 was roofed, although the detailed evidence for this interpretation is not presented in print. Given that the central square space is thought to have been a later modification, it would make sense if (3) and (5) were originally part of the same large courtyard. Room 6 has ventilation openings facing (5) that might suggest it had a role in food preparation comparable to (h) at Ammotopos, which is also adjacent to the courtyard and has comparable features. Room 4 resembles the anteroom seen at Thasos, with two further rooms behind it. Even so, there are some odd features of the plan: the courtyard is towards the northern, rather than the southern end of the house, with the largest rooms to the south, rather than to the north – an arrangement which distinguishes it from most of the single-entrance, courtyard houses discussed here, but which is also found in the hearth-room houses at Ammotopos and Kassope. Could this be because of the location of the house in relation to neighbouring buildings, or due to local topography, either of which might have affected the light entering the interior? More detailed study of the urban context, architecture, and ideally also the artefact inventories of the rooms, might help to bring a better understanding of the use of space in the house and the reasons for its unusual linear layout.

Elsewhere, fragmentary evidence of two houses at Aigeira, in the northern Peloponnese, built in the second quarter of the fourth century and destroyed around 300 BCE, was uncovered during a rescue excavation. Although they were poorly preserved, they have yielded some identifiable features: both had andrones with coloured mortar floors, and other evidence of decoration included a terracotta architectural decoration (a sima) in house 2 and the remains of a pebble mosaic floor in the fill of house 1, which had seemingly fallen from an upper storey room. In addition to finds of domestic artefacts such as fine ware cups and bowls, and terracotta loom weights, house 1 yielded a number of transport amphorae from the eastern part of the structure, which seemed to have been turned into a workshop.

In addition to excavated evidence, geophysical survey of several cities, such as Sikyon (where it was coupled with intensive field survey), Stymphalos and Tegea, has revealed the location and layout of residential quarters which, like Halieis, are organised in blocks with standard dimensions. At Tegea these are long and narrow, with similar proportions to some of the early ones in Greek settlements in southern Italy, suggesting that they may predate those at Halieis, perhaps originating as far back as the sixth century BCE. When the results of these projects are published in full it may be possible to comment on the layout of individual buildings, although the question of dating will be difficult to resolve with certainty without excavation. At Stymphalos, as at Tegea, the individual blocks were long and narrow, measuring about 30 by 100 metres. Excavation within this grid, in an area adjacent to the southern section of the city wall, has revealed the remains of two, poorly preserved, houses dating to around 350 BCE, but little evidence survived of their original layout since they underwent a series of substantial modifications until their final abandonment in the first century CE.

A smaller community is located at Ano Siphai, in Boiotia, where surface remains have been studied but extensive excavations have not been carried out. Here, a fortification wall with at least five towers encircles a group of more than fifty structures, consisting of a temple and numerous two- and three-room buildings. Across the site a common construction technique was used, with polygonal stone socles about a metre high and

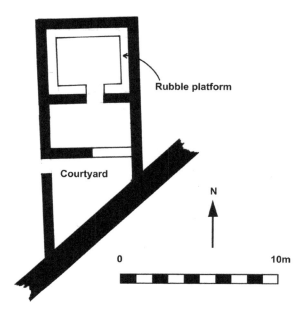

Rubble platform

Courtyard

N

0   10m

Figure 4.19 Ano Siphai, small house, plan.
(After Nevett 1999, Fig. 18.)

superstructures in mud brick. The building published in the most detail
was examined by the German Archaeological Institute (DAI) in 1975 and
interpreted as a house. It was built up against the fortification wall and
incorporates an enclosed courtyard, rectangular antechamber and a square
inner room with a platform around the walls (Figure 4.19). The total area is
a little less than 100 m², including the irregular courtyard. The doorways
are clearly reconstructable: the different spaces were entered in sequence.
The layouts of two further, slightly smaller, structures were published by
Richard Tomlinson and John Fossey in 1970. In these the plans were less
clear owing to dense vegetation cover. One of them, building k, may have
had a similar layout to that examined by the DAI, since it has an elongated
shape with cross walls dividing it into three unequal sections. The other,
building W, is rather different (Figure 4.20), with a square form subdivided
into a large southern section and three smaller northern ones arranged
side-by-side in a plan which it is tempting to interpret as a courtyard with
rooms to the north, although the rooms are apparently reached sequentially rather than individually. Given that only limited field work has been
undertaken, the buildings are difficult to date: Ernst-Ludwig Schwandner
places the structure studied by the DAI in the fifth or fourth century BCE,

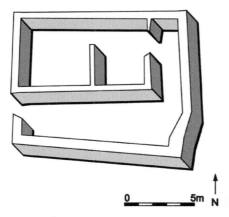

Figure 4.20 Ano Siphai, building W.
(Drawn by Max Huemer based on Tomlinson
and Fossey 1970, Fig. 6.)

but sherds from the Archaic to Hellenistic periods have been found across the site as a whole.

Ano Siphai illustrates some of the particular difficulties of assessing the roles played by small buildings: the size and layout of these structures are comparable to the smallest we have seen at urban sites such as Athens and Olynthos and are thus compatible with their interpretation as small houses. Nevertheless, by definition there are none of the kinds of characteristic features such as androns or bathing rooms, which might confirm their domestic use. A further obstacle is the absence of excavation which would reveal the range of artefacts present (or even the occupation dates). Indeed, Richard Tomlinson and John Fossey interpreted the site as a temporary military installation, believing that permanent settlement there would have been impossible because of a lack of fresh water. There is, nonetheless, evidence of cisterns for the collection of rainwater, and the similarities between the buildings here and the smallest houses found elsewhere suggest that the interpretation of the DAI team, that this is a small settlement with about fifty houses, is possible. If it is correct, the houses themselves would have been fairly basic. A courtyard would have provided space for carrying out some domestic tasks in warm, dry weather. Inside, the small number of rooms would have meant that each one was used for a variety of activities and would have been occupied simultaneously by different members of the household, offering little scope for privacy. If the courtyard was the main light source, the sequential arrangement of the interior rooms may have made the inner ones dark.

Ano Siphai may have resembled some of the deme or village sites of Attica, such as Ano Voula, discussed in Chapter 3, and there are other comparably small settlements in southern Greece which seem to have consisted of similarly irregularly planned houses. At Elean Pylos, for example, rescue excavation revealed the partially preserved remains of what John Coleman, the excavator, describes as a 'village', dating to the later fifth and earlier fourth centuries BCE. The size and organisation of the individual structures are difficult to make out due to the poor preservation. They nevertheless seem to represent buildings of a variety sizes, in some cases with perhaps no more than two rooms while others may have had five or six. Some of the individual complexes were separated by passageways less than a metre wide. Elsewhere, large, irregularly shaped courtyards or enclosures lay between the buildings. The publication includes artefact inventories and Coleman comments that the number and range of objects from the courtyards suggest that these spaces were used intensively for domestic tasks. They were not, however, integrated with the other domestic spaces in a comparable manner to the single-entrance, courtyard layout. Even in the larger structures, the courtyard was peripheral to the complex of rooms, at least some of which were entered in series, and Coleman emphasises the differences in layout between Pylos and urban sites such as Olynthos and Halieis. Such sites suggests that small, village communities in which the organisation of domestic space did not follow the more standardised patterns seen in larger cities were not only confined to Attica but probably were distributed more widely.

In southern Greece outside Athens, then, fully excavated houses of Classical date are relatively scarce. This is particularly noticeable for the Peloponnese, which has yielded very few complete structures. The presence of the single-entrance, courtyard house at Halieis suggests that in at least some settlements in this region comparable factors influenced house layout to those which seem to have guided spatial organisation at Athens and in the northern part of mainland Greece. At the same time, it is clear that, just as in Attica, beyond the larger urban settlements there were small communities like those at Ano Siphai and Elean Pylos, in which households generally had lower standards of living than those of their urban counterparts, their dwellings often consisting of relatively confined spaces without access to some of the more specialised domestic facilities of urban houses, such as andrones and baths. Interestingly, while the small number of rooms offered limited potential for the kind of architectural expression of social values which we have seen was probably integral to the single-entrance, courtyard house, in some of them there still seems to have been a concern to separate the interior of the house from the street outside. At Ano Siphai, for example, the exterior courtyard seems to have been walled off from the street. In a variety of locations including Halieis, the domestic sphere was an important locus of both agricultural and craft production, as it was in communities in other regions.

Conclusion: Classical Housing in Greece: Urbanism and Urbanisation

Current evidence suggests that the principles of domestic organisation in many parts of mainland Greece were similar to those seen in Athens and Attica. Examples of single-entrance, courtyard houses are found widely in the form of spacious buildings with a common set of features and organisational characteristics: one street entrance; a central or southern courtyard, normally with a portico on at least one side which provides access to the interior rooms; and four or more separate rooms entered individually from the court or portico. Additional features which are present in some cases include a decorated andron and bathing facilities. The occurrence of this distinctive house-form across all but one of the regions surveyed in this chapter suggests that there was a shared set of conceptions about how domestic space should be organised. It also points to the pervasive character of some of the social values underpinning the type, namely the integrity of the household in relation to the wider community and the consequent status of the householder himself. In addition, the presence of decorated andrones in most of the different regions suggests that there was common support for a more specific set of aspirations (whether or not they were fulfilled) to participate in the culture of the symposium. It seems likely that this pattern of domestic organisation arose gradually across a wide area as ideas about household practices and house-forms were shared between communities, with the social requirements imposed on domestic space developing in comparable ways. Given that the underlying principles result in a variety of architectural forms, it seems likely that it is those principles themselves which were shared, rather than simply architectural models.

In the hearth-room houses, the hearth-room created a somewhat different dynamic from that of the pastas, prostas and peristyle forms, reducing the importance of the courtyard both as an activity area and as a nexus of communication around the house. Instead, the hearth-room took over some of its role as a circulation space and perhaps also as a setting for domestic tasks. This layout nonetheless maintained the essential characteristics of separation from the street and transparency from the perspective of the interior. The reasons for its creation are uncertain: a concentration of examples in Epiros might indicate that this was a regional house-form which may have been geared to a specific local mode of domestic organisation. Further detailed study of the assemblages associated with such buildings would provide a better understanding of the way interior space was used, enabling comparisons between the domestic cultures of different communities.

While the single-entrance, courtyard house-form is found widely across the Greek mainland, the degree of uniformity between the houses within an individual settlement varies quite significantly. Despite the large sample of houses excavated on the North Hill at Olynthos, that community stands out for the strong resemblance between them in terms of both size and the frequency of various interior features such as andrones and bathing spaces. This relative standardisation cannot be attributed solely to the gridded layout of the streets, since it does not apply equally to other gridded settlements such as Halieis, where, although andrones are frequent, there is significant variation in house-size even between the five examples which have been most extensively investigated. Instead, the degree of similarity between buildings is perhaps explained by the particular historical circumstances of their construction, including factors such as the speed with which they were erected, the identities of the builders and the political or social context which led to the settlement of the North Hill district. The unusual degree of standardisation may result from a need for rapid provision of a new housing area for households moving into the city during a period of organised consolidation of several communities in one location (as suggested by textual sources).

As noted in Chapter 3, adherence to the organising principles of the single-entrance, courtyard house may have been a visible symbol of the occupants' membership of their community. Nevertheless, the use of decorative elements such as mosaics, coloured wall plaster or stone architectural features, suggests that the desire to belong and fit in was also sometimes in tension with another wish, namely, to stand out. Thus, for instance, despite the degree of standardisation of the houses at Olynthos, some had decorated andrones while others did not, while as already noted, the courtyards of a small number were adorned with mosaic floors and even complete peristyles. The use of such symbols perhaps asserts that although the occupants belong, they are also superior. This idea is explored further in the following chapters.

Despite the presence of the single-entrance, courtyard house in most regions of mainland Greece, it is clear that in none of them was it the only form used. In some of the larger settlements such as Athens and Limenas, small houses with only two or three rooms co-existed side-by-side with them and seem likely to have represented the dwellings of groups lower down in the socio-economic hierarchy. As far as we can see, some small communities, for example that found at Ano Siphai, apparently consisted entirely of such modest structures, implying that their residents had a relatively low standard of living, although it could be that there were originally neighbourhoods of larger houses which have not so far been identified. From the preserved remains, small houses appear not to have served as status symbols; nor is there evidence of the materialisation of pretentions to participate in symposium culture. Nevertheless, it is possible that archaeologically invisible means were used to ensure some degree of comfort was attained, to individualise a building to some degree and/or to make statements about the status of a household. While there is no architectural indication of this which would parallel the towers of the Attic demes (for example), it could have been done using media such as wood or textiles, which do not preserve archaeologically under normal conditions.

The picture emerging from the mainland Greek evidence is thus a complex one: the architecture and layout of any one house must have been influenced by a variety of different factors which are clearest when a number of structures are compared. Within an individual settlement, house-size, the degree of decoration and the presence of amenities are likely to have depended, in part, on the relative socio-economic status of the inhabitants. The size and design of the courtyard may have been influenced to some degree by local topographical factors such as the steepness of the site and also partly by cultural ones which determined the proportions of the houses and hence the arrangement of the interior space they could accommodate. The availability of construction materials such as long roof timbers may also have set some of the parameters for basic features such as room-size. At the same time, the strength of local cultural traditions and the intensity of contact with the wider world must have varied across the Greek mainland, leading to the survival of distinctive local building traditions to different extents.

This list only begins to hint at some of the many factors which must have shaped housing in different regions. In the light of this variety it is perhaps surprising that the ideals underlying the single-entrance, courtyard house are visible over such a wide area. To what extent is it also found further afield, amongst the culturally Greek communities located in the areas we think of today as the Asia Minor coast, southern Italy and Sicily, Crete, and even coastal north Africa or the northern Black Sea coast? This is the question addressed in the next chapter.

5 | Housing Greek Households in the Eastern, Western and Southern Mediterranean and Northern Black Sea Littoral

The Boundaries of an Ideal?

This chapter explores the extent to which the single-entrance, courtyard house is found in culturally Greek settlements lying beyond the modern-day Greek mainland and Aegean islands, in the southern, eastern and western Mediterranean and on the northern Black Sea coast. Discussion focuses on the extent and nature of variation in house-forms across time and space, and on what that variation might have to say about these different communities in social and cultural terms. How might the inhabitants have been presenting themselves through the architecture, organisation and furnishings of their homes? And how similar or different were their statements from those we have seen being made by their counterparts in mainland Greece?

Study of communities in these areas which appear in some way to be culturally Greek (when judged according to evidence such as their ceramic traditions, building forms and written texts) has frequently been framed around the question of the origins of the people who once lived in them. Commentators since the Classical Athenian historian Thucydides have attempted to trace the migration of Aegean Greeks outwards through the Mediterranean and beyond. In many contexts, modern scholars have discussed these communities in reductive terms, asking whether the occupants were 'Greek' or 'indigenous'. The evidence of housing cannot tell us 'who' the residents of a structure were in a literal (genetic) sense. Nevertheless, recent research in other fields shows that genetic origins represent only one of a number of ways in which individuals and groups can be categorised – or categorise themselves: in practice, identities are often socially constructed, fluid, contextually specific, intersectional, and can change rapidly. Material culture is an important instrument used for self-presentation, and the physical environment of a house offers one dimension in which this can be done. In the ancient context, the archaeological remains of houses, therefore, offer a means to investigate the complex issue of how former residents represented themselves and how they wished to be viewed by others. Archaeologists can attempt to understand some of the ways in which this was accomplished, by studying the architecture, decoration and organisation of the domestic environment, as well as through study of the selection and pattern of use of the artefacts within the house (where these have been recorded). Such examination reinforces the complex and multi-layered character of identity formation, exposing the inadequacy of simple binary models such as 'Greek or non-Greek' for describing ancient communities.

In this chapter, a focus on the single-entrance, courtyard house, and in particular on its geographical and temporal limits, provides the basis for selecting evidence for discussion. This does not imply that the single-entrance, courtyard house was in some way co-terminous with groups considering themselves culturally Greek: on the contrary, we have already seen that there was significant variability in the house-forms in use even in the Greek mainland and islands. As we shall see further in Chapter 6, there is also evidence for the emulation of the house types of some socio-economic groups by members of others. What is of interest here, then, is the degree to which the values implied by the adoption of the single-entrance, courtyard house can be traced across the Mediterranean and beyond. The majority of sites discussed are on the west coast of Asia Minor (present-day Turkey) and in the area of modern southern Italy and Sicily. More limited comparisons are also drawn with settlements located in the southern Mediterranean (on the island of Crete and the northern coast of modern Libya), and to the north on the northern shore of the Black Sea. While some degree of regionalism can be detected in styles of domestic architecture in these different communities, what seems more striking is that in most (although not all) of these regions the single-entrance, courtyard house was widespread. This distribution suggests that a shared sense of what the role of a house should be and how its occupants should live their lives, came to prevail over a broad geographical area, from Euesperides (on the coast of modern Libya) in the southwest, to Priene (on the western coast of Turkey) in the northeast. As on the Greek mainland, however, this ideal was not uniformly followed and seems to have been adopted at different times in different locations. Such variation means that in some cases (for example Crete and the Black Sea) it is useful to include evidence from the Hellenistic period, which provides a clearer sense of when the single-entrance, courtyard form became firmly adopted – either (in the case of the former) because the evidence from the Classical period is relatively limited, or (as in the latter) because the single-entrance, courtyard house-form does not seem to have been widely used in Classical times.

Greek Settlements in Coastal Asia Minor

As we have seen in Chapter 2, in the Early Iron Age there were settlements along the Asia Minor coast with houses similar to those from the Greek mainland and islands, including curvilinear structures. During the Archaic and Classical periods, however, culturally Greek cities in Asia Minor famously cultivated their own distinctive identity through a variety of means, including the architectural styles of their monumental religious and civic buildings. This distinctiveness was also picked up in the domestic sphere, where the dominant layout was the prostas-type house in contrast with the prevalence of the pastas house, which we have seen in much of the Greek mainland. As on the Greek mainland, however, there are some exceptions to this pattern.

Some of the changes taking place are exemplified at Old Smyrna, in the present-day city of Izmir. The small, oval house mentioned in Chapter 2 dates to the late tenth century BCE and covered an area of about 10 m². It was built of mud brick on a stone socle and probably had a thatched roof which was supported by two internal posts. The entrance was at the north end, and the interior was not subdivided. A small area in front of the house seems to have been enclosed to make a forecourt or garden, but there is no suggestion of a wall enclosing multiple structures like those found at Eretria and Skala Oropou. At Old Smyrna, as in communities on the Greek mainland and islands, curvilinear buildings were gradually replaced by rectilinear ones. By the seventh century BCE, one of the excavated areas, Area H, offers evidence of a dense complex of rectangular rooms sharing party walls (Figure 5.1). Some of these (in its south-eastern corner) resemble the earliest phase of the houses at Zagora (see Chapter 2) and apparently consisted of a single large room with a porch in front. Others (in its northern area) may be interpreted either as similar, single-room structures or as a single unit consisting of a cluster of rooms with a southern courtyard and transverse space giving access individually to a range of rooms on its north side. Variations in the building style of the wall socles suggest that the complex grew up over time. The layout of the northern sector resembles the single-entrance, courtyard house, but even if the interpretation as a single complex is correct, the idea of creating such a structure does not seem to have caught on: in a subsequent phase the portico had disappeared, and rooms were arranged on all sides of a narrow corridor.

Extensive evidence for housing of the eighth to the sixth centuries BCE comes from Miletos, further to the south (Figure 5.2). The community of

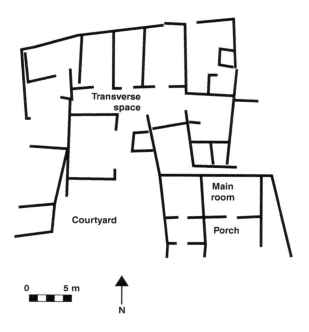

Figure 5.1 Old Smyrna, Area H, second half of the seventh century BCE.
(Drawn by the author based on Akurgal 1983, Fig. 19.)

this period was focused on the steep hill of Kalabaktepe, at the southern end of the site, but housing of similar date has also been found widely spaced in a variety of other areas on the peninsula occupied by the later city. In the eighth century, curvilinear and rectilinear houses co-existed, but during the seventh century the oval ones were replaced by larger, orthogonal ones, often with multiple rooms. These were constructed of mud brick on stone socles and probably had flat, clay roofs. Exclusive use of this rectilinear building-type enabled relatively dense occupation in several parts of the site, as on the slopes of Kalabaktepe and in the area around the later temple of Athena. In these districts, different structures frequently share the same general orientation and sometimes even party walls – although the intervening streets often seem to be arranged somewhat haphazardly. In the area west of the Classical bouleuterion, a block of buildings dated to the sixth century BCE was uncovered which, despite the steep contours of the underlying rock, had a more regular layout with adjacent single-room houses sharing party walls. By the later sixth century BCE, there is also clear evidence for attention paid to finishing the interiors of some of these structures, for example with carefully plastered floors. The size and layout of the houses at Miletos and the ways in which they

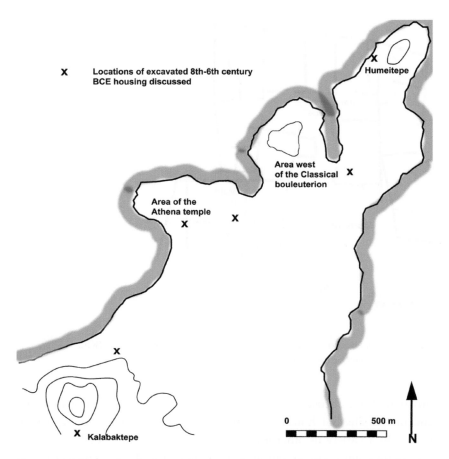

Figure 5.2 Miletos, sketch plan of the peninsula showing the locations of excavated housing dating between the eighth and sixth centuries BCE, mentioned in the text. (Drawn by the author based on information from Hoepfner and Schwandner 1994, Fig. 11 and Lang 1996, Fig. 71.)

changed through time, thus parallel what we have seen on mainland Greece, although even by the sixth century BCE there is nothing to suggest the presence of the single-entrance, courtyard layout. Unfortunately, housing of the fifth and fourth centuries BCE has not yet been excavated at Miletos.

Other evidence, which covers the transition from the Archaic to the Classical period, comes from further north at Neandria. Here, an architectural survey team was able to plan about 230 surviving buildings, the majority of them interpreted as residential. The core of the settlement dates back to the sixth century BCE, but it was expanded considerably during the fourth century BCE. Its various phases are detectable through differences in the urban plan, with an Upper City consisting of irregularly shaped house blocks on a variety of orientations set within an irregular street network, while a New City to the east seems to have been planned on a regular orthogonal grid with six houses per block (Figure 5.3). Extensive excavations have not been carried out, although some small soundings have been made. Dating and functional evaluations, therefore, have to be based on the plans of individual buildings and areas, and on masonry styles, together with parallels from other sites. The large numbers of houses planned made it possible for Thomas Maischatz, who published the material, to distinguish a variety of different house-forms and to study their occurrence across the settlement. The smallest, which are concentrated in the Upper City, consist of only two rooms with a courtyard, although they are quite spacious, offering a total of 100–150 m^2 in living space. Other houses in the Upper City are somewhat larger, courtyard structures, offering three to six rooms and occupying an area of 200–300 m^2. These probably date to the fifth and fourth centuries BCE. A third house-type found is the pastas house, which is concentrated in the New City and probably dates to the fourth century BCE. The individual houses there measure about 20 × 25 m, giving an unusually large ground area of about 500 m^2.

An example of a pastas house from Neandria is house 10.5.10 in the Lower City (Figure 5.4). The exterior walls include carefully laid masonry blocks, and the building probably had only a single storey, with a tiled, gabled, roof. No stone threshold was found, and the entrance is assumed to have lain on the west side, leading directly into a courtyard which ran the whole width of the building. Three rooms lay side-by-side to the south; a further three, larger ones, lay to the north, their entrances sheltered by a pastas. The interior walls generally seem to have been plastered. Since no significant excavation has been carried out, the doorways are unknown and the organisation of activities within the house is difficult to reconstruct in detail. The surveyors identified the main living room and an andron in the northern part of the house, the latter in the north-west corner. Its identification rests on its shape and dimensions which are suitable to accommodate 11 couches of 1 metre by 1.8 metres. Its presence may have been highlighted by the andesite blocks which were found in the back wall of the pastas in this area. Although it is impossible to know how most of the spaces in this and other houses at Neandria were used without further fieldwork, the presence of the pastas form (and the presence of androners, if these are correctly identified) suggests that at least some households at the settlement may have had some of the same aspirations as their

Figure 5.3 Neandria, city plan showing the remains recorded in the Upper (left) and the Lower City. (After Maischatz 2003. Beilage 1. Copyright Dr. Rudolph Habelt GmbH, Bonn, reproduced by permission.)

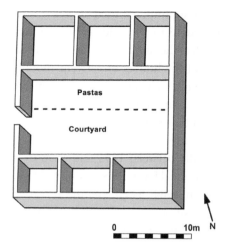

Figure 5.4 Neandria, pastas house 10.5.10 in the Lower City
(doorways not recorded).
(Drawn by Max Huemer based on Maischatz 2003, Abb. 4.)

contemporaries in other parts of the Greek world. Nevertheless, the limited subdivision of space also suggests that there were differences in their patterns of domestic social life, with much of the activity of the household taking place within sight of other household members.

The information from the different housing districts at Neandria offers a tantalising glimpse of some of the ways in which accommodation may have varied across time and space within a single settlement. It seems possible that the organisation of the houses in the Upper City might represent the survival of earlier housing quarters, while the very generously proportioned properties of the Lower City result from a later extension (a situation that would be comparable with that at Olynthos, for example, where different house-types are also present in different urban districts: see Chapter 4). Even within the Upper City there were differences in the scale of the houses, which might result from a gradual expansion of the settlement that was accompanied by a growth in house size or may alternatively suggest occupation by households of differing compositions or socio-economic statuses.

The presence of pastas-type houses at Neandria suggests that, by the fifth or fourth century BCE, at least some of the city's residents may have been representing themselves as members of a wider cultural group which shared some cultural values with residents of mainland Greek cities. As noted above, however, the more common house form in this region was the prostas-type, which was first identified in the context of the city of Priene.

This is the site which still provides the largest sample of such houses from a single community. The earliest of them date to the mid fourth century BCE, when the city was re-founded after the inhabitants moved their settlement from another location. Many of the houses underwent modification and reconstruction over the following two centuries until a major earthquake struck. At that time, a significant amount of the western part of Priene was destroyed, although the neighbourhoods on the eastern side continued to be occupied into the first century BCE.

Priene was first explored archaeologically between 1895 and 1898 by a German team led by Theodore Wiegand and Heinrich Schraeder, whose investigations were published promptly in 1904. Their volume recorded streets and buildings carved into the rock on a steep hill but nevertheless laid out on a regular grid. The steepness of the location (Figure 5.5) may

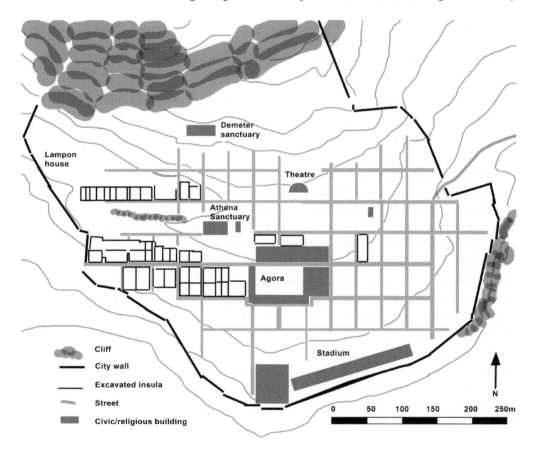

Figure 5.5 Priene, plan of the city.
(Drawn by the author based on Raeck 2005, Fig. 1 and Rumscheid 2014 Figs. 1 and 3.)

explain the small dimensions and narrow houses comprising the insulae between. Wiegand and Schraeder were able to locate and excavate a sanctuary and other public buildings. At the same time, parts of at least 24 residential insulae comprising at least 70 houses were partly or fully excavated. As is the case with most projects of this era, the excavators' main interest was in the architecture. Although a few selected finds are discussed, there is only very limited information about the context in which each was recovered. Based on these early excavations, Wolfram Hoepfner and Ernst-Ludwig Schwandner reconstructed what they saw as an original 'type-house' from Priene, dating to the earliest, fourth century BCE, phase of occupation (Figure 5.6). They argued that this represented a standard allocation of accommodation to an individual citizen, suggesting that originally a single insula comprised eight, long, narrow houses measuring about 9 by 21 m each, arranged in a double row of four. They reconstructed a second storey above the northern range of rooms of each house, providing additional living accommodation. According to this plan, space in each house is organised in three sections, with clusters of rooms to the north and south divided by a large central courtyard. A deep prostas gave access to three rooms to the north comprising a living-room with smaller side-room, and an andron which was entered separately via the prostas but had no anteroom of its own. Although there were no mosaic floors, the room is identified by its square shape and elaborate masonry style wall decorations. A living room or oikos was located alongside the andron and was sometimes furnished with a stone hearth in one corner. A further room was located to the side. To the south of the courtyard, further rooms are interpreted as comprising storage facilities, workshops and stables.

As reconstructed, the houses of Priene look somewhat different from most of those we have seen so far: their long, narrow plots must have been partly responsible for this, giving them a modular feel. The presence of the andron suggests that some of the traditions surrounding the symposium may have been followed by these households, and this has been assumed by commentators including David Small. The separate andron space offered the possibility of entertaining visitors away from the rest of the household and in a location designed to display some of the wealth and perhaps also 'stylishness' of the householder through its decoration. At the same time, the andron at Priene was generally of modest size (around 9 m^2, large enough for only three couches). This, together with its lack of a dedicated anteroom and its location next to the oikos, mean that the andron at Priene was suited to relatively intimate, and perhaps more subdued, social occasions than some of its larger, more architecturally separate, mainland

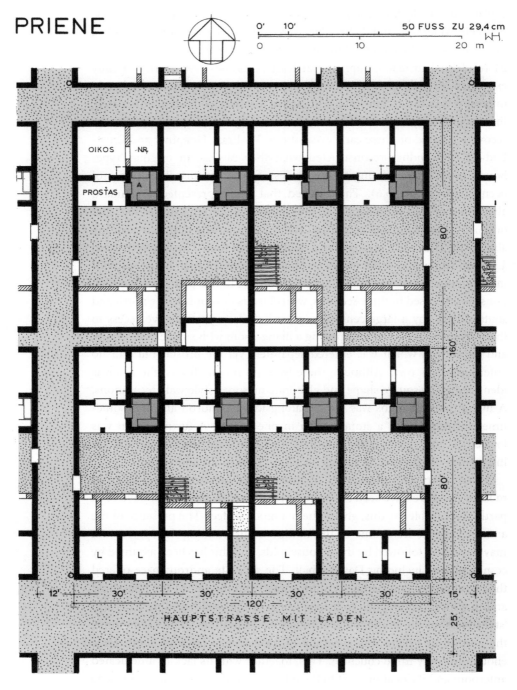

Figure 5.6 Priene, Hoepfner and Schwandner's hypothetical plan of an insula from the fourth century BCE.
(After Hoepfner and Schwandner 1994, Fig. 208, courtesy of Wolfram Hoepfner.)

counterparts. The relatively small scale of the andron is in keeping with the size of the excavated houses. Those reconstructed by Hoepfner and Schwandner cover approximately 200 m^2 in ground area, which is 30 per cent smaller than the pastas houses at Olynthos (although the latter are atypically large).

An unusually extensive proportion of the total ground area is occupied by the unroofed courtyard space, while the interior rooms are relatively limited, both in area and in number. This must surely have had consequences for the lives of the occupants. An individual space here must necessarily have been multi-functional. Exactly what this would have meant in terms of social relationships is difficult to infer: we cannot, unfortunately, know whether the composition of the households at Priene tended to be similar to those occupying the pastas-type houses of the mainland. It is possible that, in general, there were fewer individuals accommodated here (perhaps, for example, fewer enslaved household members or extended family). If the households were of a similar size, then the occupants would have had to share space to a greater extent than their mainland contemporaries. Whichever is the case, the contrasts in scale and layout seem indicative of underlying differences in patterns of domestic life.

Hoepfner and Schwandner's model for the organisation of the fourth-century BCE phase of the Priene houses is based partly on archaeological evidence for early building phases in examples which seem to have undergone only limited modification during later periods, in contrast with the majority of those excavated. Nevertheless, more recent work in the north-west residential quarter at Priene has suggested that, although there was probably a basic house design which was often followed when the housing blocks were first constructed, there was actually also some variation in plot size originating at the time of the initial laying-out of the properties. Ground areas seem to have ranged from about 50 m^2 at the edge of the city to around 500 m^2 near the centre. While the organisation of the larger ones is unclear, they may have offered space for bigger groups to be accommodated, either as residents, or as visitors in more spacious androines.

Further important evidence for prostas houses comes from Kolophon, which was investigated by an American team whose work was severely curtailed by political events in 1922, after they had carried out only a single season's work. The resulting publication is, therefore, preliminary and only a little is known about the urban plan. A rocky akropolis seems to have lain at the core of a larger settlement, the extent of which can be estimated today only through an extensive set of city walls. The excavated houses are located on a series of terraces below the akropolis in what is assumed to be an older neighbourhood. Here, the streets seem to follow the natural contours. The lack of a regular urban grid means that the boundaries between properties are not always clear, especially since internal doorways sometimes eluded the excavators. In total, approximately eight separate dwellings were uncovered, either in their entirety or in part. The team dated them to the fourth century BCE, although subsequent re-evaluation has suggested that they may be somewhat earlier, dating to the fifth century BCE and falling out of use around 300 BCE, when a stoa was constructed over some of them. House size seems to be variable, ranging between 100 m^2 and 200 m^2, with the majority of properties occupying around 160 m^2.

Despite the interpretative difficulties posed by the circumstances of excavation and publication, when the different structures at Kolophon are compared, the spatial syntax and range of architectural features are very similar. House IV serves as an example (Figure. 5.7): at the core lies an open courtyard which seems to have played a range of roles: while artefacts are not reported consistently or in detail, the features and selected finds from such areas typically attest to storage of agricultural produce in large jars and the provision of water from wells or cisterns. In some cases, traces of burning seem to indicate cooking of food and/or the burning of offerings

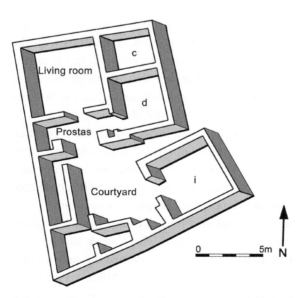

Figure 5.7 Kolophon, house IV.
(Drawn by Max Huemer, based on Holland 1944, Plate X.)

to the gods: in several instances ashes are found in connection with small, built structures which may represent altars (houses II and III as well as house IV). The principal rooms are generally located towards the north and are reached via a prostas. This varied in size from house to house but normally seems to have had a relatively wide opening onto the court. Behind, it gave access through a narrower doorway to a large living room. In some cases, a small side-chamber was apparently reached from there (in house IV this is room c, although in this house the entrance could not be located). At right angles to this axis lies a further room, also entered from the prostas. Few features or finds are recorded to give a sense of how these spaces may have been used. In any case, the circulation patterns and property boundaries apparently changed significantly through time.

On the southern side of the courtyard the rooms are generally smaller and, in at least some instances, may have been used for further storage. An exception is a large, square room frequently found close to the entrance. Its walls tend to be well-built and in one case (house IV, room i) the side facing the street is accented on the exterior by a facing of well-cut limestone blocks. Inside, these rooms had coloured plaster walls, sometimes with contrasting panels and dados. In certain cases, a cement floor was also provided. These decorative features led the excavators to propose that such rooms were used as androns, a hypothesis supported by their square shape and the placement of the doorways, which are generally off-centre. The accenting of them on the exterior of the house echoes a practice already noted for androns in Greek mainland communities as at Athens and Halieis. A flight of stairs frequently ascends across the façade of this room, giving access to a gallery which sheltered the entrance and led to an upper room. (For this reason, the excavators also refer to this room as the 'pyrgos' – 'tower'.) It is unclear whether there was additional upper storey space over any of the other rooms in these houses.

The Kolophon structures conform quite closely to a standardised layout, even though the shapes and sizes of the individual spaces vary from one house to another. That layout is somewhat similar to the organisation of some of the houses at Halieis (for example house 7). The range and distribution of different activities also appears comparable to that seen in mainland Greece: the central court and portico served as a route for communication between the main rooms. In addition, the portico seems to have been used for cooking, to judge by hearth installations present in some cases. The single decorated room seems likely to have served as an andron and although it is normally accessed from the court, it is unlike the pattern in most other communities we have seen in that it stands away from the main living quarters. None of these andrones has an anteroom, but the portico supporting the gallery overhead would have sheltered the doorway, and the room itself was provided with closable doors which could have been used to separate the occupants from the rest of the household.

The sites just discussed comprise only a small number of settlements. Even so, they suggest that a single community in this region could include a range of different house-forms, encompassing buildings of contrasting sizes, with differing facilities (such as andrones) and even different architectural types (prostas and pastas). Some of this variation is probably due to factors such as differences in the wealth of the occupants, which constrained the amount of land and the resources available to them. In other cases, the reasons are less clear. The choice between the pastas- or prostas-form is one example: while in many instances the decision to construct one rather than the other may have depended on the size and proportions of the house plot, this may not be the whole story. In some communities, such as Priene, there would have been the opportunity to extend a portico across the façades of at least two rooms. This would have offered more semi-outdoor space but would have resulted in a reduction, both of the amount of interior space, and in the quantity of direct light entering the main room from the courtyard. There were, therefore, possibly differences between the patterns of activity in households living in the pastas houses and those in the prostas houses.

Greek Settlements in the Southern Mediterranean: Crete and the North African Coast

The island of Crete has a long-standing relationship with the Greek mainland similar to that of the Asia Minor coastal sites. In recent years, new archaeological evidence has been emerging for the character of Cretan housing during the first millennium BCE. In contrast with the Greek mainland and islands, there seems to have been a strong degree of continuity in domestic organisation from the Late Bronze Age through the Early Iron Age into Classical times, although the amount of material from the Classical period itself is currently still limited. At present, there is little evidence for the adoption of the single-entrance, courtyard house among Cretan communities. Two different patterns of domestic spatial organisation are found: one features an irregular cluster of rooms which are interconnected and seem to have grown up over time; the other forms a

Figure 5.8 Kavousi Kastro, house A from above, showing the layout and steep local topography.
(Author's photograph reproduced by permission of the Ephorate of Antiquities of Lasithi. The rights to the monument shown belong to the Hellenic Ministry of Culture and Sports (Law 3028/2002). Kavousi Kastro is under the supervision of the Ephorate of Antiquities of Lasithi, Ministry of Culture and Sports.)

linear arrangement in which several different spaces communicate directly and are entered in series. The two types of plan are exemplified by various settlements in eastern Crete. House A at Kavousi Kastro demonstrates the latter pattern: it was built in the later eighth century BCE and abandoned in the late seventh century. Its location, in a small settlement perched high on a steep hillside, is typical for the island (Figure 5.8). The house itself consists of a series of five separate spaces which are built end-to-end along a narrow terrace. A paved central area about 2 metres wide was open on its eastern side, possibly offering an exterior courtyard. The presence of an oven and a range of pottery suggests that food was prepared here. Two pairs of rooms were entered sequentially from its north and south sides, although those to the north may also have been reachable directly from the exterior. Three contain storage facilities, while the fourth, the most secluded at the southern end of the house, had a hearth and may have been a living space.

More recent excavations at nearby Azoria have provided detailed information about the way in which house-forms in the area changed through
time. The earliest material at the site dates to the seventh century BCE. At
this time, the houses were composed of clusters of rooms that seem to have
grown up over time to accommodate related groups of individuals, a
pattern comparable with earlier communities at nearby Karphi and
Vronda (both occupied around the turn of the first millennium BCE).
An extensive reconfiguration of Azoria around 600 BCE erased this previous settlement and, in its place, created a more densely packed built
environment which seems to have been planned collaboratively. Like
Kavousi Kastro, the site was steeply sloping, and the new settlement was
characterised by a series of what the excavators term 'spine walls', providing terraces on which to build. Perhaps because of the difficult terrain, its
houses appear to have persisted in approximately the same form until the
site was abandoned, a little over a century after its re-organisation.
Preliminary reports of the work carried out at Azoria reveal details of
household organisation and the activities taking place in these later houses,
based not only on architecture and artefact distributions, but also on
zooarchaeological and archaeobotanical remains.

Although no two examples of these houses are identical, the project's
Director, Donald Haggis, and his colleagues have convincingly identified a
number of recurring patterns in the layout and use of space. At the time of
writing, one of the most extensively investigated of the published domestic
structures is the unusually large Northeast Building. Like house A at
Kavousi Kastro, it is located on a narrow terrace and is composed of a
series of spaces reached in sequence (Figure 5.9). It was approached from
the northwest, via an exterior activity area. The entrance led via a vestibule
into a 'hall' covering almost 30 m². This lacks any architectural features
which might point to its use, and the eclectic assemblage of artefacts
suggested to the excavators that it played multiple roles, including as a
location for dining. Behind, a slightly larger room is interpreted as a storage
space: it contained stands for large jars, as well as two preserved examples
of the jars themselves, fragments of others, and soil samples yielding
evidence for a variety of crops including olives, grapes, chickpeas, barley
and wheat. Beyond, residents of the house would have passed via a
combination of steps and ramps, into an open courtyard. On the opposite
side lay a partially preserved cooking area. Its role is identified on the basis
of a fixed hearth in its south-west corner, together with a range of food
remains and equipment for processing food. According to the plan, it

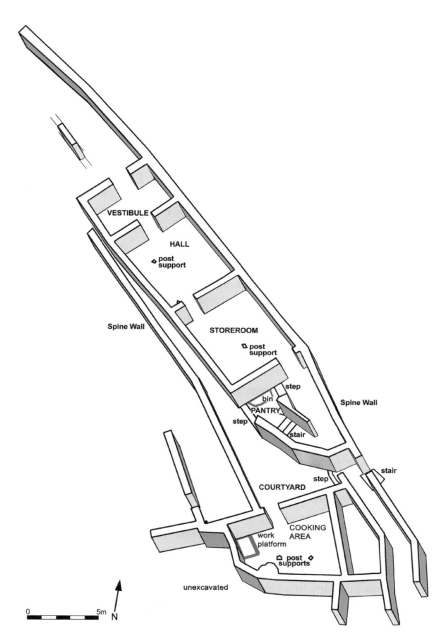

Figure 5.9 Azoria, Northeast Building.
(Drawn by Lorene Sterner based on Haggis et al. 2007, Fig. 1 and Fig. 2.)

seems that the courtyard was accessible from a street area behind, via a staircase, so that the house had two entrances.

The excavators note that the Northeast Building is representative of others at Azoria in several respects. First, it incorporates a range of types of space which seem to have played distinctively different roles within the complex as a whole – namely the multi-functional 'hall', the storage room, the open courtyard and the cooking area. Second, it locates the hall next to the storage room, implying that there was a connection between the two – perhaps for purposes of control of agricultural produce, and/or their display to visitors, which was sometimes enhanced by the use of monumentally sized, elaborately decorated, jars. Finally, it reflects a trend towards the separation of the cooking area from the other interior spaces by means of a courtyard. The repetition of such patterns across the settlement offers a tantalising glimpse of some of the social norms or ideals of its original inhabitants, which may have involved those occupying the hall engaging in surveillance or exercising control over access to the stored goods, although they were separated from food preparation. This may indicate a level of mistrust between individuals or groups within the household. At the same time, the separate access via the courtyard implies that the accessibility to outsiders of the cooking area and those working there was not a significant concern. This interpretation is supported by the fact that access to the exterior activity areas in front of the house and in front of the cooking area, was not restricted. Within the house itself, the linear plan would have compelled residents to walk through intervening spaces in order to move between (for example) the hall and courtyard, or cooking area and storeroom, thus viewing the activities taking place in those intervening areas.

Alternative patterns of organisation to the linear and agglomerative patterns are also occasionally found on Crete: for instance, in what might be interpreted as two adjacent three-room houses at Onithe (late seventh to early sixth century BCE). In the southern house, extensive evidence of storage was provided in a complex with a narrow anteroom and a row of three rooms lying behind (Figure 5.10). Although partially unexcavated, the pattern is reminiscent of a pastas, but it is a layout which does not appear to have caught on in Crete. Rather, the type of linear arrangement seen in the later phase at Azoria continues to be favoured, for example at Lato, another hillside settlement occupied perhaps from the mid fourth to the second century BCE. House Δ sits against a vertical rock face and consists of two rooms arranged one behind the other and reached

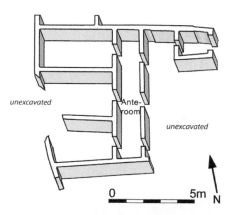

Figure 5.10 Onithe, south house.
(Drawn by Max Huemer based on Psaroudakis 2004, Fig. 3.)

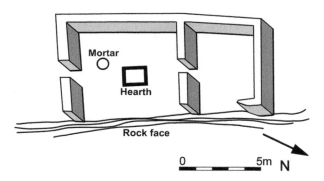

Figure 5.11 Lato, House Δ.
(Drawn by Max Huemer based on Hadjimichali 1971, Fig. 9.)

sequentially (Figure 5.11). The front room has a hearth and was therefore perhaps a living area. In the southernmost of two further houses north of the prytaneion, space was divided into three rooms, including an anteroom in front of the hearth-room.

The same linear arrangement was used in a house at Eleutherna Nissi (fourth century BCE to first century CE: Figure 5.12) and might also have been used at Trypetos (third to second century BCE), although the partial preservation of the structures at Trypetos makes their original layout difficult to reconstruct. As well as an apparently sequential arrangement of space, the dwellings in some of these settlements also share another

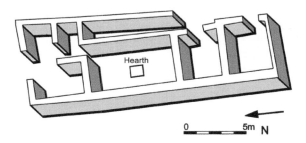

Figure 5.12 Eleutherna Nissi, house A.
(Drawn by Max Huemer, based on Tsatsaki 2010, Fig. 2.)

Figure 5.13 Trypetos, hearth-room.
(Author's photograph, reproduced by permission of the Ephorate of Antiquities of Lasithi. The rights to the monument shown belong to the Hellenic Ministry of Culture and Sports (Law 3028/2002). Trypetos is under the supervision of the Ephorate of Antiquities of Lasithi, Ministry of Culture and Sports.)

feature, namely a large 'hearth-room': in each house this room often dominates due to its size and in many cases it includes a substantial built hearth at the centre (Figure 5.13). While these rooms may seem superficially similar to the hearth-rooms found in some sites in the western Greek mainland (see Chapter 4) they do not appear to have played entirely the same role. Instead of circulation spaces with several rooms radiating from them, as at Ammotopos or Kassope, the Cretan hearth-rooms typically represent one of a series of spaces arranged in a linear sequence. The occupants, therefore, did not have the same potential for surveillance as those of the mainland hearth-rooms. Unlike either the hearth-room houses or the single-entrance, courtyard houses, in the larger houses of this type, movement between various clusters of rooms or even into and out of the house as a whole, must have been relatively free, since it could not have been monitored from a single space.

A further characteristic shared by the Cretan houses is that there is a complete lack of any evidence for a domestic andron from the entire island. This phenomenon may support the suggestion that in the cities of the Peloponnese and Crete, male citizens did not participate in the symposium. Indeed, according to textual sources they did not entertain their associates at home or even eat at home themselves, but instead participated in a communal banquet (syssition) which took place in a specialised dining building, examples of which have been identified both in the sixth-century phase BCE at Azoria and also nearby at Praisos. Such a pattern is in keeping with the comments of ancient authors who thought of the settlements on Crete as culturally different from the major mainland cities such as Athens. (These authors also claim that the communities of the Peloponnese were similar to those of Crete, but as we have seen, little evidence of Classical housing is presently known from the Peloponnese, so it is difficult to test this idea.)

In sum, while evidence for the Classical period is scarce, the continued use in Crete of houses arranged on a sequential plan suggests that social practices would have been distinctively different from those prevailing in a single-entrance, courtyard house. Access to the household by outsiders could have been much freer, and while the more spacious houses would have provided a comfortable living environment, there is little evidence of architectural elaboration to indicate that the house played a significant role as a status symbol.

Further to the south of Crete, on the northern coast of Africa, the presence of Greek and Greek-style pottery from a number of locations including the sites of the ancient cities of Cyrene, Tocra and Euesperides (all in present-day Cyrenaica, Libya: Map 2), suggest the locations of culturally Greek settlements there from at least the mid seventh century BCE. In most cases, the remains of the early houses are obscured by the more substantial civic and residential buildings of later settlements, which make it impossible to gain a detailed or comprehensive picture of earlier occupation in this region. At Euesperides, the fragmentary remains of two Archaic houses have been reported briefly on the hill of Sidi Abeid. David Gill suggests that one of these, in the southeastern part of the site, may have

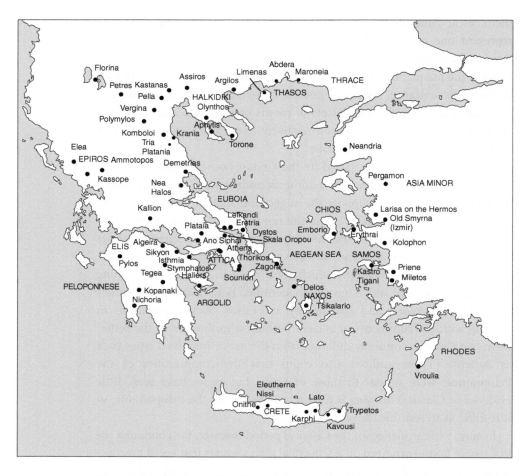

Map 1 Map showing the locations of sites mentioned in the text that are on the Greek mainland and islands and on the Asia Minor coast.

been built up against the city wall as its southeastern wall is abnormally thick (Figure 5.14). If reconstructed correctly, the house is laid out in a manner not paralleled by any houses we have seen so far: an oven or kiln lay in the street outside. The entrance led from the street into an interior room which gave access both to a further, rear room (which was paved) and to a western courtyard with a third room beyond. The poor preservation of the building makes it difficult to be certain about patterns of access, but it seems that (in contrast with the single-entrance, courtyard house) the courtyard here did not represent a route for moving around the house. It is more likely that it was one of several spaces entered in sequence. This would mean that it offered a similar kind of accommodation to that

Map 2 Map showing the locations of sites mentioned in the text that are in modern Italy and on the coasts of the Black Sea and north Africa.

identified at the Cretan sites discussed above, although space was laid out somewhat differently and the spaces are also differently proportioned. A Cretan connection for the early community here has already been suggested by Gill, based on literary and ceramic evidence, as well as on similarities in plan between this house and those at Lato.

Fragmentary remains of a second building, also interpreted as a house, have been uncovered built up against the city wall in Area H, also on Sidi

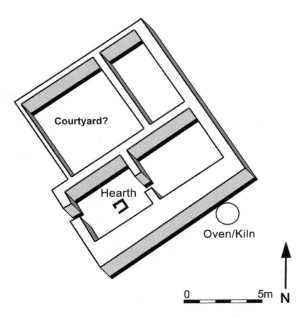

Figure 5.14 Euesperides, Sidi Abeid house A.
(Drawn by Max Huemer based on Gill and Flecks 2007, Fig. 22.3. (Note: this
is a tentative reconstruction since, from the published plan, it is unclear
whether parts of some of the walls had to be extrapolated and it seems that
the locations of most of the doorways are unknown.)

Abeid Hill, during more recent work at the site. This may originally have
been organised in a similar manner as a series of rooms leading from one to
the next, although the overall plan and identification are uncertain because
part of the structure was destroyed by recent bulldozing. In and around the
house were an oven, well and mortar-lined pit, perhaps for storage.
A central room preserved evidence of fish processing in the form of bones
and scales, as well as a hearth in one corner. Two further structures were
built in succession in the same location. The later one represents part of a
small house occupied into the late fourth to early third century BCE. Space
was organised around a cobbled courtyard with rooms to north, east and
west, although there was no evidence of a portico. Elsewhere on the site,
fragmentary remains of later housing include mosaics, some comprising
both pebbles and tesserae in a single floor. Elaborate moulded and coloured
wall plaster found alongside them appears to be from richly decorated
andrones, although the complete structures cannot be reconstructed due to
later disturbance. Despite being very incomplete, this material does suggest
that during the earlier period the organisation of space in houses at

Euesperides may have been linear, and comparable to that of Crete or Early Iron Age Greece, but that by the end of the fourth century BCE things may have been changing: the organisation of space around a central courtyard may mean that movement around the house could potentially be monitored from here, as in the single-entrance, courtyard house. At the same time, the use of mosaic decoration suggests that domestic architecture had become a medium for displays of status. (This practice is explored in detail in Chapters 6 and 7.)

Greek Settlements in the Western Mediterranean: Sicily and Southern Italy

Some of the most prosperous Greek cities of the Classical period were located in the southern coastal area of the Italian peninsula and, especially, on the coast of the island of Sicily (Map 2). Greek settlement in this part of the Mediterranean goes back at least to the eighth century BCE. Communities sharing aspects of their material culture with Greek mainland populations co-existed with others showing more affinities with indigenous people or with the Punic culture of Carthage (modern Tunis). In many cases, the material record suggests that the inhabitants of a single settlement expressed a range of cultural traits – some related to those of mainland Greece, others closer to what might be thought of as belonging to indigenous groups, and still others which seem to be innovations, suggesting the forging of new cultural forms. At the same time, there was evidently change through time in the extent and ways in which different identities were expressed. For example, the inland Sicilian site of Morgantina supports a variety of interpretations of the extensive range of excavated civic and domestic buildings constructed at different times, and of the ceramics accompanying them.

Houses with a number of different organisational patterns are represented in this region, but there are also features which are shared. Some of the most extensive evidence comes from Megara Hyblaia, in southeastern Sicily, where the earliest material dates to around 700 BCE. Land seems to have been divided on a notional grid system into rectangular plots within which the individual buildings were placed. The houses of this period consist of rectangular, single-room structures with an area of about 25 m^2. The buildings were sometimes expanded later by the construction of a further unit or units, sharing party walls and placed within the original plot. The plans of the resulting houses are varied, but overall, this process seems to have led to the gradual creation of small structures, each with an unroofed courtyard to the south, which was often furnished with a well, and two or three rooms to the north. Conceptually, these were perhaps similar to the houses seen at eighth century BCE Skala Oropou and Eretria, discussed in Chapter 2, where several separate buildings standing within an enclosure wall may together have formed a single functional unit. At Megara Hyblaia, however, the layout was quite different, with the architectural spaces adjoining and sharing party walls. In one case (house 23,5) a portico facing onto a courtyard to the east sheltered the entrances to two west-facing rooms (Figure 5.15: a third space to the north – not shown – was entered separately and may or may not have been part of the same unit). The excavators identify this portico as a forerunner to a later, more substantial pastas. A comparable layout has been found at Monte San Mauro (Figure 5.16). Here, the houses range in size from 58 m^2 to 165 m^2, each consisting of a transverse room with one, two or three rear rooms. There is no demarcated courtyard space, and the transverse room is often relatively large in proportion to those behind. Artefact distributions suggest some organisational patterns: the transverse room contained artefacts used for a range of activities including food storage and preparation. In one of the smaller houses, a bathtub was also found here, while in house 4, one was located in one of the inner rooms – a space also containing weaving equipment. Archaic houses with transverse rooms have also been found elsewhere on Sicily, for example at Monte Iato, as well as on the Italian mainland, as at Policoro and Velia.

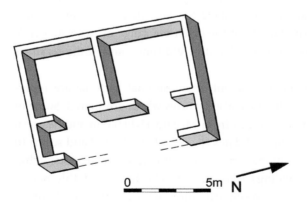

Figure 5.15 Megara Hyblaia, house 23,5, showing the portico and two rear rooms.
(Drawn by Max Huemer based on Gras et al. 2004, Fig. 388.)

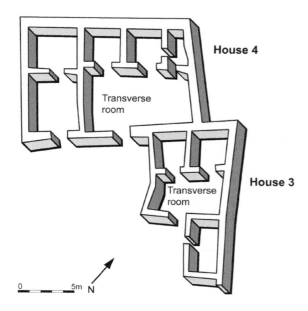

Figure 5.16 Monte San Mauro, houses 3 and 4.
(Drawn by Max Huemer based on Belvedere 2000, Fig. 2.)

Extensive evidence of housing has been excavated at Himera, in eastern
Sicily, where two successive settlements lie superimposed, one upon the
other. The earlier one is planned on a grid and probably dates to the late
seventh century BCE. Only the walls of a few scattered structures are
preserved, mostly on a north-west/south-east orientation. The community
was abandoned during the early sixth century and then completely rebuilt
shortly afterwards, when it was laid out on a new grid of long building
blocks running directly east-west. These incorporated houses of varying
dimensions. The sizes of the individual rooms and their arrangement were
also very diverse. For example, in insula II, block 1 (Figure 5.17), an area
roughly equivalent to a single space in the northern part of the building
(space 1: ca. 49 m^2) is occupied by at least five different spaces in its
southern part (spaces 4 to 6, 35 and the space west of 6: ca. 55 m^2). In
some cases, the layout may have resembled a central courtyard with rooms
radiating from it in a comparable manner to the single-entrance, courtyard
house (for example insula I, block 4: Figure 5.18). Their interpretation is
complicated, however, by the fact that the extant walls were not all constructed simultaneously, and the locations of the entrances to many of the
spaces are uncertain. While these houses yielded relatively large numbers of
artefacts which were published in detail, consistent patterning in their

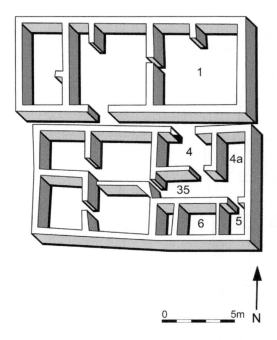

Figure 5.17 Himera, insula II, block 1 (locations of some doorways unclear).
(Drawn by Max Huemer based on Allegro et al. 2008, Fig. 1.)

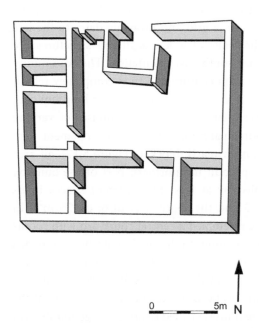

Figure 5.18 Himera, insula I, block 4 (locations of some doorways are undetermined).
(Drawn by Max Huemer based on Allegro et al. 2008. Fig. 43.)

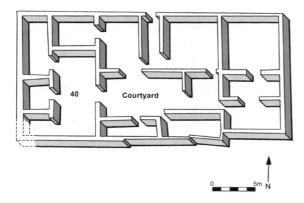

40 Courtyard

0   5m N

Figure 5.19 Himera, insula VI, house 5.
(Drawn by Max Huemer based on Belvedere 2013, Fig. 7.)

distribution is difficult to detect on a large scale. It is possible that in some cases the catalogues may include a combination of material either from different occupation phases, or from different types of context (including post-abandonment debris), or both. Nonetheless, a comprehensive and detailed analysis of the architecture and artefacts of one large, late-fifth century BCE house, VI 5, by Oscar Belvedere, has produced fruitful insights. The house was created by joining two smaller, earlier structures and had a relatively large courtyard at its heart, with separate suites of rooms to the east and west (Figure 5.19). Based on his analysis of circulation patterns and artefact distributions, Belvedere has suggested that the building was broadly divided into areas reserved for the household (to the west) and areas used for entertaining visitors (to the east), while the central courtyard would have been frequented by both groups. Space 40 might have functioned like the transverse rooms of the houses at Monte San Mauro. The layout is somewhat different from many of the houses we have seen in Chapters 3 and 4 in that some rooms to the east of the courtyard were entered in sequence. Belvedere nevertheless suggests that it conformed to the principles of the single-entrance, courtyard model, presumably because it potentially catered to the separation of visitors from household members.

Similar houses dating to the fifth century BCE have been found among Greek communities elsewhere in Sicily and southern Italy and they show a comparable lack of standardisation. At Gela, for example, a group of four small structures with areas of between 100 m^2 and 180 m^2 each possess a courtyard or light well (Figure 5.20). As at Himera, the locations of the doorways are difficult to reconstruct, but the arrangement of the spaces is

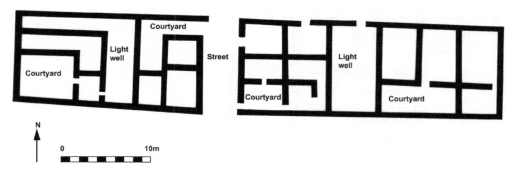

Figure 5.20 Four houses from Gela.
(After Nevett 1999, Fig. 45.)

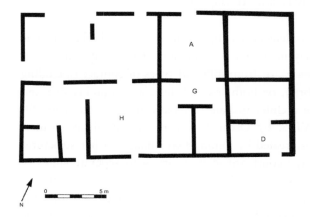

Figure 5.21 Naxos (Sicily), insula C4, house 1-2 (locations
of some doorways undetermined).
(Drawn by the author based on Lentini 1990, Fig.2.)

such that this open area cannot have played the dominant role in circulation characteristic of the single-entrance, courtyard arrangement. A further
group of houses, from Sicilian Naxos (insula C4), was also constructed
during the fifth century BCE and destroyed towards the end of that same
century. Again, the layout is irregular and it is difficult to make out the
boundaries of the individual properties or to understand the use of space
because the doorways are mostly not reconstructable. Maria Lentini, who
published them, emphasises the fact that despite the organisation of the
streets into a regular grid plan, the houses themselves are very variable in
size, and even the largest, house 1-2 (Figure 5.21), is relatively small
compared with those in other Greek settlements on Sicily. Lentini notes

that in the excavated area there are no signs of luxury such as mosaic floors, coloured wall plaster, baths or columned peristyles, although finds of decorative antefixes on the wider streets suggest that houses abutting these thoroughfares were designed to catch the passer-by's attention from the exterior. Lentini suggests that in house 1-2, residential accommodation may have been combined with commercial. She interprets (A) as an entrance hall, (H) as a courtyard, (G) as a pastas and (D) (based on the artefacts recovered) as a storeroom, although she notes a scarcity of tiles which makes it difficult to distinguish exterior from interior spaces. Notwithstanding the problem of reconstructing circulation patterns, it is clear that the organisation of space here was quite different from that in the single-entrance, courtyard house, even though at least some of the dwellings appear to be larger than the smallest units at Athens or on Olynthos' North Hill.

Towards the end of the fifth and into the fourth century BCE, more frequent evidence is found of single-entrance, courtyard-type houses in this region, a trend which comes together with an increase in the size of the largest known properties. At Kaulonia in Calabria on the Italian mainland, for example, three houses dating to the fourth century BCE each have an area of around 240 m². Although none of them is completely preserved, the surviving evidence suggests that each one was divided into at least six different spaces (including the courtyard) and there was a covered portico in front of the main range of rooms.

During the Classical period, then, there was some variation in house forms in this region. As in others we have looked at, the evidence for Classical houses was eclipsed (and in some cases literally built over) during the Hellenistic period that followed, when properties of a larger size and more substantial construction were widespread, attesting both to the prosperity of these communities in general, and to the role that housing came to play as a symbol. This evidence is considered in detail in Chapter 7.

Greek Settlements on the North Coast of the Black Sea

Greek artefacts dating back at least to the mid seventh century BCE have been found in settlements on the Black Sea coast, although the number of locations in which they occur is small and the area over which they were distributed increased relatively slowly through time in comparison with the rapid penetration of such material in the western Mediterranean. By the late sixth century BCE, however, such material was much more common, particularly large transport amphorae from the Aegean islands which may have contained imports of wine (at Berezan, ancient Borysthenes, for instance, these made up 70–90 per cent of the ceramic assemblage, attesting, perhaps, to the importance of wine to such communities). The earliest houses currently known in this region are single-room, subterranean or semi-subterranean structures unlike anything else considered in this volume. They do, however, contain large percentages of pottery like that used on the Greek mainland, alongside hand-made wares which more closely resemble those used by some of the local groups in the surrounding area. At Berezan, for instance, a combination of hand-made pottery in local styles alongside vessels imported from Ionia and the Aegean islands occurs from approximately 650 BCE onwards. An unusually large and well-constructed example of a pit-house here, house 47, offers an indication of the kind of architectural context in which such material is found. The house dates to the second quarter of the sixth century BCE and was in use for about forty years (Figure 5.22). It had an area of 38 m² and was cut about a metre into the ground, with mudbrick walls projecting above the surface and a thatched roof on top. At least one wall was reinforced using wattle and the floor was surfaced with successive layers of clay. The excavators suggest that although the house consisted only of a single room, the interior fell into two functionally distinct halves. To the northwest lay a cooking area of about 28 m² furnished with a series of ovens and hearths which were rebuilt through time. Alongside these were pits which held storage vessels. Further south a living area was identified.

At nearby Olbia, the earliest structures containing Greek material lie in the Upper City and date to the second quarter of the sixth century BCE. In

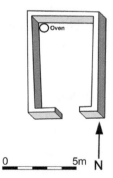

Figure 5:22 Berezan, house 47.
(Drawn by Max Huemer based on
Solovyov 1999, Fig. 43.)

the last quarter of the sixth century BCE and early fifth century BCE, construction extended to a new district, the Lower City. This is the location of the earliest known houses at the site to have been built above ground which were small, single-room habitations. Earth Dwelling 730 in Sector NGS, for example, was a rectangular mud-brick building; like the others of this type, it lies beneath later construction, and the plan could not be fully recovered, but the excavated area measured 3.6 × 2.6 m. A rectangular bench occupied the southwest corner. Few artefacts were recovered from the interior: only fragments of drinking cups, a bowl imported from Asia Minor, and transport amphorae from the Aegean islands of Chios and Lesbos.

At Berezan, pit houses began to be replaced by larger structures at ground level during the third quarter of the sixth century BCE. An example, house 2, was constructed at around this time (Figure 5.23). Initially it covered 123 m². A walled courtyard, entered through a door at the south, was provided with a well, an underground storage pit and an altar. Two rooms lay side-by-side along its western perimeter, the southern one apparently used for cooking. Around 500 BCE the building was enlarged to cover 236 m². Two further ranges of rooms were added on the northern and eastern sides of the court, and a paved (and, therefore,

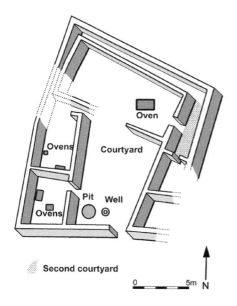

Figure 5.23 Berezan, house 2, phase 2 (shaded area is paved).
(Drawn by Max Huemer, based on Solovyov 1999, Fig. 51.)

presumably unroofed) area was created on the northeast corner of the plot. Based on the distribution of architectural features, this enlarged compound seems to have been functionally divided, with residential quarters to the west, a cooking area to the east, and additional rooms on the north. The fragmentary preservation of this and other dwellings of the period at Berezan means that thresholds are rarely in evidence, so that it is difficult or impossible to reconstruct circulation patterns. Nevertheless, if these different spaces were indeed complementary, then the building was presumably still home to a single household (and, indeed, still provided less space than, for example, one of the houses from the North Hill at Olynthos). There is little evidence to suggest that it bore a resemblance to the single-entrance, courtyard house, or that any of the social pressures underlying that house-type were at work here.

During the Classical period, a number of settlements on the Black Sea coast were laid out on grid plans, with regularly sized housing blocks between. In the Lower City at Olbia, the Classical houses were destroyed during an episode of widespread burning across the site. Those replacing them were laid out in regularly shaped blocks. The roads between them were often quite narrow – sometimes less than one metre in width and were laid out on an approximately orthogonal plan, although each one continued only for one or two blocks, so there was not a regular grid. Within each block, the houses shared party walls; judging from their size and contents, they seem to have belonged to households of relatively modest means. In each individual structure, space was typically organised around a courtyard with rooms ranged around two or three sides. The courtyard was generally surfaced with clay, although a couple of paved examples have also been found. In one partially preserved house, stone bases suggest the presence of a portico along the north side. The entrances to the individual rooms are frequently impossible to identify, but where they do survive, they seem unusually narrow compared with houses in other parts of the Greek world – only 0.9–1.1 metres in comparison with 1.5 or even up to 2 metres at Olynthos, for instance. Where spatial syntax can reliably be reconstructed it is rather variable. A single entrance to the house which led into the courtyard seems to have been normal and in some of the better preserved houses this took the form of a narrow passage.

An example, house II.3 (Figure 5.24), had an area of about 200 m^2, including an open courtyard covering about 40 m^2. The entrance led, via a corridor in the northwest corner, into a courtyard which was partially paved in stone. According to the excavators, an unpaved section to the north may have been roofed to form a portico. This lay against the

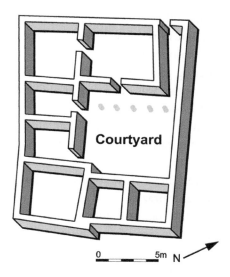

Figure 5.24 Olbia, house II.3.
(Drawn by Max Huemer based on Lejpunskaja et al. 2010, Plate 11.)

northern boundary of the house, with the rooms arranged in a 'U' shape around the other sides, so it could only have formed a sheltered outdoor workspace and not a covered walkway between the rooms. Five out of a probable total of seven or eight rooms in the house were reasonably well-preserved. Evidence for the doorways of several survived, leading directly from the court. In addition to these spaces at ground level, there were also basements beneath two of the rooms on the house's southwestern side. The artefacts found include large quantities of roof tile and ceramics. The latter comprise imported fine table wares, both wheel-made and hand-made cooking wares, and significant numbers of imported transport amphorae, most of them from the eastern Aegean island of Rhodes. All artefact types were found throughout the house, although with some changes in the relative proportions of material from room to room. There is some evidence for post-abandonment squatter occupation, so that it is unclear whether the finds from the floors and fills relate to the primary habitation phase or to later re-use of the building, perhaps for dumping debris after a catastrophic landslide which hit the area at the end of the third century BCE. Nevertheless, the architecture suggests that whoever built this house may have been familiar with the single-entrance, courtyard form and may have been aiming at a similar organisational effect here. It is perhaps not coincidental, however, that the northern side of the courtyard is without rooms leading off it, even though in many other Greek communities the north side of the courtyard of such a house is often where the main domestic apartments were located: one reason for such an arrangement was to avoid the mid-summer sun entering and heating up the interior excessively, but the local climate meant that that was not a danger at Olbia.

In sum, an unusually large amount of evidence of Archaic housing has been investigated in this region, and the pit-houses offer a tantalising glimpse of the lives of the inhabitants of the early settlements with Greek material: like the hearth-room houses of Epiros, this type may stem from the very different climatic conditions here. The narrow streets and door-ways, the evidence for multiple hearths and braziers, and the lack of a consistent orientation may be linked with the cold prevailing climate. The subterranean construction perhaps offered a means of insulation in these relatively harsh conditions. Superficially, such structures seem rather different from the dwellings from other regions. Nevertheless, while the sunken aspect is unusual, it is also relevant to remember that, based on current evidence, single-room buildings constitute a significant proportion of houses attested even on the Greek mainland during the sixth century BCE. So, although the pit houses would have been unfamiliar architecturally to any traders and migrants from the Aegean, the concept of living in a single space may not have been. At the same time, the range of ceramic material present shows that these households had access to goods obtained through long-distance trading networks, which offered a means by which to express or affirm affiliations or cultural affinities with the Mediterranean communities who produced them.

There is a general typological change through time, away from the Archaic pit houses towards multiple-room, courtyard houses, although Classical material is relatively less abundant, so that the date and nature of the process are hard to pinpoint precisely. Development was not invariably unlinear, however. At Berezan, for instance, there are some areas where pit-houses were replaced by structures above ground, which in turn seem to have been succeeded by further pit-houses. By the fourth century BCE, however, many features of the single-entrance, courtyard house-form are seen in combination, including: a single entrance which was sometimes separated from the street; a central courtyard, sometimes with evidence of a portico along one side; and rooms which were entered individually from the courtyard. The occupants of these structures may have used adherence to this organisational scheme in order to express their support for some of the ideals underlying the single-entrance, courtyard house in the Aegean and elsewhere.

Conclusion: Housing Greeks 'Overseas'

From the eighth century BCE onwards material culture originating in mainland Greece and the islands became distributed over a wide geographical area encompassing a variety of physical and cultural landscapes. Contrasting patterns of subsequent occupation have contributed to differing states of preservation. At the same time, diverse national research traditions have emphasised varying components of the archaeological record or have focused specifically on the evidence of some cultures but have sometimes neglected (and hence underestimated the contribution of) others. There is good evidence for Archaic housing in Crete, in Sicily and the south of modern Italy, as well as in the northern Black Sea littoral. By contrast for the Classical period, evidence is scarce in Crete and the northern Black Sea coast, while the Asia Minor coast and Sicily together with southern Italy are both well-represented. Despite this uneven sample, the surviving evidence suggests that in most of these regions the basic organisational properties of the single-entrance, courtyard house came to prevail sooner or later even where – as in the northern Black Sea – climatic conditions may have hindered the use of the open courtyard as an activity area. The practical advantages of the in-turned spatial arrangement in providing security may have been a major element in its adoption as well as the cultural norms or aspirations it implied. There are, however, noticeable differences in the degree to which houses were standardised in different settlements and regions. There are also a range of ways in which the social conventions of the single-entrance, courtyard house were satisfied. What seems to have happened, therefore, was a convergence of ideas about how domestic space should be organised and about the facilities to be expected, and this may indicate a growing sense of cultural unity. In some areas, a variety of aspects of the single-entrance, courtyard model were well represented by the Classical period (as in Asia Minor); in others (such as the Black Sea littoral) this may not have happened strongly or (in Crete) at all (although new evidence could change the picture). Alongside this cultural convergence, starting in the earlier fourth century BCE another trend is also visible, towards increasing inequality between households in the resources spent on their housing. It is the scope of this inequality that is explored in the final two chapters of this volume.

6 | Housing, Power and Wealth in Greek Communities during the Late Classical and Early Hellenistic Periods

Stretching the Ideal?

This chapter explores some of the roles played by the domestic buildings of the wealthier and more powerful members of society in Greek communities, particularly during the fourth and third centuries BCE. Over time, there was a dramatic growth in the size and opulence of the largest houses. One reason for this may have been that the symbolic role of the house began to shift, with owners using their properties as statements of their own personal power and wealth to an extent which had not been acceptable before. As we shall see, although such changes are visible across the Greek world, they are most obvious in the late Classical and Hellenistic periods at royal cities such as Vergina and Pella (Greek Macedonia). In those locations, monumental palatial buildings were constructed which covered thousands of square metres and included numerous decorated rooms of different sizes, arranged around multiple courtyards.

To some extent, the emergence of these structures can be viewed as the continuation of a trend towards building larger, more elaborately decorated houses, which is already visible by the earlier fourth-century BCE in cities like Olynthos and Priene. As Ian Morris has argued, the creation of large, ornate houses is likely to have been partly a response to a long-term increase in per capita wealth, which provided the necessary resources. Another aspect seems to have been an increase in the gulf between the wealthiest and poorest households. This was coupled with changes in the broader political and cultural climate from the mid fourth century BCE onwards, which may have made large, elaborate houses more desirable and expenditure on them more socially acceptable. The rapid incorporation of individual citizen-states into larger kingdoms during the later fourth century BCE saw monarchs like Philip II of Macedon (responsible for besieging and destroying Olynthos), his son Alexander the Great, and their successors, construct monumental buildings which served as settings for the reception of visitors and, presumably, as residences for the monarch (an interpretation picked up later in this chapter). These 'palaces', as they are usually termed today, were used not only as symbols of monarchical power but probably also as tools for maintaining royal authority. From the perspective of domestic architecture, their creation is likely to have been a catalyst which sped up changes already taking place. Palatial architecture offered a model suggesting what the backdrop of a powerful individual might look like, how such a building might enhance personal status or prestige, and what some of the roles were that it might play. But what was the conceptual relationship between palaces and houses? Were they simply different from each other in scale, or were they also distinctively different in kind? And what might housing be able to tell us about some of the social consequences of the kinds of profound political changes taking place in the Greek world during the late Classical and Hellenistic periods? In order to address these issues, we begin by exploring surviving evidence from palatial buildings before moving on to look at some examples of large-scale, private houses of the fourth century BCE, in order to consider the relationship between the two types of structure.

Palatial Buildings

Application of the term 'palace' in the Greek context is in some ways problematic, since it encourages us to think of the rather specific sets of roles performed by palaces in other cultures, such as the monumental official residences belonging to the European monarchs of recent historical periods. Nevertheless, it seems helpful to apply it (albeit cautiously) since not only is the term in widespread use among scholars, but also, the texts show that the idea that a ruler (basileos) possessed a monumental residence (basileion) existed from at least the eighth century BCE (Text Extract 15). Familiarity with the concept does not, however, mean that such structures were necessarily being built in Greek communities during that period. The Homeric descriptions perhaps relied on memories of the large, administrative structures which existed in Greece during the Late Bronze Age but which were lost in the turmoil accompanying the end of the societies of that period. Later discussions may draw inspiration from buildings in the Near East. Some scholars have argued that the construction of palatial buildings continued in Greece after the end of the Late Bronze Age, through the Early Iron Age and Archaic periods, even if they were smaller in scale and less sophisticated in technology than their predecessors. One might consider the Lefkandi Heröon (if it was actually ever intended to be lived in – see Chapter 1) to be an example, although to date scholars have struggled to identify anything else quite comparable. The leaders of Early

Iron Age communities may have occupied houses that were somewhat larger than those of their peers and may have secured the most desirable locations within a settlement; their dwellings might even have begun to take on ritual significance, as suggested by Alexander Mazarakis Ainian. On present evidence, though, the houses themselves seem not to have differed radically from the others around them in terms of the materials used, their appearance or their internal organisation.

By the Archaic period textual references imply that rulers like Polykrates of Samos or Dionysios I of Syracuse, constructed large, elaborate residences; yet physical evidence for these has been difficult to find. In the context of Athens, earlier scholars raised the possibility that the mid sixth-century BCE ruler Peisistratos may have resided on the Akropolis, and that only later did the precinct there gain an exclusively sacred role. Fragments of early pedimental sculpture from the Akropolis have been suggested to have come from the exterior of such a building. There is, however, no strong reason to interpret the sculptures as domestic rather than cultic – since all the other known uses of pedimental sculpture during the Archaic period connect it with sacred architecture. Another structure which has been suggested as a possible 'palace' for Peisistratos is 'Building F' in the Athenian Agora (Figure 6.1), erected just after the mid sixth century BCE.

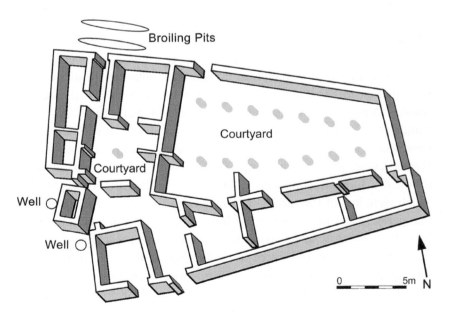

Figure 6.1 Athens, Agora, 'Building F'.
(Drawn by Laurel Fricker based on Thompson 1940, Fig. 13.)

This is a large courtyard building with an irregular plan. A few of the 'rooms' were free-standing, but the complex as a whole covered over 450 m². The excavators reconstruct a colonnaded court to the east and a further, smaller one with a porch, to the west. Two of the rooms off this western court seem to have been used for storage, and a free-standing bake-house occupied the southwest corner. Water was provided by two successive wells. Just outside the building, to the north close to the entrance into the smaller courtyard, two pits and numerous animal bones were found, seemingly residues from cooking. This area was accordingly understood by the excavators as a service wing for the main building centred on the eastern, colonnaded court, where the more spacious rooms were located. Initially Building F was published as a house, and it does incorporate features which later became characteristic of the larger houses in many Greek communities, namely a central courtyard, and rooms reached via a portico. As we shall see later in this chapter, the arrangement of space around two separate courtyards performing separate service and reception roles is one that is also found in later residential structures. Nevertheless, the scale and syntax of Building F are difficult to read as domestic. The structure is very large: an area of over 450 m² would be generous for a residential building in any period (compare the spacious houses at Olynthos, which cover about 290 m²). Building F could also be entered through two different doorways and there were doors directly linking some of the rooms, facilitating movement around the interior. Information about any artefacts found here might help to reveal whether the structure may have played a domestic role (for example loom weights would attest to cloth production which often took place in domestic contexts), but the remains are fragmentary since it was replaced by a later civic building (the tholos, thought to have served as a base for the city's prytaneis or magistrates). Given these facts, an equally plausible interpretation of the building is that it played a civic role, just like its successor.

At Athens, then, conclusive evidence for a monumental, Archaic, residential building has proved impossible to identify securely. While there is certainly variation in the scale of residential buildings in other Greek communities during the sixth and fifth centuries BCE, it is difficult to point to structures which seem in any way 'monumental' on account either of their size or of their decoration. In parallel with Athens, even where there are historical records of tyrants and oligarchs, buildings associated with them have not been located. Important work by Inge Nielsen has done much to address the origins and roles played by a variety of palaces, as well as to explore some of the influences by which they were shaped. Nielsen has shown that, on the fringes of the Greek world, there are examples of monumental administrative buildings which might be termed 'palaces'. The earliest excavated instances for which good evidence of the layout and use of space survives lie in areas under Persian influence such as at Larisa on the Hermos (in western Asia Minor) and Vouni (on Cyprus). In such places local monarchs and Persian governors built structures which drew on the architectural traditions of a variety of cultures. As well as deriving inspiration from the palaces of the Persian kings themselves (such as the series of building complexes at Persepolis in modern Iran) Egyptian elements were also incorporated.

The structure on the akropolis at Vouni is a relatively well-preserved example. In scale and construction, it is quite unlike anything we have encountered so far – it covered an area of over 5,500 m^2 (eleven times the size of the Lefkandi Toumba building). The walls were of mud brick while the socles were of carefully cut masonry blocks, and there was a ceremonial stone staircase (a feature of some of the Persian imperial palaces, including that at the capital Persepolis itself). As Nielsen points out, a striking feature of the Vouni building is its large central courtyard which had colonnades on three of its four sides, a feature sometimes attributed to Egyptian influence. In its original phase, dating to ca. 500 BCE, the Vouni building was also equipped with two small, service courtyards.

As we shall see, both the multiple courtyards and the colonnaded central court found at Vouni subsequently became key features of palatial buildings on the Greek mainland. These elements may have been developed independently in the context of the later structures (perhaps based on features found in smaller, domestic, ones), but the Vouni structure raises a possibility that Persian models may have had some influence over expectations about architectural form. There is a gap in the archaeological record of palatial buildings between about 500 BCE when Vouni was constructed, and the palaces of the Macedonian monarchs dating to the later fourth century BCE and later. Such buildings seem not to have been a feature of most communities for political and cultural reasons: at Athens, at least, the democratic ethos of the Classical era emphasised popular participation in the civic sphere. The comparable roles played by citizens in the political process may have discouraged individual shows of status in the domestic realm. Instead, the single-entrance, courtyard model was a means of demonstrating the cohesive nature of society and the participation of individual householders. On the whole, throughout the Archaic and Classical periods it seems to have been more acceptable to use dedications at sanctuaries or funeral rites as contexts for the display of wealth and status, rather than the domestic sphere. Judging by the archaeological evidence, the same seems to have been true of many other culturally Greek settlements.

The most complete evidence of a Macedonian palace comes from Vergina (ancient Aigai), historic capital of the Macedonian kings. The palace here was built in the late fourth century BCE, probably on the site of an earlier structure. Its location was dramatic: the building was perched on the edge of a set of hills and looked down on the adjacent settlement below. Its commanding view is emphasised by a terrace running its whole length on the north side (Figure 6.2a). The main part of the palace was organised around a vast peristyle and covered over 9000 m². Angeliki Kottaridi, who has undertaken fresh re-investigation and restoration at the site, has noted the enormous amounts of raw materials required to construct it, including cut stone blocks for the socle and mud brick for the superstructure. There was probably also an upper storey over at least the east wing, reached via sets of stairs occupying the narrow chambers at each end of the portico on this side, although nothing is known of the features or finds which may have come from this upper level, and therefore of the activities which took place there. Based on her recent investigations, Kottaridi considers the second, smaller, western courtyard to have been constructed at the same time as the main peristyle.

The Vergina building was clearly intended to be impressive when seen from the exterior, as well as being awe-inspiring inside. The main, eastern façade was painted in red and blue. It was decorated with a columned portico rising up two storeys, which incorporated the Doric architectural order below and the Ionic above. At its centre, a propylon (monumental entrance) led through a series of three ante-chambers into the peristyle. Nielsen suggests that the king would have used the inner space of this propylon as a formal audience chamber in which to receive visitors. There was also a secondary entrance on the south side of the peristyle, enabling the building to be accessed without the necessity of passing through the propylon.

Much of the interior of the Vergina palace is occupied by decorated rooms of different sizes, arranged around three sides of the main peristyle. Originally these had painted plaster walls and floors of marble or mosaic, with plain or raised borders suggestive of the positioning of couches around the walls. Such features parallel those of domestic androemes, suggesting that the rooms may have been used for the drinking- or dining-parties which ancient authors suggest were frequently held by some of the Macedonian monarchs. On the south side of the peristyle there is a three-room suite containing a central exedra (a chamber open to the courtyard along one wall) which gave access to a relatively small, decorated inner couch-room on each side. The entrances to those on the north side may

(a)

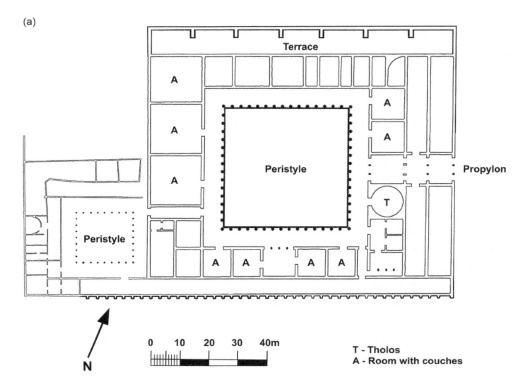

(b)

Figure 6.2 Vergina, palace. a. Reconstruction with all of the walls restored (drawn by Laurel Fricker based on Saatsoglou-Paliadeli 2001, Fig. 1 and Kottaridi 2011b, Fig. 32b); b. Photograph of the building viewed from the southeast, following the recent restoration work. (Robert Harding/Alamy.)

possibly have been arranged in a similar way although their entrances are no longer preserved. It is impossible to say for certain whether all of the couch-rooms were used simultaneously, but the fact that chambers of the same dimensions are duplicated suggests that at least some of them probably were on some occasions. Kottaridi reconstructs couches two metres in length and assumes two people per couch. On this basis as many as four hundred people could have been accommodated at once if all of the rooms were filled to capacity simultaneously.

Socially, the occasions taking place in most of these spaces must have been rather different in atmosphere from those held in cosy, domestic androns. While the smallest room would only have held seven couches, the largest could have had thirty. The distance across a room like this to those facing on the other side would have been more than sixteen metres. Add to that the effects of voices echoing off the hard surfaces of the floor and walls, and it must have been difficult or impossible to hold a conversation with anyone but those reclining on the same couch or an adjacent one. Such conditions suggest that the purpose of the events held here was different from the symposia envisaged as taking place in private houses. Participants were presumably expected to experience the spectacle of the monarch's hospitality, and perhaps of the monarch himself, but probably not to engage in much meaningful debate or dialogue with the group as a whole.

Evidence of other activities taking place in this building is conspicuously difficult to find. A room on the east side of the main peristyle is known as the 'tholos', owing to its circular interior shape (visible in the centre of Figure 6.2b). Its original use is unclear but in its later phase it was equipped with a throne and statue busts. Based on a cult inscription found nearby, the space has been suggested to have played a religious role. The recent investigations also located a room furnished with shelves which may have served as a library or archive. If the Vergina building served as a residence as well as being used for formal reception of guests, there are few clues as to where day-to-day life would have taken place. (It is important to note, however, that it was first explored during the nineteenth century and that the original excavators interpreted it as a prytaneion – a civic building - so indications of domestic activities may have been missed during the initial investigation, and indeed there is little evidence of artefacts which might reveal some of the activities that once took place here.) Bathing facilities, for example, are absent, even though, as we have seen, these had been incorporated into a number of the private houses at nearby Olynthos by the mid fourth century BCE. Service quarters which supplied refreshments to the various reception spaces are also not easy to identify. The relatively small rooms of the north wing and the upper storey over the east wing are two possible locations for household use. The second peristyle may also have provided a setting for some of these activities, since it is constructed in a more utilitarian fashion than the main peristyle, on a smaller scale and without evidence of lavish decoration. It was also equipped with its own entrance through which supplies could be brought in.

In sum, at Vergina, ostentatious display seems to have been a major role of the palace building, both as it was viewed from the exterior and as it was experienced by anyone entering through the main door and using the interior space. The columns of the façade and peristyle, the monumental entrance, the decorated couch rooms and the terrace overlooking the settlement below, would all have provided theatrical backdrops against which the monarch could have appeared with, and before, various groups of supporters, cementing his social bonds and power networks as well as enhancing his personal prestige. Because the large, peristyle courtyard was crucial to circulation patterns, any residential accommodation in the lower story of the main courtyard would have been closely intermingled with the spaces used for official functions. Nevertheless, the secondary court and upper storey also provided a possible location for living and service activities.

Although Vergina was once the capital of the Macedonian kings and retained a ceremonial importance, by around 400 BCE it had already begun to be eclipsed by the settlement at Pella, which became the new royal capital. Here, a much more extensive palatial complex became the main royal seat. This is located to the north of the settlement at the top of a gentle, southward sloping hill. The surviving remains cover a minimum area of 75,000 m^2 and consist of at least seven separate buildings which were constructed over an extended period of time (Figure 6.3). The palace's northern boundary is marked by a fortification wall (which encloses both it and the city) and the southern takes the form of a monumental facade, but to the east and west only the contours of the landscape can be used to suggest where the complex may have ended – its full extent is unknown.

Buildings I and II represent the core of the original structure. They were probably laid out during the third quarter of the fourth century BCE and provided the main ceremonial and reception spaces. Later construction added a variety of ancillary functions including comfortable living quarters (IV), a palaistra or exercise complex (V), baths (VI), storage areas (III, a building to the west of III and a building east of I and IV), stables (a building east of I and IV) and workshops for craft production (III).

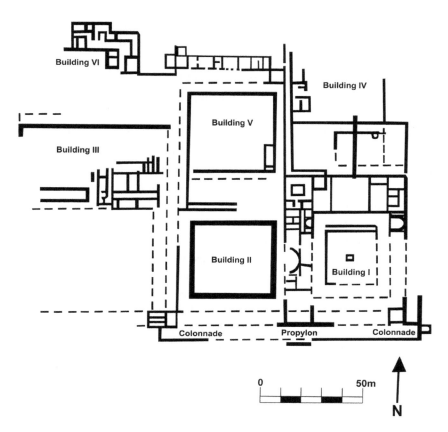

Figure 6.3 Pella, plan of excavated areas of the palace complex.
(Drawn by Laurel Fricker based on Tsigarida et al. 2021.)

Although the Pella palace is on a completely different scale from that at
Vergina, some features are shared by both. The city of Pella is located less
than 400 metres to the south of the palace and at a somewhat lower
elevation. As at Vergina, the architecture of the palace's exterior is used
to create an impressive stage for the monarch. The southern façade, facing
the city, was adorned with a colonnade pierced by a monumental entrance
(propylon). Here, too, emphasis was given to elaborate reception facilities.
In building I, for example, the northern colonnade of the peristyle is deeper
than those on the other three sides. Its importance is emphasised by an
apse at each end. Behind, also in a symmetrical arrangement and placed
centrally on the axis of the peristyle, are the largest, most highly decorated
rooms yet found here. They consist of a central chamber which is flanked
by smaller side-rooms. This may have resembled the exedra-complex
found at Vergina, although the locations of the entrances at Pella have

not been identified for certain. Many architectural elements recovered from this northern area of the peristyle testify to the lavish decoration of these and the surrounding rooms.

Although it is difficult to be precise about the roles played by individual spaces (and those roles presumably changed through time as additional courtyards were added to the original core of the building) it seems clear that the Pella palace fulfilled a range of functions necessary to support not only the ceremonial activities of the king but also the day-to-day requirements of a large retinue. To some extent this range mirrors that found on a small scale in houses: storage areas; decorated rooms for living and entertaining; courtyards for light, ventilation and access; and even craft production facilities. Nevertheless, in addition to the fact that the scale is vast, there are also striking functional differences: the reception rooms included some areas for large-scale audiences as well as others designed like andrones. As at Vergina, the andrones themselves are generally vast and must have been geared more towards spectacle than participation. In addition, the workshops may have been dedicated to fulfilling the needs of the household (in its broad sense) rather than to production for a market, as is likely for many workshops found in truly domestic contexts. There are also some components of the Pella palace which look more like those found in civic buildings – such as the palaistra (exercise building) in building V. Overall, this wide range of activities, as well as the colossal scale, must have made the complex feel like a small town, while various aspects of the architecture blurred the boundaries between housing and monumental civic buildings.

A somewhat similar situation may have prevailed at the so-called anaktoron (literally, 'palace', a name given by modern archaeologists) at Demetrias in Thessaly, central Greece. Its role is disputed but the excavated remains were probably part of a larger complex, similar to, but on a smaller scale than, the Pella palace. Unlike the buildings we have looked at so far, the low hill on which the anaktoron sits is located centrally within the city, close to a fortified akropolis or citadel, and to an agora (public square). The anaktoron represents the last in a succession of large buildings on this site: three predecessors have been interpreted as having filled a similar role. The first seems likely to have been laid out, as was the city itself, during the early third century BCE. Remains of these earlier buildings are only fragmentary, but it seems that the immediate forerunner of the anaktoron may have been organised around several courtyards, one of which was a decorated peristyle while another gave access, among other things, to a store of transport amphoras.

The anaktoron in its final phase was built in the late third century BCE. Like the structures it replaced, it is relatively poorly preserved, with the result that the location of the main entrance (or entrances) to the building and the form it (or they) took, are unclear. In plan, the most extensively investigated part is approximately square (ca. 60 by 61 m), with square towers on three of the corners and possibly also on the fourth. At its centre lies a peristyle. The north portico is wider than the other three and is distinguished from the them by its architectural decoration. The rooms on this side are also deeper. Plaster fragments suggest that the columns and walls of the peristyle were decorated with stucco painted to resemble marble, while the walls of some of the rooms were coloured a deep red. In some cases, doorways appear to have been placed off-centre, suggesting to the excavators that the rooms were furnished with couches and served as andrones. A further court or courts were located to the west, although little is known of the layout or role of these other areas.

A grouping of separate, but possibly functionally related, buildings at Pergamon in Asia Minor, has also been interpreted as palatial in function. The topography here represents a strong contrast with both Vergina and Pella: a precipitously steep akropolis dominates the town on the lower slopes below, and its fortification walls enclose a variety of structures including a theatre, cult buildings, and an arsenal, together with several peristyle buildings, all of which are built on a succession of terraces. The prominent location of the peristyle buildings – above and separated from the city, in a seemingly civic area – as well as their lavish decoration, has led the excavators to suggest that they must have been occupied by the royal household, and this is supported by the frequent occurrence of the word 'basiliki' (royal), stamped onto roof tiles found in them. Building I originated in the first half of the second century BCE. Its remains are much disturbed by later activity and cannot be reconstructed in detail, but it appears that the interior was organised around a peristyle which had rooms on two sides – the northeast and southeast, while the other two were enclosed by a wall. Nothing is known of the decoration, and recent discussion has been cautious about its potential use, suggesting it may have served as a barracks rather than as a royal residence.

The two best-preserved, residential buildings from this akropolis area are the so-called palaces IV and V, which both date to the first half of the second century BCE (Figure 6.4). They lie adjacent to each other and are interpreted by Inge Nielsen as parts of a single unit, although they are oriented differently and are not physically interconnected. Building V, to the south, occupies an irregular plot of about 2400 m^2, arranged around a

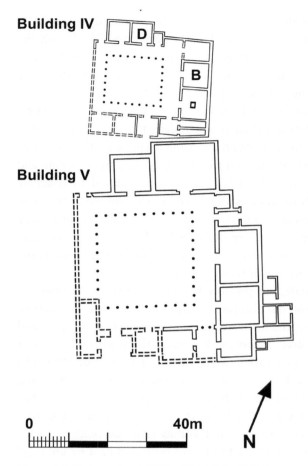

Figure 6.4 Pergamon, palatial buildings IV and V from
the akropolis.
(Drawn by Laurel Fricker based on Hoepfner 1996, Fig. 16.)

single large peristyle. As restored, there are two entrances: a monumental
one with a recessed prothyron leads into the western end of the southern
colonnade, while a smaller, simpler entrance opens from the north of the
building into the northern colonnade. The interior rooms are arranged on
three sides, while the fourth, the west, was probably enclosed by a wall.
There is no evidence of any attempt at symmetry or axiality in the
organisation and alignment of the different rooms. In the largest, on the
northern side towards the eastern end, the walls were stuccoed and painted
to resemble marble. The floor was destroyed by subsequent building
activity in the area, but the floor of the neighbouring room was decorated
with a polychrome mosaic. Both rooms contained the remains of marble
architectural elements.

To the east of the peristyle, the smallest, northernmost room is the most intensely decorated surviving space, with a marble socle and a fine polychrome mosaic floor depicting theatrical masks and patterned panels, which is signed by the mosaicist. A marble base found here was interpreted by the excavators as an altar. Insufficient evidence of the rooms further south is preserved to enable them to be discussed, although the smaller chambers behind them seem to have been entered only from the outside.

Building IV, to the north, covers approximately 1050 m², a smaller area than its neighbour, and both the central court and the individual rooms are on a more modest scale. As reconstructed, this also has dual entrances: again, the more elaborate one is on the south side of the building, this time leading into an anteroom, while a second, simpler doorway gives onto the northwestern corner of the peristyle. In parallel with building V, the interior rooms are arranged on three sides of the peristyle, with an enclosure wall on the fourth, to the west. Those that are preserved best are in the northern and eastern parts of the building: the largest has at its centre a marble block interpreted as a hearth or altar. Traces of coloured plaster and mosaic in the fill here suggest that the walls and floor were decorated. Fragments of painted wall plaster were also found in the neighbouring room, B and in the northwest room, D. Room D also had a mosaic floor, and a variety of elaborate architectural mouldings were also recovered from here. It is, therefore, possible that these spaces were reception or living rooms, although no further conclusions can be drawn.

Buildings IV and V are different in scale from each other, but they do seem to represent similar patterns of organisation and roles which are – as far as the limited architectural evidence suggests – comparable. This raises the possibility that they may have accommodated two separate households, although in the absence of information about the artefact assemblages it is impossible to investigate this further. Given the location, the residents may well have been members of the royal family, and if so, their separation in self-contained quarters on a relatively intimate scale is striking compared with the more integrated arrangement of the Vergina palace and presumably the earlier phases of the Pella palace as well. Furthermore, at Pergamon the monarch was enclosed within a fortification wall which separated him, along with a variety of civic facilities, from the hustle and bustle of the remainder of the city. The scale of the two buildings suggests use by small residential groups who entertained only limited numbers of individuals, in contrast with the massive scale of the Macedonian palaces. The Pergamene 'palaces' by themselves, therefore, gain their symbolic weight in a different way from those at Vergina and Pella – from the monumental, often religious, buildings located around them on the akropolis, or perhaps from the akropolis as a whole, arranged as it was on a series of dramatic terraces scaling the hillside. As Inge Nielsen suggests, such contrasts may reveal differing roles played by the monarchs in the two kingdoms in relation to their subjects, with those at Pergamon set up as remote, inaccessible figures, while the kings of Macedon invited a more personal relationship and closer interaction with their people.

In sum, although the Vergina palace may have had an earlier phase which now lies inaccessible, there is little to suggest that such structures had a long history in Greece, stretching back into the Archaic period. To what extent and in what ways might the introduction of these large, palatial buildings have related to the design and decoration of contemporary residential structures? During the late Classical period, experimentation took place with domestic structures which were built on alternative plans, and on different scales, from their predecessors, and which seem to some extent to have been connected with the kinds of palatial buildings we have just examined. It is to these new types of houses that we now turn.

Changing Scales: Double-courtyard Houses

Elements of the monumental palaces just discussed are most obviously found in some smaller-scale residential buildings in which space is arranged around two courtyards. This pattern of organisation is normally found in houses of a relatively large size, although they are not invariably larger than their single courtyard counterparts. How, then, did the roles played by these double-courtyard structures compare with those of their palatial peers?

Examples of double-courtyard houses dating from the fourth century BCE onwards have so far been found in a small number of widely scattered locations: at Eretria (Euboia), Maroneia (Thrace), Erythrai (Asia Minor), Priene (Asia Minor), and, on a larger scale, at the centre of the city of Pella, below the palace. At Eretria at least three different double-courtyard houses have been excavated in the area close to the West Gate. One of these, the House of the Mosaics, covers about 625 m² and is organised around two adjacent courtyards which were apparently divided by a wall (Figure 6.5). The location of the doorway(s) connecting the two parts could not be discovered from the evidence preserved. There was no sign of stairs, so there may only have been a single storey.

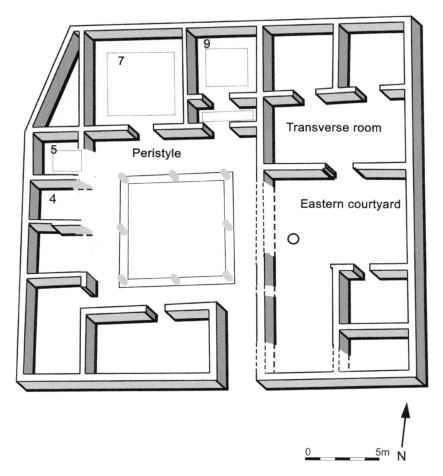

Figure 6.5 Eretria, House of the Mosaics.
(Drawn by Max Huemer based on Ducrey 1993, Fig. 25.)

In the western courtyard a peristyle gave access to a variety of rooms, several of which were decorated in an elaborate manner: the excavators found here a number of terracotta plaques and stone architectural mouldings. In the courtyard, outside room 4, the base was located for a marble sculpture of a young man. (Such an object is an unusual find in a domestic building at this date. This might be because it remained here when the rapid destruction of the house by fire in the early third century BCE caused the owners to abandon an item of a kind which, when other houses were abandoned in different circumstances, would normally have been removed.) Three rooms of different sizes leading off the western courtyard were paved with figural pebble mosaics with plain borders (Figure 6.6).

Figure 6.6 Eretria, House of the Mosaics, detail of the mosaic floor in room 9 (rear) and its anteroom (foreground). (The walls and roof are a modern restoration). (Christos Salas/Alamy.)

They could accommodate, respectively, three couches (room 5), seven couches (room 9) and eleven couches (room 7). The different scales involved, and the contrasting numbers of individuals who could comfortably have used each room, may have resulted in gatherings which varied in their character and level of intimacy. We cannot say for sure whether these rooms were used simultaneously or at different times (or a combination of these options on different occasions). But it is interesting that spaces of equal size were not simply duplicated. Instead, the rooms might have been designed to offer a choice of settings for different scales of event, or to create some form of hierarchy among guests, according to whether they were placed in a smaller, more intimate space, or a larger one with more fellow participants. The spaces for couches and the decoration in these rooms seem to fit them for the formal reception of visitors at the kind of symposium discussed in Chapter 3. The single street door of the house leads directly into the western courtyard via a corridor. From the entrance a passer-by or visitor would have glimpsed the doorway to andron 9 beyond the columns of the peristyle, but interestingly, this is the only one of the couch rooms that had an anteroom. This anteroom together with the alignments of the various other doors would have meant that the occupants of any of the rooms are unlikely to have been visible to passers-by in the street even when the house door was open.

If the western courtyard was a complete peristyle, then in order to support its roof the wall separating the eastern and western courtyards may have risen to roof height along most of its length, with a doorway (or doorways) giving access to the eastern part of the house (the exact form of the wall is uncertain because it is not completely preserved). The eastern courtyard was less formal in character than the west. The excavators suggest that it may have been planted as a garden. Rooms led off here to both north and south. To the north is a transverse anteroom with two adjacent rooms behind, similar to those in the two houses near the Silenos Gate at Limenas on Thasos. In the House of the Mosaics, there is no evidence for the original height of the outer wall of the anteroom, which could either have been solid up to roof level, or could have been a low structure supporting columns or pillars, which would have enabled light to penetrate the rooms behind. (The latter arrangement has been suggested by Karl Reber for the wall between room 9 and its anteroom, where a carved stone mullion implies an opening between the two.) Although the rooms in the eastern part of the house lacked the figured mosaic floors and raised borders of their western neighbours, they were still relatively carefully built: four of them boasted plain mosaic floors while the two northernmost also featured painted plaster walls.

Direct evidence for the role played by this eastern section of the house is scarce. The separation of the two parts raises the possibility that they may have been occupied independently by two different (although not necessarily unrelated) households. Yet the apparent complementarity of the rooms in each one argues against such an interpretation, as, perhaps, does the fact that there seems to have been a single street entrance serving both (although this is a situation not unknown in apparently separate residential units elsewhere in the ancient world). Another possibility is that the activity taking place in the western court was not strictly 'residential' in nature: could some of these rooms have been 'rented out' to diners or drinkers? Or were they used as settings for some kind of official or business dealings? Could either the western part of the building, or the structure as a whole, have played a role which, from a modern western perspective, might seem 'non-domestic'? Such suggestions are hard to evaluate on the basis of the published evidence. As noted above, the sculpture is a very uncommon find in a domestic building of this date, although statues are found more frequently in such contexts by the second and first centuries BCE. Information about the other artefacts recovered from the different spaces, which might serve to identify some of the activities taking place, has not so far been published. Furthermore, while the neighbourhood in which the building was located seems to have had a residential character, we have seen in previous chapters that in Greek cities some neighbourhoods (and even single buildings which can be interpreted as houses) were also used for a range of purposes, which in the context of other cultures would not necessarily be thought of as residential. In short, then, neither the evidence available from the structure itself, nor its context, is conclusive.

An additional way to address the interpretation of the House of the Mosaics is through comparison with other, similar buildings. As noted above, although its double-courtyard form is rare, it is not unique among late Classical and Hellenistic buildings interpreted as houses. Two larger, double-courtyard houses have been excavated in the same area of Eretria. One of them, house IV, incorporated what we would today think of as commercial activity in the form of a potter's workshop in its western section (Figure 6.7). This arrangement dates to the third century BCE

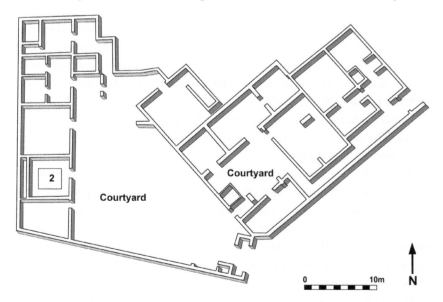

Figure 6.7 Eretria, house IV, phase 2B and 2C.
(Drawn by Max Huemer based on Reber 1998, Fig. 138.)

and the two courtyards of the house originally formed the nucleii of two separate properties, so the parallel is only a superficial one. Interestingly, the first phase of the building's western half, dated to the start of the fourth century BCE, was decorated with the Doric order and was equipped with three square rooms, one of which had a raised border (2). Based on their shape, all three rooms were identified by Reber as andrones, and he proposed that, in its original phase, this part of the building had a civic function. Another adjacent structure, House I, also appears to have had multiple courtyards, but again, this seems to have resulted from combining pre-existing properties rather than designing a double-courtyard building from the beginning.

A closer parallel for the House of the Mosaics is a building of around 640 m² at Maroneia in Thrace, perhaps built in the fourth century BCE (artefacts found there range in date from the fourth to the second century BCE) (Figure 6.8). The walls are preserved only to a maximum of 45 cm in height and the interior is not excavated completely to the southern perimeter across its full extent. Nevertheless, there is clearly a comparable spatial division between one area reconstructed by the excavators as a peristyle,

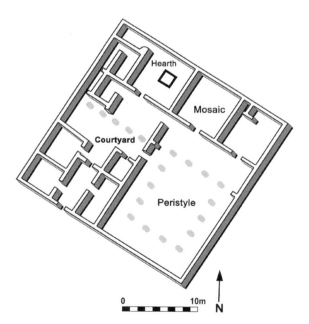

Figure 6.8 Maroneia, double-courtyard building (southwestern area reconstructed by the excavators).
(Drawn by Max Huemer based on Lavas and Karadedos 1991, Fig. 1.)

and another focused around a smaller courtyard, in this case to the west. The two sections seem to have been partitioned from each other by a wall, but to have communicated in at least two places, through the northern portico and through the courtyard. Giorgos Karadedos, who published the house, records extensive use of coloured wall-plaster, present in all the rooms, which usually formed a grey or grey-blue dado and an upper zone in red, yellow or white, or in a mixture of those colours. The exterior of the house, too, was covered in a pinkish-red waterproof mortar. While plaster may have been poorly preserved and under reported in many houses of this date, the extensive use of coloured plaster here (in other Classical houses the main colour in use was often plain white except in a few locations where colour was used for emphasis, as, for example, at Olynthos) suggests a concern with the appearance of the majority of spaces.

It is important to recognise that there are significant differences between the Maroneia building and the House of the Mosaics. For example, the peristyle at Maroneia is significantly larger, composed of fourteen columns rather than eight. The number of rooms leading off the peristyle is smaller, consisting of only two, which are of equal size. The western room had a mosaic floor with a plain border and is probably to be identified as an andron which the excavators estimate would have held eleven couches. Although the walls of the second room were fairly well preserved, little evidence is recorded of its decoration or contents to suggest how it may have been used.

The organisation of the second court is more complex. To the north the excavators reconstruct a colonnade continuing the line of the northern portico of the peristyle. Behind lies a large room with a monumental marble hearth at its centre. A series of walls in the north-eastern corner of the house mark out three further spaces. Although the area in the southwest was not excavated to floor level, Karadedos suggests that there were several spaces there including an entrance lobby which was the location of a single street door serving the entire house. Overall, the evidence currently available about the Maroneia structure suggests that it was a residential building divided between a peristyle potentially used for entertaining (although other activities may have taken place there as well) and domestic quarters (featuring the large hearth room) centred around a smaller second courtyard. In contrast with the House of the Mosaics, if the location of the entrance is reconstructed correctly, the arrangement of space would have brought any visitors through the domestic area before they entered the peristyle. The builders would then seem to have privileged display of their domestic arrangements over total separation between the two spheres. The colonnade, and perhaps also the marble hearth, if that could be glimpsed through an open door, may then have been designed not only to create a comfortable living environment for the residents, but also to catch the eye of visitors as they moved through to the peristyle. If so, this may represent a parallel to the way in which the inhabitants of Olynthos sometimes drew attention to their own courtyards using coloured plaster, architectural elaboration and even occasionally mosaic. There, too, the andron was sometimes placed away from the entrance to the house and any visitors would have had to traverse the courtyard in order to get to it (see Chapter 4). While the scale of the peristyle at Maroneia may have made it impressive, the more restricted range of decorated rooms suggests the hosting of social occasions which may have been more modest (since there is lower capacity in total) and more standardised (since there is no choice of different sizes of room).

Across the Aegean, in the city of Erythrai, a further building on this plan with architectural features of Roman date was apparently originally constructed in the fourth century BCE (Figure 6.9). While somewhat smaller in scale than the House of the Mosaics, and rectangular in plan, rather than square, it shares some of the same features. Few details have been published by the original excavator, Ekrem Akurgal, but according to a reconstruction by Wolfram Hoepfner, a wall divided the interior into two parts. To

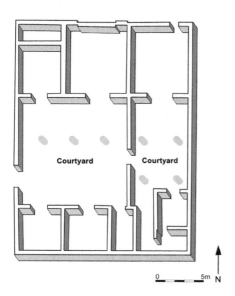

Figure 6.9 Erythrai, double-courtyard building.
(Drawn by Max Huemer, based on Hoepfner 1999, figure on page 451.)

the east lay a narrower area centred on a paved open court. A single large room to the north had an arrangement of stone slabs at the centre which have been interpreted as the base for a wide table. The room's wide doorway may have compensated for the reduction in daylight caused by a deep porch in front and by the relatively small size of the unroofed court. A further complex of rooms to the south of the court is interpreted as a cooking area. The broader part of the building, to the west, is organised around a larger courtyard furnished with a pastas on its northern side. Four different rooms on the north and south sides were arranged as banqueting rooms by the Roman period (a space similar to the Greek andron but with couches running along only three of the four walls). The main street entrance for the building led into the larger courtyard. The smaller one could be entered through a door in the dividing wall, which was placed off axis in relation to the street door. A secondary entrance appears to have led directly into the hearth room through the north wall, interrupting the line of sight from the doorway into the eastern courtyard. It is unclear to what extent the organisation and decoration of the rooms reflect those of the pre-Roman phases. If they do, then the structure prompts similar questions to those raised by the House of the Mosaics about the identities of the users of the multiple couch–rooms and the types of occasions on which those rooms were occupied.

The double-courtyard plan is also sometimes found in Greek settlements of the western Mediterranean. At Megara Hyblaia, for example, the Archaic structures mentioned in Chapter 5 were succeeded by larger, more substantial ones in the Classical, Hellenistic and Roman periods. These include a late-fourth century BCE, double-courtyard building, house XV B (also known as 49,19). Recent re-examination of its surviving remains has yielded new insights into its history and plan. It seems that this was conceived from the beginning as a double-courtyard house, with an open courtyard to the north and a second to the south that had porticoes on its west, south and east sides, and rooms to its east and west (Figure 6.10). While information on the associated artefacts is not available, the architecture suggests that this southern peristyle may have performed the role of a reception area, while its northern counterpart may have supported domestic activities. In its first phase the house is reconstructed as having had two separate entrances, one for each court, each of which led in from the road on the house's eastern side, via a foyer. To the north, (B6) had a pair of doorways, a narrow one for pedestrians and a wider one for wheeled vehicles whose ruts were found on the threshold block. The second, to the south (B4), led into the peristyle. As Annette Haug and Dirk

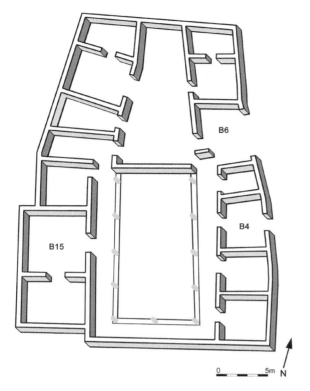

Figure 6.10 Megara Hyblaia, house XV B, phase 1.
(Drawn by Max Huemer based on Haug and Steuernagel 2018, Fig. 272.)

Steuernagel point out in their recent and detailed analysis of the building, because the doorways are more-or-less aligned, there would have been a view to the opposite side of the colonnaded court, where the doorway of the largest room (B15) would have been visible. By the time of the house's destruction this, and a small room created inside its neighbour to the south, stood out from the rest of the rooms in their level of decoration: instead of beaten earth, the floors were made of a thin layer of polished mortar and the walls were plastered. In the house's second phase, though, the entrance to the peristyle had been relocated southwards into a lobby area with a second doorway into the courtyard that was off-set, effectively obstructing the view into the house. While the entrance arrangements of this house are somewhat different from those of most of the other double-courtyard buildings we have looked at, the overall division of space seems similar, with one simpler courtyard which may have hosted the more domestic areas, and a second, more elaborate one that seems to be designed as a more impressive, perhaps pretentious, space. It also shows an awareness of sightlines and a desire for visual privacy that echoes some of the Classical single-entrance, courtyard houses.

Multiple courtyards, on a much larger scale, are also used in the House of Dionysos, south of the agora at Pella, which dates to the last quarter of the fourth century BCE. Here, the excavated area covers more than 3000 m². Only the floors and some of the stone socles of the walls survive. Patterns of access are not always clear, but the general layout can be reconstructed (Figure 6.11). A single street door was located at the centre of the east wall and was highlighted on the exterior by two Ionic columns. Beyond lay an antechamber with a larger room behind. From here it was possible either to move to the south into an extensive peristyle courtyard, or north into a somewhat smaller one. On two sides of the southern

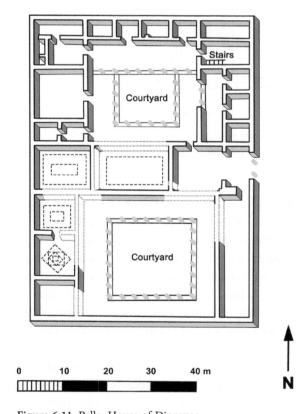

Figure 6.11 Pella, House of Dionysos.
(Drawn by Max Huemer, based on Makaronas and Giouri 1989, foldout plans 1 and 7. The locations of missing walls and the layouts of the mosaics are indicated with dashed lines.)

peristyle lie large, decorated rooms in a range of sizes, although the level of preservation is such that the entrances of most cannot be reconstructed. The surviving mosaics – including the figured scene showing the god Dionysos riding on a panther, after which the excavators named the house (Figure 6.12) – hint at the richness of the original décor: some of these rooms have floors with raised or reserved borders, suggesting that couches were placed there, although their scale is far larger than any domestic andron we have so far encountered. A number of architectural elements found in the courtyard show that this, too, was elaborately decorated, and the tiles, simas and other building materials were embellished with red, blue and yellow pigment. To the north, the second peristyle gives access to a larger number of rooms on a much smaller scale (Figure 6.13). Its northern side is deeper than the other colonnades, recalling the

Figure 6.12 Pella, House of Dionysos, pebble mosaic showing Dionysos riding on a panther.
(Science History Images/Alamy.)

Figure 6.13 Pella, northern part of the House of Dionysos viewed from the south. The room dividing the nothern and southern peristyles is in the foreground, with the Ionic columns of the restored northern peristyle visible behind.
(John Heseltine/Alamy.)

arrangement of some of the larger, palatial, peristyles. To its east a long antechamber connects to a row of three rooms behind. A staircase in the northeast corner may have led to an upper storey, at least over this part of the building. The contrast in scale and decoration between most of the rooms located here and those around the southern peristyle suggests that domestic or service quarters may have been accommodated here, while the southern courtyard may have been used for entertaining.

The House of Dionysos picks up some elements of the rare double-courtyard houses already discussed: first, a variety of decorated rooms of different sizes; and second, an apparent spatial division of large, decorated areas for living and entertaining from smaller, plainer spaces which may have been used for domestic or service purposes. Nevertheless, the scale is very different – even the smallest of the decorated rooms, at 9 m square could have held more than thirty couches. The entrance arrangements are also deliberately monumentalising. Based on the architectural elaboration of both courtyards, multiple decorated rooms and also the sheer scale, it seems likely that a residential role would have been combined with a more formal, perhaps political, one, as a location for receiving visitors and putting on a display of wealth and power – much like a monarch in his palace. Indeed, it is the surviving palatial architecture, rather than the smaller double-peristyle houses, which provides the best parallels for the level of ornamentation and the spatial syntax of the building. Despite their scale and decoration, however, these buildings probably did not belong to the monarch, who had ample quarters elsewhere. It may be that the owners of this and several other monumental neighbouring houses, were members of the Macedonian nobility who were involved in the life of the court. They may have picked up on cues such as the scale and decoration seen in the royal palatial buildings, deploying them at a (relatively) smaller scale for themselves. While comparably monumental dwellings are rare elsewhere, they are seemingly not unique to Pella: at Kastro Tigani on Samos, for example, the partial remains of an extensive double-peristyle building covering at least 50 m by 80 m by the late Hellenistic period, is similar in terms of scale and elaboration, including a southern peristyle which was left open on its south side to give a view of the sea.

What light do these comparative examples shed, first, on our interpretation of the House of the Mosaics at Eretria and second, on the relationship between domestic and palatial buildings? On analogy with the other double-peristyle structures we have looked at, it seems likely that the eastern section of the House of the Mosaics served as an informal service court, as suggested by the hearth rooms giving onto the secondary court both at Maroneia and Erythrai. At the same time, the various sizes of decorated rooms seem to provide for a range of social groups of different sizes.

On balance, it seems that at least some of these double-courtyard structures were built to be residential, even if some also incorporated activities we would not necessarily think of as 'domestic' today. Since relatively few examples are known, they were probably a rare phenomenon. In a few cases, including the fourth century BCE phase of houses C and D from near the Great Drain in the Athenian Agora, two separate single-courtyard houses were later combined into one unit. In addition to their unusual pattern of organisation, all but the Maroneia house share another characteristic which may be important to understanding them, which is the creation of multiple spaces for entertaining. This contrasts with most other houses of the fourth-century BCE, where, as we have already seen, there is generally, at most, a single andron and anteroom. Another prominent characteristic in two of our examples is the monumental hearth, which highlights the hearth's symbolic role, long recognised based on references in ancient texts. Again, this contrasts with other examples of comparable date, where although built hearths are occasionally found, they are relatively rare.

The most striking characteristic of these double-courtyard buildings is their scale: they range from covering around 50 per cent more ground area than the houses found at Olynthos, up to more than ten times that size – an indication of the population they were built to serve. It is important to note, however, that it would have been possible to build houses of this size around a single courtyard. (A single courtyard arrangement was sometimes used at a later period on Delos for houses covering 600–800 m^2 in area, although a double-courtyard plan was also in use there, too, normally for more modestly proportioned homes, and often as a result of combining two pre-existing properties.) There is, then, something deliberate about the double-courtyard arrangement, which may have been built to support a particular notion of how domestic and non-domestic roles could or should be combined. At the same time, the double courtyard was surely a mark of wealth and status, and even sometimes perhaps an allusion to palatial architecture, thus enhancing the prestige of its occupants.

A Gendered House?

One issue which has featured prominently in the discussion of several double-courtyard houses is the possibility that the spatial division between entertainment and domestic areas corresponded to a social one, between the spheres belonging to the male and female members of the household. The double-courtyard arrangement offers the closest surviving parallel for the comments of the first century BCE Roman writer Vitruvius, who describes Greek houses as offering separate areas for their male and female inhabitants (Text Extract 10). Although he was writing several centuries after the period of use of the buildings discussed above, Vitruvius' ideas echo a theme emerging from some Classical writers, that men and women habitually confined themselves to separate spaces within the house (Text Extracts 12 and 13). These passages seem to result from a general sensitivity about contact between women and unrelated men. The duplicated andrones found in most of such buildings seem designed to separate visitors from areas used by members of the household, adding an important nuance. In this connection, it is tempting to return to the question of whether several andrones may have been used simultaneously. If they were, then the gatherings inside them may have spilled out into the peristyle, with participants moving between rooms. In such a situation, the provision of a second, domestic, court would have enabled household tasks to continue relatively undisturbed while social occasions took place in and around the peristyle. At the same time, however, where the two courtyards were separated by a wall, it would not have been possible for the occupants of one courtyard, or the rooms leading off it, to monitor the movements of those in the other courtyard and surrounding rooms. Thus, while the double-courtyard house enhanced the separation between household members and guests, it also reduced the ability to command the entire household from a single location.

The range of activities accommodated in these double-courtyard buildings and the way their inhabitants used space cannot be sketched in more detail without some information about the distribution of artefacts and ecofacts through the different spaces. It remains possible that in some cases entertainment may have taken place as part of a civic duty or a commercial enterprise (for example, combining residential quarters with a larger version of the tavern identified by Evi Margaritis at Hellenistic Krania, based on archaeobotanical data). For now, rather than imposing a text-based interpretation onto the archaeological evidence, it seems preferable to view these double-courtyard buildings in the context of the prevailing single-entrance, courtyard house model, understanding them as evidence for an increasing separation between 'outward facing' and 'inward facing' spheres, rather than as dividing the two sexes per se. The inhabitants of such properties may have engaged in civic or commercial activities which involved entertaining on a larger scale and/or with greater frequency than the occupants of other contemporary houses, and it may have been this role that the two courtyards were designed to accommodate.

The use of multiple courtyards is also an obvious solution to problems of providing light, ventilation and access to many rooms, and one that could easily have been devised independently in different contexts. The colonnade could be seen as a reference to the architecture of gymnasia and other civic, or perhaps even religious, buildings, thus enhancing the prestige of the householder; but it also has a functional aspect, supporting the roof over a combined walkway and activity area alongside the courtyard, sheltering the entrances of the rooms behind from sun and rain. As previous chapters have shown, a separation between reception or living space, on the one hand, and service and/or storage facilities, on the other was fundamental to Greek houses over a long time-period and a wide geographical area. A multiple-courtyard arrangement simply accentuated a spatial separation which was already visible even in small, early houses such as those at

Zagora. While it may have served to separate domestic activities from reception of visitors, it need not necessarily have been linked to a gendered use of space per se but was part of the underpinning of a more complex web of social interactions and cultural etiquette.

Conclusion: Scale and Symbolism in the Houses of the Late Classical Period

The creation of palatial buildings and double-courtyard houses may be an indication that the symbolic role played by the domestic sphere was changing during the fourth century BCE. At least at Athens, under the democracy, textual sources indicate that it was civic life that was viewed as the proper sphere of the male citizen. Certain authors (for example, Demosthenes: Text Extract 1) suggest that lavish expenditure in the domestic sphere had increased and was immodest or even unacceptable (although, of course, this position was a rhetorical one and may have been influenced more by contemporary political events than by past cultural practices). At the same time, however, it is important to emphasise that as far as we can tell, only a small minority of buildings made use of this design in comparison with the vast majority, which continued to favour the single-courtyard layout. As we shall see in Chapter 7, large, as well as modest, houses tended to adopt a single-courtyard plan, even during the third and second centuries BCE. Within a given plot, the single-courtyard layout allowed for a larger circulation space at the centre of the house and for bigger reception rooms, creating more of a feeling of monumentality. The double-courtyard house, therefore, seems to have been an idea which had limited appeal, even among wealthy households: it may have been attractive only in specific circumstances. In the later fourth century BCE it perhaps carried connotations of an elite, or even royal, lifestyle. It also emphasised a particular set of values which involved a separation between reception of guests on the one hand, and domestic life on the other, similar to those which underpinned the single-entrance, courtyard house. In addition, from a practical point of view, it enabled the separation of reception space from the areas required to keep the household running: spaces for storing and processing food, cooking and perhaps also craft production. In the end, however, it seems to have been the importance of the house as a more general symbol for enhancing personal reputation which came to outweigh other considerations. As Greek cities were incorporated into the Hellenistic kingdoms, their residents began to use housing to symbolise different sets of ideas, as we shall see in Chapter 7.

7 | Greek Housing into the Hellenistic Period

The Transformation of an Ideal?

As we have seen in Chapter 6, during the fourth century BCE, the introduction of double-courtyard houses together with a dramatic increase in the size and decoration of the largest domestic buildings both suggest that changes were taking place among a few households in the ways that their dwellings were conceptualised. In addition to expressing support for the ideal of separating residents from outsiders, these new, large properties also seem to display individuality, symbolising the personal wealth and status of their owners. In this final chapter we see that during the Hellenistic period (from 323 through to 146 BCE) it was the second of these roles that became dominant in the designs of houses belonging to elite households, who adopted elements of the architectural vocabulary of the largest fourth-century houses: courtyards were re-envisioned as full or partial peristyles, making use of the Doric and Ionic architectural orders. The complex featuring a central exedra with flanking dining rooms, seen at Vergina, was widely used. Both floor mosaics and wall paintings became increasingly sophisticated. Using this architectural language, elite households sought to align themselves with others like themselves, forming a social and economic status group that crossed political, but also to some extent cultural, boundaries, to reach across much of the Mediterranean and even beyond. At the same time, these elites also differentiated themselves from the other members of their own communities who did not (and perhaps in most cases could not) build such houses. Among these households, too, there were changes in the dominant house-forms. The courtyard was often reduced in size and seems to have been less important than in earlier times, either as a location for domestic tasks, or as a communication route for moving around the house – a role which sometimes came to be played instead by an interior space. As we shall see, however, there is significant diversity across the Mediterranean. In mainland Greece, present evidence suggests that the peristyle was not used very frequently: rather, it is concentrated in the eastern and western Mediterranean, and is found even on the shores of the Black Sea, among communities in which the smaller houses, and the artefacts found within them, often exhibit strong elements of local cultural traditions.

One of the major factors contributing to this fragmentation in types of domestic architecture during the Hellenistic period may have been increasing inequality in the distribution of economic resources and political power, following the incorporation of Greek cities into the kingdoms which succeeded the empire of Alexander the Great. For members of the elite, the reconfigured political landscape replaced their immediate communities as a focus for group identity; instead, there was a network of geographically dispersed peers and superiors to emulate. Among the less wealthy, the decline of civic institutions perhaps removed pressure to articulate social norms concerning interaction between members of the household and outsiders, leading to the decline of the single-entrance, courtyard house.

The focus of discussion in this final chapter is on sites from the area covered by the modern Greek state, but we also draw on some well-preserved examples from further afield, in Asia Minor, in the western Mediterranean and on the northern Black Sea coast. The quantity of the available evidence, together with the diversity in the layout and architecture of the houses, makes it impossible to be comprehensive. Instead, a few examples are highlighted which demonstrate the emergence of the elite peristyle house as well as the increasing heterogeneity of the domestic arrangements among less well-off households.

The Peristyle House: Part of an Elite Cultural Koine

Houses in which a single courtyard took the form of a full or partial peristyle have their roots in the Classical single-entrance, courtyard house (several peristyles are found in houses at Olynthos, for example). In the Classical context, the courtyard's generally more modest decoration, and the utilitarian artefacts associated with it, suggest that it had a largely functional, domestic role. By the Hellenistic period, however, the importance and role of the courtyard were changing. In addition to the architectural mouldings, painted plaster and mosaic sometimes found in a Classical courtyard, sculpture became more frequent in peristyles of Hellenistic date.

Several of the sites discussed in earlier chapters continued to be occupied into Hellenistic times, and peristyle houses were sometimes created by modifying or re-building earlier structures. At Priene, for example, the prostas of an earlier house was sometimes transformed into a peristyle. Decoration became increasingly sophisticated: walls were moulded in plaster and painted to resemble large stone blocks in the andron, although no evidence has been found for mosaic floors. Such may have been the early

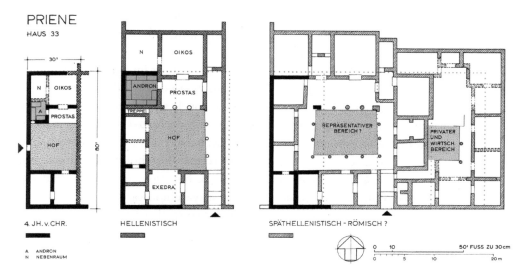

PRIENE

HAUS 33

Figure 7.1 Priene, Hopefner and Schwandner's plan of house 33 in its fourth century BCE, Hellenistic and late Hellenistic to Roman phases.
(Reproduced from Hoepfner and Schwandner 1994, Fig. 218, courtesy of Wolfram Hoepfner.)

Hellenistic form of house 33, one of those originally excavated by Wiegand and Schraeder and more recently re-investigated, with a phased plan reconstructed in detail by Hoepfner and Schwandner (Figure 7.1). Successive owners enlarged their property at the expense of those of their neighbours, and also of an adjacent street. At first the original courtyard and rooms were extended, including the andron, in tandem with the creation of additional rooms. After the earthquake and fire which hit the city in the mid second century BCE, most of the excavated houses were reconstructed, including House 33. Its owners annexed land both to the north and to the east of the original building so that by the late Hellenistic or early Roman period the structure was composed of two courtyards: the existing one was transformed into a peristyle, while a second smaller one and further rooms were added to the east. This resulted in a building resembling the House of the Mosaics at Eretria and the Maroneia house (see Chapter 6) in terms of the organisation of space, with a single entrance giving directly onto a more elaborate western courtyard which led to a variety of rooms and also to a second, smaller and more functional service court. The scale is much larger, however (the whole building covered about 1,000 m^2) so that the division between the two parts is very pronounced, with a row of rooms separating them, rather than simply a boundary wall.

A similar process of modification is also found at Kassope, where the hearth-room houses of the fourth century BCE were reconfigured, often radically, through the third, second and first centuries BCE. In the second century BCE, one of them, house 3, was enlarged by annexing land from the plot to its north (Figure 7.2). The southern courtyard now represented a full peristyle giving access to a nine-couch andron. A communicating door led from the peristyle to a smaller, less-decorated court located to the north, with a portico on its western side. Each courtyard apparently had its own separate entrance from the street so that the whole establishment was similar to Megara Hyblaia house XV B, but more permeable than was typical of most other earlier double-courtyard houses.

A comparable practice of combining two smaller houses to provide one larger, double-courtyard property is visible on the Cycladic island of Delos, where as many as 100 different residential units of various sizes and layouts have been investigated, dating mostly to the second or earlier-first century BCE. They were frequently modified, with processes of expansion and

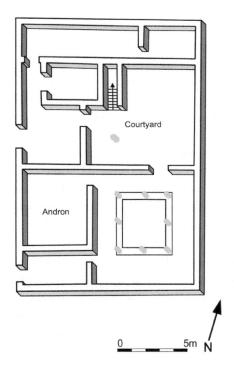

Courtyard

Andron

0   5m   N

Figure 7.2 Kassope, house 3, second century BCE phase.
(Drawn by Laurel Fricker based on Hoepfner and
Schwandner 1994, Fig. 155.)

annexation comparable to those just discussed. Interestingly, the extensive excavations here suggest that the double courtyard arrangement was never a particularly popular one: even where a sufficiently large space was available to accommodate two courtyards, an extensive, single peristyle was normally preferred. The excavated houses include many different examples arranged around a peristyle, or partial peristyle. One which seems to align quite closely with the configuration of the earlier, single-entrance, courtyard house is the Hill House, built in the second half of the second century BCE (Figures 1.8 and 7.3). It is approximately square in plan and covers an area of just over 300 m². The walls are well preserved because, like those of most of the other buildings on the island, they are constructed in stone, rather than partially in mud brick. A single entrance leads via a corridor on the west side, into the peristyle. This occupies the majority of the space and has an especially deep colonnade on its northern side. The largest rooms, to the north, are entered from here, with two smaller ones each to east and west. Although the top of the cistern, which originally underlay the peristyle, has caved in and the remains of the walls are weathered, the importance of the peristyle is still discernible to the modern viewer: not only is it large in proportion to the surrounding rooms (which

Figure 7.3 Delos, Hill House, viewed from the south looking into the peristyle.
(Author's photograph, courtesy of the Ephorate of Antiquities of the Cyclades. The rights to the monument shown belong to the Hellenic Ministry of Culture and Sports (Law 3028/2002). Delos is under the supervision of the Ephorate of Antiquities of the Cyclades, Ministry of Culture and Sports.)

are relatively few in number as a consequence), but also, the columns are worked in marble and their upper sections are fluted. Traces of painted plaster still remain on the walls, which on the eastern side of the peristyle can be seen to mimic monumental masonry. In fact, when the house was first excavated in the late nineteenth century, it was possible to reconstruct an elaborate decorative scheme which included 'masonry style' mouldings together with figurative panels.   Particularly notable are the windows, which rarely survive in the more typical mudbrick construction. The two large reception rooms at the centre and west corner of the northern range each have two large windows facing onto the peristyle, one on either side of the door. In addition, further windows opening onto the street behind the house were provided in all three of the rooms in this northern range. (A west-facing window in the northwest corner room is not visible in the photograph.) Presumably the external windows provided ventilation and some light, although because they were above head height, they were not intended to offer a view into the adjacent street; instead, in the north-western and central rooms, the attention of the occupants was focused on the view into the peristyle, through the pairs of lower, internal windows. The location of the northeastern room, tucked into a corner, may have meant that little light could enter from the peristyle, necessitating windows onto the exterior on both the northern and eastern sides.

Peristyle houses of this level of regularity and simplicity in design are rare on Delos. More typically, interior space falls into suites of rooms that are sometimes connected directly. The multi-storey Hermes House, for example, is terraced into the hillside on several levels, with a peristyle that may originally have risen three storeys (Figure 7.4). While the surviving remains suggest that it had only a single courtyard, some differentiation of space is visible, with service quarters leading off the entrance corridor at ground level (a toilet, B, along with bathing and cooking facilities, K and C) while the peristyle gave access to decorated rooms and to the upper storey, with suites of rooms entered in series as well as individually from the court. The house features a three-room group with a single outer room, and two inner rooms located side-by-side behind (rooms D, E and F).

Not all of the courtyard houses on Delos were large enough to accommodate a complete peristyle, but the concept was frequently echoed by creating colonnades along one, two or three sides, often making use of marble columns with Doric or Ionic capitals, which stood alongside painted plaster, and, on occasion, also mosaics. Even a house without a colonnade could be embellished in other ways. For example, house III S in the Theatre Quarter boasted a large marble sculpture of the goddess

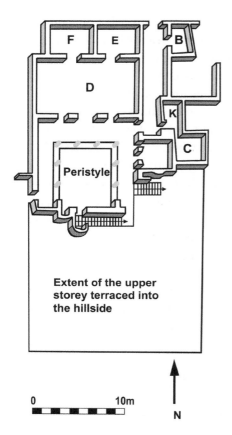

Figure 7.4 Delos, Hermes House, ground floor.
(Drawn by Laurel Fricker, based on Delorme 1953, Plate XLVI.)

Artemis killing a deer, cleverly placed in a corner of the courtyard so that it was visible even from the street, if the front door was open. Despite the large numbers of residences that have been excavated, it is mostly impossible to connect the architecture with associated artefacts. Many of the houses were uncovered at an early date and their contents were recorded as generic examples of domestic furnishings but without precise information about where they were found. Even in more recent excavations where the inventories of rooms have been studied, their interpretation is not straightforward. For example, the House of the Seals appears to have been destroyed by fire in the mid first century BCE, preserving a range of associated artefacts. Nevertheless, Monika Trümper, who studied the inventory in detail, comments that the ground floor appears to have been used for commercial production and storage, while the personal items associated with the domestic lives of the occupants apparently fell from the upper storey, their precise context lost. Similarly, the wealthy houses of the Insula of the Comedians seem to have served during their final phase as a dye works, and the artefacts recovered relate mainly to these activities rather than to the original use of the building for residential purposes. It is, therefore, safest to confine discussion to architectural evidence.

The importance placed on the courtyard at Delos, along with the attention paid to vistas into it from outside the house, suggest that although some of these structures resemble the single-entrance, courtyard house in some respects, the social context in which their residents were operating was fundamentally different. Less emphasis seems to be placed on isolating the interior and more on the house's role as a status symbol. At the same time, the productive aspect of the household also seems to take second place, with the service quarters of the larger buildings relegated to dark interior rooms, rather than being provided with their own exterior court-yard space. Two important points to keep in mind when considering these houses are their relatively late date (second to first centuries BCE) and also the character of the island's population. It is clear from epigraphic evidence that this included individuals from southern Italy and from the eastern Mediterranean. Influences from the cultures of those regions are detectable not only through a range of religious buildings that catered to them, but also in some of the motifs used in domestic contexts, which include images of the Compitalia (rituals associated with non-elite religion in southern Italy) painted and re-painted on exterior walls; the organisation of space may have been similarly influenced. Nevertheless, by creating peristyles, the owners were tapping into a set of 'globalised' ideas about elite culture which, to some extent, transcended more geographically localised cultural identities.

A similar point can be made about housing in other areas of the Hellenistic Mediterranean. Some of the most extensive and best-preserved evidence comes from the island of Sicily, which, as we saw in Chapter 5, had a long history of migration from Greece, as well as hosting settlements belonging to indigenous groups and still others established by Punic settlers. The island as a whole came under Roman control after the First Punic War in the mid third century BCE. Peristyle houses seem to have been pervasive among the elite inhabitants of settlements here with a range of cultural origins. Examples are particularly well preserved at Monte Iato (ancient Iaitai), in western Sicily, where, like Delos, the house walls were built of stone and survived up to four or five metres in height. Trial trenches across the city have suggested that there were multiple large, elaborately decorated houses located here, including both single- and double-courtyard buildings. House 1, which has a single peristyle, appears to date to the third century BCE, although it may have been occupied for up to four hundred years and there has been some debate about its precise chronology (Figure 7.5). In its first phase, the building covered approximately 665 m^2 of ground floor space, with further rooms in an upper storey. The original entrance, which led to the peristyle via a narrow corridor from the west side, was soon augmented by a second one from the south, which led into the peristyle through a large vestibule. In contrast with some of the Delian houses, the vestibule's exterior doorway and that leading into the peristyle are not aligned, as if to reduce visibility into the interior of the house from the street when the door was opened. Once a visitor was inside, the peristyle played a major role in communication around the house – comparable to the court in the single-entrance, courtyard house. The main reception rooms lie to the north and consist of an exedra (16) flanked on either side by a reception room. Unlike examples of this arrangement we have already seen (for example in the palace at Vergina), the western reception room (17) could also be entered directly from the peristyle, without passing through the exedra. Due to the excellent preservation, it is possible to see that a door and also two windows opened from the exedra into each of the flanking rooms. Thus, it seems that the exedra provided light to its neighbours, particularly to (15), which received

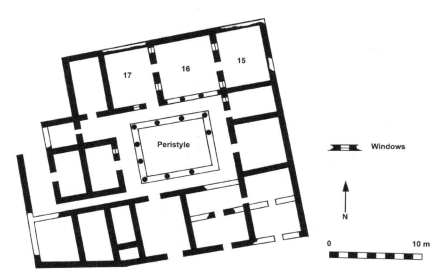

Figure 7.5 Monte Iato, peristyle house 1, phase 1.
(After Nevett 1999, Fig. 49.)

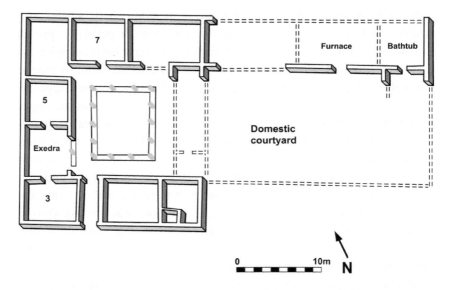

Figure 7.6 Monte Iato, peristyle house 2.
(Drawn by Laurel Fricker based on Reusser et al. 2011, plan on page 83 and Russenberger 2013, Fig. 1.)

no light directly from the peristyle. A notable feature of house 1 is a set of elaborate bathing facilities, added to the north-west corner in a later phase (not shown). These attest to an interest and investment in bathing that is an order of magnitude larger than any we have seen so far: a built tub lined with hydraulic plaster was provided with water that was heated in an adjacent room.

Another dwelling at Monte Iato, House 2, which dates to the late second century BCE was a double-courtyard building, with ornate reception rooms around a peristyle court to the west, while the domestic apartments were reached from a second courtyard to the east (Figure 7.6). Surrounding the western peristyle three different andrones were apparently provided, two of which (rooms 7 and 3) could accommodate nine couches while the third (5) had space for seven. Again, two of these (5 and 3) were arranged on either side of an exedra. Upper storey rooms lay over at least some of this part of the house, and fragments of fallen floor- and wall-decoration suggest that some of the upstairs rooms were decorated more elaborately than those on the ground floor. Like the later phase of house 1, house 2 had a sophisticated bathing facility: it was located off the domestic court and incorporated a furnace to heat the water, coupled with a large, built tub in the next room, which may have accommodated more than one bather at once. While the presence of the peristyle must have linked the occupants of these and other peristyle houses in the settlement with the elite households of other communities across the Mediterranean, the bathing facilities seem to have been characteristic of the local cultures of Hellenistic Sicily (examples of similar suites have been found elsewhere on the island, in apparently communal, as well as domestic, settings).

Examples of peristyle houses have been found in various settlements elsewhere on the island, not only those with a strong Greek material cultural heritage but also including others showing Punic or local influences. Among the former, Solunto has been extensively excavated: work began in the nineteenth century and has uncovered part of the city laid out on a grid plan, with long, narrow insulae. The excavated area includes sections of a number of different residential insulae which are terraced into the hillside, preserving parts of multiple storeys of some of the properties. The original date of their construction has been debated, with suggestions ranging between the fourth and second centuries BCE. As preserved, the architectural features of many of them suggest a second century date, with some earlier walls and some later modifications. In places, these houses are preserved to a height of over three metres owing to the steeply sloping terrain, so that evidence is preserved of their overall character and pattern of organisation in the final phase of occupation. Elaborate decoration includes opus signinum floors (made of cement incorporating ground up ceramics), painted wall plaster and peristyle courtyards in Doric and Ionic orders.

An example is the so-called Gymnasium excavated in the nineteenth century and actually a private house. It has been dated to the third century BCE based on the architecture of the Doric peristyle (Figure 7.7). The main living space was terraced into the hillside and three levels survive comprising about 630 m^2 in ground area. The lowest was on the southern, downslope side, and comprised a row of four rooms entered independently from the street, which are interpreted as shops. The main part of the house itself lies on the next level, some 4 metres above. It consists of the peristyle together with rooms surrounding it (Figure. 7.8). The central space has a vaulted cistern beneath. The twelve columns of the colonnade appear to have been connected by a low wall in a later phase, with an opening on the southern side. The main suite on this level consists of an exedra complex: the central exedra on the east side of the peristyle had a broad entrance, its opening supported by a pair of Doric columns. The flanking rooms to which it gave access are reconstructed as a seven-couch dining room to the north, and a nine-couch dining room to the south. The smaller rooms on

Figure 7.7 Solunto, view of the peristyle of the so-called 'Gymnasium'.
(REDA & Co srl/Alamy.)

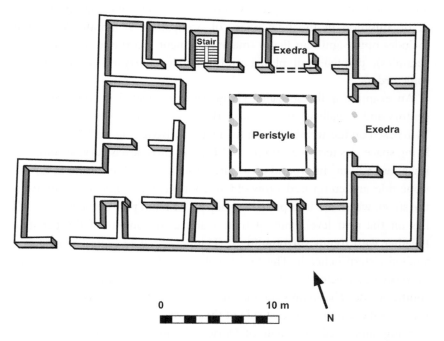

Figure 7.8 Solunto, the upper story of the so-called 'Gymnasium'.
(Drawn by Laurel Fricker based on Wolf 2003, Fig. 45.)

the northern side of the peristyle are reconstructed as a further exedra and two small side rooms – the eastern one having its own independent entrance as well as connecting with the exedra. A staircase in the north-west corner of the peristyle gave access to an upper storey at a height of about 5.7 metres above the peristyle, with further rooms behind. In this house, then, despite the Punic cultural heritage of the settlement, both the peristyle court and also the exedra with flanking dining rooms would have looked familiar to a visitor from Monte Iato or from further afield.

At Morgantina, a long-established inland community in the east of the island, the occupants of the Classical city combined both local Sikel and Greek elements in their material culture. More than 24 houses have been excavated here. Although the most common form was the pastas house, by the Hellenistic period the largest, most elaborate domestic structures were laid out on elongated rectangular plots which covered at least 600 m^2, including one or more peristyles. Some, like the House of the Official, also had space in an upper storey. Decorative features include mosaic floors and capitals making use of the Doric architectural order.

In addition to these and other sites in the western Mediterranean, peristyle houses have also been found in communities on the Black Sea coast. For example, at Olbia, Hellenistic houses in the Lower City in many ways resemble those already discussed. Relatively modest houses with a single courtyard and three to seven rooms in area NGS can be contrasted with the more pretentious dwellings of Sector NGF. Here, a pair of large houses both incorporated andrones and substantial colonnades. House 1 had an irregular plan and covered an area of approximately 540 m^2 (Figure 7.9). As reconstructed, a single entrance led via a narrow corridor on the eastern side into a trapezoidal, paved court. This had porticoes to the north and east and was surrounded on all sides by rooms. A total of eleven are reconstructed above ground, with another five in the basement, clustered in the northwest corner. The northern colonnade was deeper than that on the east and gave access to the basement via a flight of steps. An andron, complete with off-centre entrance and raised border is reconstructed beside the entrance (11). The degree to which movement around the house could have been monitored from the peristyle is unclear: in most cases it seems that the thresholds were not well preserved, although one pair of rooms in the northern range does seem to have been interconnected. (The positions of the individual interior spaces could have allowed all but those in the north-east and south-east corners to be accessed independently from each other through the courtyard.)

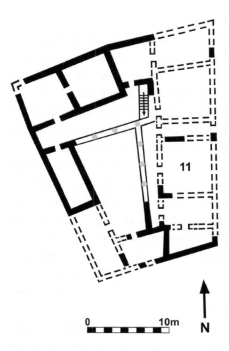

Figure 7.9 Olbia (northern Black Sea coast), area NGF, house 1.
(Drawn by Laurel Fricker based on Wasowicz 1975, Fig. 99.)

The neighbouring house, house 2, which is slightly smaller at around 414 m², was also arranged around a paved court which seems originally to have been a complete peristyle (Figure 7.10). A total of 18 rooms are reconstructed here, and the organisation of space seems to have been more complex than that of its neighbour, partly due to the location of the peristyle on the south side of the building. A group of 6 rooms clustered in the north-east corner could only be entered in series, and their design may have been influenced by the presence of basement rooms lying beneath five of them. One of the outer ones here (2) is reconstructed as an andron with a raised platform around three of the four walls. A second entrance to the house was reconstructed on the north side, although the remains here seem to have been destroyed by a pit, so the reason is not clear. Elsewhere in the settlement other architectural features are reminiscent of contemporary houses in the Mediterranean. For example, excavations in a poorly preserved house in the Upper City uncovered a figural mosaic floor, possibly associated with a domestic andron, which also had an elaborate architectural façade featuring a pediment and pilasters or columns.

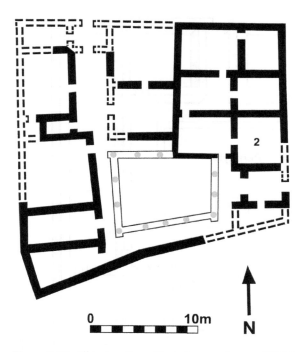

Figure 7.10 Olbia (northern Black Sea coast), area NGF, house 2.
(Drawn by Laurel Fricker based on Wasowicz 1975, Fig. 99.)

Similar structures are found at other sites around the Black Sea by the Hellenistic period: at Crimean Chersonesos, several exceptionally large properties dating from the late fourth or early third century BCE were excavated in 1908–1909. One of these covered about 650 m² (Figure 7.11). The surviving wall socles are of carefully dressed blocks which are similar to those used in the city's civic buildings. Aspects of the layout and facilities clearly parallel houses from the Mediterranean: a narrow entrance corridor on the west side led into a central peristyle furnished with a well or cistern. This courtyard gave access to a total of twelve separate rooms of different sizes which communicated only via the court except when they were located in the corners of the house, making this impossible. A further passageway to the north led up a flight of steps. It is unclear what lay beyond, although it is tempting to speculate that the house may have had a second courtyard. The walls of the rooms here were originally plastered and painted red and yellow. No evidence of floor decoration was found in the building, but elsewhere in the settlement a polychrome pebble mosaic depicting two nude women at a louterion has been interpreted as belonging to a domestic andron, although the room in which it lay seems to have been of irregular shape.

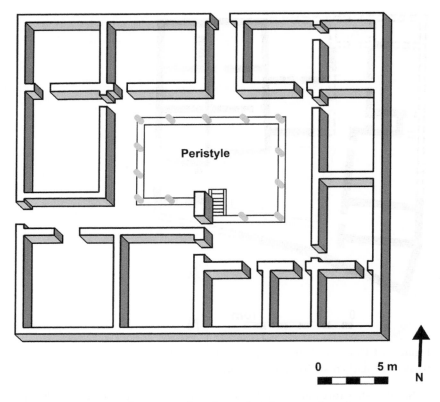

Figure 7.11 Crimean Chersonesos, large house (windows not shown).
(Drawn by Max Huemer based on Mack and Coleman Carter 2003, plan on page 82.)

Houses such as these are on a scale rivalling those of some of the wealthiest communities of the Aegean and the variety of artefacts found in some of them show that residents were able to take advantage of imported goods, such as wine and fine table-pottery, from as far afield as Asia Minor and even Attica. The wealth and the range of material possessions available at Olbia during this period may perhaps have been related to the role of the settlement as a port. The city was probably shipping out commodities including the grain for which it was well-known in Antiquity and which large Aegean cities such as Athens relied upon to supplement their home-grown supplies. At the same time, wine was imported from the eastern Aegean, together with other consumer products, some of which were possibly transhipped to neighbouring settlements. The use of peristyle courtyards, mosaic floors and architectural decoration tied the residents of both Olbia and Chersonesos into a common Hellenistic cultural network, and the presence of andrones in some of the houses may have implied that they participated in social activities resembling those of the wealthier residents of households in Greek cities in the Aegean (although it may have been this implication – rather than the actual practice of such activities – that was important to the owners of the properties). While the finds of transport amphorae suggest that wine was significant in the culinary lives of households in this region, they do not necessarily confirm that consumption took place in social contexts that were exactly comparable to those in other regions. In general, the extent to which patterns of activity in peristyle houses across the culturally Greek world and beyond might have been similar is difficult to gauge. The poor preservation of many of them, the variable information about the location of doorways and the lack of detail about the distribution of artefacts in the interior, all make the social use of space difficult to reconstruct.

Alternatives to Elite, Peristyle Houses

Alongside elite peristyle houses, a range of other forms of dwelling were created during the Hellenistic period. In some cases, these seem to have belonged to households of a more modest socio-economic status than the occupants of the peristyle houses. At Delos, for example, shops and workshops consisting of only two or three rooms may have provided living accommodation as well as business premises, although little can be said about the use of space within. Elsewhere, however, particularly where the evidence of architecture and layout is supplemented by information about some of the artefacts found in the interior, it is clear that in a few instances the residents had access to significant economic resources but that other house-forms were preferred. In some cases, the size and importance of the courtyard were diminished and there was a tendency to use an indoor room as the main circulation space (a pattern comparable to varying degrees with the hearth-room house, discussed in Chapter 4). In other instances, houses follow plans that seem to be unique to their specific communities, or even to the specific districts or neighbourhoods in which they are located. Finally, in some settlements, modestly sized houses, each with an open courtyard and only two or three undecorated rooms seem, on present evidence, to represent the majority of properties. These resemble similarly sized houses we have seen from earlier periods, for example at Ano Siphai (see Chapter 4).

One of the most recently investigated and intensively recorded Hellenistic houses is the House of Lampon, a second-century BCE dwelling at Priene. (The house was named by the excavators after the name on a ceramic mould found in the building). Through their work on this structure the excavators aimed to understand the organisation and artefact inventory of a large residence at the time of the earthquake and fire which caused widespread destruction across the city in around 140–130 BCE. This particular house was selected for detailed study because it was in an area of the city that had not been reconstructed by the residents after the earthquake (for the location see Figure 5.5) nor had it been investigated in the course of earlier archaeological work. The assemblage was, therefore, likely to be intact, and indeed preliminary publications show deposits of artefacts (mainly ceramics) apparently crushed in situ as the building collapsed.

The house has an area of approximately 260 m^2 (Figure 7.12). Unlike the later House 33, discussed in Chapter 6, the House of Lampon has

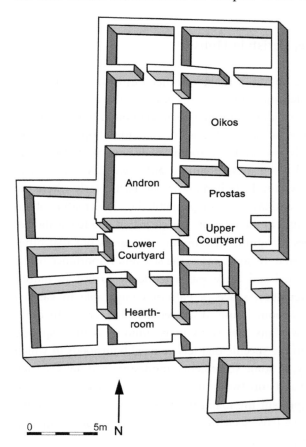

Figure 7.12 Priene, House of Lampon.
(Drawn by Max Huemer based on Rumscheid 2014, Fig. 5.)

linked courtyard areas with clusters of rooms to the north and south. The plot is irregular in shape and there are additional rooms to the west, including a large andron which in its final phase accommodated seven couches. Not all of the doorways could be located during excavation, but the layout of the house is clearly less centripetal than the single-entrance, courtyard houses explored in previous chapters. Here, both courtyards are small, and the northern and southern groups of rooms constitute clusters which are separate from them. Some of the interior spaces must, therefore, have been entered in sequence, rather than being accessed individually from the court or prostas. The House of Lampon's rectangular plot shape presumably represents a choice made by the city's earlier inhabitants, although the excavators suggest that in the first phase of construction in this location there was some unbuilt space incorporated into the insula, which presumably allowed some limited flexibility in the laying out and extension of the individual houses. The arrangement of the interior of the House of Lampon, therefore, seems to be partly the result of a conscious choice made to limit the importance of the courtyard and to enhance the role of the main internal spaces as routes for moving around the house, in a way that, to some extent, parallels the hearth-room house, discussed in Chapter 4.

Although the House of Lampon yielded evidence for ceramic production, this does not mean that the socio-economic status of its occupants was necessarily modest; in fact, the structure as a whole was among the larger and more elaborate residences found in the city. Moulded and painted wall plaster was used in at least six of the rooms, including the andron. In preliminary articles, project director Frank Rumscheid comments that the finds were unusually rich in both number and variety. Along with the usual selection of pottery, the assemblage included a gold finger-ring, a hoard of 60 bronze coins, numerous lead weights and even some fragments of coloured glass. Overall, the collection indicates a household with access to a variety of material goods and possessions. This, together with the size and decoration of the building itself, suggests that the occupants may have been among the wealthier inhabitants of the city during this period. By contrast, while they and their peers were adorning their homes with such architectural decoration and costly possessions, some of their neighbours came to occupy only parts of the house-plots belonging to previous generations, which had now been subdivided between more households.

The catastrophic destruction and detailed recording of the House of Lampon arguably offer a uniquely detailed window into the standard of living of a single Hellenistic household. It is difficult to compare this building – which apparently collapsed rapidly during an earthquake – with others that suffered the more common fate of falling gradually into disuse while their occupants (or neighbours) may have removed at least some of their most prized possessions along with re-usable building materials, and perhaps also dumped rubbish in the vacated property. Nevertheless, houses elsewhere show comparable characteristics in their layouts. For example, some of those at Nea Halos, in Thessaly, follow a similar pattern. The city had a short lifespan: it was founded at the very end of the fourth century BCE and abandoned during the mid third century BCE. A regular street grid enclosed a series of houses with rectangular plans of which eight have been excavated. The individual plots varied in size, ranging between about 190 and 265 m². (Dimensions are sometimes approximate because the remains were found so close to the modern ground-surface that preservation is not always complete.) Although each house has a courtyard, it seems that in at least some cases this was more important as an activity area than as an access route. In the House of the Coroplast, for instance, a large courtyard takes up most of the western half of the building and seems to have been used for craft production (Figure 7.13). The eastern half, which is likely to have been residential, consists of a suite of several small, interconnected rooms. In other houses, less emphasis appears to have been

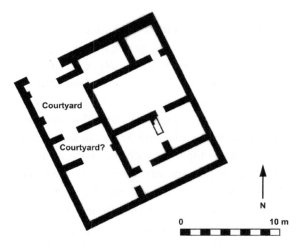

Figure 7.13 Nea Halos, House of the Coroplast.
(After Nevett 1999, Fig. 38.)

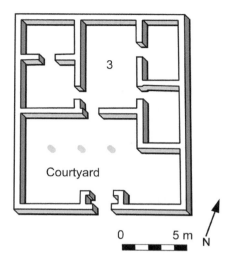

Figure 7.14 Nea Halos, House of the Geometric Krater,
Phase 1.
(Drawn by Laurel Fricker, based on Haagsma 2003, Fig. 2.19.)

placed on craft production but the interior rooms are often still arranged in suites. For example, in the House of the Geometric krater (Figure 7.14) the reconstructed plan suggests that the single largest room (3) served as the major hub for communication, rather than the courtyard. The organisation of space in some of these dwellings, therefore, looks more like that of the hearth-room houses than it does the pastas or prostas type. A comparable layout is also found elsewhere: for example, at Polymylos in western Macedonia, a Hellenistic- to Roman-period housing district probably belonging to the ancient city of Evia, was located during rescue excavations. The houses are described as covering approximately 220 m² in area and organised around a central covered space.

A variety of more locally specific layouts are also found during the Hellenistic period. Often these belong to relatively small houses which lacked architectural elaboration and might have been inhabited by households of modest means. There are exceptions, however. For example, at Kallion (ancient Kallipolis) in the central Greek mainland, a row of four houses was probably built when the city was laid out during the late fourth century BCE and continued in use until their violent destruction by fire sometime between the third and mid second century BCE. They lay on a major urban thoroughfare and were excavated under rescue conditions before being submerged beneath an artificial lake. House IV offered the clearest picture of the internal arrangements at the time of the fire because subsequently it was neither reinhabited nor rebuilt. The destruction-layer preserved a rich assortment of artefacts which, like those from the House of Lampon at Priene, were presumably in use during the final moments of occupation.

House IV was square in plan and covered an area of about 270 m^2 (Figure 7.15). The courtyard constituted a narrow strip of ground dividing two ranges of rooms to its north and south. There was no evidence for any kind of portico although the extent of the roof was not absolutely clear. The excavator, Petros Themelis, compares the layout of house IV with the hearth-room type houses found at Ammotopos and Kassope, which have similarly small courtyards. Like Ammotopos house 1, Kallion house IV had a large living room or oikos with a monumental hearth at its centre, marked by marble slabs. Not all of the doorways were marked by stone thresholds, which meant that circulation patterns could not be reconstructed with certainty by the excavators. Nevertheless, it is clear that the courtyard was the main circulation space, rather than the hearth-room, so that in this respect the layout was more similar to the single-entrance, courtyard house.

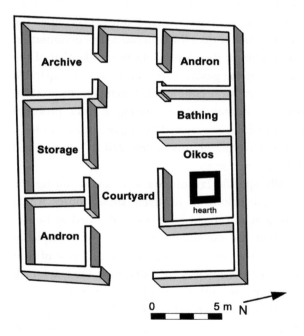

Figure 7.15 Kallion, house IV.
(Drawn by Max Huemer, based on Hoepfner 1999, figure on page 432.)

Among the other facilities in house IV were a storage room and a bathing space complete with drainage. Several mosaic floors incorporated decorative patterns, while stuccoed walls in some rooms were moulded and painted to resemble large marble blocks. Two different androns lay in opposite corners of the house. Each had an off-centre doorway, mosaic floor and raised border. Both were the same size, with space for five couches. In addition, a room referred to by Themelis as the 'archive' also had an off-centre doorway and plastered walls but no raised border or mosaic floor. This space contained more than 600 clay sealings, apparently from a collection of papyrus documents stored there at the time of the house's destruction. Themelis argues for the existence of an upper storey over at least the western part of the house, based on a variety of finds which had apparently fallen from above. They included: a group of loom weights (which were scattered on both sides of the south wall of the western andron); a range of decorative and personal items found in the storeroom; and pieces of a mosaic found above the floor level of the bathing room. The nature of these artefacts suggests that important living space was located upstairs in addition to that found at ground level.

Other evidence for the furnishings was also found: fragments of engraved ivory located with the sealings may once have decorated the exterior of some kind of box; small silver nails with decorative heads may have been part of a casket; and a variety of bronze fixtures and fittings found throughout the building probably came from furniture and interior doors. There were also a variety of decorative artefacts, including a terra-cotta statuette with applied gold and three large, marble statuettes which, again, appear to have fallen from above. In addition, the destruction level yielded a variety of fine pottery vessels including cups and jugs in red-figure and west-slope ware, some of which were apparently stored on shelves in one of the androns.

This building presents something of an interpretative challenge in that it yielded evidence potentially suggestive of what, in a modern western context, we might think of as both 'domestic' and also 'non-domestic' activities. The collection of documents to which the sealings were once fixed might be viewed as an indication that the users of the property were active in both commercial and civic capacities (the sealings suggested to Themelis that some records had a personal, and others a more official, character). Furthermore, the two separate, comparably sized androns imply that two gatherings of similar numbers may have taken place here simultaneously and perhaps separately – again possibly implying a com-mercial or civic function (such as the individual rental of dining rooms or the entertainment of two groups simultaneously by different officials). But the finds of loom weights suggest that the building's role was, at least in part, residential. Despite its relatively modest size, the furnishings and decoration such as the sculptures, stucco decoration and mosaic floors, imply that this property would have provided a comfortable living environment. Activity areas cannot be reconstructed in detail because the full inventories and details of the artefact distributions are not, so far, available. It is, therefore, difficult to know whether any domestic activities were carried out in the small courtyard, apart from washing which was provided for by a louterion set into a pebbled surface in front of the storeroom. Although the court was central to communications, the narrowness of the space may have limited the tasks taking place there. The lack of a pastas or prostas may also have made the courtyard less practical to use in hot or wet weather, although its small size may have meant that it was shaded by the upper storey of the house for some of the day. The space between the western andron and archive may have been roofed to provide a portico-like area.

In common with the occupants of the House of Lampon at Priene, those of Kallion house IV had access to a wide range of material goods requiring either specialist manufacturing techniques, or imported materials, or both. Thus, despite the relatively modest scale of the building, its inhabitants probably had significant financial resources at their disposal. While it is impossible to know how representative the assemblage in this house is of other houses of comparable date and size, what it does suggest is that building an elaborate peristyle courtyard was not the only means by which householders in the Hellenistic period may have used their houses to assert their status. Instead, the occupants created decorated rooms and furnished their homes with a range of prestige items. These two examples also indicate that by the second century BCE some households were gaining access to an increasing number and diversity of consumer goods, including exotic materials such as ivory and glass, alongside the ceramics and metalwork typical of earlier periods.

A different scale of dwelling, and a much more restricted assemblage, prevails among a group of relatively small houses in the Rachi settlement, at Isthmia, which was occupied ca. 350–210 BCE. Both the location and the character of the evidence from here are somewhat reminiscent of the material from the Koile Valley in southwest Athens, discussed in Chapter 3. Excavation has revealed a variety of rock-cut features clustered onto a rocky ridge and terraced into the slope below on the south side (Figure 7.16). Although some of the site has been destroyed by recent

Figure 7.16 Rachi, Isthmia, plan of the settlement.
(After Anderson-Stojanović 2016, Fig. 4.2, courtesy of the Trustees of the American School of Classical Studies at Athens.)

quarrying, it is still possible to get a sense of the ancient settlement once located here. The rock-cut features originally served as the bases of walls, and as the floors for living spaces. Each structure originally had low wall-socles which combined field stones and cut stone blocks, with mud brick above and a tiled roof. Occasionally the rock surface seems to represent a basement and there is evidence of a floor at a level above that was originally supported by columns (of which the bases survive) or by beams for which sockets were cut into the vertical rock-face. Virginia Anderson-Stojanovic, who published the material, estimates that, in all, about twenty to twenty five houses have been revealed, although a number of factors make them difficult to reconstruct and interpret: excavation took place in two separate episodes and the infor-mation available from the earlier one is limited. The degree of preservation is also variable. At the same time, party walls are shared by different buildings, so that the boundaries of each property are not always very clear. Finally, the alleys giving access to the houses followed the natural contours rather than being arranged on a grid. These alleys were only 1–1.2 m wide, making them potentially difficult to distinguish from interior spaces. (Flights of rock-cut steps also provided access in the steepest locations.)

Based on the published plan, it appears that the houses at Rachi range in size between about 55 m^2 and 80 m^2 and generally comprise two or three rooms together with an open courtyard – sometimes identified by the presence of a rock-cut cistern in one corner. Where evidence of doorways is preserved, the entrance from the street seems to have led into this courtyard – in a comparable manner to the arrangement seen, for example, in some of the smallest houses near the Agora at Athens. The organisation of interior space is not standardised, although Anderson-Stojanovic was able to identify a number of recurring elements. Basement rooms seem to have served for storage, while those at ground level contained evidence for domestic activities such as weaving. Many properties included workshop space, identified by a cement floor and/or by circular, rock-cut vats and rectangular tanks. For example, house II (Figure 7.17) comprised an open courtyard (C), an irregular sunken basement with cuttings for shelves (B) and a room above. Two further rooms lay at ground level (A and D). The circulation patterns between spaces could not be reconstructed because of the absence of evidence for doorways. While much of C and D had been destroyed by quarrying, careful study of the preserved artefacts from A and B suggested functional differences between them: room B contained items associated with domestic chores including weaving and grinding grain. By contrast in room A the most prominent finds were table wares and lamps.

The Rachi settlement is interesting for the relatively small size of the individual domestic units and for the prominence of facilities for

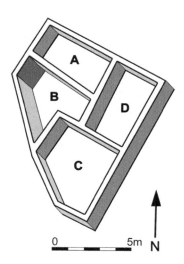

Figure 7.17 Rachi, house II (doorways not indicated).
(Drawn by Max Huemer, information from Anderson-Stojanović 2016, Fig. 4.4.)

production. While in the past an attempt was made to identify the site as a specialised facility for cloth production and dyeing, more recent study suggests that it may have hosted a wider variety of productive activities. In common with some of the other small houses we have seen elsewhere, this community is also interesting for what the houses do not offer: andrones are entirely absent and only a single bath was discovered, in a room which seems to have been entered directly from the street and may therefore possibly have been communal. The occupants of this settlement thus appear not to have had access to the kind of lifestyles enjoyed by the residents of larger houses, either for social, or for economic reasons, or both.

A different form of house has been found at Elea. This was a maritime city less than 20 km from Kassope (discussed in Chapter 4), but the hearth-room layout adopted at Kassope appears not to have been used at Elea. In fact, amongst the excavated areas, no house types can be identified which are repeated elsewhere on the site. Instead, the individual structures seem to be strongly influenced by the steeply sloping topography. At least one of the houses here (house 27) dates back to the late fourth century BCE, perhaps a generation or two after the construction of the Kassope houses. By the time Elea was destroyed (probably in 167 BCE by the Roman army) the division of space between houses was less regular than it may have been originally, but it is the pattern of organisation of the earlier second century BCE which is visible in the plans and finds from the excavated houses. In one neighbourhood, south of the town's agora, the streets are laid out in parallel although the walls of the intervening buildings do not quite abut at right-angles, perhaps because of the way in which they were terraced into the hillside with the walls of individual houses also acting as retaining walls for the construction terraces. An example of one of the smallest structures, house 18 comprises only three spaces (Figure 7.18). These were reached sequentially from the street, resembling the arrangement of some of the smallest houses at Classical Athens. A number of artefacts suggest some of the activities which may have taken place in each space at the time the settlement was destroyed: in particular, the innermost room seems to have been used for storage since it contained fragments of both large storage jars and transport amphoras. The middle space was furnished with a bathtub.

By contrast, neighbouring house 27 (Figure 7.19) is an example of one of the larger structures at the site, with an area of approximately 200 m². Its six rooms are organised around a central courtyard, although the two to the east were at a higher level and had to be reached via a wooden staircase whose stone base was found still in situ. The excavators suggested that this upper level contained a loom, since ten stamped loom weights were found tumbled into the northeastern corner of the courtyard. On the lower level, on the north side, a room with a cement floor and a drain was provided with three terracotta louteria. The excavators identify a square room on the west side of the building as an andron, presumably on the basis of its shape. The houses of Elea were, thus, of modest proportions, and construction was relatively utilitarian, with socles of large, uncut boulders. No evidence of decoration, such as fragments of painted plaster, architectural decoration or mosaic, are noted from the site. The larger houses were, nevertheless, furnished with bathing facilities and enough different rooms to enable

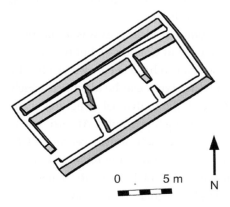

0   .   5 m   N

Figure 7.18 Elea, house 18.
(Drawn by Laurel Fricker based on Riginos and Lazari 2008, plan
p. 42.)

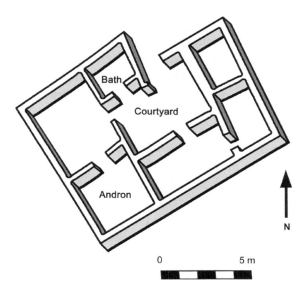

Figure 7.19 Elea, house 27.
(Drawn by Laurel Fricker based on Riginos and Lazari 2008, plan p. 42.)

some separation of various activities and individuals within the domestic sphere. Movement around the house could have been controlled from the courtyard, as in the single-entrance, courtyard model, although some spaces were interconnected and there is no surviving evidence of any attempt to block the view between the street and the courtyard.

Small Hellenistic structures have also been uncovered on Aghios Panteleimon hill (ancient Lynkestis), in the modern city of Florina. The houses are long-lived, having been constructed in the mid fourth century BCE but survived into the first century BCE. The majority consist only of a few rooms each (usually three to five). Most had storerooms with reserves of grain and there was also evidence for a range of craft production, including weaving, metallurgy, potting and manufacture of terracottas. Although some of the walls were plastered, the excavators recorded little evidence of other decoration and the houses seem above all to have been of a utilitarian character. Comparable houses have also been found elsewhere, including at Abdera. For instance, a house on the Avramoglou plot inhabited during the second half of the fourth century or early third century BCE seems to have consisted of three rooms, including a bathing area equipped with a drain and hydraulic cement floor.

Similarly modest domestic buildings have also been found elsewhere in neighbourhoods which also included larger properties. For example, at

Limenas on Thasos, the lone house forming insula II near the Silenos Gate was located close to the single entrance, courtyard houses in insula I (discussed in Chapter 4), but retained a much less complex layout from its construction in the mid fourth century BCE to the time the area was abandoned in the early third century BCE. The building consisted of an extensive southern courtyard with two large rooms to the north (Figure 7.20). It covered approximately 110 m^2, two thirds of the area of its neighbours, but the occupants made do with only the two rooms, which were approximately equivalent to the larger ones in houses Ia and Ib. The excavators reconstruct an open courtyard which was approximately the same area as the courts and pastades of its larger neighbours in insula I but was composed of beaten earth rather than paved with stones, except in front of the entrance. As with the smaller Classical properties we have seen at Athens and Olynthos, the single street door led directly into an open courtyard. A wall constructed in the final phase may have obstructed the view into the interior, or acted as the base for a walled pastas like those in the houses of insula I. The two spaces behind the courtyard were each reached separately but also had a connecting doorway between them. The eastern room contained a bath in the final phase, which may suggest a domestic role for the building as a whole since domestic contexts are where

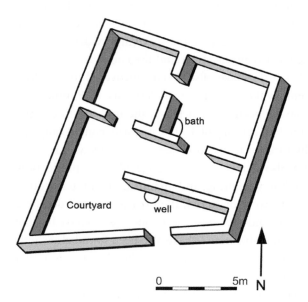

Figure 7.20 Limenas, Thasos, house in insula II near the Silenos Gate, final phase.
(Drawn by Max Huemer based on Grandjean 1988, Plate 86.)

such individual bathtubs are normally found. There are few other clues to suggest how the rooms and courtyard may have functioned.

Different layouts were found at the site of Petres, near Florina. This was another settlement founded in the mid fourth century BCE, on a steep hillside. Its final form, as recovered by the excavators, dates to the third and second centuries BCE. The different neighbourhoods had distinctively different characters. The Fountain District, on the southeastern slope, had wide streets and houses provided with central courtyards. On the South Plateau, however, multi-storey houses were terraced into the steep slope of the hill and lacked open courtyard spaces (Figure 7.21). Living rooms on the top level included decorated androness, some with wall plaster painted in coloured panels. Down below in a smaller space partly terraced into the hillside were stables and storerooms. An external staircase seems to have given access to a balcony which may have provided outdoor work-space as well as offering an access route (Figure 7.22). Finds of fine pottery include cups and amphoras. The agricultural basis of the economy of some of these southern households is attested by the remains of cultivation equipment in some of the rooms. In addition, archaeobotanical remains recovered include grapes, wheat, barley and lentils. In the final years before

Figure 7.21 Petres, houses of the South Plateau.
(Author's photograph. The rights to the monument shown belong to the Hellenic Ministry of Culture and Sports (Law 3028/2002). Petres is under the supervision of the Ephorate of Antiquities of Florina, Ministry of Culture and Sports.)

Figure 7.22 Petres, reconstruction of houses from the South Plateau. (After Adam-Veleni 2000, Fig. 40. Courtesy of the Ephorate of Antiquities of Florina, © Hellenic Ministry of Culture and Sports.)

the destruction of the community there seems to have been an intensification of craft activities such as production of pottery and terracottas.

The houses of the South Plateau possess their own characteristic domestic organisation which seem to point to local building traditions and to distinctive local social conventions. As additional information becomes available about the settlement it will be interesting to try to compare the two residential quarters in more detail to understand the underlying causes for the differences in the design of their houses, whether socio-economic, cultural or chronological. Overall, however, it is not clear that the inhabitants did not have resources to build single-entrance, courtyard houses: one factor in the choice of layout may have been the steep terrain, but we have seen that in other settlements (such as Priene) the single-entrance, courtyard house was used. It seems, then, that the residents of Petres may have chosen to cater for a different pattern (or patterns) of domestic social life.

These various examples demonstrate the diversity of the housing of comfortably off to relatively modest households during the Hellenistic period. What is striking about them is that, even in the larger properties, the model of the single-entrance, courtyard-house, which seemed so pervasive during Classical times, seems mostly to have fallen out of favour. Instead, the importance of the courtyard as a circulation space often seems to have diminished. Spatial syntax has become more diverse, and it must have been less feasible to survey or control movement into and around the house from a single location. This diversity suggests that no single new social model replaced the underlying ideas materialised in the single-entrance, courtyard house. Instead, individual communities and the households of which they were made up, adopted differing solutions to the problem of how to organise their domestic space. These solutions may have been influenced by a number of factors including the availability of economic resources, local topography and divergent local norms of social behaviour. This development took place alongside the emergence of the monumental, peristyle houses, but the cultural and aesthetic influences of the Hellenistic elite koine did not always play an influential role – even where, as at Kallion, households seem to have had access to significant economic resources. Instead of looking outwards to other communities, regions and social groups for their inspiration, some households seem to have relied on what made sense given their individual needs and the local topography and resources. Whether there was also symbolic value in adopting patterns of spatial organisation that were different from the typical layout of the Classical urban housing is unclear. The trend may equally stem from underlying changes in the activities and relationships the buildings were constructed to support.

The evidence discussed above covers a variety of settlement types, from large cities through to small, rural villages. Settlement in isolated farms in the rural hinterlands of these settlements also continued through the late Classical and Hellenistic periods, and it is to these establishments that we now turn.

Rural Housing in the Hellenistic Period

Some of the variety of organisational patterns already seen in urban and village housing can also be identified in individual farmsteads. Patterns of rural occupation and the organisation of the rural economy are likely to have varied regionally across mainland Greece and to have changed through the period covered by this book. In the area of modern Greece, it has long been noted that the density in the occupation of the countryside by small farms detected in data from a number of field surveys appears to have reached its peak during the fifth and fourth centuries BCE in many places, followed by a decline starting in the third or second century BCE (the dating schemes of different projects varied, as well as possibly the timing of this decline itself). Among those establishments that continued into the Hellenistic period, in some locations modestly sized rural farmsteads seem to have continued to be organised around a central courtyard and pastas. An excavated example on Delos, for example, the Farm with the Granite Jambs was built during the Classical period with four rooms opening off a large courtyard, but it grew in size through time, and by the Hellenistic period a pastas had been added, along with further rooms. Curiously, the excavators note that although the location amid a landscape terraced for cultivation strongly suggests that the building was associated with farming, the architecture and finds themselves yielded little sign of the agricultural activities that might be expected to have taken place there.

By contrast, in Pieria, in northern Greece, large farming complexes were in use during the Hellenistic period which clearly produced significant quantities of crops such as grapes, olives and grain. They have their own characteristic ranges of facilities and patterns of organisation which are likely to be linked to bulk production for sale, particularly, perhaps, of wine. An example is located at Komboloi, on the eastern slopes of Mount Olympos. It was constructed in the mid fourth century BCE and was destroyed by fire at the start of the third century BCE (Figure 7.23). The complex covers some 1,350 m^2 and was constructed with a stone socle consisting of unworked or partially worked blocks and a mudbrick superstructure which was plastered, at least in part. Floors were composed of a variety of materials including beaten clay and pebbles. The main excavated section of the complex was organised around a central courtyard which had rooms on all four sides, their entrances apparently sheltered by porticoes. Beneath the eastern side of the house was a basement level which had an area of about fifty square metres. Thickened walls above may have supported a tower. A further storage area lay outside this courtyard on its western side, and there was probably a second courtyard to the east. Extensive evidence of agricultural production was recovered from both the basement and the storage area. Archaeobotanical sampling revealed that the basement contained grapes, olives and cereals. Evidence of cultivation equipment was also located here. By contrast the storage complex contained evidence only for grapes. A series of large storage jars held both

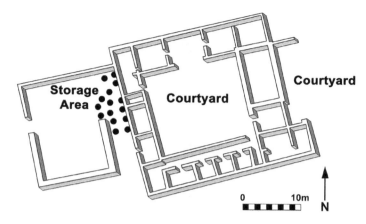

Figure 7.23 Komboloi, farm building (some doorways unlocated).
(Drawn by Max Huemer based on Adam-Veleni et al. 2003, figure on page 65.)

pips and skins, together with pine resin, and may have been used for fermenting resinated wine. Other facilities at the complex include a ceramic kiln. Among the artefacts, a variety of utilitarian pottery included transport amphorae and cooking vessels as well as black-slipped cups, plates and jugs. A second structure at nearby Tria Platania yielded similar evidence (Figure 7.24). This is a still larger building of comparable construction. Its first phase is dated to the late fourth century BCE. Much of the 2,340 m² area of the complex is taken up by an internal courtyard. In the northeast corner a storeroom originally contained twenty-two large storage jars which were dug into the ground and contained grape pips and olive pits. Evi Margaritis, who carried out the archaeobotanical study of both this and Komboloi, estimated the capacity of each one at 2,200–2,300 litres. The storeroom must thus have held a minimum of 48,400 litres. At the centre of the courtyard were the foundations for a tower, with a stone-built kiln alongside. The finds from the building included a variety of fine table vessels. A range of household pottery was also found, among which were transport amphorae, cooking pots, ladles and bowls. Other domestic equipment included loom weights and knives.

Given that these two farms both seem to cater, at least in part, to production of surplus agricultural goods for sale, it is tempting to wonder whether agricultural intensification might have been one potential source of the elite wealth which must have supported the construction of the larger, more elaborate houses being built in the late Classical and Hellenistic periods. Nevertheless, the excavated portions of the two complexes fall comfortably within the range of sizes that have been suggested

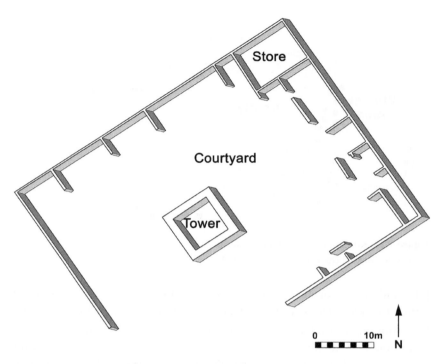

Figure 7.24 Tria Platania, farm building, phase 1.
(Drawn by Max Huemer based on Adam-Veleni et al. 2003, figure on page 58.)

for Classical farms further south in Greece, based on data from field survey. Such figures are approximate, and the surface remains are not all well-dated nor their extents well-defined, but this comparison suggests that the Pieria examples may not have been exceptional. What cannot be determined, however, is the numbers of such large establishments relative to those of subsistence farms in either the Classical or the Hellenistic period.

Elsewhere in the Greek world there is some evidence of a progressive filling up of the landscape with farming complexes. On the northern Black Sea coast, in the hinterland of Chersonesos, for instance, a remarkably well-preserved ancient landscape extends over the Heraklian Peninsula of modern Crimea. A regular grid of stone-paved roads and field boundaries incorporates rural farmsteads constructed in the late fourth or early third century BCE and often occupied for several centuries. There is frequent evidence of extensive cultivation of vines and the presence of pressing equipment suggests production beyond the subsistence needs of a single household. Among the excavated examples, the layouts are variable, but they typically include a walled courtyard with one or two entrances. Several rooms lead off on two or more sides,

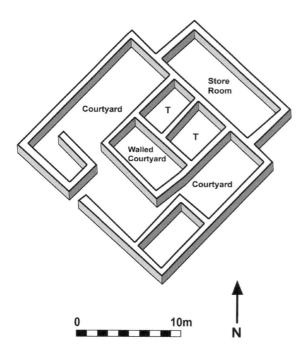

T - Ground floor room in the tower

Figure 7.25 Hinterland of Crimean Chersonesos, farm 151. (Some doorways are unlocated.)
(Drawn by Max Huemer based on Coleman Carter et al. 2000, Fig. 12.)

the number increasing through time. These rooms are usually entered from the courtyard but sometimes also interconnect.

A well-documented example, farm 151 (Figure 7.25), seems, like its neighbours, to have grown up through time. In this case, a square, fortified tower and an adjacent walled courtyard with a plaster floor were both constructed late in the fourth century BCE. The socles for the walls are built of irregular masonry and survive in places to a height of up to two metres; the upper part of the tower would have been mud brick. On the ground floor of the tower pressing equipment for wine production was located. Next door, a storeroom had five large storage jars set into the floor, estimated to have held a total of up to 4,000–5,000 litres. The upper rooms are thought to have consisted of domestic quarters, reached via a wooden ladder inside the tower. Finds of coarse cooking pottery and fine, black-slipped table wares support the identification of the tower as residential as well as agricultural. The excavators also found evidence for religious worship in the form of a small shrine to the hero Herakles and a terracotta incense burner depicting the god Dionysos. Gradually, further rooms were added to the compound inside the courtyard wall, until the tower collapsed and the farm went out of use in the second century BCE. While the layouts of the farms at Chersonesos were quite variable, a tower, a walled courtyard and several rooms leading off the courtyard seem to be common elements. Many of the farms appear to have associated vineyards and it is assumed that wine was produced and sold in bulk. The scale of these establishments is, nonetheless, of an order of magnitude smaller than even the excavated portions of the buildings in Pieria.

In the western Mediterranean, in the territory of Metaponto in southern Italy, the farms look somewhat different. Here, a series of ancient land divisions has been reconstructed from features visible in historical aerial photographs. Alongside these, a number of farming establishments yielding Greek and Greek-style ceramics are present from the Archaic period onwards. The sizes range from approximately 100–300 m^2 in area, and the plans of those that have been excavated are difficult to reconstruct: the buildings are typically only partially preserved or partially excavated, and the locations of the doorways were not always reconstructable. A Hellenistic farmhouse at San Biagio is organised in a similar way to Classical farmhouses from southern Greece, such as the Dema and Vari houses discussed in Chapter 3, with an approximately southern courtyard, northern pastas and single rows of interior rooms arranged around three sides. In other cases, however, the plans seem to have been rather different. The late-fifth century BCE Fattoria Fabrizio, fourth century BCE Fattoria Arezzo and Fattoria Stefan, and third century BCE Pantanello farmhouses all seem to lack a central courtyard and pastas, consisting instead of clusters of rooms which have been compared with the farms of some of the local population of the region. The palaeobotanical evidence from the Fattoria Fabrizio suggested to the publication team that, in addition to the cultivation of crops, pastoralism played a significant role in the economy of the region during the late Classical period, even though animal bone was scarce in and around the farmhouse itself. These establishments thus seem to have been part of a mixed subsistence economy. The uses of interior and exterior space are likely to have been very different from those seen in the courtyard establishments of mainland Greece and Chersonesos, where the interior rooms must have been brighter and better ventilated because they each had access to the courtyard space.

While this discussion of Hellenistic farmhouses is indicative rather than comprehensive, it does suggest that, as with the contemporary houses from nucleated settlements, there was significant variation in the scale and organisation of space. A central courtyard with rooms leading off it was probably an efficient arrangement which provided both exterior workspace and well-lit and -ventilated interior rooms. This seems to have been favoured particularly where large-scale production was taking place. The biggest buildings provide evidence of covered work areas alongside the courtyard. Furthermore, the farms from the hinterland of Metaponto show that spatial organisation could also be specific to local circumstances.

The Single-Entrance, Courtyard House Superseded

By the third and second centuries BCE, then, the layout and range of sizes of residential buildings among culturally Greek communities had become increasingly variable. As with the material covered in previous chapters, the evidence for Hellenistic housing is unevenly distributed: fewer examples are available from the southern Greek mainland than from Sicily (for example); the larger, better-built houses of the wealthy are also more readily identified and interpreted than the smaller properties of their less well-off contemporaries. Nevertheless, the pattern that begins to emerge is of an increase in the diversity of house-layouts during the Hellenistic period. The decline in the popularity of the single-entrance, courtyard house that seems to have begun in some elite contexts in late Classical times appears to have become widespread. By the early Hellenistic period, the ideal of belonging to a community with shared ideals and a common housing culture, which had been materialised by the single-entrance, courtyard house, seems to have lost its attraction across a broad socio-economic spectrum. Existing courtyard-centred buildings were adapted in various ways, and new ones adopted a variety of different forms. More modest structures with idiosyncratic layouts often seem to have been relatively localised in their distribution and perhaps indicate the fore-grounding of a sense of local or regional identity.

For wealthier households, the peristyle house emphasised their difference from their less well-off neighbours, becoming a vehicle for establishing membership of an elite status group that constituted a network spread across the Mediterranean and beyond. Some of the precise ways in which this group was materialised through the house may have taken shape through emulation of, or in dialogue with, the kinds of palatial buildings discussed in Chapter 6. The idea of the peristyle courtyard seems to have been an important element (even where space was lacking for a full peristyle) as were architectural features such as painted wall plaster, mosaics and an exedra-complex. At the same time, however, these elite households also drew upon more localised influences in shaping their domestic environments, as the example of Sicilian bathing culture shows. The timing of these developments may have varied: for example, in southern Greece, while large peristyle houses are found in Eretria, they seem to have been rare in other regions before the Roman period. This may be an accident of our present archaeological knowledge, but it also may attest to differing social and economic trajectories in different communities. In place of architecture, alternative means may have been used by households in some locations to differentiate themselves from their neighbours. For example, the evidence from Kallipolis indicates how this might have been done by expenditure on costly movable furnishings placed in the building. The choice of whether to adopt the peristyle may also have been influenced by cultural conventions or social and political aspirations. In Macedon, for example, attitudes towards the overt display of personal wealth and power were different from those found in Athens, leading to the use of earlier and more extreme symbols of status by elites in various contexts, including in their domestic buildings. In the Macedonian heartland, some of the wealth invested in monumental houses may have accrued from spoils of the rapid expansion of the kingdom and empire. But there were, perhaps, other factors involved as well: there seems to have been a gradual increase in standards of living throughout Greece. As noted above, one source of wealth that may have helped to support this change might have been an intensification of agricultural production in some regions.

Epilogue: The Single-Entrance, Courtyard House and Beyond

The concept of the single-entrance, courtyard house offers a means of exploring the relationship between cultural expectations about domestic life, and the physical form taken by the house itself. It re-focuses attention away from superficial aspects of the appearance of the buildings themselves and instead places the emphasis on how the spaces they created may have worked as lived environments. The model highlights the pervasiveness in Greek cities during the Classical period of the interior courtyard which provided a relatively secure exterior activity space while creating an isolated domestic environment which permitted a high degree of oversight over movement around the house. At the same time, it also provides a frame for thinking beyond the environment of the prosperous Classical urban-dweller, to encompass the houses – and the experiences – of other social groups, including the less wealthy inhabitants of those urban settlements; those resident in the villages and farmsteads of the Greek countryside; occupants of the Early Iron Age and Archaic villages and towns; households in culturally Greek settlements across the western Mediterranean and beyond; and finally, those dwelling in the cities, villages and rural landscapes of the Hellenistic world. In broadening the perspective in this way while at the same time distinguishing between these different groups of evidence, it becomes clear that, although the Classical model is striking for its widespread use and for the variety of architectural forms through which it was materialised, it was actually a relatively socially restricted and short-lived phenomenon.

Evidence from the Early Iron Age suggests that during this period buildings were typically differentiated from each other only by scale, if at all. Following the Late Bronze Age collapse, the concept of a house (as contrasted with a structure built to fulfil other, more communal, roles) may not have been widespread until the eighth century BCE when separate cult buildings were created (which initially used the same designs and technology as residential structures). Even through the Archaic period the dominant form of residence seems to have been relatively small in size, with one to three rooms. Only in the late Archaic or early Classical period do we have evidence of the widespread use of a more spacious house-type in which access from the exterior was restricted, a greater variety of separate interior spaces was included, and an enclosed courtyard was provided from which most of those spaces were reached individually. The exact timing of the introduction of this arrangement is difficult to pinpoint precisely owing to the sparseness of the evidence from the sixth century BCE: its various components almost certainly came together in different ways at different times, and in different places. It is only from the fifth century BCE, however, that this single-entrance, courtyard house-form is found widely across the Greek world. As well as embodying specific ideals or assumptions about how the residents should interact with each other and with the wider community, such houses typically provided generous amounts of roofed and unroofed space in which a range of domestic tasks could be carried out, often including the processing and storage of agricultural produce; preparation and consumption of food and drink; production of textiles and other manufactured goods for domestic use and/or for sale; and entertaining visitors from outside the household. Although these activities were surely part of the role of domestic buildings in earlier times as well, in the single-entrance, courtyard house they, along with the individuals performing them, could be separated spatially. In aggregate, these houses were also substantially larger than their predecessors. It therefore seems possible that a larger household could have been accommodated, perhaps incorporating a more extended family group and/or dependent or enslaved individuals, whose presence is revealed in some of the Classical Athenian texts. We cannot know, however, the sizes of the households once living in any of the houses discussed in this volume, nor the nature of the relationships between any of their former residents. It is also the case that, in relation to any single structure, both the number of residents and the nature of the social relationships between them will have fluctuated through time with the life-cycles of individual households. Not all households had such spacious quarters at their disposal: while our archaeological sample is likely to be biased towards the larger properties, there are also significant numbers of smaller ones which seem likely to have accommodated households of lower socio-economic status who were presumably unable to afford more space or a wider range of architectural features. (There is no way to know whether the households themselves were also smaller than those of their neighbours residing in single-entrance, courtyard houses, but this seems possible, particularly if the larger households included some unrelated individuals.)

This gulf in the resources expended on the largest and the smallest houses widened dramatically during the later Classical period. By the early fourth century BCE we already start to see the appearance of a small number of exceptionally large houses that were built on a double-courtyard plan. While they normally retained a single street entrance, they appear to have created two separate spheres for the entertainment of visitors and performance of household tasks, respectively. Each was organised around a separate courtyard: the rooms used for entertaining were normally arranged around a peristyle while those used for domestic purposes may either have been focused around a second peristyle or around a courtyard and pastas. To the extent that it was impossible to see between the two courtyards, such houses may have represented a step away from the single-entrance, courtyard model by diminishing the ability to monitor or even control movement around the whole house from a single location. A widespread abandonment of the single-entrance, courtyard plan seems to have followed within a couple of generations as a variety of patterns of domestic organisation came to be adopted by different communities at a range of socio-economic levels. The peristyles and dining rooms exemplified by some of the double-courtyard buildings, and especially by the Macedonian palaces, came to be adopted across the Mediterranean and beyond. Such features were surely a tool through which individual households laid claim to elite status and to bonds with those of similar status living in other communities. Such symbols must have had a powerful effect, since both colonnaded courtyards and decorated dining rooms continued in use in the larger houses of numerous regions until Late Antiquity. In southern Italy the peristyle was adopted as an element of the well-known atrium house at settlements such as Pompeii and Herculaneum (destroyed in the first century CE). In communities in the Greek east such as Ephesos, the peristyle was the central courtyard space around which the rooms of the houses were organised, well into the Roman period. Viewed from this perspective, it seems that the single-entrance, courtyard house was desirable only as long as there was support for the values by which it was underpinned. The diversity of the structures that succeeded it suggests the need for detailed analysis from a regional perspective in order to arrive at a more nuanced understanding of the significance the forms adopted subsequently in different areas. In the meantime, however, it is striking that at a global level what stands out is the enduring power of domestic architecture to articulate social and economic status.

The broad outlines of this picture are supported by a variety of architectural, artefactual, and textual evidence. Nevertheless, the particular strengths of the archaeological material are its quantity, its distribution through time, its representation across geographical space and the range of social groups to which it provides access. The archaeology, therefore, offers the potential to nuance more generalised models by focusing on particular contexts. Narrowing the focus in this way highlights variation between and within communities, at different times and in various places, in the amount of living space available, its organisation and the resources spent on it. While the focus of this volume has been on the Greek mainland and Aegean islands, there is much scope for constructing more comprehensive analyses of culturally Greek settlements elsewhere in the Mediterranean and beyond. In addition, as we have seen, even in relation to the Greek mainland and islands, in-depth investigation can be carried out to varying extents in different periods and regions: thus, while it is possible to construct a relatively complex picture of Classical Athens and Attica (for example), evidence for the entire Greek mainland during the later Archaic period is currently very scarce. It is to be hoped that future discoveries in the field will bring more evidence to light which will fill such lacunae. Advances in the way in which the archaeological record is conceptualised can also assist in interpreting individual buildings and assemblages in order to arrive at a better understanding. At the same time, an interest in addressing new questions, together with developments in archaeological field techniques, may widen the scope of what can be inferred from the material record. In particular, application of various kinds of scientific methods may contribute: at its best, geophysical imaging can sometimes give an impression of the type, scale, and even the layout, of buildings without excavation, improving our ability to evaluate the extent to which individual excavated houses can be taken as representative of wider neighbourhoods, districts or settlements. In addition, various forms of geoarchaeological and chemical study have the potential to extend the range of activities discoverable through excavation, providing more detail about domestic organisation and thus enabling a wider range of issues to be addressed more satisfactorily. In short, there is still much work that remains to be done to improve our understanding of Greek households during the first millennium and future work is sure to clarify, extend and probably also modify, the picture presented here.

Glossary

Amphora – describes two different types of vessels: 1. Amphora or table amphora: a smaller ceramic or metal vessel with a high base, flaring body, narrow neck and two handles; 2. Transport amphora: a large coarse ware pottery vessel used to transport or store foodstuffs.

Andron (pl. andrones) – term used in the ancient texts and usually translated as 'men's space'; in archaeological contexts it is usually applied to a room possessing an off-centre doorway, interior decoration and a raised platform around the walls, that is assumed to have been used for drinking and perhaps also dining.

Anta (pl. antae) – stub wall on the long side of a rectangular building that projects beyond its meeting point with the cross wall.

Apsidal – having a curved end or apse.

Architectural order – architectural style (see also 'Doric' and 'Ionic', below).

Architrave – architectural moulding running across the tops of columns or other supports, or around doorways and window openings.

Ashlar masonry – built out of cut stone blocks of standardised, rectangular shape.

Asia Minor – the land mass separating the Mediterranean from the Black Sea and approximating to the area occupied by the modern nation of Turkey.

Attica – the territory of the city of Athens.

Bouleuterion – building for meetings of the boule or council of representatives of the city.

Capital – decorative architectural moulding at the top of a column.

Demes – political and administrative subdivisions of the Classical Athenian state; those located outside the city were centred on villages or small towns – the deme centres.

Doric order – architectural style which included pillowy column capitals particularly characteristic of mainland and western Mediterranean communities, which was originally developed to elaborate religious buildings

Exedra – a room open on one side to a colonnade or courtyard.

Gunaikon (or gunaikonitis) – a term used in textual sources which is generally translated as 'women's space'.

Hekatompedon – literally a structure measuring 100 feet in length, but generally referring to a monumental early temple, such as the one at Eretria.

Herm (Hermaic stele) – sculpted bust of religious significance.

Insula (pl. insulae) – block of buildings defined by surrounding streets or other open spaces.

Ionic order – architectural style particularly characteristic of eastern Aegean communities, featuring column capitals with volutes (spirals) and originally created for religious buildings.

Koine – a common language, either a literal one, or – as used here – in the sense of a shared repertoire of material culture.

Kottabos – a drinking game, thought to have been played at symposia, in which players flicked the dregs of the wine from their cups at a target placed across the room.

Krater – a deep, open-footed ceramic vessel associated by archaeologists with mixing wine and water, especially in the context of a symposium (see Figure 3.5).

Kylix (pl. kylikes) high-stemmed cup with a wide, flat body (see Figure 3.9).

Loom weights – weights for keeping the vertical threads of a loom taut through the process of weaving yarn into textiles.

Masonry style – a style of wall decoration in which plaster is molded and painted to represent monumental stone blocks composing a series of horizontal registers.

Megaron (pl. megara) – rectangular room or building with an entrance, sheltered by a porch, on one of the short sides.

Mullions – solid architectural elements separating the different parts of a window opening.

Oikos – two related meanings are: 1. in ancient texts: the household; 2. in archaeological contexts: the main living room of a house; hence 'oikos unit' – a group of three rooms, first identified by J. Walter Graham at Olynthos, comprising a living room with adjacent flue- and bathing-areas.

Orthogonal – constructed with straight walls or streets, crossing at right angles.

Pastas – wide portico or colonnade adjacent to an open courtyard and sheltering the doorways of rooms behind it (see Figure 1.7).

Pediment – architectural feature filling the triangular space at the gable end of a pitched roof.

Peribolos (plural periboloi) – boundary wall.

Peristyle – portico running around multiple sides of a courtyard, its roof supported by decorative columns (see Figure 1.8).

Polychrome – multi-coloured.

Polygonal masonry – built of stone blocks of irregular shapes.

Prostas – narrow porch adjacent to a courtyard and sheltering the doorways of one or two rooms (see Figure 1.6).

Prothyron – lobby at the street door of a house.

Prytaneion – building in which a city's prytaneis (magistrates) would have met.

Pyre – ashy deposit resulting from an episode of deliberate burning.

Spindle whorl – a weighted disc used for spinning raw wool fibres into a thread prior to weaving it into cloth.

Stele (pl. stelai) – upright stone marker, often with an inscription and/or carved relief.

Stratigraphy – the vertical sequence of archaeological deposits.

Symposium (pl. symposia) – male drinking party (see Figure 1.9).

Tesserae – small cut stones used to compose a mosaic.

Selection of Ancient Texts in Translation[1]

Text Extract 1: Demosthenes 3.25–26. (Similar passages occur also at Demosthenes 13.29 and 23.207.)

Their [the Athenians' ancestors] status among the Greeks was thus: look around this city and see what kind of men they were in public and in private. On the one hand, from state funds they constructed public buildings and other such things for us, as sanctuaries and offerings, so that none of their descendants could surpass them. But in private they were so modest and very public spirited that if any of you knows the house of Aristeides or Miltiades or of other famous men from that time, you can see that it is no more elaborate than any of the neighbours'.

Adapted from Vince, J. H. 1930. *Demosthenes*, (London, Heinemann).

Text Extract 2: Xenophon *Hiero* 11.2

First, which do you think would bring the most credit, to have a house [oikia] adorned with elaborate decoration or to have adorned the whole city with walls and temples and stoas and public squares and harbours?

Adapted from Marchant, E. C. 1925. *Xenophon Scripta Minora*, (Cambridge, MA, Harvard University Press).

Text Extract 3: Plutarch *Lykourgos* 13.3

Another [speech] was against extravagance, so that every house should have an upper storey fashioned with an axe, and its doors only with a saw, and not with any other tools. For, as in later times they say Epaminondas said at his own table, this kind of virtue does not go along with treachery. So Lykourgos was the first to realise that such a house does not go with luxury and extravagance. Nor is any man so vulgar and senseless as to bring into a plain and common house silver-footed couches, purple throws, gold cups, and the extravagance that goes with them, but by necessity the couch should be in keeping with, and appropriate to, the house, the throws to the couch, and this to the rest of his goods and possessions. It was because he was used to this, they say, that Leotychides the Elder, when he

[1] All the original texts are in Greek except Extract 10 which is in Latin.

was dining in Corinth and saw the roof of the house was decorated with expensive panels, asked his host if trees grew square in that area.

Adapted from Perrin, B. 1914. *Plutarch. Plutarch's Lives*, (Cambridge, MA, Harvard University Press.)

Text Extract 4: Herakleides Kritikos Frag. 1.1, describing Athens

It is badly organised because of its age, for many of the houses are well-built but few are convenient.

Adapted from Robinson, D. M. and Peters, A. 1946. Testimonia Selecta ad Domum Graecam Pertinentia. In D. M. Robinson *Excavations at Olynthos Vol. XII Domestic and Public Architecture*, (Baltimore, Johns Hopkins University Press).

Text Extract 5: Plutarch On Curiosity 3

It is not legitimate to go through the door into some else's house without knocking; indeed, now there are doormen, but in the past, there were knockers on the doors to give notice so that an outsider would not come upon the lady of the house busy, or a daughter, or a servant being corrected, or the maids screaming.

Adapted from Helmbold, W. C. 1939. *Plutarch. Moralia,* (Cambridge, MA, Harvard University Press.)

Text Extract 6: Plato *Symposium* 212 C-D

... suddenly there was knocking on the door into the courtyard, much noise as if from party-goers, and the voice of the flute player was to be heard. So Agathon said to the servants 'Go and see, and if it is one of our good friends, invite him in: but if not, say we are not drinking, but already going to sleep.' And not much later the voice of Alkibiades was to be heard in the courtyard, very drunk and shouting loudly, wanting to know where Agathon was, and asking to be taken to Agathon.

Adapted from Fowler, H. 1925. *Plato, Volume 9*, (Cambridge, MA, Harvard University Press).

Text Extract 7: Lysias 3.6

So, hearing that the boy was at my place, he came to my house at night, drunk; having broken down the doors, he went into the women's quarters [gunaikonitis]: inside were my sister and my nieces, who have lived so modestly that they are embarrassed to be seen, even by their male relatives. Such was the level of arrogance this man reached, that he did not want to go away until the men who came upon him, and those who came with him, drove him out by force, thinking he had behaved badly by walking in on young girls and orphans.

Adapted from Lamb, W. 1930. *Lysias*, (Cambridge, MA, Harvard University Press).

Text Extract 8: Plato *Protagoras* 314C–315D

Now, it seems to me that the doorkeeper, who was a eunuch, heard us; perhaps the large number of sophists* had made him annoyed with comings and goings to the house; anyway, so after we knocked on the door, he opened it and seeing us, said 'Ha, some sophists! He has no time!' And, at the same time, he took the door with both hands and slammed it as hard as he could. And we knocked again, and answering through the closed door he said, 'Gentlemen, have you not heard, he has no time?' 'But, sir,' I said, 'we have not come to see Kallias, nor are we sophists. But take heart: for we have come wanting to see Protagoras; so, go and announce us.' So, then the man reluctantly opened the door for us and when we had come in, we met Protagoras walking in the portico [prostöon]...

*travelling scholars

Adapted from W. Lamb 1967. *Plato, Volume 3*, (Cambridge, MA, Harvard University Press).

Text Extract 9: Example of an Olynthian sale document, inscribed in stone and found to the right of the street door of house D v 6.

> God. Direct sale.
> When Aristoboulos son of Kallikrates
> was priest. In the month
> of Thargaleon. Zoilos,
> son of Philokrates, [received] from
> Diopeithos son of
> Antipater, the house
> which he owned next to the house of
> Diokles son of Charon
> and that of Apollodoros'
> children, for 1200 drachmai. The guarantor
> was Polemarchos son of Straton.
> The witnesses were Diokles son of Charon,
> Euxitheos son of Xanthippos and
> Philon son of Theodotos.

Author's translation.

Text Extract 10: Vitruvius *De Architectura* 6.7.1–5: his description of a Greek house:

Because the Greeks do not use atria, they do not build them, but for people entering from the front door, they make corridors, not very wide, with stables on one side and doorkeepers' rooms on the other and shut off by inner doors. This place between the two doors is called the 'thurorion' in Greek. From here, one enters the peristyle. This peristyle has porticoes on three sides, and on the side facing the south it has two antae, a considerable distance apart, carrying an architrave ... Some call this space the 'prostas', others the 'pastas'. 2. In these areas, facing inwards, are the large living rooms in which the mistresses of the households hold court with their wool spinners. To the right and left of the prostas there are chambers, one of which is called the 'thalamos', the other the 'amphithalamos'. All round the colonnades are dining rooms [triclinia] for daily use, small rooms [cubicula], and service rooms [cellae familiaricae]. This part of the building is called the 'gynaeconitis'. 3. Connected with these there are larger suites with more splendid peristyles ... Such apartments have distinguished vestibules [vestibula] with their own imposing front doors; the colonnades of the peristyles are decorated with polished stucco in relief and plain, and with coffered wooden ceilings; off the colonnades that face northwards are Cyzicene dining rooms [triclinia] and picture galleries [pinacothecae]; to the east, libraries; exedrae to the west; and to the south, large square rooms of such ample size that four sets of dining couches can easily be arranged in them, with plenty of space for serving and for entertainment. 4. In these rooms, men's dinner parties are held; for according to Greek custom, it was not the practice for the lady of the house to recline there. Such peristyles are, therefore, called the men's apartments [andronitides], because men stay in them without interruptions from women. Furthermore, to the right and left small sets of apartments are built with their own front doors and comfortable dining rooms [triclinia] and small rooms [cubicula], so that guests arriving can be received, not in the peristyles, but rather in these guest-apartments. For when the Greeks became more luxurious, and their fortunes greater, they began to provide their arriving guests with dining rooms [triclinia], small rooms [cubicula], and rooms with provisions ... 5. Between the two peristyles and the guests' apartments are the corridors called 'mesauloe' because they are located in the middle between two courts; but our people called them 'androns'. This, however, is a very strange thing, for the term does not fit either the Greek or the Latin use of it. The Greeks call the large rooms in which men's dinner parties are usually held 'androns', because women do not go there ...

Translation adapted from Granger, F. 1934. *Vitruvius On Architecture* Volume II, (Cambridge, MA, Harvard University Press).

Text Extract 11: Aristotelian *Constitution of Athens* 50.2.

And just as they [the magistrates] see that no dung-gatherer leaves dung near the city walls, so they prevent building on the roads, balconies overhanging the roads, raised pipes with overflows onto the road and windows [thyrides] that open onto the road...

Adapted from Rackham, H. 1952. *Aristotle*, Volume 20, (Cambridge, MA, Harvard University Press).

Text Extract 12: Xenophon *Oikonomikos* 9.2–10: the speaker describes showing his new wife around his house.

... 'I decided first to show her [my wife] the benefits of our house. For it is not elaborately decorated, Socrates, but the rooms are built to provide convenient locations for the things to be put in them, so each room received what was suited to it. (3.) So the inner-room [thalamos], being secure, was suitable for the most valuable blankets and utensils, the dry covered rooms for the grain, the cool ones for the wine, the bright ones for those tasks and utensils that need light. (4.) I showed her decorated living-rooms for people, that are cool in summer but warm in winter. I showed her that the whole house faces south, so that it is obvious that it is sunny in winter but shady in summer. (5.) I showed her the women's quarters [gunaikonitis] too, separated by a bolted door from the men's quarters [andronitis], so that nothing might be taken from inside which should not be, and the household slaves may not bear children without our agreement...' (6.) 'But when we had gone over these things,' he said, 'we immediately began dividing the furnishings according to their type. We began first' he said 'by gathering together the things we use for sacrifice. After that we separated out the women's finery used for festivals, and the men's festival and war clothes, blankets in the women's, blankets in the men's quarters, women's shoes, men's shoes. (7.) Another group consisted of weapons, another of wool working equipment, another was for bread-making, another for cooking, another the things required for bathing, another those things needed at the kneading-trough, another for table use. All these things we divided up, those for daily use and those for feast days. (8.) We also took out the things used up in a month and set apart the supplies calculated to last for a year....'.

Adapted from Pomeroy, S. 1994. *Xenophon, Oeconomicus*, (Oxford, Clarendon).

Text Extract 13: Lysias 1.9: addressing a jury, the speaker explains his domestic arrangements.

So first, gentlemen (for I must tell you these things), my little house is two-storey, with equal space above and below for the women's quarters [gunaikonitis] and men's quarters [andronitis], respectively. But when our baby was born its mother fed it; so that, when she had to wash it, she would not endanger herself coming down the stairs, I spent my time upstairs while the women were below.

Adapted from Lamb, W. 1930. *Lysias*, (Cambridge, MA, Harvard University Press.)

Text Extract 14: Demosthenes 47.55–56: addressing a jury, the speaker relates some events that happened at his house while he was absent.

What is more, gentlemen of the jury, my wife happened to be eating lunch with my children in the courtyard, along with my nurse, who is now elderly ... As they were eating lunch in the courtyard, these men burst in and found them and were grabbing the furniture. The other female slaves (for they were in the tower [pyrgos], where they lived), when they heard the outcry, closed the tower, and the men did not get in there, but they took away the furnishings from the rest of the house ...

Adapted from Murray, A. T. 1939. *Demosthenes with an English Translation*, (Cambridge MA, Harvard University Press.)

Text Extract 15: Homer *Odyssey*, book 7, 84–130: the hero Odysseus' first sight of the palace of King Alkinöos of the Phaeacians.

... Odysseus went to the glorious halls [domata] of Alkinöos; his heart pondered many things as he stood, before he approached the bronze threshold; for there was a gleam like the sun or moon on the high-roofed hall [doma] of great-hearted Alkinöos. For bronze walls ran this way and that, from the inside to the threshold, and along them was a blue cornice. Gold doors enclosed the interior of the well-built house, and silver door-posts stood on the bronze threshold. The lintel above was silver and the handle gold. There were gold and silver dogs on each side, which Hephaestos* had made with cunning skill, guarding the hall [doma] of great-hearted Alkinöos, immortal and ageless all their days. Inside, chairs were fixed along the wall this way and that, continuously from the thresh-old to the innermost place, and on them were thrown coverings of fine, well-woven fabric, the work of women. There sat the leaders of the Phaiakians, drinking and eating, for they had many supplies. And golden youths stood on well-made pedestals, holding shining torches in their hands lighting the night for the diners in the halls [domata].

*the smith god

Adapted from Murray, A. T. 1919. *The Odyssey with an English Translation*, (Cambridge, MA, Harvard University Press).

Bibliographic Essay

Preface

In addition to Nevett 1999, other volumes bringing together evidence for ancient Greek housing from a range of ancient sites include several edited collections: Westgate et al. 2007; Ladstätter and Scheibelreiter 2010; Glowacki and Vogeikoff-Brogan 2011; a monograph: Morgan 2010; and a special issue of the Greek popular magazine Αρχαιολογία και Τέχνες (vol. 113, 2009).

For comprehensive discussion of Greek identity, as a step towards **defining the Greek world**, see, for example, Hall 1997; Hall 2002.

I have addressed some of the **interpretative potential and challenges posed by Greek domestic material** in, for example, Nevett 2010, 3–21; Nevett 2021. My basic theoretical perspective is outlined in Nevett 1999, 29–33 and I have continued to develop and refine my ideas over the years: for a recent example, see Nevett 2018.

Chapter 1:

For depictions of **the house and household, or oikos, in ancient Greek literature**, see, for example, Napolitano 2013. On **punishment by kataskaphe**, see Connor 1985. Interestingly, by contrast with this deliberate act, it seems that poverty alone did not entirely deprive a man of his sense of home, see Rougier-Blanc 2013. On the character of **domestic religion**, see Faraone 2008 and on the closely related topic of family religion, Boedecker 2008. Aspects are also discussed by Janette Morgan (Morgan 2010, 143–66). For a full treatment of the significance of domestic **herms** and of the circumstances surrounding their mutilation at Athens, see Osborne 1985; Crawley-Quinn 2007.

The **exterior features of Classical and Hellenistic houses** are discussed in more detail in Nevett 2009b. For an example of a **smoke-vent tile** (opaion tile) at Eretria, see Reber 1998, 126; for the chimney pot from Athens see discussions in Lawall et al. 2001, 173–75 and Tsakirgis 2007, 230–31. The **roof elements** from the House of Dionysos at Pella are discussed and illustrated in Makaronas and Giouri 1989, 88–123. For **Greek mosaics**, see Dunbabin 1999, 5–37, and **wall painting** Kakoulli 2009. Hellenistic domestic decoration more generally, including the 'masonry style', is discussed by Westgate 2000.

The **window mullions** from the houses at Eretria, are discussed by Reber (Reber 2010), with previous references. On **lighting** domestic interiors see Parisinou 1998; Parisinou 2007; Tsakirgis 2010. **Toilets** in Classical Greece are discussed by Antoniou 2010, with earlier references, and a terracotta urinal and toilet seat from Olynthos are shown in Robinson and Graham 1938, Plates 54 and 55. The child's potty from the Agora is discussed in Papadopoulos and Lynch 2006. **Bathing** is explored in Trümper 2010.

The **inscription from Black Corcyra** is discussed by Cahill 2002, 219–221. For the **inscription from Pergamon**, see Saba 2012. For Cahill's reconstruction of the **planning and building process** of houses within the orthogonal grid on the North Hill at Olynthos see Cahill 2002, 202–204; Sewell's discussion is at Sewell 2010, 87–109. The possible social context for planning and construction is also explored in Nevett in press.

On domestic **furniture** see Andrianou 2009, with further references. For the **Attic Stelai,** see Amyx 1958; Pritchett 1953; Pritchett 1956.

The **scarcity of pottery at Olbia** is discussed in Guldager Bilde 2010, 118–19. The existence of '**modest housing**' alongside larger, more elaborate properties on Delos is discussed by Trümper 2005b. For epigraphic evidence of **multiple dwellings** (synoikiai) see, for example, Vial 1984, 347. **Building Z** from the Kerameikos in Athens is discussed below in Chapter 3.

On the circumstances surrounding the **destruction and abandonment of Olynthos**, see Cahill 2002, 45–49. Thucydides' description of the **abandonment of the Attic countryside** is at Thucydides II.14.1. The **leases for the Delian farmsteads** are discussed in Kent 1948. The **farmhouses at Vari and near the Dema wall, in Attica,** are discussed further in Chapter 3 below.

Examples of **pyre deposits** found around the Athenian Agora include those in houses C and D near the Great Drain, and in the eastern house on the north slope of the Areopagos. A comprehensive account, with earlier references, is given in Rotroff 2013.

Production and workshops in the domestic context have also been studied from Athenian texts: see, for example, Harris 2002.

Organic remains: the potential offered by **archaeobotanical sources** is discussed, for example, by Margaritis 2014. References to Tria Platania, Lefkandi and Thorikos are given in Chapters 7, 2 and 3, respectively. For an overview of evidence from **Karanis**, see Husselman 1979. (Although the main aim of the excavations there was to find papyrus texts, Francis Kelsey, who conceived of the project, thought that the buildings and artefacts should be recorded to set those texts in context.) The **wooden artefacts from the Athenian Agora** well deposit are published in H. Robinson 1959, 108–09.

Interpretation of artefacts found in domestic contexts has become increasingly sophisticated in recent years: an early (and in retrospect rather uncritical) attempt to use such information, is Nevett 1999, 53–79. A more nuanced account, with additional references, can be found in Nevett 2021. (For a comprehensive discussion of the 'formation processes' giving rise to archaeological deposits in general, see Schiffer 1996.) The **koprones** at Halieis are described by Bradley Ault: Ault 1999, 550–56 and Ault 2005, 63–65; the **re-used vessel at Olynthos** comes from the 'House of Many Colours': Robinson 1946, 197; the **pottery sherds in the mortar matrix** of House I at Eretria are discussed by Reber 1998, 115.

Further discussion of **architectural typologies for Greek houses** can be found in Nevett 1999, 22–25. The definition and character of the andron is discussed further in Chapter 3. Some of the pitfalls of the use of **ancient terminology** by modern scholars are discussed by Allison 1999.

The **distribution of artefacts at Nichoria** is plotted in Fagerström 1988a, Fig. 5.

The **landmark studies of the 1980s** are Walker 1993 (first published in 1983) and Hoepfner and Schwandner 1994 (the first edition of which was published in 1986). The **hearth-room house** is described and discussed by Dakaris 1989 and Hoepfner and Schwandner 1994, 146–54. Evidence from **Crete** is covered extensively in Glowacki and Vogeikoff-Brogan eds. 2011, and an overview of the Classical material is presented by Westgate 2007b.

Preliminary comparative data on **pottery from a single house at Olynthos** recovered during more recent excavations are available in Ault et al. 2019. The data on the **ceramic finds from House 7 at Halieis** are summarised in Ault and Nevett 1999, 49–53 and Ault 2005, 19. The excavations at **Euesperides**, **Benghazi** are reported in Lloyd et al.

1995; Buzaian and Lloyd 1996; Lloyd et al. 1998 and discussed further in Chapter 6. For the **geophysics** at Plataia, see Konečny et al. 2012; for those at Olynthos, see Nevett et al. 2017 and Nevett et al. 2020.

Chapter 2

An introduction to the Early Iron Age is provided in Dickinson 2006, summarised on p. 23. I have added a coda to this Chapter covering the Archaic period since, as far as it is possible to see from current evidence, there is some continuity in house-forms, although excavated examples are extremely scarce compared with the preceding and subsequent periods. The dates given are all approximate and rely on the conventional, ceramic-based chronologies. (Findings at Assiros, in northern Greece, suggest that those absolute dates for the Early Iron Age pottery sequence may in fact need to be adjusted upwards by some fifty years: see Wardle et al. 2014 with earlier references). In addition to Dickinson's book, other classic treatments of this period include Snodgrass 2001 and Coldstream 2003. While some scholars would still like to use the Homeric poems, which were probably written down during the eighth century BCE, as evidence for the social and cultural context of the period discussed here (for example Raaflaub 2006), it seems safer to accept that they represent, at best, an amalgam of influences from different periods and locations: see, for instance, Whitley 1991; Morris 2001.

Early Iron Age housing in general receives exhaustive discussion in Fagerström 1988a; Mazarakis Ainian 1997; and Morris 1998a; their catalogues, together with a few additions, form the dataset on which the generalisations made here about Early Iron Age housing are based. For more in-depth discussion of the range of Early Iron Age Greek house-types, their distribution through time and space, and their possible social significance, see Nevett 2010, 22–42; Lippolis 2013. Early Iron Age housing is also the subject of a number of the papers in two edited collections, see: Westgate et al. eds. 2007; Glowacki and Vogeikoff-Brogan eds. 2011. The broader settlement context for the housing of early Greek communities is discussed by Lang 2002, summarising some of the ideas in her book-length study: Lang 1996. In some regions (particularly Crete and northern Greece) Early Iron Age house forms may have been influenced by those of the preceding Late Bronze Age. Nevertheless, in central southern Greece the abandonment of monumental, ashlar architecture and the complex, redistributive economy of that period seems to have been accompanied by a new concept of built space in which there was a lack of differentiation between domestic and other types of structures.

Nichoria: the original data on Unit IV.1 are published in Coulson 1983; my description of the architecture follows the reconstructions of Fagerström 1988b and Mazarakis Ainian 1992 together with Fagerström's discussion of finds distribution. For a reconstruction of the Greek economy between the Early Iron Age and Classical periods, see Morris 2004 and Morris 2005a. The potential **symbolism of storage jars (pithoi)** is discussed by Whitley 2018, with previous references.

For the apsidal houses of phase 1 at **Assiros**, see Wardle and Wardle 2000, with previous references. For **Old Smyrna**, see Akurgal 1983, 17–18 (the oval house and other buildings at the site are discussed further in Chapter 5).

Different approaches to **estimating the number of inhabitants** of a building are summarised briefly by Kent Flannery (Flannery 2002, 423, with further references). The nature of the **connection between house size and social status** in an ethnographic context has been addressed, among others, by Carol Kramer (Kramer 1982, 126–31, with reference to rural western Iran). Information about apartments at **Guangzhou**, China, is taken from the exhibition 'Solos: Tulou/Affordable Housing in China', held at the Smithsonian's Cooper-Hewitt, National Design Museum 3 October 2008 through 8 May 2009, curated by Matilda McQuaid: www.cooperhewitt.org/exhibitions/fall-design/Solos-Tulou/, accessed 6 October 2010.

Eretria: area by the seashore: I have taken as representative Kahil's excavation of the **Roussos plot:** Kahil 1981, summarised by Mazarakis Ainian 1987 and discussed further in Morris 1998a, 18; my phasing of the plot is taken from Mazarakis Ainian 2007, Fig. 17.6. **Themelis' excavations** are summarised in Mazarakis Ainian 1987, whose numbering of the structures I follow here; Mazarakis Ainian also lists the previous publications. Additional information is provided by Themelis 1992. More recent work on an adjacent plot to the south which confirms the results of the earlier excavations is reported in Reber et al. 2009. **Area of the later Apollo sanctuary:** my discussion greatly simplifies this very complex site but does try to take full account of renewed excavation between 1998 and 2003, published in full in Verdan 2012a. My numbering system for the buildings follows that used there and in the preliminary reports of those excavations published in *Antike Kunst*. Additional evidence for metalworking during the eighth century in the area outside the northwest corner of the seventh-century temple is discussed by Verdan 2002, 130; for evidence of the hearth in front of building 5, see: Verdan 2004. Verdan argues that buildings 1 and 150 were both religious in character throughout their periods of use: Verdan 2012a, 180; Verdan 2012b, 184–86. **Pausanias' description** of the cult building in the Apollo sanctuary at Eretria is at Pausanias 10.5. Alexander Mazarakis Ainian's ideas about the **connection between elites, religion, houses and temples** are set out at length in Mazarakis Ainian 1997 and summarised in Mazarakis Ainian 2001. There are additional models for the creation of sanctuaries (for example in association with natural topographic features), but, given the diversity of Early Iron Age society, it would not be surprising to see religious spaces forming in a variety of different ways in different locations.

Skala Oropou: at the time of this writing, preliminary results of the excavations in the south and west sectors have been reported in *Πρακτικά της Αρχαιολόγικης Εταιρείας* and *Έργον της Αρχαιολόγικης Εταιρείας*. Detailed summaries appear in several articles and chapters, including Mazarakis Ainian 1998; Mazarakis Ainian 2002a. Mazarakis Ainian's ideas about the role of the boundary walls or periboloi are explained in detail in Mazarakis Ainian 2002b and Mazarakis Ainian 2007 (see p. 166 for discussion of ethnographic parallels and functional specialisation within individual compounds). The possible relationship between the aristocracy and metal working is explored in Mazarakis Ainian 2006 and in Doonan and Mazarakis Ainian 2007. For ethnographic examples of multiple households co-resident in a single compound see, for example, the Malay village of Galok, discussed in Tsubouchi 2001, 120.

Emborio: the settlement, its houses and some of the associated artefacts are described in Boardman 1967.

Zagora has figured in numerous discussions of Greek society during the eighth century BCE. The original data are published in Cambitoglou et al. 1971 and Cambitoglou et al. 1988. The results of a more recent project at the site (see Beaumont et al. 2012; Beaumont et al. 2014; Miller et al. 2019/ 2020) have yet to be published in detail at the time of this writing. The social implications of the architecture of the houses at Zagora are discussed, among others, by Morris 1999, 309 whose interpretation is followed by various others including Coucouzeli 2007, especially p. 181 and Mazarakis Ainian 2007, 168. All view the creation of the enclosed courtyard as evidence of the kinds of gendering of space seen at Athens and elsewhere in the Classical period (see Chapter 3). A more recent analysis is Mann 2015. The chapter by Lin Foxhall mentioned in my discussion is Foxhall 2009.

The Lefkandi Toumba building: the building and its finds are published in full, and the stratigraphy discussed in detail, in Catling and Lemos 1990 and Popham and Sackett eds. 1993, the latter featuring an architectural reconstruction of the building by Jim Coulton. More recently Georg Herdt has suggested a less structurally ambitious restoration than Coulton's, on the grounds that the original reconstruction would not have been sufficiently sturdy: Herdt 2015. (Given that its scale is, as far as we know, unprecedented and the building does not seem to have stood for very long, it also seems possible that the builders' design was in fact flawed, leading to its collapse.) The primacy of the female burial is raised as a possibility by Carla Antonaccio: Antonaccio 2002. On the concept of monumentality in early Greece, including at Lefkandi, see Osborne 2005; on the emergence of monumentality in architecture, specifically, see Coulton 1977, 30–50. The development of specialised building forms is discussed by Franziska Lang in Lang 1996, summarised in Lang 2005 and Lang 2007. **Xeropolis site:** for a preliminary summary of some of the more recent work, see Lemos 2007. The analogy between the Lefkandi Toumba building and Amazonian long houses is made by Alexandra Coucouzeli: Coucouzeli 1998.

The term '**wanax**' is taken from a word found in Mycenean documents and survives into later Greek. '**Chief**' and '**big man**' are borrowed from anthropological studies of tribal societies in the present or recent past. There is extensive debate on the **nature of Early Iron Age society**, particularly over the validity of using various strategies as aids to understanding the extent and nature of social hierarchy, including the means through which it was created and maintained. Many of the issues are discussed in Whitley 1991. Other approaches are included in, for example, Deger-Jalkotzy and Lemos eds. 2006. Some of the discussions on the nature of Early Iron Age elites are reviewed by Ulf 2007.

For the occupation sequence at **Assiros**, see the discussion by Ken Wardle: Wardle 1996 esp. 446–52; **Kastanas** is published in detail in Hänsel 1989.

Aspects of the significance of the changes taking place in housing during the seventh and sixth centuries BCE are discussed by Lang 1996, who includes a consideration of the apsidal building at **Larisa on the Hermos** at p. 227.

For **Vroulia**, the original publication is Kinch 1914. The site is significantly eroded, and the complete plans of the individual buildings are difficult to reconstruct. The plan of the settlement is discussed by Melander 1988. The illustration here is based on the reconstruction by

Franziska Lang (Lang 1996, Fig. 64). The history of excavations together with recent work at the site by the Ephorate of the Dodecanese and the Danish Institute at Athens are discussed in Kaninia and Schierup 2017. The single room at **Limenas** on Thasos is under the northeast corner of insula I (Grandjean 1988, 389 n. 30). Preliminary information about the site of **Hypsele** is presented in Televantou 2011.

A brief account of **house k at Dystos** can be found at Schwandner 1999, 355–56. The **Kopanaki** building is described by Kaltsas 1983. The houses of **insula II near the Hermes Gate at Limenas**, Thasos are referred to in Grandjean 1990, 384 and discussed in detail in Grandjean 1988, 283–88 and 447–48. On the 'three-room group' see Krause 1977; Reber's discussion is in Reber 2001. The **Argilos** house is discussed by Bonias and Perrault 1996. The orthogonal **Archaic building in the west quarter at Skala Oropou** is discussed in Mazarakis Ainian 1996, 28–33 (the terracotta tiles are mentioned on p. 30).

Chapter 3

The **movement of female members of citizen families outside the house**, including restrictions implied in some of the textual sources, is discussed in detail in Nevett 2011b. My **statistics about Athens and Attica** in this Chapter are taken from Morris 2009, 115. Émile **Burnouf's investigations** are described briefly in Burnouf 1856, Burnouf 1878 and Burnouf 1879, 312–19. Thucydides' reference to the occupation of land within the **Long Walls** is at Thucydides II.17.3. A recent project to map the layout of the streets in Classical Athens is published in the series *Topografia di Atene*, by the Italian School at Athens.

For traces of **housing which pre-dates the Persian sack** of Athens, see Shear 1973, 147–50. For summaries of **archaeological evidence for Classical housing** found in Athens and Attica see Graham 1974 and Ellis Jones 1975, the latter supplemented by Ellis Jones 2007. More recent, though less comprehensive discussions of Athenian urban houses include Goldberg 1999 and Tsakirgis 2009. At the time of this writing, detailed publication of some of the **houses from the vicinity of the Agora** is still in preparation. Preliminary publications of them constitute the most detailed picture of the city's Classical housing, providing plans of the excavated structures together with discussion of how they changed through time, information about a few of the architectural features and examples of associated finds. These are summarised, with previous references, in

Thompson and Wycherley 1972, 173–185: their discussion covers the various urban Athenian houses discussed in Chapter 3.

The character of **house façades** generally in the Classical and Hellenistic periods is discussed more fully in Nevett 2009b. A possible **balcony** is identified in a house southwest of the Agora: Young 1951, 247. The location of **ounai or mortgage inscriptions** in situ on the façades of Athenian houses such as the **House of Aristodemos**, is described in Thompson 1966, 53.

The argument that **pits in streets and courtyards** were for planting trees is made by Lin Foxhall (Foxhall 2007b, 235–40). By contrast, Maureen Carroll-Spillecke suggests that the courtyards of Classical Greek houses generally were too small to be planted with trees, that their roots would undermine house foundations and that growth would have been impeded by the habitual use of cobbled or cement surfaces in some settlements during some periods (Carroll-Spillecke 1989, 19–21). The Athenian evidence for the pits, including textual sources for waste disposal, is outlined by Eddie Owens (1983); Bradley Ault offers detailed analysis of comparable features from Halieis: Ault 1999, 550–59; see also below Chapter 4.

For detailed discussion of the origins and cultural significance of **symposia**, with references to the very extensive previous scholarly literature on the subject, see respectively, Wecowski 2014; Hobden 2013, especially 2–21. Examples of andrones found during rescue excavations include Threpsiadis 1960 and Alexandri 1967. For the House of the Greek Mosaic, see Thompson and Wycherley 1972, 182–84, with previous references. The construction techniques used for the so-called **House of the Parakeet Mosaic** (also sometimes called the House of the Roman Mosaic) is described in Thompson 1966, 53 with Plate 18. For **House Θ'**, see Eleutheratou 2010, 148.

Kathleen Lynch provides detailed analysis of material from one of the **well-deposits** from the Agora, which she interprets as containing domestic material associated with drinking: Lynch 2011. The **artefacts** associated with the Agora houses more generally have yet to be published in detail, so my reconstruction of the range of activities carried out in them relies on occasional items mentioned in the preliminary excavation reports, together with discussions of the material found in the Agora generally, for which see Sparkes and Talcott 1970. The figures for the relative abundance of different pottery types come from Rotroff 1999. On **hearths, braziers and cooking**, see Tsakirgis 2007 and Foxhall 2007a, with previous references. Use of **communal serving dishes** instead of personal plates or bowls has been suggested for Roman Pompeii by Penelope Allison: Allison 2009, 24 and (again in the Roman context) has been viewed as a practice belonging to the lower social orders (as opposed to elites): Hudson 2010.

Evidence for domestic production and workshops at Athens is discussed in Tsakirgis 2005 and Tsakirgis 2016. The Π-shaped structures on the Hill of the Nymphs and adjacent areas are discussed in Lauter-Bufe and Lauter 1971, and the cuttings around Aghia Marina reinterpreted as the remains of a sanctuary of Zeus by Lalonde 2006, 20, with note 23 (I am indebted to the late Barbara Tsakirgis for pointing this out). The evidence for **building Z in the Kerameikos** is published fully in Knigge 2005 and summarised in Ault 2016.

The **social make-up of Athenian households** is a complex question: for discussion of some of the main issues, with references to previous literature, see Cox 1998, 130–208; Patterson 1998, 107–225. Similar conclusions have been reached for Ptolemaic Egypt, based on rather different evidence: see Bagnall and Frier 1994. Some of the difficulties of identifying the individuals resident in an excavated house are discussed in Nevett 2011a. The use of **surveillance** as a mechanism for social control is discussed by Hunter 1994, 81–85. **Women's access to water** in domestic contexts is touched on by Walker 1993, who also discusses the gendering of those contexts. The topic of **gender separation** in Greek houses is also discussed in Nevett 1994; Nevett 1995; Nevett 1999; Goldberg 1999; Antonaccio 2000. The possible **social significance of possessing an andron** is explored by Lynch 2007, especially 248–49 and Nevett 2010, 43–62.

The major surviving source of historical information about the context for the expansion of **Peiraios** is Aristotle's *Politics* (2.5.1267 b 22 – 1268 a 14). The general urban context and history are provided by Garland 1987. Information about the layout and housing is presented by George Steinhauer and Ioanna Kraounaki in collaboration with Hoepfner and Schwandner: Hoepfner and Schwandner 1994, 24–43; summarised by the same authors in Hoepfner 1999, 217–20. The connection between orthogonal grid plans and equality is argued by Hoepfner and Schwandner 1994.

The physical form and layout of the **Attic demes** are discussed by Steinhauer 1994. The layout and probable date of the deme centre at **Sounion** are discussed in Goette 2000, 49–51 which is the record of an architectural survey carried out after the vegetation cover burned off during a forest fire in 1993. The houses there were found to be roughly square in form, measuring approximately 16 by 16 m, with elaborate façades and open central courtyards. No recent excavations have been carried out, however, and the layouts of individual houses cannot be reconstructed in detail from the survey. **Thorikos** has a long history of excavation and has been revealed extensively. Information about some of the work of the Belgian School at Athens between 1963 and 1989 is given in Mussche 1998. Following the resumption of work at the site in 2004, Docter and Webster eds. 2018 offer a preliminary view. For attempts to identify an enslaved population there, see Morris 1998b. The evidence from **Ano Voula** is summarised in Andreou 1994. Domestic material from both Thorikos and Ano Voula is explored, and further references listed, in Nevett 2005, where the significance of these house-forms is discussed in more detail. Epigraphic evidence is discussed by Jones 2004, 111–16.

The use of **towers** as locations in which to lock up enslaved people is argued in Morris and Papadopoulos 2005 (evidence for barring the doors internally and externally is discussed at 188–92). Morris and Papadopoulos explicitly dismiss any reading of towers as markers of wealth and status on the grounds that the owners would not have been the individuals actually living in the properties. Nevertheless, in arguing that the towers were built for one specific purpose they contradict a mass of evidence showing that different spaces in ancient Greek houses tended to be used flexibly and were generally multi-functional. Their arguments also depend upon the coincidence of towers with areas of intensive mining or agriculture; nevertheless, these areas not only relied partly on enslaved labour but also provided the surplus wealth which, as Morris and Papadopoulos point out, was necessary to finance such structures. It seems unlikely that these communities were occupied only by enslaved people since facilities such as the theatre, which continued to be used – and enlarged – into the fourth century BCE, surely catered primarily to a free audience. It thus seems likely that towers – especially those incorporated into settlements, as at Thorikos and Ano Voula – had a range of different practical and symbolic functions.

Settlement evidence from the deme of **Atene** is set out in detail by Lohmann 1993. The remains of **rural towers in the area around Sounion** are described by Young 1956, with earlier references. The **Dema house** is published in Ellis Jones et al. 1962. For the **Vari house** see Ellis Jones et al. 1973 and for the **Zoster house** Stauropoullou 1938. For further discussion of the issues surrounding rural residence see also Foxhall 2004 and Winther-Jacobsen 2010. The suggestion that the Dema and Vari houses are atypical of rural houses in general was originally made by Winther-Jacobsen based on their ceramic assemblages, but, as indicated here, it also accords with their scale. Evidence for ore washeries in southern Attica, including examples where an andron is present, are discussed by

Ellis Jones 2007. The debate over the extent of **rural residence** is outlined, with further references, in Osborne 2010, 127–38. McHugh 2017 offers a recent overview of evidence for ancient Greek farmsteads generally.

The concept of the **single-entrance, courtyard house** was first laid out in Nevett 1999. **Perikles' citizenship law** is alluded to in Plutarch's *Life of Perikles* (37.2-5) and the Aristotelian *Constitution of the Athenians* (26.3). Its socio-political context and consequences are discussed, for example, by Josine Blok: Blok 2009; Blok 2017. The possible **link between house-form and citizen ideology** is discussed further in Nevett 1999, 167–68; Nevett 2009a; and argued in more detail in Westgate 2007a.

Chapter 4

Olynthos: the original excavations were published promptly and in great detail by the site's first excavator, David Robinson: Robinson 1929–1952. Evidence of burned destruction and looting are found, for example, in Section O (Robinson 1946, 264–65). Smaller scale investigations were carried out by Ioulia Vokotopoulou and the Greek Archaeological Service between 1988 and 1994 (Drougou and Vokotopoulou 1989; Protopsalti 1993; Vokotopoulou and Protopsalti 1994; Protopsalti 1994). The most recent program of investigations on both North and South Hills, by the Olynthos Project, was undertaken as a synergasia (collaboration) between the Greek Archaeological Service and the British School at Athens between 2014 and 2019. Study for the publication is ongoing and, like so many other things, has been severely delayed by the Covid-19 pandemic, but preliminary information about this work, including summaries of the geophysical evidence for the layout of the different districts, is published annually in *Archaeological Reports* for those years, while fuller discussions are given in Nevett et al. 2017 and Nevett et al. 2020. For the inscriptions (ounai) see Nevett 2000; Cahill 2002, 294–99. More recent discussion by Game 2008, 43–74 includes all of the Olynthian texts as well as commentaries and previous references in the context of a broader treatment of the significance of such documents from northern Greece, the Cyclades and Sicily. (The sale document in Text Extract 9 is translated from the text edited by Game 2008, 57–58 and originally published by Robinson 1938, 47–50.)

My interpretation of the **organisation of domestic space at Olynthos** is based on statistical analysis of the architecture and artefact distributions presented in Nevett 1999, 53–79; see also Cahill 2002, *passim*, where the material is evaluated using an alternative statistical technique and with a different emphasis. (For further discussion of the limitations of statistical analysis to understand spatial organisation in the houses, see also Cahill 2010.) House A vii 4 is described in Robinson and Graham 1938, 118–21. Even before the excavation of house B ix 6, stratigraphic study was shown to be important by the work of Vokotopoulou and colleagues, mentioned above (see especially Drougou and Vokotopoulou 1989, 343). This reinforced the significance of such information in enabling functional assemblages to be reconstructed, observing that in some spaces material was found in two different strata associated with different patterns of spatial usage.

The possible roles played by the various artefacts – especially pottery – encountered during excavation of Classical houses such as those from Olynthos are explored in detail in Nevett 1999, 34–52 and Nevett 2021; see also Rotroff 1999.

For information on **water systems in Greek cities**, including at Olynthos, see: Crouch 1993. On **commercial and craft production facilities integrated into domestic space at Olynthos**, see Robinson and Graham 1938, 211–13; Cahill 2002, 236–61; Cahill 2005, 54–60. For discussion of the possible **role of upper floors** in Olynthian houses, see Nevett 1999, 75–76.

Hoepfner and Schwandner's ideas on equality are set out in detail in Hoepfner and Schwandner 1994, 312–13 and are also discussed in Chapter 3. On the **political and economic situation at Olynthos,** and its possible effects on property ownership, see Hatzopoulos 1988. Ian Morris' discussion of **Athens as a stimulus for cultural change** across the Greek world appears in Morris 2009.

Thasos: evidence from the houses at the Silenos Gate in Limenas is published in Grandjean 1988, 67–238. An overview of these and other houses on the island, along with further references, is provided by Grandjean 1990, who traces the pastas-type plan back as far as the sixth century BCE on the island, although a domestic function for the earliest examples is not certain. The **farms at Marmaromandra and Glykadi** are described in Bonias 1999.

Torone: house 3 is discussed in Cambitoglou and Papadopoulos 2001, 142–70. **Abdera:** The dating of the houses near the West Gate has been debated. Their original excavator, Dimitris Lazaridis, placed them in the third or second century BCE (e.g. Lazaridis 1971, with references to earlier articles in *Πρακτικά* and *Αρχαιολογικόν Δελτίον*), while J. Walter Graham placed them in the fourth century BCE: Graham 1972, 299. (Graham's date was based, among other criteria, on the style of masonry used and the dates of the associated artefacts.) Artefacts found in the northern part of the site in the Avramoglou plot show that settlement there dates back as far as the Archaic period, but suggest that the architectural remains date from the late fourth or early third century BCE: Koukouli-Chrysanthaki 1991; Skarlatidou 1992. **Aphytis:** information is taken from one of the preliminary reports: Missailidou-Despotidou 2007. **Aiani:** a summary appears in Karamitrou-Mentessidi 2011.

Ammotopos and Kassope: because of their proximity and similarities the houses at the two sites are often discussed in tandem: see Dakaris 1989; Hoepfner and Schwandner 1994, 114–179; and Dakaris, Gravani and Schwandner in Hoepfner 1999, 368–411, with previous references. (The term 'hearth-room' is borrowed from Hoepfner and Schwandner's discussion of the 'Herdraum'.) For an early treatment of Ammotopos see also Hammond 1953. Elsewhere in the region housing has also been excavated at **Vitsa**, revealing a settlement of small, single-room houses dated somewhere between the ninth- and fourth-centuries (see Dakaris 1982; Vokotopoulou 1986 for a summary). These should not necessarily be taken as representative of the houses constructed in permanent settlements in the region: it has been argued that they were occupied in the summer months by pastoralists bringing their animals up into the mountains to graze. However, seasonality information from, for example, archaeobotanical or faunal evidence, is not reported, and this suggestion may have been made based on assumptions about what permanent houses and settlements ought to look like during this period. For housing at **Arta**, see summaries by Catherine Morgan and others of work by the Greek Archaeological Service between 2000 and 2014, in *Archaeology in Greece Online*; for **Leukas**, see Manuel Fiedler's contribution to Hoepfner 1999 and also Fiedler 2005. On the **political organisation of Epiros** during the Classical period and its gradual cultural alignment with cities further south and east, see Hammond 1967, 487–524 with Hammond 2000.

Halieis: the houses are described in detail and the finds discussed in Bradley Ault's publication of the houses: Ault 2005 (which includes references to earlier work). The mean minimum number of vessels per house is calculated by Robin Osborne who also usefully highlights some similarities and differences in the ranges of pottery types found in the different houses: Osborne 2006, 445. The koprones and oil presses are discussed in detail in Ault 1999. On the role of olive production in the economy of the Southern Argolid, see Jameson et al. 1994, 383–86; 393–94. The possible association between elite households and olive oil is discussed in Foxhall 2007b, 132, and her comments on the Halieis facilities are at pp. 143–48.

Dystos: the site was investigated by Wolfram Hoepfner and Ernst-Ludwig Schwandner in 1976. Their account of its houses appears in Hoepfner 1999, 352–67. Earlier discussions include Luce 1971. For **Aigeira** see: Kolia 2007–2008. On **Sikyon**: Lolos et al. 2007. **Stymphalos**: Williams et al. 1998; Williams et al. 2002, 138–41. **Tegea**: Ødegård 2010.

The work of the DAI at **Ano Siphai** is discussed by Schwandner: Schwandner 1977, 516–19. The DAI house is contextualised architecturally and culturally in Hoepfner and Schwandner 1994, 322 and Hoepfner and Schwandner 1999, 138–39. For Tomlinson and Fossey's work and a plan of the whole site: Tomlinson and Fossey 1970. For the rescue excavations at **Elean Pylos** see Coleman 1986, 66–116.

Fuller discussion of the relative **standardisation of houses** in a range of gridded settlements is provided in Nevett 2016.

Chapter 5

The potential of housing as a source for investigating cultural identity is explored in more detail in Nevett 2010, 63–88. Some of the problems with using the archaeological evidence to think about identity in the study of Greek cultures of the western Mediterranean are discussed perceptively by Antonaccio 2005; she brings up the context of Archaic Morgantina, specifically, in Antonaccio 1997.

Asia Minor: in addition to the comprehensive discussions of Hoepfner and Schwandner 1994, Lang 1996 and Hoepfner 1999, which all contain information about Asia Minor, among other areas, a more specific and focused discussion of housing along the northern part of the Asia Minor coast (the Troad) can be found in Aylward 2005.

Old Smyrna: evidence for housing is discussed in Akurgal 1983, although the interpretation is heavily dependent on a framework established using the ancient literary sources. The oval house is described at pp. 17–18; the later complex of rooms is that in squares B to G, described at pp. 35–39.

Miletos: The complex occupation histories and buildings of the different areas during the Geometric and Archaic periods are summarised by Lang 1996, 198–217, with further references. Aspects are summarised in a narrative account by Greaves 2002. Greaves suggests that the Archaic settlement was organised in a binary pattern similar to that seen in some of the Greek islands in more recent times, with part of the community exploiting the defensive qualities of Kalabaktepe, while the remainder was sited to take advantage of the natural harbours of the peninsula to its north-east. Alternatively, it seems possible that occupation here took the form of scattered nuclei of housing (as we have seen during the Geometric period at Eretria, see Chapter 2), while Kalabaktepe may have formed a defensive stronghold to which the population could withdraw if necessary.

Neandria: the survey of the site as a whole is published in Maischatz 2003; house 10.5.10 is described at p.43. Maischatz's interpretation of the social dimension of the housing is strongly influenced by the work of Moritz Kiderlen, discussed above in Chapter 2. For an earlier overview of the material, see Maischatz 1994. A single, well-preserved house is described in detail by Fatmann-Rey 1996, although he comments that it is atypically large.

Priene: the houses were originally published in Wiegand and Schraeder 1904, 285–468. Discussion of their organisation can be found in: Hoepfner and Schwandner 1994, 208–225 and also in Hoepfner 1999, 344–51. In the past few decades, there have been a variety of general publications about the site; see for example, Rumscheid 1998; Dontas and Hoepfner 2005, Ferla ed. 2006. For the urban layout, see Raeck 2005; for variation in the size of houses from the period of the city's initial construction see Raeck 2009; Rumscheid 2015. For David Small's treatment of symposiastic activities, see Small 2009, 214; Small 2010, 149. The results of more recent work at the site are discussed in Chapter 7.

Kolophon: the excavations are published in a preliminary fashion in Holland 1944. The features and dating are re-evaluated by Wolfram Hoepfner and Ernst-Wilhelm Osthues (Hoepfner 1999, 280–91). Work at the site resumed in 2013 under a joint Turkish and Austrian initiative: at the time of this writing, their focus has been on surveying the city and its chora and studying the cemeteries, so they have not as yet added to our knowledge of the houses (see, for example, Bammer et al. 2014 and Gassner et al. 2014). For property boundaries apparently changing through time, see for example room IIId, which seems to have been transferred from house III to its neighbour, house IV, prior to its abandonment. For andrones with plaster walls featuring contrasting panels and dados, see house II, room g. Examples of cement floors in the andron include house IV, room I and house VI room f.

Crete: Cretan housing from the Neolithic to Roman periods is the subject of the conference volume Glowacki and Vogeikoff-Brogan eds. 2011. Evidence from the Classical and, especially, Hellenistic periods has been summarised by Ruth Westgate, with further references: Westgate 2007b. For the Cretan Early Iron Age cultural- and settlement-contexts, see Wallace 2010, especially 231–62 and 267–85. A summary of findings at **Kavousi Kastro** is offered in Coulson et al. 1997. For recent work at **Karphi**, with previous references, see Wallace 2005. On **Kavousi Vronda**, see Day et al. 2009 and Day and Glowacki 2012.

Azoria: at the time of this writing, work is still on-going; for preliminary interpretations of the evidence for housing, with earlier references, see Haggis et al. 2011; Haggis and Mook 2011; Haggis 2014. Fitzsimons 2014 offers revisions of some of the original interpretations (see for example p. 245, n. 1). The Northeast Building is discussed in Haggis et al. 2007, 246–52 where it is interpreted as domestic in character.

Onithe was originally published by Nikolaos Platon and re-studied by Kyriakos Psaroudakis (see Psaroudakis 2004 for Psaroudakis' discussion together with previous references). Two sections of 'house A' have been variously interpreted as parts of a single dwelling or as subdivided. They are separated by an east-west wall and cover a total area of about 400 m^2. Given the extensive evidence for storage, Psaroudakis may be correct in questioning whether the role of the building could have been communal rather than domestic. **Lato**, see Picard and Ducrey 1996; **Eleutherna Nissi**, see Tsatsaki 2010; and **Trypetos, see** Vogeikoff-Brogan 2011, all with earlier references.

For detailed discussion of the similarities and differences between **symposium and syssition**, see Rabinowitz 2009. Rabinowitz 2011, also discusses the role of Archaic drinking practices in the construction of male identity on Crete, including the literary and epigraphic sources. The **andreion at Praisos** is discussed by Whitley 2011; the **communal dining building at Azoria** is discussed in Haggis 2013, 77–78 with previous references.

North Africa: the distribution of early Greek ceramic material from Cyrenaica is summarised in Boardman 1966. Evidence from Benghazi (ancient **Euesperides**) is summarised, with an emphasis on Archaic housing represented in earlier excavations, in Gill 2003; Gill 2006 and Gill and Flecks 2007. The more recent work is published in preliminary form in *Libyan Studies*: see, for the Archaic building in area H: Lloyd et al. 1998. For the remains of the early Hellenistic courtyard house see Buzaian and Lloyd 1996 and for the Hellenistic domestic architecture at Euesperides more generally, Wilson et al. 2004 (both with further references).

Sicily and southern Italy: twentieth-century evidence for culturally Greek housing is summarised in Barra Bagnasco 1996 and De Miro 1996. Some of the earliest houses associated with Greek material found in the western Mediterranean are those at Pithekoussai on the island of Ischia, which date back to the eighth century BCE (see, for example, Ridgeway 1992, 91–93; De Caro 1998). Evidence for Archaic housing in this area is reviewed by Oscar Belvedere, who compares the organisation of activities in the houses of western settlements like Monte San Mauro, Sicilian Naxos and Velia, with those of mainland Greek settlements such as Thorikos and Zagora (Belvedere 2000). **Morgantina** is discussed further below. Anne Cordsen makes a case for the identification of early pastas houses in Sicily in Cordsen 1995, discussing blocco 1 at Agrigento at pp. 115–16 (originally described by De Miro 1979, 713–14).

Megara Hyblaia: the Archaic houses are published in Vallet 1976 and Gras et al. 2004, 465–71. **Monte San Mauro:** my observations summarise those of Belvedere 2000, 80. At **Monte Iato**, Archaic houses west of the better-known Hellenistic peristyle house 2 are mentioned by Reusser et al. 2011, 88–95. The transverse room is house 1, room 2. As Belvedere 2000 notes, similar arrangements have been found in a seventh century house of unusually large size (about 115 m^2) at **Policoro** (ancient Siris) on the Italian mainland. This includes a formal court as well as a transverse anteroom, although details of the objects found during excavation are unknown so that it is not possible to comment on the distribution of activities. The settlement at **Velia** also incorporates both transverse ante-room and formal courtyard space: see Cordsen 1995, noted above.

Himera: the major reports include Adriani et al. 1970; Allegro et al. 1976; Allegro et al. 2008. The chronology of settlement has been debated and varies somewhat from neighbourhood to neighbourhood, but my discussion of the dates relies on Allegro 1996. A brief discussion of evidence from the earlier publications, including the distribution of artefacts, is given in Nevett 1999, 129–33. For a more recent consideration see also Harms 2010. Belvedere's detailed functional analysis of house VI 5 is Belvedere 2013. He suggests that house VI 5 broadly conforms to the single-entrance, house arrangement at p. 243. Comparative evidence from **Gela** is discussed in De Miro 1979, 710. The large *pastas* house and the organisation of Archaic and Classical **Sicilian Naxos** are discussed in Lentini 1998 and insula C4 in Lentini and Garaffo 1995; see also Lentini 1990. The houses from **Kaulonia** are described by Orsi 1914.

The northern Black Sea coast: much of the primary literature on this area is in Russian and Ukrainian and inaccessible to readers who (like me) cannot read these languages, but some is also in French and in the past couple of decades increasing numbers of summaries and reports have also appeared in English. Collections of papers on the region in antiquity include, for example, Grammenos and Petropoulos eds. 2003 and 2007; Bresson et al. eds. 2007. My discussion here draws only on a small selection of the potential sites and sources. Varying opinions have been offered about the extent to which the pit houses belonged to, or followed the traditions of, indigenous cultural groups. The debate is briefly summarised in Morel 2010, 283–84. Valeria Bylkova suggests that the house-form is different from those of indigenous groups in the region and must, therefore, have belonged to the Greek settlers: Bylkova 2007. **Berezan:** Solovyov observes similarities between handmade pottery found in the houses and the styles of local Thracian and Scythian groups: Solovyov 1999, 43. He suggests that the large number and wide distribution of the pit houses exclude the possibility that they were all inhabited by Greek settlers, ibid. 63, although he also acknowledges that the use-life of each building was probably very short – perhaps on occasion as little as 7 years: ibid. 40–41. **Olbia:** the houses of the Lower City discussed here are published in detail in Lejpunskaja et al. 2010.

Chapter 6

Ian Morris' argument for **long-term economic growth** in Greece between 800 and 300 BCE can be found in Morris 2004 and Morris 2005a.

For discussion of Alexander **Mazarakis-Ainian's argument** for the ceremonial role played by chief's houses in the Early Iron Age see above, Chapter 2.

Archaic Athens: for discussion of the possible location of a palace for Peisistratos at Athens, see Nielsen 1994, 73–75 with previous references. **Building F** is described in detail in Thompson 1940, 15–33 (where it is referred to as a house) and summarised in Thompson and Wycherley 1972, 27–28 (where a civic function is proposed). Various interpretations (including that this, rather than a structure on the Akropolis, was a palace for Peisistratos) are discussed by Boersma 2000, 54–55. Lin Foxhall has suggested that building F was the home of the chief magistrate (archon) and his family: Foxhall 2009, 504.

Palatial buildings: on the concept of the palace in the Hellenistic world and the vocabulary used by the ancient sources, see Hoepfner 1996, 1; Morgan 2017, 32–35. For more detail on textual sources, see Braund 2001.

Hansen and Fischer-Hansen 1994 point out the lack of archaeological evidence for palatial buildings in the Archaic period, and suggest that until the late fifth century BCE the concept of monumentality was applied only to religious buildings. An extreme contrary argument, that palaces (as opposed to relatively large houses) continued to be built through the Early Iron Age and Archaic periods, is proposed by Moritz Kiderlen (Kiderlen 1995; compare also Lippolis 2013, 207–17). Some of the problems with Kiderlen's theory are highlighted by, for example, Nevett 1997 and Ault 1998. A comprehensive summary of the archaeological evidence for the later palaces, including most of the buildings discussed here, is given by Nielsen 1994; for her important work on the origins and social significance of some architectural features of palaces, see also Nielsen 1996. Heermann 1986 also offers an architectural analysis of the Macedonian palaces. More recently Ferrara 2020 presents a detailed exploration of their architecture and roles.

Smaller but still elaborate structures have also been found in the western Mediterranean, for example at Torre di Satriano, southern Italy, which, while only covering an area of ca. 300 m, yielded elaborate architectural terracottas and Attic black-figure pottery alongside the local types (see Osanna and Capozzoli eds. 2012).

Vergina: a summary with previous references is given in Saatsoglou-Paliadeli 2007. On early research on the building, with further references, as well as the role played by the tholos, see Saatsoglou-Paliadeli 2001. For the significance of some of the architectural elements of the palace, see Brands 1998. On the recent cleaning, restoration and re-dating of the building and its components, see Kottaridi 2011a; Kottaridi 2011b. Based on these investigations Kottaridi suggests that the second peristyle was integral to the original design of the building. (Janett Morgan's assertion, 2017, 41, that the building could not have been residential fails to take account of the fact that the original excavations took place in the nineteenth century and little is known of the artefacts found, which could provide evidence for domestic activities.)

Pella palace: although excavation of the palace is incomplete owing to the vast scale and variable preservation of the building, there are many preliminary reports detailing different aspects of its construction and layout. My discussion here draws, in particular, on Siganidou 1981; Siganidou 1987; Siganidou 1996; Chrysostomou 1996 and Tsigarida et al. 2021. At the time of this writing, work to restore the propylon for viewing by visitors has just been completed, with further restoration and also research excavation, planned elsewhere in the building.

Demetrias: the excavated peristyle of the anaktoron is published in Theocharis 1976 and Marzolff 1996. Excavations since 1991 by the Greek Archaeological Service have revealed a number of additional features including more of a second courtyard to the west of this peristyle, see Batziou forthcoming. **Pergamon**: For the palatial buildings on the akropolis, see Zimmer 2014. Inge Nielsen's correlation between different forms of palatial building and the type of monarchy is based on a comparison between Macedon and Hellenistic Palestine: Nielsen 1997.

The **double-courtyard houses of the fourth century BCE** are referred to by Wolfram Hoepfner as 'palace-like', because of their layout (Hoepfner 1999, 325). **Eretria**: for the **House of the Mosaics**, see Ducrey et al. 1993. In addition, the interpretation of the decorative schemes of the individual rooms is discussed in detail in Westgate 2010, 497–504 and Hardiman 2011. The wall between rooms 8 and 9 is discussed by Reber 2007, 282–283, with earlier references. The evidence from the other houses of the **West Gate Quarter**, including House IV, is set out in detail by Reber 1998, where some of the earlier preliminary interpretations of the material are revised. (For Reber's suggestion that the original, western section of house IV served a non-domestic purpose, see 91–92; see also the comments on this subject by Monika Trümper: Trümper 2002, 629–30; and Craig Hardiman: Hardiman 2011, 196–99.) The set-up of this house in fact parallels that of **houses C and D** near the Great Drain in the Athenian Agora, which at one stage were combined, with one courtyard serving as a metal workshop (see Chapter 3).

Maroneia: an overview is presented in Karadedos 1990 and details of construction and decorative schemes are provided by Lavas and Karadedos 1991, both with further references. **Erythrai**: Hoepfner's account and reconstruction are in Hoepfner 1999, 450–51. For discussion of the differences between the Greek andron and Roman triclinium, together with their social implications, see Dunbabin 1998.

Megara Hyblaia house XV B: my discussion here is based on Annette Haug and Dirk Steuernagel's re-analysis of the architecture following a new documentation project (Haug and Steuernagel 2014; summarised in Haug and Steuernagel 2018). This reading of the evidence differs significantly from that given by Vallet 1983, 45–48, hence the present treatment supersedes Nevett 1999, 144–46. (Major differences between the earlier and more recent interpretations include the attribution of the northern courtyard to the first phase of construction, and the exclusion of the southernmost range of rooms, which are now viewed as part of a separate structure.)

The **House of Dionysos at Pella** was one of several luxurious residences excavated south of the agora at Pella: for this, and the neighbouring house of the Abduction of Helen, see Makaronas and Giouri 1989. On **changing social customs associated with dining rooms** with different patterns of layout, see the useful and perceptive comments of Inge Nielsen: Nielsen 1998. On specifically Hellenistic dining patterns, see also Hellström 1996. John Ma has suggested that these Pella houses represent a diffusion of the culture of the royal court into the behaviour of its aristocratic members: Ma 2011, 541.

The building at **Kastro Tigani on Samos** is described in Tölle-Kastenbein 1974 where it is suggested that its scale suggests a public, rather than strictly private, role (Tölle-Kastenbein 1974, 14).

For textual references to the **purchase of neighbours' property** to combine with one's own, see, for example, Isaios 5.11, in which the speaker relates how a house was purchased by a neighbour, although in this case it was demolished to make a garden. On the **symbolism of the hearth** in Greek literature and thought, see Vernant 1983.

There is an extensive literature on **male and female spaces** in Greek houses. My argument is set out in full, with earlier references, in Nevett 1995 and Nevett 1999, 70–74. For more recent discussion see, for example, Antonaccio 2000; Foxhall 2013, 114–21. See also the discussion above in Chapter 3.

For **the tavern at Krania**, see Margaritis 2014.

The possibility of a shift in expenditure of wealth from funerary and sanctuary contexts to domestic ones is explored in Nevett 2007. On **Demosthenes and domestic architecture**, as well as the possible **relationship between palatial buildings and large houses**, see Nevett 2022. With reference to another passage in which Demosthenes criticises domestic luxury, this time that of Meidias (Demosthenes 21.159), Marden Nichols makes the helpful observation that the point is not the luxury per se but the impression it creates in the civic sphere that is important (Nichols 2017, 93).

Chapter 7

A number of scholars have noted that earlier Greek ideals of **self-restraint in domestic architecture** seem to have been abandoned from the late fourth century BCE onwards in favour of conspicuous consumption: for example, Walter-Karydi 1998; Rumscheid 2010, 131.

Examples of **peristyle houses with a single courtyard** are rare on the Greek mainland before the Roman period, although this may be the result of chance factors. Those that have been excavated include some in the West Quarter at Eretria during certain phases (for example, House II in its first phase: see Reber 1998). In addition, as noted in Chapter 3, the House of the Greek Mosaics, near the Athenian Agora, was interpreted by Homer Thompson as having had 'porticoes' on three of its four sides, but his discussion does not make clear whether these were original to the house, which was occupied down to at least the fourth century CE. (Thompson 1966, 52). A further Classical Athenian house on the north shoulder of the Areopagos is normally represented as having had a central peristyle (see Chapter 3). The building was occupied into the Roman period and the excavator, T. Leslie Shear, argued that the presence of foundations for two columns at approximately the Classical floor level showed that the house had a peristyle in its Classical phase as well as later (Shear 1973, 153). (Barbara Tsakirgis suggested that this reconstruction was purely hypothetical: Tsakirgis 2005, 80 n. 5).

The phasing of **Priene house 33** is discussed by Hoepfner and Schwandner 1994, 225. They also explore the development of **house 3 at Kassope:** Hoepfner and Schwandner 1994, 158–59.

Evidence for the houses at **Delos** is published in Chamonard 1922, Deonna 1938, Bruneau et al. 1970 and Siebert 2001. Information from these and from preliminary reports in the *Bulletin de Correspondance hellénique* is summarised by Trümper 1998, who identifies a penetration of elite architectural and decorative styles among the larger residences of the community. An example of a double-courtyard house on Delos, created by amalgamating two earlier domestic units is the **House of Cleopatra and Dioscorides**. This house, along with patterning in the architecture of Delian housing more generally, is discussed in Nevett 2010, 63–88. The Hill House is documented in Chamonard 1922, 411–16. The Hermes House is described by Delorme 1953. Sculptural decoration among Delian houses, including the house in the Theatre Quarter displaying a figure of Artemis in the courtyard, is explored by Kreeb 1988. The assemblage in the House of the Seals is discussed by Trümper 2005a, who argues that even in the context of detailed evidence, the question of the cultural origins of the house's last occupants is impossible to answer. The evidence from the **Insula of the Comedians** is set out in detail in Bruneau et al. 1970. The paintings of the **Compitalia** are discussed by Hasenohr 2003, Nevett 2005.

House 1 from Monte Iato is published by Dalcher 1994 and Brem 2000 with a more recent reconsideration by Aiosa 2017, who includes a summary of the debate concerning the chronology at p. 234, n. 3. Preliminary accounts of **House 2** are given by Reusser et al. 2011 and Russenberger 2014. The **bathing culture** of the settlement is discussed in Russenberger 2013 and that of Sicily more generally by Trümper 2014. On **Solunto** see Wolf 2003 and Helas 2012. **Morgantina:** the Classical city provides evidence for increasing local cultural influences, see Walsh 2011/ 12. It is challenging to engage in detailed discussion of this evidence because the house-plans have yet to be fully published. At the time of this writing, a definitive publication of the Hellenistic houses from the site by the late Barbara Tsakirgis is forthcoming, based on her original doctoral dissertation, Tsakirgis 1984. At present, the most complete information relates to the House of the Official: Stillwell 1963, 166–68 (with plan, Fig. 11); see Nevett 1999, 148 (for a summary of this house and full references). Work on domestic buildings at Morgantina is still ongoing, see for example, Souza et al. 2019.

Olbia: the Hellenistic houses of area NGF are described in Wasowicz 1975, 94–98, with Figs. 85, 88 and 89, summarising information originally published by Sergei Kryžicki. The Hellenistic houses from the city of **Chersonesos** are summarised in Mack and Coleman Carter 2003, 74 and 82–83.

Helpful preliminary accounts of the **House of Lampon at Priene** are given in Rumscheid 2014 and Rumscheid 2015. Evidence from **Nea Halos** is summarised in Haagsma 2003 and discussed in more detail in Haagsma 2010. Houses there with a more conventional courtyard plan include the House of the Ptolemaic Coins. **Polymylos** is described briefly in Karamitrou-Mentessidi 2012 and summarised in Whitley 2007, 49. (Unfortunately, at the time of this writing, no published plan is available.) Findings at **Kallion** are summarised in Themelis 1979, Themelis 1998, 47, and Themelis 1999. The nature of the archive is discussed in detail by Pantos 1984, who suggests a later destruction date than Themelis, based on the evidence of the sealings.

Rachi, Isthmia: some of the rock-cut features here, including a well and cistern, were originally published as the remains of a facility for producing and dyeing cloth on a large scale: Kardara 1961. Excavation was subsequently extended further east revealing a settlement, identifiable not only through the wider range of rock-cut features but also based on the variety of domestic pottery such as tablewares and coarsewares used for transportation and storage of foodstuffs. My discussion is based on Virginia Anderson-Stojanovic's reports (Anderson-Stojanovic 1996; Anderson-Stojanović 2016). In support of her conclusion that this represents a small agricultural community, Lin Foxhall also interprets the facilities here as encompassing a variety of agricultural and craft production activities, rather than solely the manufacture of textiles (Foxhall 2007b, 153–59).

For housing at **Elea** see Riginos and Lazari 2008, with previous references. The settlement on **Aghios Panteleimon hill in Florina** is summarised in Akamatis and Lilimbaki Akamati 2006. My information on the Abramoglou plot at **Abdera** is taken from Skarlatidou 1992, 685–87. Insula II near the Silenos Gate at Limenas on **Thasos** is described in Grandjean 1988, 199–235. My discussion of **Petres** is based on information from Adam-Veleni 1995, Adam-Veleni 1996 and Adam-Veleni 2000. (For a full list of preliminary publications, see Naoum 2019, 63 n. 1.)

Rural housing: a pioneering overview of evidence from a range of field survey projects, which points to a decline in the numbers of small sites from the Hellenistic or early Roman periods is Alcock 1993 (for a more up-to-date summary, see also Alcock 2012). On regional variability in rural occupation during the Classical period, see, for example, Osborne 1994, 59–62. More recently, Carl Reber has also suggested a contraction in rural settlement: Reber 2007, 285–88. For the **Farm with the Granite Jambs, Delos**, see Brunet 1989 and Brunet 1990, with previous references. The **large Hellenistic farms in Pieria** are published in Adam-Veleni et al. 2003. Evi Margaritis discusses the importance of both farms as evidence for the Hellenistic rural economy generally in Margaritis 2016. Maeve McHugh explores the size-range of rural sites detected by a variety of field survey projects, with estimates ranging up to 1,380 m^2 in Methana, 3,000 m^2 in the southern Argolid and 7,000 m^2 in Lakonia (McHugh 2017, 56–57), although presumably these figures represent the extent of the associated material, with the buildings themselves covering a smaller area.

Chersonesos: an early English language discussion of the fossilised agricultural landscape was included in Pecirka 1973. Detailed discussion of four different farm sites is included in Saprykin 1994. More recent summaries, including information about Farm 151, are given in Coleman Carter et al. 2000 and Mack and Coleman Carter eds. 2003, 120–27.

Metaponto: my discussion here is based on a range of farmhouses in the chora of Metaponto and further afield in southern Italy summarised by Lanza Catti and Swift in Lanza Catti et al. 2014, drawing on earlier work by Joseph Coleman Carter. Lanza Catti and Swift point out the similarities in organisation between the farms in the Metapontine chora and those of the local population at p. 104. Assunta Florezano draws conclusions about the agricultural regime around the Fattoria Fabrizio at pp. 133–138.

Epilogue

Advances in archaeological interpretation: here, I am thinking of how the relationship between the material record and the processes by which it is shaped tend to be conceptualised, see for instance Nevett 2021. For an example of what can be done with **geophysical evidence**, see the work at Olynthos by the Olynthos Project, reported in preliminary fashion in Nevett et al. 2017, 12–15 and 34–35; Nevett et al. 2020, 14–20. For an example of the application of a wider range of **geoarchaeological techniques**, see the experimental work by Carla Lancelotti in house B ix 6 at Olynthos, reported briefly in Nevett et al. 2020, 34–36. Full publication of these Olynthos Project data is in preparation.

References

Adam-Veleni, P. 1995. Πέτρες 1995, η συνοικία της κρήνης, *Αρχαιολογικό Έργο στη Μακεδονία και στη Θράκη*, 9: 15–23.

1996. Πέτρες Φλώρινας: δώδεκα χρόνια ανασκαφής, *Αρχαιολογικό Έργο στη Μακεδονία και στη Θράκη*, 10: 1–18.

2000. *Πέτρες Φλώρινας*, (Thessaloniki: second edition).

Adam-Veleni, P., Poulaki, E. and Tzanavari, K. 2003. *Ancient Country Houses on Modern Roads: Central Macedonia*, (Athens: Archaeological Receipts Fund).

Adriani, A., Bonacasa, N., di Stefano, C., Joly, E., Piraino, M., Schmiedt, G. and Cutroni, A. 1970. *Himera I: Campagne di Scavo 1963–1965*, (Rome: 'L'erma' di Bretschneider).

Aiosa, S. 2017. La Casa a Peristilio 1 di Monte Iato: considerazioni per una nuova ipotesi ricostruttiva. In L. M. Caliò and J. de Courtils, eds., *L'architettura greca in Occidente nel III secolo a.C.: atti del convegno di studi, Pompei-Napoli, 20–22 maggio 2015*, (Rome: Edizioni Quasar), 233–48.

Akamatis, I. M. and Lilimbaki Akamati, M. 2006. *The Hellenistic City of Florina*, (Thessaloniki: Ministry of Culture).

Akurgal, E. 1983. *Alt-Smyrna I: Wohnschichten und Athenatempel*, (Ankara: Türk Tarih Kurumu Basımevi).

Alcock, S. E. 1993. *Graecia Capta: The Landscapes of Roman Greece*, (Cambridge: Cambridge University Press).

2012. The Essential Countryside: The Greek World. In S. Alcock and R. Osborne, eds. *Classical Archaeology*, (Oxford: Wiley Blackwell, second edition), 124–43.

Alexandri, O. 1967. Γ Εφορεία κλασικών Αρχαιοτήτων Αθηνών: Μενάνδρου 9, *Αρχαιολογικόν Δελτίον* 22, Χρονικά: 98–100.

Allegro, N. 1996. Le fasi dell'abitato di Himera. In H. P. Isler, D. Käch and O. Stefani, eds. *Wohnbauforschung in Zentral- und Westsizilien, Sicilia occidentale e centro-meridionale: ricerche archeologiche nell'abitato*, (Zürich: Archäologisches Institut der Universität Zürich), 65–80.

Allegro, N., Amico, A., Badagliacca, F., Danile, L., d'Esposito, L., Grotta, C., et al. 2008. *Himera V. L'abitato: isolato ii. i blocci 1–4 della zona 1*, (Palermo: Università di Palermo, Dipartimento di Beni Culturali).

Allegro, N., Belvedere, O., Bonacasa, N., Bonacasa Carra, R. M., di Stefano, C. A., Epifanio, E., Joly, E., Manni Piraino, M. T., Tullio, A. and Tusa Cutroni, A., eds. 1976. *Himera II: campagne di scavo 1966–1973*, (Rome: Bretschneider).

Allison, P. 1999. Labels for Ladles: Interpreting the Material Culture of Roman Households. In P. Allison ed. *The Archaeology of Household Activities*, (London: Routledge), 57–77.

2009. Understanding Pompeian Household Practices through Their Material Culture, *Facta* 3: 11–33.

Amyx, D. A. 1958. The Attic Stelai: Part III, *Hesperia* 27: 163–310.

Anderson-Stojanovic, V. 1996. The University of Chicago Excavations in the Rachi Settlement at Isthmia, 1989, *Hesperia* 65: 57–98.

2016. The Domestic Architecture of the Rachi Settlement at Isthmia. In E. Gebhart and T. Gregory, eds. *Bridge of the Untiring Sea: The Corinthian Isthmus from Prehistory to Late Antiquity*, (Princeton: Hesperia Supplement).

Andreou, I. 1994. Ο δήμος των Αιξωνίδων Αλών. In W. Coulson, O. Palagia, T. L. Shear Jr., H. Shapiro and F. Frost, eds. *The Archaeology of Athens and Attica under the Democracy*, (Oxford: Oxbow), 191–209.

Andrianou, D. 2009. *The Furniture and Furnishings of Ancient Greek Houses and Tombs*, (Cambridge: Cambridge University Press).

Antonaccio, C. 1997. Urbanism at Archaic Morgantina, *Acta Hyperborea* 7: 167–93.

2000. Architecture and Behavior: Building Gender into Greek Houses, *Classical World* 93: 517–33.

2002. Warriors, Traders, Ancestors: The 'Heroes' of Lefkandi. In J. M. Hojte, ed. *Images of Ancestors (Aarhus Studies in Mediterranean Archaeology, Volume 5)*, (Aarhus: Aarhus University Press), 13–42.

2005. Excavating Colonization. In H. Hurst, and S. Owen, eds. *Ancient Colonizations*, (London: Duckworth), 97–113.

Antoniou, G. 2010. Ancient Greek Lavatories: Operation with Reused Water. In L. Mays, ed. *Ancient Water Technologies*, (Heidelberg: Springer Netherlands), 67–86.

Ault, B. A. 1998. (M.) Kiderlen Megale Oikia. Untersuchungen zur Entwicklung aufwendiger griechischer Stadthausarchitektur von der Früharchaik bis ins 3 Jh. v. Chr., *Journal of Hellenic Studies* 118, 244–45.

1999. Koprones and Oil Presses at Halieis: Interaction of Town and Country and the Integration of Domestic and Regional Economies, *Hesperia* 68: 549–73.

2005. *The Houses: The Organization and Use of Domestic Space. The Excavations at Ancient Halieis, 2* (Bloomington: Indiana University Press).

2016. Building Z in the Athenian Kerameikos: House, Tavern, Inn, Brothel? In A. Glazebrook and B. Tsakirgis, eds. *The Archaeology of Brothels, Houses and Taverns in the Greek World*, (Philadelphia: University of Pennsylvania Press), 75–100.

Ault, B. A. and Nevett, L. C. 1999. Archaeologies of Classical and Hellenistic Domestic Assemblages. In P. Allison ed. *The Archaeology of Household Activities*, (London: Routledge), 43–56.

Ault, B. A., Lynch, K. M., Panti, A., Archibald, Z. H., Nevett, L. C. and Tsigarida, E. B. 2019. The Olynthos Project: Classical Pottery in an Urban and Domestic Context. In E. Manakidou and A. Avramidou, eds. *Classical Pottery of the Northern Aegean and Its Periphery (480–323/300 BC)*, (Thessaloniki: University Studio Press), 423–30.

Aylward, W. 2005. Security, Synoikismos, and Koinon as Determinants for Troad Housing in Classical and Hellenistic Times. In B. A. Ault and L. C. Nevett, eds. *Ancient Greek Houses and Households*, (Philadelphia: University of Pennsylvania Press), 36–53.

Bagnall, R. and Frier, B. 1994. *The Demography of Roman Egypt*, (Cambridge: Cambridge University Press).

Bammer, A., Draganits, E., Gassner, V., Grammer, B., Gretscher, M., Mariaud, O. and Muss, U. 2014. Colophon 2013, *Forum Archaeologiae, Zeitschrift für klassische Archäologie* 71 / VI / 2014.

Barra Bagnasco, M. 1996. La casa in Magna Grecia. In F. D'Andria and K. Mannino, eds. *Ricerche sulla casa in Magna Grecia e in Sicilia*, (Lecce: Congedo), 41–66.

Batziou, A. Forthcoming. The Palace of Demetrias: Location, Organisation and Role. In A. Skitsa and E. Tsigarida, eds. *The Hellenistic Palaces*, (Thessaloniki: Archaeological Museum of Pella).

Beaumont, L. A., McLoughlin, B., Miller, M. C. and Paspalas, S. A. 2014. Zagora Archaeological Project: The 2013 Field Season, *Mediterranean Archaeology* 27: 115–121.

Beaumont, L. A., Miller, M. C., Paspalas, S. A., Bassiakos, Y., Cantoro, G., Déderix, S., McLoughlin, B., Papadopoulos, N., Sarris, A. and Wilson, A. 2012. New Investigations at Zagora (Andros): The Zagora Archaeological Project 2012, *Mediterranean Archaeology* 25: 43–66.

Belvedere, O. 2000. Osservazioni sulla cultura abitativa greca in eta arcaica. In I. Berlingó, H. Blanck, F. Cordano, et al., eds. *Damarato: studi di antichita classica offerti a Paola Pelagatti*, (Milan: Electa), 58–68.

    2013. Himera. Casa VI 5: un tentativo di analisi funzionale. In S. Bouffier and A. Hermary, eds. *L'occident grec de Marseille à Mégara Hyblaea: hommages à Henri Tréziny*, (Aix-en-Provence: Publications du Centre Camille Jullian), 241–63.

Blok, J. 2009. Perikles' Citizenship Law: A New Perspective, *Historia* 58: 141–70.

    2017. *Citizenship in Classical Athens*, (Cambridge: Cambridge University Press).

Boardman, J. 1966. Evidence for the Dating of Greek Settlements in Cyrenaica, *Annual of the British School at Athens* 61, 149–56.

    1967. *Excavations in Chios 1952–1955: Greek Emporio*, (London: Annual of the British School at Athens Supplement 6).

Boedecker, D. 2008. Family Matters: Domestic Religion in Classical Greece. In J. Bodel and S. M. Olyan, eds. *Household and Family Religion in Antiquity*, (Oxford: Blackwell), 229–47.

Boersma, J. 2000. Peisistratos' Building Activity Reconsidered. In H. Sancisi-Weerdenburg, ed. *Peisistratos and the Tyranny: A Reappraisal of the Evidence*, (Amsterdam: Gieben), 49–56.

Bonias, Z. 1999. Οι αγροικίες τις Θάσου και τα λατόμια μαρμάρου. In C. Koukouli-Chrysanthaki, A. Muller and S. Papadopoulos, eds. *Thasos, Matières premières et technologie de la préhistoire à nos jours, Actes du Colloque intern. de Thasos*, (Athens-Paris: Boccard), 102–15.

Bonias, Z. and Perreault, J. 1996. Άργιλος, πέντε χρόνια ανασκαφής, *Αρχαιολογικό Έργο στη Μακεδονία και στη Θράκη* 10, 663–80.

Brands, G. 1998. Halle, Propylon und Peristyl: Elemente hellenistischer Palastfassaden in Makedonien. In W. Hoepfner and G. Brands, eds. *Basileia: die Paläste der hellenistischen Könige*, (Mainz: von Zabern), 62–75.

Braund, D. 2001. Palace and Polis: Dionysus, Scythia and Plutarch's Alexander. In I. Nielsen, ed. *The Royal Palace Institution in the First Millennium*, (Aarhus: Aarhus University Press), 15–31.

Brem, H. 2000. *Das Peristylhaus 1 von Iaitas: Wand- und Bodendekorationen*, (Zurich: Huber).

Bresson, A., Ivantchik, A. and Ferrary, J.-L. ed. 2007. *Une koinè pontique: cités grecques, sociétés indigènes et empires mondiaux sur le littoral nord de la mer Noire (VIIe s. a.C-IIIe s. p.C.)*, Collection Mémoires 18, (Bordeaux: Ausonius Éditions).

Bruneau, P., Vatin, C., Bezerra de Meneses, U., Donay, G., Lévy, E., Bovon, A., Siebert, G., Grace, V., Savvatianou-Pétropoulakou, Lyding Will, E. and Hackens, T. 1970. *Exploration archéologique de Délos XXVII: L'îlot de la maison des comédiens*, (Paris: Boccard).

Brunet, M. 1989. Ferme aux jambages de granit, *Bulletin de Correspondence Hellénique* 113, 754–61.

1990. Ferme aux jambages de granit, *Bulletin de Correspondence Hellénique* 114, 906–08.

Burnouf, E. 1856. Notice sur le plan d'Athènes, *Archives des Missions Scientifiques et Littéraires* 5, 64–88.

1878. Maisons privées de l'ancienne Athènes, *Revue Générale de l'Architecture et des Travaux Publics* 35, 129–34.

1879. *Mémoires sur l'antiquité: l'age de bronze; Troie; Santorin; Délos; Mycènes; Le Parthénon; Les courbes; Les propylées; Un faubourg d'Athènes*, (Paris: Maisonneuve).

Buzaian, A. and Lloyd, J. 1996. Early Urbanism in Cyrenaica, *Libyan Studies* 27, 129–52.

Bylkova, V. 2007. Scythian and Olbian Settlements in the Lower Dnieper Region. In R. Westgate, N. Fisher and J. Whitley, eds. *House, Settlement and Society in the Aegean and Beyond*, (British School at Athens Studies, 15, London: British School at Athens), 297–306.

Cahill, N. 2005. Household Industry in Greece and Anatolia. In B. Ault and L. C. Nevett, eds. *Ancient Greek Houses and Households: Chronological, Regional and Social Diversity*, (Philadelphia: University of Pennsylvania Press), 54–66.

2010. Functional Analyses of Ancient House Inventories. In S. Ladstätter and V. Scheibelreiter, eds. *Städtisches Wohnen im östlichen Mittelmeerraum 4. Jh. v. Chr. - 1. Jh. n. Chr.*, (Vienna: Verlag der Österreichischen Akademie der Wissenschaften), 477–95.

Cahill, N. D. 2002. *Household and City Organization at Olynthus*, (New Haven: Yale University Press).

Cambitoglou, A., Birchall, A., Coulton, J. and Green, J. R. 1988. *Zagora 2: Excavation of a Geometric Town*, (Athens: Athens Archaeological Society).

Cambitoglou, A., Coulton, J. J., Birmingham, J. and Green, J. R. 1971. *Zagora 1: Excavation Season 1967, Study Season 1968–9*, (Sydney: Sydney University Press).

Cambitoglou, A. and Papadopoulos, J. K. 2001. The Excavations of 1975, 1976, 1978. In A. Cambitoglou, J. K. Papadopoulos and O. Tudor Jones, eds. *Torone I*, (Athens: Athens Archaeological Society), 89–272.

Carroll-Spillecke, M. 1989. *ΚΗΠΟΣ Der antike griechishe Garten*. (Munich: Deutscher Kunstverlag).

Catling, R. W. V. and Lemos, I. 1990. *Lefkandi II: The Protogrometric Building at Toumba. Part 1, The pottery*, (London: British School at Athens).

Chamonard, J. 1922. *Exploration archéologique de Délos VIII*, (Paris: École française d'Athènes).

Chrysostomou, P. 1996. Το Ανάκτορο της Πέλλας, *Αρχαιολογικό Έργο στη Μακεδονία και στη Θράκη* 10(A), 105–42.

Coldstream, J. N. 2003. *Geometric Greece*, (London: Routledge).

Coleman, J. 1986. *Excavations at Pylos in Elis*, (Princeton: American School of Classical Studies, Hesperia Supplement 21).

Coleman Carter, J., Crawford, M., Lehman, P., Nikolaenko, G. and Trelogan, J. 2000. The Chora of Chersonesos in Crimea, Ukraine, *American Journal of Archaeology* 104, 707–41.

Connor, W. R. 1985. The Razing of the House in Greek Society, *Transactions of the American Philological Association* 115, 79–102.

Cordsen, A. 1995. The Pastas House in Archaic Greek Sicily. In T. Fischer-Hansen, ed. *Ancient Sicily: Acta Hyperborea 6*, (Copenhagen: Museum Tusculanum Press, University of Copenhagen), 103–21.

Coucouzeli, A. 1998. Architecture, Power, and Ideology in Dark Age Greece: A New Intepretation of the Lefkandi Toumba Building. In R. Docter and E. Moorman, eds. *Proceedings of the XV International Congress of Classical Archaeology, Amsterdam July 12-17*, 1998, (Amsterdam: Allard Pierson Museum), 126–29.

2007. Architecture and Social Structure in Early Iron Age Greece. In R. Westgate, N. Fisher and J. Whitley, eds. *Building Communities. House, Settlement and Society in the Aegean and Beyond*, (British School at Athens Studies 15, London: British School at Athens), 169–82.

Coulson, W. 1983. The Architecture: Area IV. In W. A. McDonald, W. D. E. Coulson and J. Rosser, eds. *Excavations at Nichoria in Southwest Greece*, (Minneapolis: University of Minnesota Press), 18–56.

Coulson, W., D. Haggis, M. Mook and J. Tobin 1997. Excavations on the Kastro at Kavousi: An Architectural Overview, *Hesperia* 66, 317–90.

Coulton, J. J. 1977. *Greek Architects at Work*, (London: Paul Elek).

Cox, C. A. 1998. *Household Interests. Property, Marriage Strategies and Family Dynamics in Ancient Athens*, (Princeton: Princeton University Press).

Crawley-Quinn, J. 2007. Herms, Kouroi and the Political Anatomy of Athens, *Greece and Rome* 54, 82–105.

Crouch, D. 1993. *Water Management in Ancient Greek Cities*, (Oxford: Oxford University Press).

Dakaris, S. 1982. Von einer kleinen ländlichen Ansiedlung des 8.-4. Jhs. v. Chr. zu einer spätklassischen Stadt in Nordwest-Griechenland. In V. M. Strocka and D. Papenfuss, eds. *Palast und Hütte: Bauen und Wohnen im Altertum*, (Mainz: von Zabern), 357–74.

Dakaris, S. I. 1989. *Κασσώπη. Νεώτερες Ανασκαφές (1977–83)*, (Ioannina: Ioannina University).

Dalcher, K. 1994. *Das Peristylhaus 1 von Iaitas: Architektur und Baugeschichte*, (Zurich: Studia Ietina VI, Zurich Archäologisches Institut).

Day, L. P. and Glowacki, K. T. 2012. *Kavousi IIB: The Late Minoan IIIC Settlement at Vronda: The Buildings on the Periphery*, (Philadelphia: INSTAP Academic Press).

Day, L. P., Klein, N. L. and Turner, L. A. 2009. *Kavousi IIA: The Late Minoan IIIC Settlement at Vronda. The Houses on the Summit*, (Philadelphia: INSTAP Academic Press).

De Caro, S. 1998. Novità pitecusane. L'insediamento di Punta Chiarito a Forio d'Ischia. In B. D'Agostino and M. Bats, eds. *Euboica*, (Naples: Centre Jean Bérard), 337–53.

De Miro, E. 1979. La casa greca in Sicilia. In *Φιλίας Χάριν: Miscellanea in onore di Eugenio Manni*, (Rome: Bretschneider), 709–57.

1996. La casa greca in Sicilia. In F. D'Andria and K. Mannino, eds. *Ricerche sulla casa in Magna Grecia e in Sicilia*, (Galatina: Congedo), 17–40.

Deger-Jalkotzy, S. and Lemos, I., eds. 2006. *Ancient Greece: From the Mycenean Palaces to the Age of Homer*, (Edinburgh: Edinburgh University Press).

Delorme, J. 1953. Le maison dite de l'Hermès à Délos, *Bulletin de Correspondance hellénique* 77, 444–96.

Deonna, W. 1938. *Le mobilier délien. Exploration archéologique de Délos XVIII*, (Paris: École française d'Athènes).

Dickinson, O. T. P. K. 2006. *The Aegean from Bronze Age to Iron Age*, (London: Routledge).

Docter, R. and Webster, M., eds. 2018. *Exploring Thorikos*, (Gent: University of Gent).

Dontas, N. and Hoepfner, W. 2005. *Priene*, (Cambridge, MA: Harvard University Press).

Doonan, R. and Mazarakis-Ainian, A. 2007. Forging Identity in Early Iron Age Greece: Implications of the Metal Working Evidence from Oropos. In A. Mazarakis-Ainian, ed. *Oropos and Euboea in the Early Iron Age*, (Volos: University of Thessaly Publications), 361–78.

Drougou, S. and Vokotopoulou, I. 1989. Όλυνθος – η οίκια BVII1, *Αρχαιολογικό Έργο στη Μακεδονία και στη Θράκη* 3, 339–50.

Ducrey, P., Metzger, I. and Reber, K. 1993. *Eretria: Fouilles et recherches VIII: le quartier de la Maison aux Mosaïques*, (Lausanne, École suisse d'archéologie en Grèce).

Dunbabin, K. 1998. *Ut Graeco more biberetur*: Greeks and Romans on the Dining Couch. In I. Nielsen and H. Sigismund Nielsen, eds. *Meals in a Social Context*, (Aarhus: Aarhus University Press), 81–101.

Dunbabin, K. M. D. 1999. *Mosaics of the Greek and Roman World*, (Cambridge: Cambridge University Press).

Eleutheratou, S. 2010. Ανασκαφή οικοπέδου Μακρυγιάννη για την ανέγερση του Νέου Μουσείου Ακροπόλεως, *Αρχαιολογικόν Δελτίον 56–59*, Χρονικά Β'1, 147–52.

Ellis Jones, J. 1975. Town and Country Houses of Attica in Classical Times. In H. Mussche, P. Spitaels and F. Goemaere-De Poerck, eds. *Thorikos and Laurion in Archaic and Classical Times*, (Ghent: Miscellanea Graeca), 63–140.

2007. 'Living above the Shop': Domestic Aspects of the Ancient Industrial Workshops of the Laureion Area of South-east Attica. In R. Westgate, N. Fisher and J. Whitley, eds. *Building Communities. House, Settlement and Society in the Aegean and Beyond*, (British School at Athens Studies 15, London: British School at Athens), 267–80.

Ellis Jones, J., Graham, A. J. and Sackett, L. H. 1973. An Attic Country House below the Cave of Pan at Vari, *Annual of the British School at Athens* 68, 355–452.

Ellis Jones, J., Sackett, L. H. and Graham, A. J. 1962. 'The Dema House in Attica', *Annual of the British School at Athens* 57, 75–114.

Fagerström, K. 1988a. *Greek Iron Age Architecture*, (Göteborg: SIMA Volume 81).

1988b. Finds, Function and Plan: A Contribution to the Interpretation of Iron Age Nichoria in Messenia, *Opuscula Atheniensia* 17, 33–50.

Faraone, C. 2008. Household Religion in Ancient Greece. In J. Bodel and S. M. Olyan, eds. *Household and Family Religion in Antiquity*, (Oxford: Blackwell), 210–28.

Fatmann-Rey, G. 1996. Versuch der Rekonstruktion eines Wohnhauses von Neandria, *Asia Minor Studien* 22, 15–42.

Ferla, K., ed. 2006. *Priene*, (Athens: Foundation of the Hellenic World).

Ferrara, F. M. 2020. *Basileus e basileia. Forme e luoghi della regalità macedone*, (Rome: Quasar).

Fiedler, M. 2005. Houses at Leukas in Akarnania: A Case-study in Ancient Household Organization. In B. A. Ault and L. C. Nevett, eds. *Ancient Greek Households: Chronological, Regional and Social Diversity*, (Philadelphia: University of Pennsylvania Press), 83–98.

Fitzsimons, R. 2014. Urbanization and the Emergence of the Greek Polis: The Case of Azoria, Crete. In A. T. Creekmore and K. D. Fisher, eds. *Making Space in Ancient Cities: Space and Place in Early Urban Societies*, (Cambridge: Cambridge University Press), 220–56.

Flannery, K. 2002. The Origins of the Village Revisited: From Nuclear to Extended Households, *American Antiquity* 67, 417–33.

Foxhall, L. 2004. Small Rural Farmstead Sites in Ancient Greece: A Material-cultural Analysis. In F. Kolb, ed. *Chora und Polis*, (Munich: Schriften des Historischen Kollegs), 249–70.

2007a. House Clearance: Unpacking the 'Kitchen' in Classical Greece. In R. Westgate, N. Fisher and J. Whitley, eds. *Building Communities: House, Settlement and Society in the Aegean and Beyond*, (British School at Athens Studies 15, London: British School at Athens), 233–42.

2007b. *Olive Cultivation in Ancient Greece: Seeking the Ancient Economy*, (Oxford: Oxford University Press).

2009. Gender. In K. Raaflaub and H. van Wees, eds. *Companion to Archaic Greece*, (Oxford: Blackwell), 483–507.

2013. *Studying Gender in Classical Antiquity*, (Cambridge: Cambridge University Press).

Game, J. 2008. *Actes de Vente dans le Monde grec: témoinages epigraphiques des ventes immobilières*, (Lyon: Travaux de la Maison de l'Orient et de la Mediteranée).

Garland, R. 1987. *The Piraeus from the Fifth to the First Century B.C.*, (London: Duckworth).

Gassner, V., Muss, U., Grammer, B., Gretscher, M. and Mariaud, O. 2014. The Urban Organization of Kolophon and Its Necropoleis: The Results of the 2011–2014 Surveys', *Hesperia* 86, 43–81.

Gill, D. 2003. Euesperides: Cyrenaica and Its Contacts with the Greek World. In K. Lomas, ed. *Greek Identity in the Western Mediterranean: Papers in Honour of Brian Shefton*, (Leiden: Brill), 391–410.

2006. Early Colonization at Euesperides: Origins and Interactions. In G. Bradley, and J.-P. Wilson, eds. *Greek and Roman Colonization: Origins, Ideologies and Interactions*, (Swansea: Classical Press of Wales), 1–24.

Gill, D. and Flecks, P. 2007. Defining Domestic Space at Euesperides, Cyrenaica: Archaic Structures on the Sidi Abeid. In R. Westgate, N. Fisher and J. Whitley, eds. *Building Communities: House, Settlement and Society in the*

Aegean and Beyond, (British School at Athens Studies 15, London: British School at Athens), 205–12.

Glowacki, K. and Vogeikoff-Brogan, N., eds. 2011. *STEGA: The Archaeology of Houses and Households in Ancient Crete, Hesperia Supplement 44*, (Princeton: American School of Classical Studies at Athens).

Goette, H. R. 2000. *Ὁ ἀξιόλογος δῆμος Σούνιον: Landeskundliche Studien in Südost-Attika*, (Rahden: Marie Leidorf).

2001. *Athens, Attica and the Megarid*, (London, Routledge).

Goldberg, M. 1999. Spatial and Behavioural Negotiation in Classical Athenian City Houses. In P. Allison, ed. *The Archaeology of Household Activities*, (London: Routledge), 142–61.

Graham, J. W. 1972. Notes on Houses and Housing-Districts at Abdera and Himera, *American Journal of Archaeology* 76, 295–301.

1974. Houses of Classical Athens, *Phoenix* 28, 45–54.

Grammenos, D. V. and Petropoulos, E. K., eds. 2003 and 2007. *Ancient Greek Colonies in the Black Sea Volumes 1 and 2*, (Thessaloniki/Oxford: Archaeological Receipts Fund/British Archaeological Reports, International Series).

Grandjean, Y. 1988. *Études Thasiennes XII: recherches sur l'habitat Thasien à l'époque grecque*, (Athens: École française d'Athènes).

1990. Les formes predominantes de la maison Thasienne. In *Μνήμη Δ. Λαζαρίδη: Πόλις και Χώρα στην Αρχαία Μακεδονία και Θράκη*, (Ministry of Culture: Archaeological Museum of Kavala), 379–90.

Grandjean, Y. and Marc, J.-Y. 1996. La Ville de Thasos. In *L'espace grec: cent cinquante ans de fouilles de l'École française d'Athènes*, (Paris: Fayard), 74–80.

Gras, M., Tréziny, H. and Broise, H. 2004. *Mégara Hyblaea 5: La ville archaïque: l'espace urbain d'une cité de Sicile orientale*, (Rome: École française de Rome).

Greaves, A. 2002. *Miletos: A History*, (London: Routledge).

Guldager Bilde, P. 2010. The Finds: A Brief Introduction. In N. A. Lejpunskaja, P. Guldager Bilde, J. Munk Højte, V. Krapivina and S. D. Kryžickij, eds. *The Lower City of Olbia (Sector NGS) in the 6th Century BC to the 4th Century AD*, (Aarhus: Aarhus University Press), 117–20.

Haagsma, M. J. 2003. The Houses of New Halos. In H. Reinder Reinders and W. Prummel, eds. *Housing in New Halos, a Hellenistic Town in Thessaly, Greece*, (Lisse: A. A. Balkema), 37–80.

2010. *Domestic Economy and Social Organization in New Halos*. Doctoral dissertation, University of Groningen, Netherlands.

Hadjimichali, V. 1971. Recherches à Lato: III. Maisons, *Bulletin de Correspondance Hellénique* 95, 167–222.

Haggis, D. 2013. Social Organization and Aggregated Settlement Structure in an Archaic Greek City on Crete. In J. Birch, ed. *From Prehistoric Villages to*

Cities: Settlement Aggregation and Community Transformation, (New York: Routledge), 63–86.

2014. Excavations at Azoria and Stratigraphic Evidence for the Restructuring of Cretan Landscapes ca. 600 BCE Models of Urbanization on Crete. In O. Pilz, and G. Seelentag, eds. *Cultural Practices and Material Culture in Archaic and Classical Crete*, (Berlin/Boston: De Gruyter), 11–39.

Haggis, D. and Mook, M. 2011. The Archaic Houses at Azoria. In K. Glowacki and N. Vogeikoff-Brogan, eds. *ΣΤΕΓΑ: The Archaeology of Houses and Households in Ancient Crete*, (Princeton: American School of Classical Studies at Athens), 367–80.

Haggis, D., Mook, M., Fitzsimons, R., Scarry, C. M. and Snyder, L. 2007. Excavations at Azoria, 2003–2004: part 1: The Archaic Civic Complex, *Hesperia* 76, 243–321.

Haggis, D., Mook, M. Fitzsimons, R. D., Scarry, C. M. and Snyder, L. 2011. The Excavation of Archaic Houses at Azoria 2005–2006, *Hesperia* 80, 431–90.

Hall, J. M. 1997. *Ethnic Identity in Greek Antiquity*, (Cambridge: Cambridge University Press).

2002. *Hellenicity: Between Ethnicity and Culture*, (Chicago: University of Chicago Press).

Hammond, N. G. L. 1953. Hellenic Houses at Ammotopos in Epirus, *Annual of the British School at Athens* 48, 135–40.

1967. *Epirus*, (Oxford: Clarendon Press).

2000. The Ethne in Epirus and Upper Macedonia, *Annual of the British School at Athens* 52, 345–52.

Hänsel, B. 1989. *Kastanas*, (Berlin: Wissenschaftsverlag Volker Spiess).

Hansen, M. H. and Fischer-Hansen, T. 1994. Monumental Political Architecture in Archaic and Classical Greek Poleis: Evidence and Historical Significance. In D. Whitehead, ed. *From Political Architecture to Stephanus Byzantinus*, (Copenhagen: Historia Einzelschriften 87), 23–90.

Hardiman, C. 2011. Wrestling with the Evidence: Decorative Cohesion and the House of the Mosaics at Eretria. In D. Rupp and J. E. Tomlinson, eds. *Euboea and Athens: Proceedings of a Colloquium in Memory of Malcom B. Wallace*, (Athens: Canadian Institute in Greece), 189–207.

Harms, A. 2010. Himera. Überlegungen zur Stadtentwicklung und Wohnarchitektur einer nordsizilianischen Stadt. In S. Ladstätter and V. Scheibelreiter, eds. *Städtisches Wohnen im östlichen Mittelmeerraum 4. Jh. v. Chr. – 1. Jh. n. Chr.*, (Vienna: Verlag der Österreichischen Akademie der Wissenschaften), 333–46.

Harris, E. M. 2002. Workshop, Marketplace and Household. In P. Cartledge, E. Cohen and L. Foxhall, eds. *Money, Labour and Land: Approaches to the Economies of Ancient Greece*, (Routledge: London), 67–99.

Hasenohr, C. 2003. Les compitalia à Délos, *Bulletin de Correspondence Héllenique* 127, 167–249.

Hatzopoulos, M. B. 1988. *Actes de Vente de la Chalcidique centrale*, (Paris: Boccard).

Haug, A. and Steuernagel, D. 2014. *Das Haus XV B (Maison 49,19) von Megara Hyblaia*, (Wiesbaden: Dr. Ludwig Reichert Verlag).

2018. La ville classique, hellénistique et romaine. In H. Tréziny and F. Mège, eds. *Mégara Hyblaea*, (Rome: École française de Rome).

Heermann, V. 1986. *Studien zur makedonischen Palastarchitektur*, (press and location not indicated).

Helas, S. 2012. *Selinus II: Die punische Stadt auf der Akropolis*, (Rome: Deutsches Archäologisches Institut).

Hellström, P. 1996. The Androlnes at Labraynda. Dining Halls for Hellenistic Kings. In W. Hoepfner and G. Brands, eds. *Basileia: die Paläste der hellenistischen Könige*, (Mainz: von Zabern), 164–69.

Herdt, G. 2015. On the Architecture of the Toumba Building at Lefkandi, *Annual of the British School at Athens* 110, 203–212.

Hobden, F. 2013. *The Symposium in Ancient Greek Society and Thought*, (Cambridge: Cambridge University Press).

Hoepfner, W. 1996. Zum Typus der Basileia der königlichen Androlnes. In W. Hoepfner and G. Brands, eds. *Basileia: die Paläste der hellenistischen Könige*, (Mainz: von Zabern), 1–43.

1999. Die Epoche der Griechen. In W. Hoepfner, ed. *Geschichte des Wohnens*, (Ludwigsburg: Wüstenrot Stiftung), 123–608.

Hoepfner, W. and Schwandner, E.-L. 1994. *Haus und Stadt im Klassischen Griechenland*, (Munich: Deutscher Kunstverlag; second edition).

1999. Dystos. Eine Kleinstadt auf Euboea. In W. Hoepfner, ed. *Geschichte des Wohnens*, (Ludwigsburg: Wüstenrot Stiftung), 352–67.

Holland, L. B. 1944. Colophon, *Hesperia* 13, 91–171.

Hudson, N. 2010. Changing Places: The Archaeology of the Roman *Convivium*, *American Journal of Archaeology* 114, 663–95.

Hunter, V. 1994. *Policing Athens: Social Control in the Attic Lawsuits, 420–320 BC*, (Princeton: Princeton University Press).

Husselman, E. 1979. *Karanis Excavations of the University of Michigan in Egypt, 1928-1935: Topography and Architecture*, (Ann Arbor: University of Michigan Kelsey Museum of Archaeology Studies, 5).

Jameson, M., Runnels, C. and van Andel, T. 1994. *A Greek Countryside: The Southern Argolid from Prehistory to the Present Day*, (Stanford: Stanford University Press).

Jones, N. 2004. *Rural Athens under the Democracy*, (Philadelphia: University of Pennsylvania Press).

Kahil, L. 1981. Erétrie à l'époque Géometrique, *Annuario della Scuola Archeologica di Atene e delle Oriente N.S.* 43, 165–73.

Kakoulli, I. 2009. *Greek Painting Techniques and Materials*, (London: Archetype).

Kaltsas, N. 1983. Η αρχαϊκη οικία στο Κοπανάκι της Μεσσηνίας, *Αρχαιολογική Εφήμερις*, 122, 207–37.

Kaninia, E. and Schierup, S. 2017. Vroulia Revisited: From K. F. Kinch's Excavations in the Early 20th Century to the Present Archaeological Site, *Proceedings of the Danish Institute at Athens* 8, 89–129.

Karadedos, G. 1990. Υστεροκλασικό Σπίτι στη Μαρώνεια Θράκης, *Εγνατία* 2, 265–97.

Karamitrou-Mentessidi, G. 2011. Aiani: Historical and Geographical Context. In R. Lane-Fox ed. *Brill's Companion to Ancient Macedonia*, (Leiden: Brill), 93–112.

2012. Λ' Εφορεία Προϊστορικών και Κλασικών Αρχαιοτητών. In *2000–2010 από το Ανασκαφικό Έργο των Εφορειών Αρχαιοτήτων*, (Athens: Ministry of Culture and Tourism), 223–30.

Kardara, C. 1961. Dyeing and Weaving Works at Isthmia, *Hesperia* 65, 261–66.

Kent, J. H. 1948. The Temple Estates of Delos, Rheneia and Mykonos, *Hesperia* 17, 243–338.

Kiderlen, M. 1995. *Megale Oikia. Untersuchungen zur Entwicklung aufwendiger griechischer Stadthausarchitektur*, (Hürth: Lange).

Kinch, K. 1914. *Vroulia*, (Berlin: Georg Reimer).

Knigge, U. 2005. *Der Bau Z: Kerameikos: Ergebnisse der Ausgrabungen XVII*, (Munich: Deutsches Archäologisches Institut/Hirmer Verlag).

Kolia, E. 2007–2008. Παράκτιος Οικισμός της κλασικής εποχής στην ανατολική Αιγαλεία, *Athens Annals of Archaeology* 40–41, 41–60.

Konečny, A., Boyd, M. J., Marchese, R. T. and Aravantinos, V. 2012. The Urban Scheme of Plataiai in Boiotia: Report on the Geophysical Survey, 2005–2009, *Hesperia* 81, 93–140.

Kottaridi, A. 2011a. Appendix: The Palace of Philip II in Aegae. In A. Kottaridi and S. Walker, eds. *Heracles to Alexander*, (Oxford: Ashmolean Museum), 233–36.

2011b. The Palace of Aegae. In Lane-Fox, R., ed. *Brill's Companion to Ancient Macedon: Studies in the Archaeology and History of Macedon, 650 BC–300 AD*, (Leiden: Brill), 297–334.

Koukouli-Chrysanthaki, Ch. 1991. Ανασκαφή αρχαίων Αβδήρων, 1991, 193–211.

Kramer, C. 1982. *Village Ethnoarchaeology: Rural Iran in Archaeological Perspective*, (New York: Academic Press).

Krause, C. 1977. Grundformen des Griechischen Pastashauses, *Archäologische Anzeiger* 1977, 164–79.

Kreeb, M. 1988. *Untersuchungen zur Figürlichen Ausstattung Delischer Privathäuser*, (Chicago: Ares Publishers).

Ladstätter, S. and Scheibelreiter, V., eds. 2010. *Städtisches Wohnen im östlichen Mittelmeerraum 4. Jh. v. Chr. – 1. Jh. n. Chr.*, (Vienna: Verlag der Österreichischen Akademie der Wissenschaften).

Lalonde, G. V. 2006. *Horos Dios: An Athenian Shrine and Cult of Zeus*, (Leiden: Brill).

Lang, F. 1996. *Archaische Siedlungen in Griechenland: Struktur und Entwicklung*, (Berlin: Akademie-Verlag).

2002. Housing and Settlement in Archaic Greece, *Pallas* 58, 13–32.

2005. Structural Change in Archaic Greek Housing. In B. A. Ault and L. C. Nevett, eds. *Ancient Greek Houses and Households*, (Philadelphia: University of Pennsylvania Press), 12–35.

2007. House – Community – Settlement: The New Concept of Living in Archaic Greece. In R. Westgate, N. Fisher and J. Whitley, eds. *Building Communities. House, Settlement and Society in the Aegean and Beyond*, (British School at Athens Studies 14, London: British School at Athens), 183–94.

Lanza Catti, E., Swift K. and Coleman Carter, J. 2014. *The Chora of Metaponto 5: A Greek Farmhouse at Ponte Fabrizio*, (Austin: University of Texas Press).

Lauter-Bufe, H. and Lauter, H. 1971. Wohnhäuser und Stadtviertel des klassischen Athen, *Mitteilungen des deutschen archäologischen Instituts Athenische Abteilung* 86, 109–24.

Lavas, G. and Karadedos, G. 1991. Mauerwerk, Bodenbeläge und Anstrichtecknik eines spätklassischen Hauses in Maroneia, Thrazien. In A. Hoffmann, E.-L. Schwandner and W. Hoepfner, eds. *Bautechnik der Antike*. (Diskussionen zur Archäologischen Bauforschung Band 5, Mainz: Philipp von Zabern), 140–47.

Lawall, M., Papadopoulos, J. K., Lynch, K., Tsakirgis, B., Rotroff, S. and MacKay, C. 2001. Notes from the Tins: Research in the Stoa of Attalos, Summer 1999, *Hesperia* 70, 163–82.

Lazaridis, D. 1971. *Αβδήρα και Δικάια*, (Athens: Centre of Ekistics).

Lejpunskaja, N. A., Guldager Bilde, P., Munk Højte, J., Krapivina, V. and Kryžickij, S. D., eds. 2010. *The Lower City of Olbia (Sector NGS) in the 6th Century BC to the 4th Century AD*, (Black Sea Studies, Aarhus: Aarhus University Press).

Lemos, I. 2007. Recent Archaeological Work on Xeropolis Lefkandi: A Preliminary Report. In A. Mazarakis Ainian, ed. *Oropos and Euboea in the Early Iron Age*, (Volos: University of Thessaly), 123–33.

Lentini, M. C. 1990. Naxos: alcune case dell'isolato C 4 (V secolo a.c.) *Xenia* 20, 5–22.

1998. Le ultime esplorazioni a Naxos (1983–1995). In M. C. Lentini, ed. *Naxos, a quarant'anni dall'inizio degli scavi, Atti della tavola rotonda, Giardini Naxos*, (Messene: Museo Archeologico di Naxos), 71–100.

Lentini, M. C. and Garraffo, S. 1995. *Il Tesoretto di Naxos (1985). Dall'isolato urbano C4, casa 1–2*, (Rome: Istituto Italiano di Numismatica).

Lippolis, E. 2013. L'oikos come spazio architettonico e soziale, *Seminari Romani di Cultura Greca* II(1), 203–39.

Lloyd, J. A., Bennett, P., Buttrey, T. V., Buzaian, A., El Amin, H., Fell, V., Kashbar, G., Morgan, G., Ben Nasser, Y., Roberts, P. C., Wilson, A. I. and Simi, E. 1998. Excavations at Euesperides (Benghazi): An Interim Report on the 1998 Season, *Libyan Studies* 29, 145–68.

Lloyd, J. A., Buzaian, A. and Coulton, J. 1995. Excavations at Euesperides (Benghazi), 1995, *Libyan Studies* 26, 97–100.

Lohmann, H. 1993. *Atene. Forschungen zu Siedlungs- und Wirtschaftsstruktur des klassischen Attika*, (Cologne: Böhlau Verlag).

Lolos, Y., Gourley, B. and Stewart, D. 2007. The Sikyon Survey Project: A Blueprint for Urban Survey? *Journal of Mediterranean Archaeology* 20, 267–96.

Luce, J. V. 1971. The Large Houses at Dystos in Euboia, *Greece and Rome* N.S.18, 143–49.

Lynch, K. M. 2007. More Thoughts on the Space of the Symposium. In R. Westgate, N. Fisher and J. Whitley, eds. *Building Communities. House, Settlement and Society in the Aegean and Beyond*, (British School at Athens Studies 15, London: British School at Athens), 243–49.

2011. *The Symposium in Context: Pottery from a Late Archaic House Near the Athenian Agora*, (Princeton: American School of Classical Studies at Athens).

Ma, J. 2011. Court, King, and Power in Antigonid Macedonia. In R. Lane-Fox, ed. *Brill's Companion to Ancient Macedon: Studies in the Archaeology and History of Macedon, 650 BC–300 AD*, (Leiden: Brill), 521–543.

Mack, G. and Coleman Carter, J., eds. 2003. *Crimean Chersonesos: City, Chora, Museum and Environs*, (Austin: Institute of Classical Archaeology; National Preserve of Tauric Chersonesos).

Maischatz, T. 1994. Untersuchungen zu einer Stadterweiterungsphase im 4. Jh. v. Chr. In E. Schwertheim and H. Wiegartz, eds. *Neue Forschungen zu Neandria und Alexandria Troas*, (Bonn: Dr. Rudolf Habelt Gmbh), *Asia Minor Studien* 11, 49–64.

2003. *Neandria: Untersuchungen zur Bebauung und Stadtentwicklung*, (Bonn: Rudolf Habelt).

Makaronas, C. and Giouri, E. 1989. *Οι Οικίες Αρπαγής της Ελένης και Διονύσου, της Πέλλας*, (Athens: Athens Archaeological Society).

Mann, K. 2015. Mutable Spaces and Unseen Places: A Study of Access, Communication and Spatial Control in Households at Early Iron Age (EIA) Zagora on Andros, *Archaeological Review from Cambridge* 30, 52–62.

Margaritis, E. 2014. The Kapelio at Hellenistic Krania: Food Consumption, Disposal and the Use of Space, *Hesperia* 83, 103–21.

2016. Agricultural Production and Domestic Activities in Rural Hellenistic Greece. In E. Harris, D. M. Lewis and M. Woolmer, eds. *The Ancient Greek Economy: Markets, Households and City-states*, (Cambridge: Cambridge University Press), 187–206.

Marzolff, P. 1996. Der Palast von Demetrias. In W. Hoepfner and G. Brands, eds. *Basileia: die Paläste der hellenistischen Könige*, (Mainz: von Zabern), 148–63.

Mazarakis Ainian, A. 1987. Geometric Eretria, *Antike Kunst* N.S. 30, 3–24.

1992. Nichoria in the Southwestern Peloponnese: Units IV-1 and IV-5 Reconsidered, *Opuscula Atheniensa* 19, 75–84.

1996. Ανασκαφή Σκάλας Ωρωπού (1985–1987). *Πρακτικά της Αρχαιολογικής Εταιρείας* 1996, 21–124.

1997. *From Rulers' Dwellings to Temples: Architecture, Religion and Society in Early Iron Age Greece (1100–700 B.C.)*, (Jonsered: Paul Åströms Forlag).

1998. Oropos in the Early Iron Age. In M. Bats and B. d'Agostino, eds. *Euboica: l'Eubea e la presenza Euboica in Calcidica e in Occidente*, (Naples: Centre Jean Bérard), 179–215.

2001. From Huts to Houses in Early Iron Age Greece. In J. R. Brandt and L. Karlsson, eds. *From Huts to Houses. Transformations of Ancient Societies*, (Stockholm: Åström), 139–61.

2002a. Recent Excavations at Oropos (northern Attica). In M. Stamatopoulou and M. Yeroulakou, eds. *Excavating Classical Culture*, (Oxford: Archaeopress), 149–78.

2002b. Les fouilles d'Oropos et la fonction des périboles dans les agglomérations du début de l'Age du Fer, *Pallas* 58, 183–227.

2006. The Archaeology of Basileis. In S. Deger-Jalkotzy and I. Lemos, eds. *Ancient Greece: From the Mycenean Palaces to the Age of Homer*, (Edinburgh: Edinburgh University Press), 181–212.

2007. Architecture and Social Structure in Early Iron Age Greece. In R. Westgate, N. Fisher and J. Whitley, eds. *Building Communities: House, Settlement and Society in the Aegean and Beyond*, (British School at Athens Studies 15, London: British School at Athens), 157–68.

McHugh, M. 2017. *The Ancient Greek Farmstead*, (Oxford: Oxbow).

Melander, T. 1988. Vroulia: Town Plan and Gate. In S. Dietz and I. Papachristodoulou, eds. *Archaeology in the Dodecanese*, (Copenhagen: National Museum of Denmark).

Miller, M. C., Paspalas, S. A., Beaumont, L. A., McLoughlin, B. M., Wilson, A. and Thomas, H. 2019/2020. Zagora Archaeological Project: The 2014 Season, *Mediterranean Archaeology* 32/33, 217–226.

Missailidou-Despotidou, V. 2007. Aphytis 2004, Αρχαιολογικό Έργο στη Μακεδονία και στη Θράκη 21, 311–21.

Morel, J.-P. 2010. Quelques aspects de la culture matérielle dans le Pont Nord: vers une koinè entre Grecs et indigènes?. In H. Tréziny, ed. *Grecs et indigènes de la Catalogne à la Mer Noire*, (Paris: Centre Camille Jullian), 279–89.

Morgan, J. 2010. *The Classical Greek House*, (Exeter: Bristol Phoenix Press).

2017. At Home with Royalty: Re-viewing the Hellenistic Palace. In A. Erskine, L. Llewellyn-Jones and S. Wallace, eds. *The Hellenistic Court: Monarchic Power and Èlite Society from Alexander to Cleopatra*, (Swansea: Classical Press of Wales), 31–67.

Morris, I. 1998a. Archaeology and Archaic Greek History. In N. Fisher and H. van Wees, eds. *Archaic Greece: New Approaches and New Evidence*, (London: Duckworth), 1–91.

1998b. Remaining Invisible: The Archaeology of the Excluded in Classical Athens. In S. Murnaghan and S. R. Joshel, eds. *Women and Slaves in Greco-Roman Culture*, (London: Routledge), 203–20.

1999. Archaeology and Gender Ideologies in Early Archaic Greece, *Transactions of the American Philological Association* 129, 305–17.

2001. The Use and Abuse of Homer. Revised edition. In D. Cairns, ed. *Oxford Readings on Homer's Iliad*, (Oxford: Oxford University Press), 57–91.

2004. Economic Growth in Ancient Greece, *Journal of Institutional and Theoretical Economics* 160, 709–42.

2005a. Archaeology, Standards of Living, and Greek Economic History. In J. G. Manning, and I. Morris, eds. *The Ancient Economy: Evidence and Models*, (Stanford: Stanford University Press), 91–126.

2009. The Greater Athenian State. In I. Morris and W. Scheidel, eds. *The Dynamics of Ancient Empires*, (Oxford: Oxford University Press), 99–177.

Morris, S. and Papadopoulos, J. 2005. Greek Towers and Slaves, *American Journal of Archaeology* 109, 155–225.

Mussche, H. F. 1998. *Thorikos: A Mining Town in Ancient Attika*, (Gent: Belgian Archaeological School in Greece).

Naoum, E. 2019. Πέτρες 2011–2014, *Αρχαιολογικό Έργο στη Μακεδονία και στη Θράκη* 2014: 63–70.

Napolitano, M. ed. 2013. *Oikos: spazio architettonico, sociale, letterario*, (Rome: Quasar).

Nevett, L. C. 1994. Separation or Seclusion? Towards an Archaeological Approach to Investigating Women in the Greek Household in the Fifth to Third Centuries B.C. In M. Parker Pearson and C. Richards, eds. *Architecture and Order: Approaches to Social Space*, (London: Routledge), 98–112.

1995. Gender Relations in the Classical Greek Household: The Archaeological Evidence, *Annual of the British School at Athens* 90, 363–81.

1997. Review of Megale Oikia by Moritz Kiderlen, *American Journal of Archaeology* 101, 602–03.

1999. *House and Society in the Ancient Greek World*, (Cambridge Cambridge University Press).

2000. A 'Real Estate Market' in Classical Greece?: The Example of Town Housing, *Annual of the British School at Athens* 95, 329–43.

2005. Between Urban and Rural: House-form and Social Relations in Attic Villages and Deme Centres. In B. A. Ault and L. C. Nevett, eds. *Ancient Greek Households: Geographical, Regional and Social Diversity*, (Philadelphia: University of Pennsylvania Press), 83–98.

2007. Domestic Architecture and Household Wealth: The Case of Ancient Greece. In R. Beck, ed. *The Durable House: Architecture, Ancestors and Origins*, (Carbondale: University of Southern Illinois Press), 365–79.

2009a. Domestic Culture in Classical Greece, *Bulletin Antieke Beschaving Supplement*, 59–66.

2009b. Domestic Façades: A Feature of the Greek 'Urban' Landscape? In S. Owen, and L. Preston, eds. *Inside the City in the Greek World*, (Oxford: Oxbow), 118–30.

2010. *Domestic Space in Classical Antiquity*, (Cambridge: Cambridge University Press).

2011a. Family and Household: Ancient History and Archaeology: A Case-study from Roman Egypt. In B. Rawson, ed. *A Companion to Families in the Greek and Roman World*, (Oxford: Blackwell), 15–31.

2011b. Towards a Female Topography of the Ancient Greek City: Case-studies from Late Archaic and Early Classical Athens (c. 520–400 BCE.), *Gender and History* 23, 548–75.

2016. Understanding Variability in Ancient House Forms: A Preliminary Discussion. In A. di Castro, C. Hope and B. E. Parr, eds. *Housing and Habitat in the Mediterranean World: Cultural and Environmental Responses*, (Leuven: Bulletin Antieke Beschaving Supplement), 145–51.

2018. 'Least Talked About Among Men?': The Verbal and Spatial Rhetoric of Women's Roles in Classical Athens (ca. 450–350 BCE), *Archaeology and Text* 2, 7–24.

2021. The Complicated Problem of Seasonality at Classical Olynthos, Greece. In A. Lichtenberger and R. Raja, eds. *The Archaeology of Seasonality*, (Turnhout: Brepols), 381–92.

2022. Architectural Rhetoric and the Rhetoric of Architecture: Athens and Macedon in the Mid Fourth Century BCE. In J. Baird and A. Pudsey, eds. *Housing in the Ancient Mediterranean World: Material and Textual Approaches*, (Cambridge: Cambridge University Press), 212–28.

in press. Vernacular Architecture and Beyond: The Changing Form and Scale of Buildings and Settlements in the First Millennium BCE Greek World. In F. Keshk and B. Schaefer, eds. *Vernacular Architecture as a Frame of Life in Historic and Ancient Communities*, (Berlin: Deutsches Archäologisches Institut).

Nevett, L. C., Tsigarida, E. B., Archibald, Z. H., Stone, D. L., Ault, B. A., Akamatis, N., Cuijpers, E., Donati, J. C., Garcia-Granero, J. J., Hartenburger, B., Horsley, T., Lancelotti, C., Margaritis, E., Alcaina-Mateos, J., Nanoglou, S., Panti, A., Papadopoulos, N., Pecci, A., Salminen, E., Sarris, A., Stallibrass, S. M., Tzochev, C. and Valdembrini, C. 2020. Constructing the Urban Profile of an Ancient Greek City: Evidence from the Olynthos Project, *Annual of the British School at Athens* 115, 329–378.

Nevett, L. C., Tsigarida, E. B., Archibald, Z., Stone, D. L., Horsley, T., Ault, B. A., Panti, A., Lynch, K., Pethen, H., Stallibrass, S., Salminen, E., Gaffney, C., Sparrow, T. J., Taylor, S., Manousakis, J. and Zekkos, D. 2017. Towards a Multi-Scalar, Multi-Disciplinary Approach to the Classical Greek City: The Olynthos Project, *Annual of the British School at Athens* 112, 155–206.

Nichols, M. 2017. *Author and Audience in Vitruvius' De Architectura*, (Cambridge: Cambridge University Press).

Nielsen, I. 1994. *Hellenistic Palaces*, (Aarhus: Aarhus University Press).

1996. Oriental Models for Hellenistic Palaces. In W. Hoepfner and G. Brands, eds. *Basileia: die Paläste der hellenistischen Könige*, (Mainz: von Zabern), 209–12.

1997. Royal Palaces and Type of Monarchy: Do the Hellenistic Palaces Reflect the Status of the King?, *Hephaistos* 15, 137–61.

1998. Royal Banquets: The Development of Royal Banquets and Banqueting Halls from Alexander to the Tetrarchs. In I. Nielsen and H. Sigismund-Nielsen, eds. *Meals in a Social Context*, (Aarhus: Aarhus University Press), 102–33.

Ødegård, K. 2010. Urban Planning in the Greek Motherland: Late Archaic Tegea, *Acta ad Archaeologiam et Artium Historiam Pertinentia* 23, 9–22.

Orsi, P. 1914. Caulonia: isole di case nel quartiere orientale della citta, *Monumenti Antichi* 23, 806–27.

Osanna, M. and Capozzoli, V., eds. 2012. *Lo spazio del potere II: nuove ricerche nell'area dell'anaktoron di Torre di Satriano*, (Venosa: Osanna Edizioni).

Osborne, R. 1985. The Erection and Mutilation of the Hermai, *Proceedings of the Cambridge Philological Society* 31, 47–73.

1994. Classical Landscape Revisited, *Topoi* 6.1, 49–64.

2005. Monumentality and Ritual in Archaic Greece. In D. Yatromanolakis and P. Roilos, eds. *Greek Ritual Poetics*, (Washington, D.C.: Center for Hellenic Studies), 37–55.

2006. Review: The Excavations at Ancient Halieis Volume 1 The Fortifications and Adjacent Structures and Volume 2 The Houses, *Journal of Field Archaeology*, 31, 443–46.

2010. *Athens and Athenian Democracy*, (Cambridge: Cambridge University Press).

Owens, E. 1983. The Koprologoi at Athens in the Fifth and Fourth Centuries B.C., *Classical Quarterly* 33, 44–50.

Pantos, P. 1984. *Τα σφραγίσματα της αἰτωλικής Καλλιπόλεως*, (Doctoral dissertation, University of Athens). Chapter suummaries consulted at https://independent.academia.edu/PantosPantos; accessed 27 December 2021.

Papadopoulos, J. and Lynch, K. 2006. Sella Cacatoria: A Study of the Potty in Archaic and Classical Athens, *Hesperia* 75, 1–32.

Parisinou, E. 1998. Lighting Practices in Early Greece (From the End of the Mycenaean World to the 7th Century BC), *Oxford Journal of Archaeology* 17, 327–43.

2007. Lighting Dark Rooms: Some Thoughts about the Use of Space in Early Greek Domestic Architecture. In R. Westgate, N. Fisher and J. Whitley, eds. *Building Communities. House, Settlement and Society in the Aegean and Beyond*, (British School at Athens Studies 15, London: British School at Athens), 213–23.

Patterson, C. 1998. *The Family in Greek History*, (Cambridge, MA: Harvard University Press).

Payne, H., Dunbabin, T. and Blakeway, A. 1940. *Perachora, the Sanctuaries of Hera Akraia and Limenia: Excavations of the British School of Archaeology at Athens, 1930-1933*, (Oxford: Clarendon).

Pecirka, J. 1973. Homestead Farms in Classical and Hellenistic Hellas. In M. I. Finley, ed. *Problèmes de la Terre en Grèce ancienne*, (Paris: Mouton), 123–74.

Picard, O. and Ducrey, P. 1996. Recherches à Lato VII. La rue Ouest. Habitations et défense, *Bulletin de Correspondance Hellénique* 120, 721–45.

Popham, M. and Sackett, H. eds. 1993. *Lefkandi II: The Protogeometric Building at Toumba Part 2, The Excavation, Architecture and Finds*, (London: British School at Athens).

Pritchett, W. K. 1953. The Attic Stelai: Part I, *Hesperia* 22, 225–99.

1956. The Attic Stelai: Part II, *Hesperia* 25, 178–328.

Protopsalti, S. 1993. Νόμος Χαλκιδηκής: Ὄλυνθος, Ἀρχαιολογικόν Δελτίον 48, 339–42.

1994. Ὄλυνθος, Ἀρχαιολογικόν Δελτίον 49, 458–59.

Psaroudakis, K. 2004. Ονιθέ Γουλεδιανών: νέα μάτια στα ίχνη μίας αρχαίας Κρητικής πόλης, *Κρητική Εστία* 10, 9–50.

Raaflaub, K. 2006. Historical Approaches to Homer. In S. Deger-Jalkotzy and I. Lemos, eds. *Ancient Greece: From the Mycenaean Palaces to the Age of Homer*, (Edinburgh: Edinburgh University Press), 449–62.

Rabinowitz, A. 2009. Drinking from the Same Cup: Sparta and Late Archaic Commensality. In S. Hodkinson, ed. *Sparta: Comparative Approaches*, (Swansea: Classical Press of Wales), 113–92.

2011. Drinkers, Hosts or Fighters? Masculine Identities in Pre-Classical Crete. In O. Pilz and G. Seelentag, eds. *Cultural Practices and Material Culture in Archaic and Classical Crete*, (Berlin: de Gruyter), 91–119.

Raeck, W. 2005. Neue Forschungen zum spätklassischen und hellenistischen Priene. *Asia Minor Studien* 54, 149–63.

2009. Urbanistische Veränderung und archäologischer Befund in Priene. In A. Matthei and M. Zimmermann, eds. *Stadtbilder im Hellenismus*, (Berlin: Verlag Antike), 307–21.

Reber, K. 1998. *Eretria: Ausgrabungen und Forschungen X: Die klassischen und hellenistischen Wohnhäuser im Westquartier*, (Lausanne: École suisse d'archéologie en Grèce).

2001. Entwicklungsstufen in der Grundrissorganisation griechischer Wohnhäuser. In J. Rasmus Brandt and L. Karlsson, eds. *From Huts to Houses. Transformations of Ancient Societies*, (Stockholm: Åström), 63–69.

2007. Living and Housing in Classical and Hellenistic Eretria. In R. Westgate, N. Fisher and J. Whitley, eds. *Building Communities. House, Settlement and Society in the Aegean and Beyond*, (British School at Athens Studies 15, London: British School at Athens), 281–88.

2010. Säulen im Andron: Neues zur Innenausstattung griechischer Androns. In S. Ladstätter and V. Scheibelreiter, eds. *Städtisches Wohnen im östlichen*

Mittelmeerraum 4. Jh. v. Chr. – 1. Jh. n. Chr., (Vienna: Verlag der Österreichischen Akademie der Wissenschaften), 581–87.

Reber, K., Léderrey, C., Psalti, A., Fachard, S. and Theurillat, T. 2009. Fouilles sur la terrain O.T. 737, *Antike Kunst* 52, 114–18.

Reusser, C., Cappuccini, L., Mohr, M., Russenberger, C. and Mango, E. 2011. Forschungen auf dem Monte Iato 2010, *Antike Kunst* 54, 71–104.

Ridgeway, D. 1992. *The First Western Greeks*, (Cambridge: Cambridge University Press).

Riginos, G. and Lazari, K. 2008. *Ελέα Θεσπρωτίας*, (Athens: Ministry of Culture).

Robinson, D. M. 1929–1952. *Excavations at Olynthus, Parts I–XIV*, (Baltimore: The Johns Hopkins Press).

    1938. Inscriptions from Macedonia, 1938, *Transactions of the American Philological Association* 69, 47–76.

    1946. *Excavations at Olynthus XII: Domestic and Public Architecture*, (Baltimore: Johns Hopkins University Press).

Robinson, D. M. and Graham, J. W. 1938. *Excavations at Olynthus VIII: The Hellenic House*, (Baltimore: Johns Hopkins Press).

Robinson, H. S. 1959. *The Athenian Agora Volume V: Pottery of the Roman Period: Chronology*, (Princeton: American School of Classical Studies at Athens).

Rotroff, S. I. 1999. How Did Pots Function within the Landscape of Daily living?. In M.-C. Villanueva Puig, F. Lissarrague, P. Rouillard and A. Rouvet, eds. *Céramique et Peinture grecques: modes d'emploi*, (Paris: La Documentation française), 63–74.

    2013. *Industrial Religion: The Saucer Pyres of the Athenian Agora*, (*Hesperia* Supplement 47, Princeton: American School of Classical Studies at Athens).

Rougier-Blanc, S. 2013. Architecture et/ou espaces de la pauvreté: habitats modestes, cabanes et "squats" en Grèce ancienne. In E. Galbois and S. Rougier-Blanc, eds. *La pauvreté en Grèce ancienne: formes, représentations, enjeux*, (Bordeaux: Ausonius), 105–135.

Rumscheid, F. 1998. *Priene: A Guide to the Pompeii of Asia Minor*, (Istanbul: Deutsches Archäologisches Institut).

    2010. Fragen zur bürgerlich-hellenistischen Wohnkultur in Kleinasien. In S. Ladstätter, and V. Scheibelreiter, eds. *Städtisches Wohnen im östlichen Mittelmeerraum 4. Jh. v. Chr. – 1. Jh. n. Chr.*, (Vienna: Verlag der Österreichischen Akademie der Wissenschaften), 119–43.

    2014. Die hellenistischen Wohnhäuser von Priene. Befunde, Funde und Raumfunktionen. In A. Haug and D. Steuernagel, eds. *Hellenistische Häuser und ihre Funktionen: internationale Tagung Kiel, 4. bis 6. April 2013*, (Bonn: Verlag Dr. Rudolf Habelt), 143–60.

    2015. Urbanistische Strukturen und Veränderungen im hellenistischen Priene. Wohnbereiche. In A. Matthei and N. Zimmermann, eds. *Urbane Strukturen und bügerliche Identität im Hellenismus*, (Heidelberg: Verlag Antike), 283–99.

Russenberger, C. 2013. A New Bathtub with Hypocaust in Peristyle House 2 at Monte Iato. In S. Lucore and M. Trümper, M., eds. *Greek Baths and Bathing Culture: New Discoveries and Approaches*, (Leuven: Peeters), 189–200.

2014. 200 Jahre Wohnen im Peristylhaus 2 auf dem Monte Iato: Materialien für eine Analyse der Raumfunktionen und der Raumhierarchien. In A. Haug and D. Steuernagel, eds. *Hellenistische Häuser und ihre Funktionen*, (Bonn: Verlag Dr. Rudolf Habelt), 57–84.

Saatsoglou-Paliadeli, C. 2001. The Palace of Vergina-Aegae and Its Surroundings. In Nielsen, I., ed. *The Royal Palace Institution in the First Millennium BC*, (Aarhus: Aarhus University Press), 201–214.

2007. Το ανάκτορο των Αιγών: προδημοσίευση, *Αρχαιολογικό Έργο στη Μακεδονία και στη Θράκη* 21, 127–34.

Saba, S. 2012. *The Astynomoi Law from Pergamon: A New Commentary*, (Mainz: Verlag Antike).

Sapouna Sakellaraki, E. 1995. *Eretria*, (Athens: Archaeological Receipts Fund).

Saprykin, S. 1994. *Ancient Farms and Land-Plots on the Khora of Khersonesos Taurike*, (Amsterdam: Gieben).

Schiffer, M. B. 1996. *Formation Processes and the Archaeological Record*, (Salt Lake City: University of Utah Press).

Schwandner, E.-L. 1977. Die Böotische Hafenstadt Siphai, *Archäologischer Anzeiger* 20, 513–51.

1999. Dystos. Eine Kleinstadt auf Euböa. In W. Hoepfner, ed. *Geschichte des Wohnens: Die Epoche der Griechen*, (Ludwigsburg: Wüstenrot Stiftung), 352–67.

Sewell, J. 2010. *The Formation of Roman Urbanism: Between Contemporary Foreign Influence and Roman Tradition*, (Portsmouth, RI: Journal of Roman Archaeology Supplementary Series 79).

Shear, T. L. 1973. The Athenian Agora: Excavations of 1971, *Hesperia* 42, 123–79.

Siebert, G. 2001. *L'îlot des Bijoux, l'îlot des Bronzes, la Maison des Sceaux. Exploration archéologique de Délos XXXVIII*, (Paris: Boccard).

Siganidou, M. 1981. Ανασκαφές Πέλλας, *Πρακτικά της Αρχαιολογικής Εταιρείας* 1981, 42–54.

1987. Το ανακτορικό συνγκρότημα της Πέλλας, *Αρχαιολογικό Έργο στη Μακεδονία και στη Θράκη* 1, 119–24.

1996. Die Basileia von Pella. In G. Brands and W. Hoepfner, eds. *Basileia: die Paläste der hellenistischen Könige*, (Mainz: von Zabern).

Skarlatidou, E. 1992. Ανασκαφή αρχαίων σπιτιών στο βόρειο περίβολο των Αβδήρων, *Αρχαιολογικό Έργο στη Μακεδονία και στη Θράκη* 6, 685–91.

Small, D. 2009. The Dual-Processual Model in Ancient Greece: Applying a Post-neoevolutionary Model to a Data-rich Environment, *Journal of Anthropological Archaeology* 28, 205–21.

2010. Contexts, Agency and Social Change in Greece. In N. Terrenato and D. Haggis, eds. *State Formation in Italy and Greece: Questioning the Neoevolutionist Paradigm*, (Oxford: Oxbow), 135–160.

Snodgrass, A. M. 2001. *The Dark Age of Greece*, (Edinburgh: Edinburgh University Press.)

Solovyov, S. L. 1999. *Ancient Berezan: The architecture, History and Culture of the First Greek Colony in the Northern Black Sea*, (Leiden: Brill).

Souza, R., Walthall, A., Benton, J., Wueste, E., Tharler, A., Crowther, B. and Schirmer, C. 2019. Preliminary Report on the 2016 Field Season of the American Excavations at Morgantina: Contrada Agnese Project (CAP), *The Journal of Fasti Online*. www.fastionline.org/docs/FOLDER-it-2019-450.pdf, accessed 3 December 2021.

Sparkes, B. and Talcott, L. 1970. *The Athenian Agora Volume XII: Black and Plain Pottery*, (Princeton: American School of Classical Studies at Athens).

Stauropoullou, F. D. 1938. Ιερατική οικία εν Ζωστήρι της Αττικής, *Αρχαιολογική Εφημερίς* 10, 1–31.

Steinhauer, G. 1994. Παρατηρήσεις στην οικιστική μορφή των αττικών δήμων. In W. Coulson, T. L. Shear Jr., H. Shapiro and F. Frost, eds. *The Archaeology of Athens and Attica under the Democracy*, (Oxford: Oxbow), 175–89.

Stillwell, R. 1963. Excavations at Morgantina (Serra Orlando) 1962, Preliminary Report VII, *American Journal of Archaeology* 67, 163–71.

Televantou, Ch. 2011. Hypsele on Andros: The Geometric Phase, *Mediterranean Archaeology* 25, 83–87.

Themelis, P. 1979. Ausgrabungen im Kallipolis (Ost-Aetolien) 1977–1978, *Αρχαιολογικά Ανάλεκτα εξ Αθηνών* 12, 245.

1992. Η Ερέτρια τον 8° π.χ. αι. Εργαστήριο Χρυσοχΐας, *Αρχαιολογία* 42, 29–38.

1998. Attic Sculpture from Kallipolis (Aitolia): A Cult Group of Demeter and Kore. In O. Palagia and W. Coulson, eds. *Regional Schools in Hellenistic Sculpture*, (Oxford: Oxbow), 47–59.

1999. Die Epoche der Griechen: Ausgrabungen in Kallipolis (Ost-Aetolien). In W. Hoepfner, ed. *Geschichte des Wohnens*, (Ludwigsburg: Wüstenrot Stiftung), 427–40.

Theocharis, D. and Milojčić, V., eds. 1976. *Demetrias I*, (Deutschen Archaologischen Forschungen in Thessalien, Bonn: Habelt).

Thompson, H. A. 1940. *The Tholos of Athens and Its Predecessors. Hesperia Supplement IV*, (Princeton: American School of Classical Studies at Athens).

1966. Activities in the Athenian Agora: 1960–65, *Hesperia* 35, 37–54.

Thompson, H. A. and Wycherley, R. E. 1972. *Excavations in the Athenian Agora Volume XIV: The History Shape and Uses of an Ancient City Centre*, (Princeton: American School of Classical Studies at Athens).

Threpsiadis, I. 1960. Ανασκαφή εις το οικόπεδον της οδός Αριστείδου 6, *Αρχαιολογικόν Δελτίον* 22, Χρονικά, 29–32.

Tölle-Kastenbein, R. 1974. *Das Kastro Tigani. Die Bauten und Funde griechischer, römischer und byzantinischer Zeit. Samos 14*, (Bonn: Habelt).

Tomlinson, R. A. and Fossey, J. M. 1970. Ancient Remains on Mount Mavrovouni, South Boiotia, *Annual of the British School at Athens* 65, 243–63.

Trümper, M. 1998. *Wohnen in Delos: eine baugeschichtliche Untersuchung zum Wandel der Wohnkultur in hellenistischer Zeit*, (Rahden: Leidorf).

2002. Karl Reber: Die klassischen und hellenistischen Häuser im Westquartier, *Gnomon* 74, 627–38.

2005a. Die Maison des sceaux in Delos: Ein ‚versiegelter' Fundkomplex? Untersuchungen zur Aussagekraft und Interpretation der Funde eines durch Brand zerstörten hellenistischen Wohnhauses, *Mitteilungen des deutschen Archäologischen Instituts, Athenischer Abteilung*, 317–416.

2005b. Modest Housing in Late Hellenistic Delos. In B. A. Ault and L. C. Nevett, eds. *Ancient Greek Houses and Households: Chronological, Regional and Social Diversity*, (Philadelphia: University of Pennsylvania Press), 119–139.

2010. Bathing Culture in Hellenistic Domestic Architecture. In S. Ladstätter and V. Scheibelreiter, eds. *Städtisches Wohnen im östlichen Mittelmeerraum 4. Jh. v. Chr. – 1. Jh. n. Chr.: Akten des internationalen Kolloquiums vom 24.– 27. Oktober 2007 an der Österreichischen Akademie der Wissenschaften*, (Vienna: Verlag der Österreichischen Akademie der Wissenschaften), 529–68.

2014. Sanitary Installations in Hellenistic Houses of Sicily. A Critical Reassessment. In A. Haug and D. Steuernagel, eds. *Hellenistische Häuser und ihre Funktionen*, (Bonn: Verlag Dr. Rudoph Habelt), 87–102.

Tsakirgis, B. 1984. *The Domestic Architecture of Morgantina in the Hellenistic and Roman Periods*, (Doctoral Dissertation, Ann Arbor, University Microfilms International).

2005. Living and Working Around the Athenian Agora: A Preliminary Case Study of Three Houses. In B. A. Ault, and L. C. Nevett, eds. *Ancient Greek Houses and Households*, (Philadelphia: University of Pennsylvania Press), 67–82.

2007. Fire and Smoke: Hearths, Braziers and Chimneys in the Greek House. In R. Westgate, N. Fisher and J. Whitley, eds. *Building Communities. House, Settlement and Society in the Aegean and Beyond*, (British School at Athens Studies 15, London: British School at Athens), 225–31.

2009. Living Near the Agora: Houses and Households in Central Athens. In J. Camp and C. Mauzy, eds. *The Athenian Agora: New Perspectives on an Ancient Site*, (Mainz: von Zabern), 47–54.

2010. Lighting the Way: Windows on Behavioural Patterns in the Greek House. In S. Ladstätter and V. Scheibelreiter, eds. *Städtisches Wohnen im östlichen Mittelmeerraum 4. Jh. v. Chr. – 1. Jh. n. Chr.*, (Vienna: Verlag der Österreichischen Akademie der Wissenschaften), 569–82.

2016. Whole Cloth: Exploring the Question of Self-sufficiency through the Example of Textile Manufacture and Purchase in Greek Houses. In E. M. Harris, D. M. Lewis and M. Woolmer, eds. *The Ancient Greek Economy: Markets, Households and City-States*, (Cambridge: Cambridge University Press), 166–81.

Tsatsaki, N. 2010. Residences, Workshops or Both? A Study of Hellenistic Houses at Nissi-Eleutherna (Crete). In S. Ladstätter and V. Scheibelreiter, eds. *Städtisches Wohnen im östlichen Mittelmeerraum 4. Jh. v. Chr. – 1. Jh. n. Chr.*, (Vienna: Verlag der Österreichischen Akademie der Wissenschaften), 67–80.

Tsigarida, E. B., Skitsa, A. and Oikonomou, S. 2021. *Πέλλης Βασιλείον: Enhancement Project of the Monumental Entrance and Building I*, (Athens: Ministry of Culture and Sport/Ephorate of Antiquities of Pella).

Tsubouchi, Y. 2001. *One Malay Village: A Third-year Community Study*, (Kyoto: Trans Pacific Press).

Ulf, C. 2007. Elite oder Eliten in den Dark Ages und der Archaik: Realitäten und Modelle. In E. Akram-Stern, G. Nightingale, A. E. Bächle and S. Deger-Jalkotzy, eds. *Keimelion: Elitenbildung und elitärer Konsum von der myke-nischen Palastzeit bis zur Homerischen Epoche*, (Vienna: Verlag der Österreichischen Akademie der Wissenschaften), 317–24.

Vallet, G., Villard, F. and Auberson, P. 1976. *Megara Hyblaea: Le quartier de l'agora archaïque*, (Rome: École française de Rome).

1983. *Megara Hyblaia 3: Guida agli Scavi*, (Rome: École française de Rome).

Verdan, S. 2002. Fouilles dans le sanctuaire d'Apollon Daphnéphoros, *Antike Kunst* 45, 126–32.

2004. Sondages de contrôle dans le sanctuaire d'Apollon Daphnéphoros, *Antike Kunst* 47, 86.

2012a. *Eretria: Fouilles et recherches XXII: Le Sanctuaire d'Apollon Daphnéphoros à l'époque géométrique*. (Lausanne, École suisse d'archéologie en Grèce)

2012b. Geometric Eretria: Some Thoughts on Old data, *Mediterranean Archaeology* 25, 181–89.

Vernant, J.-P. 1983. Hestia-Hermes, the Religious Expression of Space and Movement in Ancient Greece. In *Myth and Thought Among the Greeks*, (London: Routledge and Kegan Paul), 127–75.

Vial, C. 1984. Délos Independante, *Bulletin de Correspondance Hellénique Supplement* 10.

Vogeikoff-Brogan, N. 2011. Domestic Assemblages from Trypetos, Siteia: Private and Communal Aspects. In K. Glowacki and N. Vogeikoff-Brogan, eds. *ΣΤΕΓΑ: The Archaeology of Houses and Households in Ancient Crete from the Neolithic Period through the Roman Era*, (Princeton: American School of Classical Studies at Athens), 409–19.

Vokotopoulou, I. 1986. *Βίτσα. Τα νεκροταφεία μιας μολοσσικής κώμης*, (Athens: Ministry of Culture).

Vokotopoulou, I. and Protopsalti, S. 1994. Νέα ανασκαφική έρευνα των δρόμων του οικισμού του βορείου λόφου της αρχαίας Όλυνθο 1992–1994, *Αρχαιολογικό Έργο στη Μακεδονία και στη Θράκη* 8, 295–303.

Walker, S. 1993. Women and Housing in Classical Greece. In A. Kuhrt and A. Cameron, eds. *Images of Women in Classical Antiquity*, (London: Routledge; second edition), 81–91.

2005. Last Chance to See? Karfi (Crete) in the Twenty-first Century: Presentation of New Architectural Data and Their Analysis in the Current Context of Research, *Annual of the British School at Athens* 100, 215–74.

2010. *Ancient Crete*, (Cambridge: Cambridge University Press).

Walsh, J. P. 2011/2012. Urbanism and Identity at Classical Morgantina, *Memoirs of the American Academy at Rome* 56/57, 115–36.

Walter-Karydi, E. 1998. *The Greek House: The Rise of Noble Houses in Late Classical Times*, (Athens: Athens Archaeological Society).

Wardle, K. 1996. Change or Continuity? Assiros Toumba at the Transition from Bronze to Iron Age, *Αρχαιολογικό Έργο στη Μακεδονία και στη Θράκη* 10A, 443–57.

Wardle, K. and Wardle. D. 2000. Assiros Toumba: Remains of the Later Iron Age. In P. Adam-Veleni, ed. *ΜΥΡΤΟΣ: μνήμη Ιουλίας Βοκοτοπούλου*, (Thessaloniki: Ministry of Culture), 653–673.

Wardle, K., Higham, T. and Kromer, B. 2014. Dating the End of the Greek Bronze Age: A Robust Radiocarbon-based Chronology from Assiros Toumba, *PlosOne* 9(9), 1–9.

Wasowicz, A. 1975. *Olbia pontique et sa territoire*, (Paris: Les Belles-Lettres).

Wecowski, M. 2014. *The Rise of the Greek Aristocratic Banquet*, (Oxford: Oxford University Press).

Westgate, R. 2000. Space and Decoration in Hellenistic Houses, *Annual of the British School at Athens* 95, 391–426.

2007a. The Greek House and the Ideology of Citizenship, *World Archaeology* 39, 229–45.

2007b. House and Society in Classical and Hellenistic Crete, *American Journal of Archaeology* 111, 423–57.

2010. Interior Decoration in Hellenistic Houses: Context, Function and Meaning. In S. Ladstätter and V. Scheibelreiter, eds. *Städtisches Wohnen im östlichen Mittelmeerraum 4. Jh. v. Chr. – 1. Jh. n. Chr.*, (Vienna: Verlag der Österreichischen Akademie der Wissenschaften), 497–528.

Westgate, R., Fisher, N. and Whitley, J., eds. 2007. *Building Communities. House, Settlement and Society in the Aegean and Beyond*, (British School at Athens Studies, 15, London: British School at Athens).

Whitley, J. 1991. Social diversity in Dark Age Greece, *Annual of the British School at Athens* 86, 341–65.

2007. Archaeology in Greece 2006–2007, *Archaeological Reports* 53, 1–122.

2011. Praisos V: Preliminary Report on the 2007 Excavation Season, *Annual of the British School at Athens* 106, 3–45.

2018. The Krater and the Pithos: Two Kinds of Agency. In L. C. Nevett and J. Whitley, eds. *An Age of Experiment: Classical Archaeology Transformed (1976–2014)*, (Cambridge: MacDonald Institute of Archaeology), 59–74.

Wiegand, T. and Schraeder, H. 1904. *Priene: Ergebnisse der Ausgrabungen und Untersuchungen in den Jahren 1895–1898*, (Berlin: Georg Reimer).

Williams, H., Schaus, G., Cronkite-Price, S.-M., Gourley, B., Hagerman, C. 1998. Excavations at Ancient Stymphalos, 1997, *Echos du Monde Classique/ Classical Views* 42 (N.S. 17), 261–319.

Williams, H., Schaus, G., Cronkite-Price, S.-M., Gourley, B., Sherwood, K. D. and Lolos, Y. 2002. Excavations at Ancient Stymphalos, 1999–2002, *Mouseion* 46, 135–87.

Wilson, A., Bennett, P., Buzaian, A., Fell, V., Found, B., Goransson, K., Guinness, A., Hardy, J., Harris, K., Helm, R., Kattenberg, A., Megias, E. T., Morley, G., Murphy, A., Swift, K., Twyman, J., Wootton, W. and Zimi, E. 2004. Euesperides (Benghazi): Preliminary Report on the Spring 2004 Season, *Libyan Studies* 35, 149–90.

Winther-Jacobsen, K. 2010. The Classical Farmstead Revisited. Activity Differentiation Based on a Ceramic Use Typology, *Annual of the British School at Athens* 105, 269–90.

Wolf, M. 2003. *Die Häuser von Solunt und die hellenistische Wohnarchitektur*, (Sonderschrift des Deutschen Archäologischen Instituts Rom, 14).

Young, J. H. 1956. Studies in South Attica, *Hesperia* 25, 122–46.

Young, R. S. 1951. An Industrial District of Ancient Athens, *Hesperia* 20, 135–250.

Zimmer, T. 2014. The Basileia: The Palace District of Pergamon. In F. Pirson and A. Scholl, eds. *Pergamon: A Hellenistic Capital in Anatolia*, (Istanbul: Tüpraş – Yapı Kredi Culture, Arts and Publishing), 276–87.

Index

Page numbers in italics are figures; those with 'g' are glossary terms.